READING

The Virginian

IN THE NEW WEST

Edited by Melody Graulich and Stephen Tatum

READING

The Virginian

IN THE NEW WEST

University of Nebraska Press, Lincoln and London

Chapter 2 was published as "Marrying for Race and Nation:
Wister's Omniscience and Omissions" in William R.
Handley, *Marriage, Violence, and the Nation in the American
Literary West* (Cambridge: Cambridge University Press,
2002). Reprinted with the permission of Cambridge
University Press.

Chapter 7 was published as "The Bovine Object of Ideology: History, Gender, and the Origins of the 'Classic' Western" in *Western American Literature*, vol. 35, no. 4 (winter
2001). Reprinted with the permission of *Western American
Literature*.

Library of Congress Cataloging-in-Publication Data
Reading "The Virginian" in the New West / edited by
Melody Graulich and Stephen Tatum.   p.   cm. Includes
bibliographical references and index. ISBN 0-8032-7104-2
(pbk. : alk. paper) 1. Wister, Owen, 1860–1938. Virginian.
2. Western stories – History and criticism. I. Graulich,
Melody, 1951– II. Tatum, Stephen, 1949– PS3345.V53 R43
2003 813'.52—dc21   2002028522

"N"

Dedicated to our mentors, David Levin and Don D. Walker

CONTENTS

ACKNOWLEDGMENTS

The editors would particularly like to thank Alan Barlow and Sabine Barcatta of Utah State University for excellent technical assistance, and Matt Burkhart of Utah State University and Kindra Briggs of the University of Utah for their research and editing skills. For their assistance with archival material and the preparation of illustrations we would like to thank the staff of the Manuscripts and Archives Division of the New York Public Library, the Rare Books Division of the J. Willard Marriott Library at the University of Utah, and Carl Hallberg and Leslie C. Shores at the American Heritage Center of the University of Wyoming. The University of Utah Research Committee supported this project by providing a grant for travel to research collections. The editors would also like to thank the anonymous reviewers for the University of Nebraska Press for their insightful comments and suggestions for improving the manuscript. Finally, we wish especially to acknowledge our thanks to Brock and Kathy for everything east of the sun and west of the moon.

INTRODUCTION   *Melody Graulich*

Owen Wister's *The Virginian*, published in 1902, ends with a New Western view into the twentieth century. The Virginian is no longer a prank-playing cowboy but the owner of a coal mine, conveniently serviced by a railroad line, and the West is maturing from the playground of young men that Wister documented in his earlier novel, *Lin McLean*, and getting down to the serious business of resource extraction, labor management, irrigation projects, competition for markets, railroad monopolies, foreign investment, Los Angeles real estate speculation, "cheap foreign" labor, and tourism, all mentioned in the text. Most Indian tribes have been herded onto reservations, where beef contracts provide another source of capital for enterprising entrepreneurs; agents "allow" some Crow off the reservation to sell "painted bows and arrows" to tourists, while the artistic productions of southwestern tribes, like Molly's Navajo blanket, are already being marketed beyond the region by Indian traders.[1] Other artifacts tell the same story: Molly carries her miniature portrait of her grandmother from East to West; she carries a photograph of her cowboy lover from West to East. Cattle are shipped to Omaha and packed into cans that are then shipped back to litter the Wyoming landscape.

Yet while Wister closed his frontier novel looking forward to a New West, *The Virginian* ironically initiated a backward-looking tradition, the formula western, as repeating – and perhaps as deadly – as the Winchester rifle. While the Virginian's gunfight against Trampas is presumably his only one, ending a period in his life and in the West, I well remember Saturday nights in the 1950s, black-and-white images flickering behind most suburban windows, when, at precisely eight o'clock, week after week, Marshall Matt Dillon stepped out into the dusty Main Street of Dodge City, hand hovering over his holster. Pow. Pow. *Gunsmoke*, image and word, filled the screen. In 2002, one hundred years after the publication of *The Virginian*, in a wonderfully suggestive symbol, you can still catch reruns of Matt Dillon rerunning the Virginian.

As John Cawelti argued in the 1970s, "Surely no twentieth century American needs to have the Western's importance as a cultural form demonstrated to him."[2] For the past hundred years, *The Virginian* has been an important cultural icon, one of those forefathering texts – frequently taught, often referred to – largely because of the relationship between Theodore Roosevelt and Wister and because it has been read as the progenitor of the much-critiqued and widely read western.[3] But what will the novel have to say to twenty-first-century readers? As critical responses to western American literature evolve, focusing not on a mythic Anglo-Saxon pioneer West but on change, diversity, borderlands, the Treaty of Guadalupe-Hidalgo, multiple migrations, cities, the Pacific Rim, and technology, will *The Virginian* seem hopelessly retrograde, one of those seminal patriarchal texts that we would like to bury in Boot Hill, a novel that captured, like a photograph, a static view of a West immobilized in a past that existed only fleetingly, if ever, so narrowly framed as to fence out vast expanses of western history and experience? Always challenged for its "inauthenticity," its class, racial, and sexual politics, its fairy-tale ending, decried by New Western historians as representing everything wrong with the mythic Old West, *The Virginian* receives only six brief mentions in the massive *Updating the Literary West*, sponsored by the Western Literature Association.[4] And its illegitimate sons, formula westerns, carry on its reputation for monolithic conservatism, the favorite reading of both Dwight Eisenhower and Ronald Reagan.

Yet in 2002 we have a president in the White House who wears cowboy boots for photo ops, who runs a Texas cattle ranch for a hobby and digs oil wells for profit, who leads me to look back on the Virginian as a "compassionate conservative." In 2000 the Turner network screened yet another film version of *The Virginian*; as Susan Kollin points out (chapter 11 in this volume), one hundred years after the "frontier thesis," a "new" Turner is shaping the "historic" representation of the West for the next century. As did Theodore Roosevelt and Owen Wister, contemporary figures like George W. Bush and Ted Turner use the imagery of the Old West to construct – through business, government, and media – their visions of a New West. As I write this introduction, television talking heads look back a century for western clichés to assess Bush's foreign policy: in dealing with the capture by the Chinese of a downed American spy plane, he is, they suggest, "speaking softly before pulling out his big stick."

So *The Virginian*, which sold over sixty-five hundred new paperback copies in 2000, still has a strong voice in our cultural conversations. While the novel has conventionally been read as speaking loudly and blatantly about a mythic, masculine West, we contend that, on the centennial of its original publication, *The Virginian* offers a stage for debating central issues for the next century. Its most subtle recent critics have pointed out that its politics and its messages are hardly monolithic. As Forrest Robinson has suggested in a book called *Having It Both Ways*, the novel exposes – or "actually betrays" – the myths that it simultaneously embodies. Christine Bold calls it a "fractured" text. "What makes *The Virginian* so interesting," argues Jane Tompkins, "is that it states so openly the counterargument to its own point of view." "The very ability to have things both ways led to its success," says Lee Clark Mitchell.[5]

Following these influential voices, the contributors to this volume read the novel's themes and its narrative style as dialogic rather than dialectical, acknowledging the pervasive influence of Bahktin. In *The Virginian*, says Neil Campbell, the "tensions form dialogues between movement and stasis, nature and civilization, migration and settlement, hybridity and essentialism." Campbell and his fellow contributors do not argue that Wister was not racist and misogynist and elitist and imperialist: he certainly was. But they do argue that his fine novel can and should be put to more complicated critical uses, that the novel is more fluid and mobile, more subtle and contradictory, than most critics have allowed. Its "disjunctions produce a narrative far more complicated in its formal methods and thematic effects than most critics have recognized," suggests William Handley. Like earlier critics such as Robinson and Mitchell, Handley, Stephen Tatum, Melody Graulich, and others demonstrate that the novel's wordplay, narration, and stylistic complexity reward the close reader, leading to more fully articulated social and political arguments. In these "close readings" turned "thick description," Navajo blankets are as culturally suggestive as references to George Eliot novels, labor history as significant as Shakespeare's history plays.

Unexpectedly, the essays collected in this volume demonstrate that the central tenet of one of the most apolitical recent critical theories, deconstruction, can be effectively united with socially engaged criticism and revisionist history. Contributor after contributor exposes narrative gaps, omissions, concealed themes, "displaced" histories, significance kept from "immediate view" (Handley), subjects virtually "invisible" (Jennifer Tuttle). Some suggest that the novel's dominant narrative tropes are poker and the tall tale: like its hero, the text is torn between the social power of performance, of bluffs and lies, and the emotional power of honesty. Perhaps Campbell articulates this pattern best when he asserts that "between the 'surface' of the text and its 'depth' exist other stories of contradiction and unease, where alternative American identities jostle with the 'smooth' surface of the myth." Susan Kollin provides theoretical support: "Pierre Macherey has argued that the speech of any narrative always comes from a particular silence. No book is ever fully 'self-sufficient'; each is 'necessarily accompanied by a certain absence, without which it would not exist.'"

The most dominating absence in this allegorical novel of nation building, this story of the United States of America, its "collective identity," and its literary history, is the American Indian, politically and narratively contained offstage. Do such "silences and absences structuring the text," as Kollin argues, "ultimately operate to safeguard . . . a larger social order," or is the text, like the Virginian himself, vulnerable to their off-the-reservation assaults? Do Native Americans "haunt" the text, as Tuttle argues? Does Louis Owens, an appropriately engaged "resisting reader," enact a retributive act of *survivance* – Gerald Vizenor's term – as he explores the erasure, imprisonment, and appropriation of American Indian histories, lands, and cultures?

As these questions suggest, many of the contributors to this volume use the novel as a rich textual point of departure for rethinking the cultural politics of western American studies. As Kollin argues, "*The Virginian* deserves attention less for how it functions in the development of the western than for the ways in which it intervened in debates during the period concerning labor, economy, and American national identity." Others demonstrate her point, using an analysis of the novel to suggest, as Zeese Papanikolas does, "that, far from being the sum of random acts of violent men in an untamed land, major violence was the result of wars of incorporation, where powerful interests fought among themselves for control of pasturelands and water rights, for railroads, and finally, against laboring men in an industrialized economy, just as they had earlier fought against Indians and Mexicans."

Class, labor, and property rights represent one of the critical threads in this collection. Throughout, the contributors incorporate recent approaches – cultural geography, postcolonial theory, social construction, cultural anthropology, cultural studies, gender studies, biographical criticism, Native American studies, poststructuralist theory, new historicism, visual and aesthetic studies – to provoke new insights into the text, to establish its cultural significance, and to imagine future directions for western literary criticism. Of course, approaches and recurrent themes intersect and braid. New historicist and comparativist approaches foreground formerly overlooked facts and implications about labor and property; the novel's treatment of these themes leads those influenced by postcolonial theory to analyses of nation or empire building; cultural geographers claim jump, literally and metaphorically, territory traditionally controlled by those in power; gender studies reveals the role of the marriage narrative in consolidating Wister's views on property and nation.

Throughout the collection a constellation of questions focuses on gender. Some contributors revisit familiar feminist territory: Is Molly a New Woman? Does Wister "rein her in" or, even worse, portray her as choosing subordination? What alternative views of the role of women in western settlement are offered by women writers? Does Wister presume that his readership is female? Other essayists debate whether within the novel gender is fixed and stable, where and when it breaks down. Judith Butler's concept of gender as a socially constructed, performed role is much in evidence.[6] Extending the early work of Robinson, writers explore how, in Handley's words, the novel questions "the purpose of masculinity"; the social construction of masculinity, who defines "how it must be about a man," is one of the collection's major concerns. There is considerable attention to the body, to the corporeal presence created by words and image. In his analysis of film versions of the novel, for instance, Richard Hutson illuminates how masculinity is historically contingent, depending on the viewer: "To a post–Gary Cooper viewer of these early films, the similarity in body and acting styles between Farnum and Fairbanks suggests that different historical contexts generate different styles of male cultural icons."

Several essays attend to the narrator, so peculiarly omnipresent yet obscured, whose sexual identity is one of this text's "particular silences"; he is simultaneously a presence and an absence, reifying conventional masculinity while expressing, as critics like John Seelye, Blake Allmendinger, and others have noted, surprisingly unguarded feelings of homoerotic desire in his descriptions of the Virginian's body.[7] The narrator's discourse certainly works to safeguard the body politic; his metaphors, for instance, turn the evolving relationship between Molly and the Virginian into a battleground of domination and submission, and his abstract lectures on "quality" and "equality," framing the comic scene of the Virginian's story about frog farming, recall the old southwestern humor dialectic between the unruly storyteller and the pompous, socially acceptable narrator, the storyteller's verbal highjinks framed, and contained, by the voice of the narrator. To borrow from Robinson, the contributors to this volume explore how Wister "has it both ways" in his portrayal of the narrator, using him both to espouse his own conservative politics and, covertly, to express a longing for less rigidly defined social roles.

The role of new historicism is evident throughout the collection. Several essays open with a historical stage setting – tourists encountering angry Nez Perce at Yellowstone in 1877, the Chicago World's Fair, the meeting of Wister and Remington at Yellowstone after Wister's visit to the fair. Most essayists have unearthed what Wallace Stegner's fictional historian, Lyman Ward, describes as his passion, the "quirky little things," the marker along the trail leading to deeper and broader understanding – Victoria Lamont's "maverick question," Papanikolas's gaucho poem, Tuttle's Shoshone guide, Gary Scharnhorst's Pullman strike, Graulich's pseudonymous author.[8] Obviously significant details like Molly's portrait of her grandmother are treated ethnographically, less as symbols than as cultural icons, as historical work blends into cultural criticism. Some contributors – Campbell, for example – base their readings on the work of anthropologists like James Clifford; others take an ethnographic approach to Wister's "use" of his materials, as does Tuttle when she argues that his "hunt for material resembles a form of taxidermy."

In this volume, as in some of the best earlier work on Wister, primary biographical research leads to cultural analysis. Of influential American fictions, few have received such sustained biographical attention as *The Virginian*. Ironically, one of those few – "The Yellow Wallpaper" – is frequently mentioned in this volume because of its biographical parallels to the novel. Both sent to Weir Mitchell following nervous breakdowns, Charlotte Perkins Gilman was given a "rest cure," fictionalized in her story, while Wister was given, in Tuttle's words, a "West cure," obliquely fictionalized in his novel. Biographical criticism establishes ironic historical juxtapositions that reveal larger issues, as in Mitchell's gendered prescriptions for Gilman and Wister or in Wister's presence at the Chicago World's Fair, where both Frederick Jackson Turner and Paul Groussac gave addresses describing the demise of the frontier – in the United States and in Argentina.[9] Some critics use familiar biographical materials, such as Wister's relationship with his longtime guide, George West, to new ends, while others discover suggestive implications in overlooked documents, such as Wister's photographs of the Shoshone guide Tigie discussed by Tuttle.

Looking at photographs, illustrations, Wister's stageplays, filmed versions of the novel, other western films, the influence of television shows and networks, Tuttle and other contributors carry on a long tradition in western American studies of exploring the interrelation between images and words, "artifact" and art, popular and privileged art forms. References to films, actors, performances, art, public spectacles, appear throughout the volume, and visual studies and film theory influence readings of the novel, its cultural influence, and media representations. They also draw our attention to the idea of spectatorship, to the always culturally and historically determined position of the viewer or reader.

For as this volume amply demonstrates, the text that we read as *The Virginian* is itself socially constructed, shifting in relation to the reader and the historical moment. Wister himself demonstrates that readings are contingent on gender, history, and a host of other variables in the debates between Molly and the Virginian over Austen and Turgenev. As Hutson comments, it is "next to impossible to pin down the story's meaning as it is translated from era to era." The essays themselves introduce us to a host of readers with various responses – from Henry James to Cecil B. DeMille, from Frederic Remington to Ted Turner. Gary Cooper's silent cowboy hardly resembles Lee Clark Mitchell's loquacious one. Those contributors who find themselves disenfranchised or excluded from the novel take Judith Fetterly's position as "resisting readers" and present alternative visions of the West.[10] Others self-consciously claim their own space in the text. Must the female reader "consent to her own inferiority," in Handley's view, or can she take back the text, as I attempt to do? Hutson finds in the 1929 version of the film, directed by Victor Fleming during a period when women were claiming autonomy, "a near reciprocity in the relations between the Virginian and Molly, as they dish out critiques of each other's behavior." Reflecting both the individual reader's personal engagement and the liberating influence of autobiographical literary criticism, many essayists write in unconventional critical styles – laments, ruminations, tall tales, satire.

Debates also occur around the novel's affective qualities. Is it, as Papanikolas suggests, "a nostalgia," with, in Handley's words, an "unsatisfying, sentimental resolution"? Beginning with Wister's mother and her friend Henry James, many readers have agreed that the final chapter is unsatisfying. Others – Robinson, Tatum, myself – read at least the honeymoon sequence as an uncertain, questioning counterpoint to the narrator's often dogmatic certainty. Many readers, appropriately annoyed, challenge the novel's politics, while others, notably Tatum, use a lyrical style to explore the novel's emotional resonances, without losing sight of its political implications.

As I conclude this introduction, I think of the insights of Robinson and Tompkins, both of whom argue that, on a personal and cultural level, *The Virginian* is an attempt to withdraw from adult responsibility.[11] Wister saw a future that he did not want to be part of. Now, one hundred years later, many of us read *The Virginian* as exemplifying and to some extent prophesying a past, the twentieth century, that we would like a chance to revise. At this turn into the new century, the contributors to this volume reread the myths of the past to reveal the omissions and take on the monopolies, looking toward a future based on opened boundaries, room for us all to range, and shared responsibility.

NOTES

1. Wister, *The Virginian* (NAL, 1979), 115. Page numbers for subsequent quotations will be given in the text.

2. Cawelti, *The Six-Gun Mystique*, 2. Cawelti did some of the earliest and most influential work on the formula western, focusing on generic elements: "In analyzing a popular form like the Western, we are *not* primarily concerned with an individual work . . . but with the cultural significance of the Western as a type of artistic construction. . . . Therefore the culturally significant phenomenon is not the individual work, but the formula or recipe" (25).

3. Most writers on Wister and many on Roosevelt spend some time on their friendship. The most complete analysis is contained in White, *The Eastern Establishment and the Western Experience.*

While many critics see the twentieth-century western as originating in works by Cooper and others and in dime novels, nearly everyone argues that *The Virginian* recast the genre. See, e.g., DeVoto, "Birth of an Art." Popular westerns, fiction and film, continue to receive considerable critical attention, although recent books have focused on the western's social commentary, continuing to explore *The Virginian*'s influence. See, e.g., Emert, *Loaded Fictions*; and Wallman, *The Western.*

4. See Lyon et al., eds., *Updating the Literary West.*

5. Robinson, *Having It Both Ways,* 41. Bold, *Selling the Wild West,* 74. Tompkins, *West of Everything,* 154. Mitchell, *Westerns,* 118.

6. Butler, *Gender Trouble.*

7. Seelye, introduction to *The Virginian.* Allmendinger, *Ten Most Wanted.*

8. Stegner, *Angle of Repose,* 211.

9. See Turner, "The Significance of the Frontier in American History"; and Groussac, *Popular Customs and Beliefs of the Argentine Provinces.*

10. Fetterly, *Resisting Reader.*

11. See Robinson, *Having It Both Ways;* and Tompkins, *West of Everything.*

1   PICTURES (FACING) WORDS   *Stephen Tatum*

Stephen Tatum begins his essay by exploring Wister's relationships with his illustrators, the celebrated Frederic Remington and the less well known Arthur Keller, who actually illustrated the 1902 edition of The Virginian. *Wister and his work have often been read in the context of his relationships with famous male contemporaries, notably Remington and Theodore Roosevelt, but Tatum uses biography as a background against which he "brings into the light" the complexity of the novel and what he calls the "ritual exchange between words . . . and an image." Through detailed readings of illustrations and passages, he demonstrates that this "popular" novel, so often read merely as contributing to the development of a genre, repays close, imaginative, aesthetic attention. His essay raises key interpretive questions that will recur throughout this collection: gender as performance; how to read Molly's apparent "subordination" and the critical final chapter; the novel's tendency to conceal, obscure, or render invisible ideas and meanings that nevertheless come to light; and perhaps most significantly, the "dialectical interplay" at work both thematically and stylistically, which so many of the contributors to this volume argue contributes to the novel's complexities. Finally, partially through his observations about longing and desire in the text, Tatum opens up, for readers and for himself,* The Virginian*'s emotional force; he thus begins a conversation that will continue throughout this volume about the novel's affective qualities, about reader response.*

"A LONG BOOK IS 'WAITING' FOR ME"

This was November 1901. Just before departing for Charleston, South Carolina, where he would winter and work on the manuscript of *The Vir-*

First illustration of the Virginian (unsigned; not by Frederic Remington),
from "Em'ly" (*Harper's New Monthly Magazine*, vol. 87 [1893]). The Virginian
is seated, at right.

ginian, Owen Wister severed his ties to the Harper Brothers publishing
house and signed a long-term contract with the Macmillan Publishing
Company. Corresponding with George Brett, his editor at Macmillan,
Wister acknowledged receiving from Brett a copy of Rolfe Boldrewood's
Australian frontier novel *Robbery under Arms* (1893), noting that reading
this novel had "made active again my intentions long ago expressed to
Remington, and very naturally add weight to my belief that a long book is
'waiting' for me."[1]

For Wister, declaring to turn from the short story to the novel form
would have seemed just about right, for with the publication approximately a year before of *The Jimmyjohn Boss*, his inventory of short stories
was mostly depleted. And with the long story entitled "Superstition
Trail" – eventually to become a pivotal chapter in the "long book" that he
would finally complete in the early spring of 1902 – concluding its serial-
ization in the 7 November 1902 number of the *Saturday Evening Post*, Wister was energized to rework the extant stories featuring the Virginian into
a novel during the coming winter in South Carolina.

The Virginian (middle figure), as illustrated by Remington in "Balaam and Pedro" (*Harper's New Monthly Magazine*, vol. 88 [1894]).

Still, regardless of aims and intentions, Wister's correspondence throughout the winter of 1901–2 indicates that he struggled to complete the long book that was "waiting" for him. Of course, he finally did finish *The Virginian*, and in mid-March 1902 he mailed it to Brett in New York City. Then, approximately a month before its scheduled release in May 1902, Wister wrote Brett to inform him of his hopes and his "views and intentions" regarding the novel. For one thing, Wister was somewhat apprehensive about his artist friend Frederic Remington's response to the novel's publication. Well established in the reading public's mind as *the* illustrator of Wister's stories, Remington had early and actively encouraged Wister to write a novel about the American cowboy, and both his collegial presence and his artwork had influenced the evolution of the Virginian's character over the past decade. His artistic representations of the Virginian's appearance in magazine publications of "Balaam and Pedro" (1894), "The Game and the Nation" (1900), and "Superstition Trail" (1901) document the cowboy character's transformation from his initial appearance as a provincial backwoods type into the "slim young giant,

Arthur Keller's illustration of Bret Harte's "Miggles," for William Dean Howells's *Heroines of Fiction* (1901).

more beautiful than pictures," described by Wister's tenderfoot narrator at the novel's outset.[2] As if he anticipated some personal difficulty with Remington following on the novel's publication, Wister advised Brett in early April to "write to [Remington] what seems best to you," whereas for his part Wister surmised that he "had better go and see [Remington] at New Rochelle on my return in May. For long ago when I talked the book to him he said 'Mind, nobody else is to do that with you.'"[3]

Macmillan had in fact commissioned – apparently with Wister's tacit approval – another artist to "do" the novel's illustrations.[4] That someone else Macmillan assigned to illustrate the first edition of *The Virginian* was Arthur Keller, a New Yorker born of German immigrant parents. Trained both at the National Academy of Design and in the Munich studio of Ludwig Von Loefftz, Keller had served as a member of the prestigious *Harper's* staff of illustrators throughout the 1890s, and by the time he assumed the task of illustrating *The Virginian* in the spring of 1902, he had illustrated stories and articles for all the major American magazines. In addition, during the 1890s he had illustrated books by such notable American authors as Bret Harte, John Muir, S. Weir Mitchell, and William Dean Howells. In 1903 Keller served as president of the Society of Illustrators, and as his career progressed he became well known as the illustrator both of Thomas Dixon's novel *The Clansman* (1905) and of Winston S. Churchill's popular novel *Mr. Crewe's Career* (1908).[5]

Since Keller's major assignment during the fall prior to *The Virginian* assignment was to illustrate several of the women characters discussed in Howells's two-volume critical study *Heroines of Fiction*, he undoubtedly seemed to Brett and the Macmillan staff, as well as perhaps to Wister himself, an ideal choice for the task of rendering, among other things, the Virginian's romantic interest, Molly Stark Wood.[6]

Brett did write his letter to Remington about the matter of somebody else doing the illustrations for Wister's novel, and – to assuage any possible bitterness or anger on Remington's part – he proposed a future Wister-Remington collaboration on a "picture book" that Macmillan would publish. Ironically, as this drama of personal relations during the spring of 1902 concluded, Wister became upset about the pressure that he felt Remington and the publisher R. H. Russell were placing on him to supply original verses to accompany Remington's new portfolio of drawings, *Done in the Open*.[7]

In the end, Wister and Remington did *not* meet in May in New Rochelle

Remington's final illustration of the Virginian (rear figure), in "Superstition Trail" (*Saturday Evening Post*, 7 November 1901).

(or anywhere else) to discuss either Keller's role in illustrating *The Virginian* or Wister's tardiness in writing verses for *Done in the Open*. After a series of misunderstandings created as their correspondence crossed in the mail was finally resolved, Remington was already established for the summer on his island retreat in the Saint Lawrence River by the time the novel was released. As it turned out, Remington responded to the novel's publication by devoting most of that summer to writing his own novel, *John Ermine of the Yellowstone*, which was acquired by Brett and published by Macmillan in early 1903. Although neither man could have known it at the time, Remington's last illustration for a Wister piece was the picture in the November 1901 "Superstition Trail" concluding installment in which the barely visible Virginian and the story's narrator ride toward the picture's rear plane, some horses' rumps in the foreground essentially dominating the picture's composition.

Meanwhile, immediately on receiving in mid-May an advance copy of *The Virginian*, Wister wrote Brett how pleased he was with the "look" of the final product: "I should like you to tell Mr. Keller that I did not think he (or anyone) could come so close to my own mental picture of the hero. I think he has quite wonderfully united the various qualities suggested by the text – good looks, force, humor and gravity – My two favorites are the frontispiece and the finding of Shorty's body – Mr. Keller has caught the situation extraordinarily well, to my thinking, in both instances. And I also like his landscape very much. It is very true and is also full of atmosphere. I am jubilant; and want you to feel my full appreciation."[8]

THE LETTER AND THE SPIRIT

Published originally as an *illustrated* novel, the 1902 edition of *The Virginian* displays Keller's frontispiece illustration facing the novel's title page as well as seven other halftone pictures interspersed throughout the text, each occupying its own page and facing a related page of Wister's prose. Thus, in the format for the original illustrated edition of *The Virginian*, words and pictures can be said (or seen) to mirror each other on facing pages. Moreover, an additional "doubleness" about the relation between words and pictures results when either Wister's words function as descriptive images (as they often do) or Keller's painted images contain or reference Wister's verbal discourse. On the one hand, all the novel's illustrations have captions, whether a simple title (e.g., "The Rescue") or a single line of Wister's words running just below the bottom edge of each picture. Thus, words drawn from the facing page of verbal discourse can be said (and seen) to bleed out onto and frame the page of the picture. On the other hand, Wister's verbal discourse occasionally becomes dramatically internal to the pictures themselves: in one of the two Keller illustrations that Wister singled out for praise, for instance, the Virginian holds a newspaper (we know from the text that Steve's last words are scrawled on it) while he and the novel's tenderfoot narrator survey Shorty's corpse sprawled on the ground before them.

Given this original edition's juxtaposition of Wister's words and Keller's pictures, and given further that the novel's verbal and visual discourse can be said to inhabit each other, certain questions would seem to invite our extended attention. What are the possible semantic meanings and dynamic themes generated by this close proximity of words and pictures? Indeed, if it can be said, as I think it can, that *The Virginian* is a novel centrally preoccupied with issues of masculine and feminine *decorum* – with dramatically establishing what is "proper" or "appropriate" human behavior and action as these relate to matters of "property" and "proprietorship" – then what exactly constitutes an appropriate (or inappropriate) way to conceive the relation between the novel's words and pictures? To be more specific, in what ways might Keller's pictures be said to complement or perhaps even to contradict Wister's words, to illuminate the novel's apparent themes and motifs or perhaps instead to bring into the light contradictory aims and intentions?

As we can see in the tenor of his praise for Keller's artwork, Wister himself offers one theoretical perspective on such questions. Voicing his jubilation to Brett about the way in which Keller's pictures came "so close to [his] own mental picture," how they "united the various qualities suggested by the text," and how they "caught the situation extraordinarily well," Wister discloses his belief that illustrations should be *continuous* with and *complementary* to his accumulating words' implicit intentions and explicit meanings. For Wister, in other words, "successful" illustrations would *reflect* the "qualities" and "situations" suggested by the prior written text, this reflecting function of course manifested by a format calling for illustrations to face the pages of words just as any mirror reflects whatever comes before its reflecting surface. Yet because verbal discourse always precedes the illustrations in order of creation, and also because his words (as captions) serve to frame the reader's interpretive response, Wister also clearly assumes that his written text will be authoritative, will

" 'When you call me that, smile.' "

" 'I wish I could thank him,' he said, 'I wish I could.' "

have, to use one of the words associated with the idea of decorum, "proprietorship" over the text's meaning. So just as Molly's family in Bennington, Vermont, requires (but apparently does not possess) the appropriate context with which to understand the "proper" meaning of the word *rustler* (discussed in chapter 22), so too the inherently promiscuous or indeterminate nature of visual signifiers requires the framing context of a verbal caption or an accompanying narrative line to stabilize and then communicate the "proprietary" author's aims and intended meanings. Moreover, as we learn in the novel's opening scene, the Virginian – at least to the eyes of Wister's tenderfoot narrator – is "more beautiful than pictures" (3). So regardless of any illustrator's ability to communicate the static, spatial truths of surfaces, his or her artwork – at least as Wister would have it – needs the *temporal* supplement provided by a narrative's sequential presentation of words in order fully to convey the elegance, harmony, and rhythm found in fluid things of "beauty" or things that embody the "beautiful."

Still, as his comment to Brett discloses, Wister also admires Keller's artistic ability to evoke the novel's "qualities" or overall "atmosphere," which can be only "suggested" by the novel's accumulating words. So it would also seem to be the case that Wister is jubilant about Keller's artwork precisely because it is, while continuous with and complementary to his words, at the same time neither slavishly dependent on them nor merely decorative. "Successful" illustrations ideally should function, then, both to reflect the words and to enhance and extend the words' implicit and explicit meanings. To frame the issue by using his narrator's comment, "So I perceived a new example of the old truth, that the letter means nothing until the spirit gives it life" (23), Wister hoped not only that the novel's illustrations would capture the documentary truth of "the letter" but also that they would bring into the light – to use the literal meaning of the word *illustration* – his letters' and words' essential meaning or "spirit." Figuratively speaking, just as the rustler Steve's "pencil writing" on the newspaper found near Shorty's corpse in the "Superstition Trail" chapter exists as a "message from the dead, brought by the dead" (329), so too Wister's "dead" letters on the novel's pages need the supplement of Keller's illustrations in order to be brought to "life" in the reader's consciousness. Wister's expressed jubilation about Keller's artwork's ability to catch and release the novel's "spirit" (its intangible qualities and atmosphere), however, comes with this caveat: that any visual elaboration or extension of his verbal discourse should not, finally, overwhelm, contradict, or even subvert his words' apparent meanings.

Taken together, then, Wister's comments about Keller's "success" suggest that he considered illustrations to relate to a novel's verbal discourse in the manner of an alien stock grafted onto a host plant: metaphorically speaking, Keller's illustrations are nourished by and, in turn, nourishing of the larger textual plot or verbal soil that surrounds them. Wister models for us this idealized, organic reciprocity between words and pictures in a scene in which Molly and her great-aunt study a photographic portrait of the Virginian posed in "all his cow-boy trappings, – the leathern chaps, the belt and pistol, and in his hand a coil of rope" (202). Trying to make some interpretive sense of the Virginian's visage and his cowboy getup, Molly's great-aunt back in Vermont at first wonders whether the photograph that she studies accurately reproduces the "way" cowboys really look. But she breaks off that developing thought – as if the visual signifiers of the Virginian's vivacity and potency are too prominent to ignore – in order to ask her niece if such a man has "presumed" not only to court her but also to woo her just as he might, say, woo any ordinary "biscuit-shooter" who does not possess Molly's social and cultural capital. Molly's abrupt, defensive response to the query is to rejoin, "He's not a bit like that." She immediately reconsiders this judgment, however, and decides that the photograph's visual signifiers do, in fact, accord with her personal knowledge of the Virginian: "Yes, he's exactly like that" (202). After studying "the picture closely for a minute," the great-aunt finally remarks that "it is a good face," conceding even that the Virginian is "handsome." However, just as soon as she makes this conclusion she wonders whether she can trust what the photograph presents to her eyes: "'Is the fellow as handsome as that, my dear?' More so, Molly thought" (202–3).

As is the case with verbal signifiers, visual signifiers too seem to be both accurate and deceptive, clearly adequate and yet entirely deficient in representing the "true" reality of any situation, object, or character. Inevitably, it seems, visual signifiers, whether in a photograph or in a painted picture, are destined to be both "like that" and "not a bit like that." Now Wister's omniscient narrator describes Molly's eye as growing "warlike" as she watches her great-aunt study the Virginian's photograph, and as this brief scene unfolds, their verbal jousting discloses how pictures potentially, perhaps inevitably, forward competing and even contradictory meanings. As the two women verbally wrestle for interpretive authority over the Virginian's picture, furthermore, their comments also reveal how the various visual signifiers of his "cowboy trappings" remain inherently elusive or multivalent, displaying a residue of what might be called excessive or nontranslatable or untranslatable meaning. Molly describes the Virginian as "splendid," echoing the word *splendor* used by the tenderfoot narrator in his opening verbal portrait of Wister's cowboy hero. But the great-aunt is less than certain about the ability – and hence the reliability – of Molly's word *splendid* to negotiate the gap between the manifest visual signifiers of the Virginian's "wildness" that greet her eyes and the latent signifiers *manhood* and *gentleman*. Thus, she wonders, at least initially, whether Molly has simply fallen in love with the Virginian's clothes and cowboy accessories. And she further wonders whether the Virginian's "cowboy trappings" and physiognomic features display or veil the truth about his manner of manhood and moral character: is the relation between the "letter" of surface appearances and the "spirit" of underlying truths or essences a decorous, which is to say, a proper and, hence, a faithful and trustworthy one?

Regardless of Wister's comments to his editor about Keller's illustrations, then, the interpretive gap opened up here by Molly's ambivalent response to the Virginian's photographic picture (both "like that" and "not a bit like that") and the interpretive space of difference realized during her conversation with her great-aunt suggest that pictures do not only reflect the thematic meanings and semantic forces produced by the words that precede them. Pictures may just as well, perhaps unavoidably, bring something "new" into the light and before the reader's eyes. They may just as well forward some new or unexpected meanings and forces, with the result that a novel's words might be not only amplified or enhanced but perhaps even subverted by the accompanying illustrations – just as unruly horses or men and women occasionally resist the Virginian's coiled rope and his ropes of words.[9]

With this provisional answer to the question about the relation between words and pictures in mind, I want to look in some detail at two of Keller's illustrations for the original edition of *The Virginian*. Considering the illustrations in more detail will allow us to understand better the inherent double edge to the novel's illustrations, how they not only complement and amplify but also extend and even complicate the novel's thematic aims and intentions. Molly's great-aunt's response to the Virginian's photographic portrait epitomizes, among other things, how Wister's novel is preoccupied with gender identity and the related issue of what constitutes appropriate or decorous behavior for both men and women. The dynamic relation between Wister's words and Keller's illustrations both incorporates and extends this particular thematic preoccupation, largely because nearly all Keller's illustrations feature the Virginian and Molly in some sort of physical entanglement or contact, one or both gesturing with outstretched arms and hands. Even as they instance the potential "double edge" of the novel's illustrations, Keller's "entanglement" pictures, to be specific, visually amplify and extend, complement and complicate, (1) the novel's absorption in leitmotifs of concealment (or layering) and of disclosure (or display); (2) its exploration of the contours of human desire in the face of unresponsive objects or persons; and (3) its investment in a dialectic between aggressive and erotic passions so as to announce the theme of sacrifice.

"BY HIS SIDE WALKING AND CHEERING HIM FORWARD"

Facing the title page of the novel's original edition, Keller's halftone frontispiece portrays in its foreground a cowboy, apparently suffering from a shoulder wound, astride his horse, while a young woman – on foot at his side, leading her horse – turns her body to gaze up at her mounted male companion. A single line of Wister's words, arranged just below the picture's bottom edge, offers the reader an interpretive clue: "By his side the girl walking and cheering him forward." Culled from the "Grandmother Stark" chapter from late in the novel, this framing caption contributes a narrative or temporal dimension to the illustration's spatial presence, and along with the picture's elements, it solicits readers just beginning the novel to want to read on in search of answers: Where have they been? Where are they going? Why is she "walking and cheering him forward"? While Wister's captioned words clearly serve to "frame" Keller's frontispiece, it is also the case that the frontispiece's particular composition and iconographic details provide an interpretive frame for the novel's verbal discourse. At a minimum, for instance, as the first of what will be a total of four Keller pictures featuring physical contact between the Virginian and Molly Stark Wood, the frontispiece signals readers beginning the novel that this narrative about a horseman of the plains will likely incorporate a plot of romantic passion as well as one of adventure. For Wister's contemporary readers, furthermore, this particular scene would have seemed familiar, for the idea of a man being rescued or rehabilitated through a woman's influence or good works was a cultural commonplace in the print media of American industrial popular culture at the turn of the twentieth century.

"By his side the girl walking and cheering him forward."

"The Rescue."

In the late "Grandmother Stark" chapter, which supplies the scene for the frontispiece illustration, the "delicate wound" of Cupid's arrow that had been launched when the Virginian first read Molly's letter of application for the teaching position at Bear Creek has been displaced by the bloody shoulder wound that he has suffered during an offstage skirmish with Indians. For the reader who looks back at the frontispiece after (or while) reading this chapter, the Virginian's bandaged shoulder does not index only Molly's competent ministration of his wound after she discovers his unconscious, sprawled form by a pool of water. It also indexes Molly's surprise discovery – as she rummages through his bedroll in search of material to fashion a bandage – of a handkerchief of hers that had been missing since the Virginian had, in chapter 9, rescued her from a stagecoach stranded in still another body of water. But whereas Charles M. Russell's in-text pen-and-ink drawing illustrating this chapter in the novel's "new" 1911 edition stresses the moment of Molly's startled discovery of the Virginian's dire strait (and features his prone body in the drawing's lower, foreground plane), Keller's frontispiece interestingly foregrounds Molly's performance as the wounded cowboy's rescuer, highlights her acting, to use the Virginian's admonition to her during

Charles M. Russell's in-text illustration from the "Grandmother Stark" chapter of the novel's 1911 edition.

this scene, like "the man through all this mess" (259) as the pair slowly travel together through the narrow mountain valley's drainage toward the safety of her Bear Creek cabin.

Even with the inherent limitations of the technology for halftone reproduction, Keller's frontispiece reveals three representative features of his visual style or signature: a rich application of pigment in certain passages of the picture; broad and vigorous brushwork, particularly with regard to the picture's setting; and compositionally speaking, a strategic counterpointing of pronounced horizontal and vertical lines. His expressive, gestural brushwork configuring the ground cover through which the couple and their horses pass incrementally evolves into the slightly more refined and graduated brushwork detailing the Virginian's and Molly's faces. In concert with the semirounded, inverted line of the mountain and trees in the picture's rear plane, this painterly tactic amplifies Wister's verbal description of this landscape as a "cuplike ravine" and simultaneously draws the reader's gaze toward the picture's center, where the human and animal forms create, abstractly speaking, the letter *V.* What we might call the picture's *absolute* or geometric center appears to be the layered swath of white pigment representing Molly's blouse. With regard to the picture's *balancing* center, even though the trajectory of Molly's gaze and the Virginian's privileged position atop Monte, his horse, throw its visual weight toward the viewer's left, this torque is contended against by the downwardly moving thrust of Molly's left arm and by the bulk and height of the trailing horse, whose reins she holds. So amid the dynamism promoted by Keller's brushwork and by the represented scene of humans and horses in motion, the picture's balancing center seems to rest on Molly's face or her upraised right arm helping brace the Virginian in his saddle. As a result of Keller's brushwork and the close proximity of the picture's absolute and balancing centers, the frontispiece asks readers both to imagine a line, roughly paralleling the angle of Molly's arms, connecting her gaze with the Virginian's shoulder and to recognize how Keller's chromatic parallelism unites the white bandage (covering the bullet wound) with her white blouse (covering her chest and heart).

Now the centricity of the frontispiece's composition and its chromatic parallelism effectively amplify the novel's verbal emphasis on the dialectical interplay of erotic passion and violence. But the more specific and important point to make here is that the intersection in the frontispiece of emotional affect (Molly "cheering him forward") with a seemingly unresponsive, sealed-off object (his distracted and distanced gaze) gets organized by Keller through what we might call an overall *visual rhetoric of layering*. With the phrase *rhetoric of layering* I want, first, literally to draw attention to Keller's characteristically dense and concentrated filling and covering up of the picture's available space. But with this phrase I want, second, to draw attention to Keller's apparent investment in promoting volume and depth in the picture's spatial field. In the case of the frontis-piece, this investment results in his painterly care with textured or layered representations of drapery, folds, or coverings – as in, say, the thick folds of a neckerchief or pair of chaps; the wrinkled creases of a blouse or shirt or hat; the sinuous drapery of a long skirt or jacket. Third, in contrast to a visual rhetoric of display or exposure – evinced here by the butt of the Virginian's pistol holstered on the right side of his waist – the frontis-piece's predominant visual rhetoric of layering forwards a kind of para-doxical visual logic: something will potentially achieve greater interest or intensity precisely because of any concerted, visible effort to deny, con-ceal, veil, or repress it.

At first glance, then, the frontispiece's matrix of affect ("walking and cheering him forward") and fashion (Molly's long skirt, her long-sleeved jacket with tight cuffs, and her blouse's high neckline) seemingly stresses Molly's sororal and maternal role in relation to the Virginian (who de-scribes himself to Molly as a "child" while she tends to his wounds). But Keller's frontispiece complicates this reading, for all the features that I have been singling out for notice – composition, brushwork, chromatic parallelism, the rhetoric of layering – focus attention on Molly's thick, luxuriant hair, only partially covered by her hat; her small waist, which serves, conversely, to emphasize her bust and hips; the draped, sinuous fold and pendulous shape of her long skirt as it brushes against and trails down from the Virginian's left foot in the stirrup; and the parallel V-shaped insert of her white blouse. Paradoxically, in other words, instead of working to repress or veil Molly's corporeal presence, the very shape and the contoured lines of these coverings and layers bring her potential erotic presence more fully into the light. In short, her sexualized being is exposed even as it is concealed, and this aspect of the frontispiece trou-bles its complicity with the novel's words' "official" presentation of her as standing by her man in the role of nurse-caretaker.[10]

On one level Keller's signature visual rhetoric of layering provides an interesting analogue to the fashion in Victorian interior decoration for eliminating open or negative space by covering floors, walls, and windows with numerous drapes, rugs, and hangings. But in the novel's verbal dis-course this particular Victorian *aesthetic of presentation through concealment* manifests itself most vividly as the Virginian explains his ideal of proper conduct in life through the metaphor of "winnin' poker." To illustrate what he means about the need to distinguish "quality" from "equality," the Virginian claims that "cyards are only one o' the manifestations of poker in this hyeh world. . . . If a man is built like that Prince [Hal] boy was built (and it's away down deep beyond brains), he'll play winnin' poker" (120). Admiration for Shakespeare's Prince Hal centers on his sense that the prince is so clever and composed that he would do a thing well with whatever and however minimal the resources at hand. And as we have seen in the case of Keller's visual rhetoric of layering, "winnin' poker" in affairs of cards and, by extension, in affairs of work and of the heart always involves some daring and some degree of concealment and repression – as in the necessity at times for bluffing, the so-called poker face. So on the basis of his reading of Scott's *Kenilworth*, the Virginian speculates that even if Queen Elizabeth had only an "ace high" showing, she nevertheless "could scare Robert Dudley with a full house plumb out o' the bettin'" (120).

What links Wister's words about "winnin' poker" with Keller's frontis-piece and its visual rhetoric of layering, then, is an ideal of performative resourcefulness based both on risk and on the premise of repression and concealment. The Virginian's bandaged wound, his seemingly unre-sponsive gaze marking his increasing pain and delirium, and Molly's concealed-yet-revealed erotic potential combine in the frontispiece to underline how excessive instinctual desire troubles reason's disciplined rule. As we discover through Wister's words in the "Grandmother Stark" chapter, to reach the moment on their journey depicted by the frontis-piece Molly has successfully steeled herself *not* to faint or panic at the sight of the Virginian's bloodied form lying by a pool of water. In the manner of a Prince Hal, she has resourcefully warmed the Virginian by building a fire, given him heated water with brandy, dressed his wound, reloaded his pistol, and supported him while he rides Monte toward her cabin. And in the manner of Queen Elizabeth bluffing Robert Dudley, as Molly walks and cheers him on during the last quarter mile of their journey, she intu-itively realizes that to get the injured Virginian to make this final push to her cabin she must leave off acting, per his earlier advice, like "the man through all this mess." Instead, she finds that she needs to act just "like" a woman, which is to say, feign an anxious dependency on his protection so as to draw out his protective instincts and will to survive.

Clearly, as the novel's "Em'ly" chapter and the pedagogical scenes of instruction between Molly and the Virginian disclose, a patriarchal cul-ture's ideological norm of male dominance and female submissiveness provides the dominant framework of meaning and value for Wister's words and Keller's frontispiece. Even so, as I have been suggesting, Keller's visual rhetoric of layering cannot fully displace or repress evidence of Molly's physical and erotic presence. Moreover, her performative resourcefulness in rescuing the Virginian clearly inverts the standard active/passive and male/female binary oppositions and aligns her character with those whom the Virginian idealizes as "winnin' poker" players. As both self-sacrificing nurse-caretaker and capable actor who improvises and ventriloquizes normative gender identities to ensure the pair's survival, Molly's "walking and cheering him forward" pose exposes how both gender relations per se and the decorum of gendered behavior are fungible cultural constructions. Thus, the distance or gap between established norms and the contingencies of experience in the relatively "free" environment of Wyoming Territory allows for the kind of negotiation of class boundaries evinced by the Virginian's rising class status throughout the novel. And the distance or gap between established norms and the contingencies of experience signaled by Molly Wood's successful playing at the parts of a "man" and of a "woman" serves to foster the frontispiece's abiding dual accent or double edge. So although the novel's overall conclusion suggests somewhat conventionally that Molly's particular journey to self-discovery depends ultimately on her surrendering some of her independence to her lover and the marriage contract, the frontispiece's formal design complicates the matter, indeed highlights the chapter's (and the novel's) ambivalent address to the supposedly normative and fixed decorum of gendered behavior.

I say the novel's *ambivalent* address primarily because the rescue motif in the frontispiece scene from the "Grandmother Stark" chapter binds it together, if only in an inverted way, with the rescue motif dramatized in "The Spinster Meets the Unknown" chapter, where the Virginian and Molly have their first encounter. During the stagecoach portion of her journey to Wyoming described in this chapter, Molly's stamina and face so impress one of the drivers that he impulsively asks her to marry him. When she takes leave of this driver – he is relieved by another driver, who eventually gets drunk and strands the stagecoach at a water crossing, thus occasioning the Virginian's rescue of Molly – she shakes his hand: "After all, he was a frank-looking boy, who had paid her the highest compliment that a boy or a man (for that matter) knows; and it is said that Molly Stark, in her day, was not a New Woman" (77–78). Molly Stark Wood, granddaughter of the spirited, Revolutionary War–era patriot Molly Stark and niece of Mary Stark Wood, is, like her forebears, "not a usual young lady"

(69). She is unusual because she undertakes a long, dangerous journey without a protector either accompanying her or waiting for her at journey's end and because her decision to teach school at Bear Creek represents anything but the "usual ambition for such young ladies" (69). She is also "not a usual young lady" because of her notable genealogy and her highly independent character, which leads her – when the mills fail – to help support her family by teaching music or embroidering handkerchiefs. Commenting on her work ethic, Wister's narrator acknowledges, "That machine called the typewriter was then in existence, but the day of women typewriters had as yet scarcely begun to dawn, else I think Molly would have preferred this occupation to the handkerchiefs and the preserves" (71).

On the one hand, Molly Wood's observing of social propriety in the matter of the stagecoach driver's brash proposal is said to remove her, like her fabled grandmother in her day, from the ranks of Wister's contemporary "New Woman." Yet on the other hand, given the critique of genteel public opinion in Vermont and Wyoming otherwise sustained by Wister's first-person narrator throughout the novel, and also given the novel's characterization of Molly Wood's unusual independence and resourcefulness, the discursive gap that exists between the "I" who comments on Molly's actions and the pseudo-objective collective "it is said" that comments on Molly's grandmother's behavior becomes significant, registers Wister's oblique ironizing of orthodox opinion. That is, in contradistinction to the general run of mass opinion signified by the expression *it is said*, the narrator's insertion of such pseudo-objective discourse into his own discourse provides for a possible alternative conclusion: that Molly is, in fact, just like Wister's contemporary New Woman, unconventional or unusual enough to choose to observe social proprieties in a situation where class or caste distinctions do not necessarily require their observance.

Indeed, the final point to make here about the frontispiece in relation to the novel's words is that Keller's particular visual signature and decision to illustrate this moment in the novel also situates Molly Stark Wood within the mix of other popular media representations of American "girl" power during the new experiential circumstances attending the nation's modernization. Although not as heavy lidded as the typical Howard Chandler Christy or James Montgomery Flagg "girl" popular during Wister's era, Keller's Molly Wood does possess the full lips and luxuriant hair, the straight nose slightly tipped up at the end, the vivacious full

Daisy Miller, as illustrated by Howard Chandler Christy in William Dean Howells's *Heroines of Fiction* (1901).

James Montgomery Flagg's "Two Arrivals" (*Harper's Weekly*, 23 March 1907).

figure, and the expressive face and physicality associated with these other illustrators' popular creations.[11] In addition, the character traits that both Keller's visual signifiers and Wister's words identify with Molly compare favorably with those that William Dean Howells analyzes, in his *Heroines of Fiction*, with regard to Henry James's Daisy Miller: self- styled independence or pluckiness; healthy, as opposed to immodest, physicality and athleticism; mental and verbal cleverness; personal freedom rather than self-denial (e.g., Molly's decision to leave her family and suitor and journey to Wyoming). Perhaps more important, these particular attributes, at a minimum, connect with the ongoing discursive construction of the New Woman at the turn of the twentieth century – to use the era's shorthand phrase to describe, generally speaking, women writers, artists, and social reformers whose advocacy of greater economic, political, educational, and sexual freedom for women worked to expand professional opportunities beyond the traditional ones of nursing and teaching.[12] The Virginian, as we have learned, is both like and not like the visual signifiers that beholders of his photographic portrait scan. In the novel's verbal discourse, Molly Wood seems to be both a conventional and an unusual sort of woman, still "a rebel, independent as ever" (261), both like and unlike

"Gibson Girls," from Charles Dana Gibson's *Picturesque America Anywhere along the Coast* (1900).

the kind of New Woman who in a few years just might be found working as a typist in the commercial sector instead of canning preserves or doing embroidery at home. Through its visual rhetoric of layering and spatial composition, Keller's frontispiece effectively clarifies, highlights, and extends this muted double edge within the text to the illustrated page.

THE MAGICAL HEIRLOOM

Just prior to her rescue of the Virginian, Molly Wood had sent a farewell letter to him at the Sunk Creek Ranch and had begun packing her possessions, putting away the various books and "trophies of the frontier" that had adorned her living quarters in the cabin at Bear Creek. "Amidst its emptiness of dismantled shelves and walls and floor, only the tiny ancestress still hung in her place" (249) when Molly and the wounded Virginian finally reach her cabin. Molly undresses the wounded Virginian and puts him to bed under this miniature portrait of her grandmother, designated "the empress of Molly's spirit" (76) by Wister's narrator. Told by the visiting country doctor that the Virginian must not experience any sudden shocks to his system while his wound mends, Molly plays cribbage with him and reads to him. And gradually, over the space of a few days, she returns a bearskin rug to the floor, returns books to their shelves, and re-decorates the cabin's walls with bows and arrows, a Crow warbonnet, and the skin of a silver fox. Despite her best efforts, however, the Virginian had noticed the room's initial emptiness and realized what it signified regarding her intention to leave him and Wyoming. When Molly's farewell letter finally arrives, ironically, back at Molly's Bear Creek cabin, he reluctantly confesses to her that this was "no country for a lady" – that he could not, in any case, make her "happy" (276). Molly, however, replies that she in fact now wishes that he would continue to try to make her happy. With her impromptu declaration belying the farewell letter's message, the couple embrace under the presiding gaze of Molly's fabled ancestress, "Grand-mother Stark in her frame, rosy, blue, and flaxen, not quite familiar, not quite smiling" (277).

At this point Wister begins a new chapter, the novel's shortest, entitled "No Dream to Wake From." The three-page chapter begins with the Virginian waking from a nap and wondering whether he had merely been dreaming about Molly's confession of her love for him. He recalls that she had been reading *David Copperfield* to him "when everything happened," and he reasons that if everything he imagined did in fact occur, then "there should be a hole in the book row" (278–79) of the nearby shelves. After verifying that there is indeed an opening in one of the upper rows, the Virginian then gazes at the miniature portrait of Grandmother Stark hanging on the wall opposite his chair. Remarking to himself that her painted visage is remarkably like that of Molly Wood's, he whispers aloud, "May I kiss you too, ma'am?" (279). So he rises from his chair, lets slip the Navajo blanket "striped with its splendid zigzags of barbarity" (275), and begins slowly to approach the opposite wall, finally touching the minia-ture portrait "very gently" with his lips and then promising "to make your little girl happy." As he stoops down to make this promise to the hanging heirloom, the weakened Virginian nearly falls over, but he recovers by clutching the wall with both hands. At this juncture Molly enters the cabin and, seeing him faltering in front of the miniature portrait, rushes to help him return to his chair. Once again they embrace, and the Virginian lets himself "kiss her with fuller passion" (279) before promising to be a more compliant patient in the future. As the chapter concludes, Wister invokes the Sleeping Beauty motif by having Molly claim that she had been asleep until the Virginian's kiss awakened her, all the while wondering whether she had heard his spoken promise to her grandmother's portrait.

" 'I promise to make your little girl happy,' he whispered."

In terms of the novel's chronology of events, Keller's illustration of the Virginian's direct address to the heirloom on the wall, with Molly standing in the cabin's doorway, shielded from the direct sight of her lover by the angle of the open door, follows directly on the frontispiece's rescue scene. Keller's decision to illustrate this moment further intensifies the rapid development of the novel's romance plot that has transpired in just a few pages. The Virginian's admission that in this wild country he cannot make Molly "happy" has been transformed here, as the running caption of Wister's words indicates, into his promise – sealed with a kiss as in the stories of Snow White or Sleeping Beauty – that he will make Grandmother Stark's "little girl happy." Keller's illustration also intensifies Wister's words by transposing disparate actions unfolding in a temporal sequence into a static visual image organized through spatial relations. That is, whereas Wister's words depict Molly entering the cabin and discovering that her patient is not in his chair after he had kissed the portrait, made his promise, and nearly fallen over, the captioned illustration's simultaneous presentation of Molly's entrance and the Virginian's spoken promise functions in at least two ways. It highlights the slight but nevertheless enigmatic issue as to whether Molly has heard her lover's contractual promise; more important, it highlights the heirloom's magnetic presence: not only its tutelary gaze and presiding spirit but also its very power to compel the Virginian to approach it.

In the words that surround Keller's illustration, Wister grounds the dramatic tension and thematic differences between the values of East and West, "civilization" and "savagery," by counterpointing the Navajo blanket with Molly's reading copy of *David Copperfield* (and other novels). Wister's words explicitly mark this blanket as a sign of "barbarity" that – like the activity of rustling cattle – is destined to bow to the social and legal imperatives of civilization. The Virginian's approach to the miniature portrait, which is marked by his leaving behind the Navajo blanket covering him, thus symbolically anticipates both his eventual trip back East to visit the other descendants of Grandmother Stark and the novel's plotted transformation of his boyish narcissism into responsible maturity. Wister's words, in short, work to establish thematic and imagistic binary oppositions in order, finally, to resolve them somewhat conventionally according to Manifest Destiny's ideology of "progressive" evolution through competition and the (necessary) extinction of species and races.

At first glance, Keller's illustration seems essentially to complement this aspect of Wister's words. The picture's overall perspectival arrangement and its standing human figures endow it with a pronounced verticality. This verticality – reinforced here by the perspectival, receding lines of the planks of the wooden floor and by the light framing Molly's form from behind – centers on the open door (and the floor rug's left border) that neatly bisects the picture's vertical plane into evenly divided left and right halves. On the one hand, Molly's searching gaze looks down and toward the reader's right, the foreground province marked by arranged flowers and stacked books. On the other hand, the Virginian's gaze obviously tracks in the opposite direction, directly off to the left, this midground space distinguished by the presence of the "exotic" animal skin, a warbonnet, Indian pottery, and a couple of large wooden crates or trunks. Like Wister's words, Keller seems to envision the moment primarily according to the principle of visual contrast, as if the line demarcated by the open door arranges all the objects displayed in the room according to the following opposed categories: inside/outside, masculine/feminine, the wild/the civilized. As a result, a Navajo blanket counterpoints a table covering; bright flowers contrast with a warbonnet's bright eagle feathers; an animal skin covering a wall contrasts with crumpled bed coverings; a piece of Indian pottery contrasts with the dishes on the tray held by Molly.

However, an extended study of Keller's picture reveals that, besides the different temporal effect created by his visual medium, Keller's rendering of the spatial relations between objects and humans serves to *prolong* – and as a result, to intensify – rather than to resolve the various dramatic tensions and thematic oppositions forwarded by Wister's words and the plot's developing logical trajectory. An extended glance at this picture discloses instead how Keller's composition actually strives to *harmonize through contrast* these assorted souvenirs and displayed objects and thus how, rather than merely complementing Wister's words at this point in the novel, the picture stages a syncretic vision that anticipates the novel's ending. And by thinking about the picture's overall syncretic vision, its structural or formal harmonizing of contrasting objects, we can better understand how Keller's picture complicates the novel's plot trajectory and clarifies its underlying antimodernist critique of the very modernizing process to which the Virginian will be rapidly assimilated after his rescue and rehabilitation by Molly's hands.

Three elements in Keller's picture from the "No Dream to Wake From" chapter complicate Wister's words' predilection for thematic and imagistic binary oppositions. The first, and perhaps most obvious, thing to note is how the visual display of collected objects in the picture's left vertical plane basically integrates the various "trophies of the frontier" with Molly's shelved books and, of course, her precious heirloom. And in the picture's center foreground, the rumpled Navajo rug can be seen extending through both the left and the right vertical planes of the picture. There is, in fact, no neat or clear or clean division of the signifiers *wild* and *civilized* between the picture's vertical planes, and this fact suggests that Keller particularly conceives this woven Navajo rug not so much as opposing the signs of culture – say, the vase of cut flowers and the stacked books on the nearby table – as mediating between or potentially linking the cabin's various material objects and its posed human figures. Whereas Wister's words explicitly mark this rug as a sign of "barbarity," Keller visually centers the Navajo rug and draws it as in contact with the Virginian's left foot and as contiguous with the textiles adorning both the table and the floor at Molly's feet. If the Virginian's location can be said spatially to mediate between the leading signifiers of the East (the heirloom) and the West (the Navajo rug), so too Keller's centered Navajo rug – but one in a series of woven textiles on view – literally and figuratively mediates between the two leading human representatives of the West and the East, the natural and the civilized, the masculine and the feminine.

A second way in which Keller's picture ultimately harmonizes disparate objects and humans through contrast or juxtaposition centers on highlighting *the theme of shared sacrifice*. Structurally speaking, all the textiles displayed in the picture – and particularly the Navajo rug – represent an achieved fusion of nature (the rug's raw materials) and culture (the woven design). Thinking about the rug in this way reminds us that, in fact, all the displayed "trophies of the frontier" – the Indian pottery; the mounted and cured animal hides; the Crow warbonnet – are fashioned cultural artifacts, not simply signifiers of "nature," or "barbarity," or "death," violent or otherwise. Rightly regarded, in other words, all these assorted "trophies of the frontier" – just like the books on the table and in the shelves and the heirloom on the wall – display a human culture's working over and transformation or transfiguration of nature's resources. And if by this embedded structural logic such fashioned artifacts can and should be regarded as cultural productions, then it seems to follow that, in Keller's visual discourse at least, this cabin's cultural trophies from both the East and the West are essentially analogous to or continuous with each other, different by degree rather than by kind. In addition, Keller's visual and structural logic brings into the light, on another level, how the fact that they share the cabin's interior space speaks to a shared history marked by voluntary and involuntary *sacrifice*. There are the sacrifices entailed by Molly's "tiny ancestress" during the Revolutionary War.

There are the sacrifices of animals and tribal peoples in the era of west-ward expansion. In addition, there is connoted here the individual's nec-essary sacrifice of narcissistic self-regard – the kind of sacrifice specifically displayed in this picture by Molly's nurse-caretaker role and by the Virgin-ian's contractual utterance as he beholds the painted image of Molly's exalted forebear and prepares to enter the precincts of romance and marriage.

By depicting the Virginian's arms and gaze framing the miniature por-trait on the wall, Keller renders this revelatory scene as an enchanted rit-ual exchange between words (his spoken promise) and an image (the portrait). This ritualized exchange – sealed, of course, by the Virginian's kiss and oral promise – discloses how the cabin's entire household econ-omy gets organized around and finally centered by Molly's fetishized heir-loom, this miniature visual sign that is embedded within a larger visual sign (Keller's illustration) that is, in turn, embedded within Wister's ver-bal signs.[13] The miniature oval portrait that draws the Virginian from his chair thus constitutes the scene's innermost magical object of possessive desire. As Wister develops the heirloom motif throughout the novel, Molly's miniature portrait comes to connote more than a mere physiog-nomic link between the female generations of a family. Through the prin-ciple of contiguity – Grandmother Stark's marriage; the way in which her actual or represented presence inevitably evokes stories of her and her husband's Revolutionary War exploits – both Grandmother Stark's name and her visage stand metonymically for the warrior values of General Stark and his compatriots who established the nation through their ex-ploits and sacrifices.[14]

Although clearly occasioned by his specific passion for Molly, the Vir-ginian's physical and verbal actions at this moment distance or abstract erotic desire so as to honor, first, the magical, if not mystical, force of an-cestral desire and, second (and more generally), a nostalgic desire for the (re)united ideal family. So the heirloom's magnetic, framed presence speaks to the novel's deep investment in projecting – in the face of the le-gal, political, and economic crises facing the judge and the Virginian – a fundamental continuity between the nation's vital childhood and the Wy-oming present. Regarded in this fashion, Keller's framing of the heirloom by the Virginian's face and body and by Wister's captioned words illus-trates the third way in which his artwork ultimately harmonizes and syn-thesizes the various binary oppositions and thematic tensions identified and furthered by the novel's verbal discourse.

Existing as "the empress of Molly's spirit," as well as providing a template for her facial features, the heirloom finally dramatizes – through its magical power to compel the Virginian's approach – that a kind of *metempsychosis* is under way in this chapter devoted to awakenings from dreams. Both the putative transmigration of the "spirit," as well as the nose and eyes, of Grandmother Stark into Molly Stark Wood and the metonymic link between Grandmother's Stark's visage and General Stark's warrior heroism make the heirloom itself a magical totem or powerful talisman. Existing as a totemic or talismanic object that always accompanies Molly, "even if she went away for only one night's absence" (70), it has no use value per se. What it instead possesses and communicates, what its painted surface "speaks," is symbolic value. As is the case with the assorted "trophies of the frontier" with which it shares space in Molly's cabin, the talismanic heirloom testifies to the symbolic values associated with both artisanal labor and the warrior ethos, which is to say, the nobility of character associated with adventurous hunting and military exploits (courage, honor, dignity, loyalty, valor). *The Virginian*, of course, traces the genealogy of the warrior ethos – described by Wister in his 1895 essay "The Evolution of the Cow-Puncher" as that "spirit of adventure, courage, and self-sufficiency" – to General Stark, Molly's grandfather.[15]

Having no particular use value per se, yet at the same time connoting spiritual or idealized values associated with a warrior and artisanal ethos, both the collected objects on display and the drama of aroused desire in Keller's picture of the Bear Creek cabin's interior ultimately disclose the contours of Wister's utopian vision. This utopian vision somewhat nostalgically centers on establishing the appeal and the authority of the "noble household of the soul,"[16] a household economy that opposes a modernizing society's standardized, mass-produced utilitarian objects of exchange dependent on profit calculations. Although the novel's plot trajectory comes to rest with the Virginian seemingly situated at the very center of an emergent, modern political and economic regime in Wyoming, Keller's imagined interior of Molly's cabin – its textiles and pottery and exotic wall hangings, its talismanic heirloom – not only complements Wister's words and vision. In this instance its textured depiction of the look of a "noble household of the soul," dominated by heirlooms and trophies of warrior societies, visually interrupts and thematically forestalls the novel's ineluctable narrative progression toward the dead hand of modernity's economic rationalization, an ethos emblematized in the end, not by the Virginian's violence against Trampas, but by his "strong grip" on various business enterprises.

"CAN'T YU' SEE HOW IT MUST BE ABOUT A MAN?"

While the gothic romance's "central concern is its preoccupation with the proper way to realize female identity," the western genre's central preoccupation is instead with the proper way to realize a properly masculine identity.[17] In dramatizing this preoccupation, the "western" genre that Wister helped launch at the turn of the twentieth century also characteristically displays a secondary interest: dramatizing the emergence of, and subsequent strategies to defend against, real and imagined threats to the *family*, however this is defined – as the ranch worked by a nuclear or extended family or an occupation group (like a band of cowboys) or as the territory of the nation. Matters of love and work, issues of justice and democracy – such perennial thematic concerns addressed by "westerns" in Wister's wake typically get elaborated through a single basic plot: "the family [ranch] is threatened; the family [ranch] is reunited."[18]

Yet as genre westerns in words and film typically dramatize an eventual reunion of the endangered family and the return to or recovery of the "home" ranch, the genre's investment in defining an appropriately masculine identity and decorum characteristically involves a remarkable interlude during which the principal male protagonist becomes incoherent and powerless, typically beaten or wounded and essentially given up for dead. That is to say, the "orthodox structuring code" for westerns (and other action-adventure genres) inaugurated by *The Virginian* calls for the male hero to pass, sequentially speaking, from being objectified (as an ego ideal, as a potential object of erotic interest), to being challenged and tested (being beaten, given up for dead), and then on to the seemingly miraculous recuperation of his powers so as to unleash, at narrative's end, putatively redemptive violence on behalf of the "family" and its real or imagined territory. Nowadays we call this dynamic *holding down the 'hood*.[19]

Keller's final illustration for the 1902 edition of *The Virginian*, drawn from the "With Malice Aforethought" chapter, again depicts the Virginian and Molly indoors, with the latter figure on her knees, hands outstretched and grasping her lover's waist and shoulder, her face in near profile, while the standing Virginian looks away, out a glass window and toward the town street where Trampas awaits him as the sun begins to slide below the distant mountains. Whereas in Keller's frontispiece Molly walks beside the wounded Virginian, cheering him forward, here their entangled bodies illustrate her final plea to the Virginian, that he flee with her rather than (as he does in the novel's text) say "good-by" to her

" 'For my sake,' she begged him, 'for my sake.' "

and go outdoors to confront Trampas. And whereas in the illustration depicting the interior of Molly's cabin erotic desire gets distanced and
deferred by the painted representation of Molly's grandmother, here in
Keller's final picture such desire gets registered and displaced by or onto
the Virginian's low-slung belt, holster, and pistol, the obvious signifiers –
along with his clenched right hand – of his recovered, masterful power
and authority. No longer are his legs weak and his head addled. As Dave
Hickey puts it in his discussion of the television show *Perry Mason*, "Dad-
dy's back at the head of the table."[20]

In his insightful discussion of Clint Eastwood's films, Paul Smith argues
that this orthodox plotting of the male hero's vindication and reaffirma-
tion of his special status suggests how "the pleasure proffered in action
movies can be regarded . . . not so much as the perverse pleasure of trans-
gressing given norms, but as at bottom the pleasure of reinforcing them."
In Smith's view, the "orthodox structuring code" organizing the typical
action-adventure hero's rite of passage shows how the genre's final sequences want to overdetermine whatever critique of normative political,
legal, judicial, and cultural authorities and institutions may have been
raised to the (cinematic or literary) text's surface during that lengthy interlude when the hero is either without a clue or out of commission. Even
so, Smith makes a provocative second point about this "orthodox structuring code" of western and other action-adventure movies: that the male
hero's resolution of the masochism trope (the "pleasure" of being tested,
of getting it and taking it like a man) into a fully recovered mastery at
narrative's end cannot in any case fully displace the text's evidence of "a
residual, barely avowed male hysteria." Novel readers and film viewers
glimpse this "residual, barely avowed male hysteria" precisely during
those moments when the male hero is powerless or impotent and when
he confronts danger as a result of his alliances with or dependency on
women such as, say, Molly Stark Wood. Such moments and such alliances
circulate an "underside, a double edge, or residue" as a result of the
hero's provisional abjection, and their existence thus troubles the genre
western's effort to revitalize and stabilize normative gender, race, and
class boundaries.[21]

As I have been suggesting here, Keller's illustrations for the 1902 first edition of *The Virginian* certainly on one level display a continuous and complementary relation to Wister's words. Yet each of Keller's illustrations
also means itself, also represents this particular artist's visual abstract, if

you will, of certain ungraspable ideas or essences that the novel's verbal discourse can only gesture toward – but never become fully capable of articulating. So for instance, I have drawn attention to how the frontispiece's visual rhetoric of layering both complements the novel's presiding aesthetic of presentation through concealment ("winnin' poker") and at the same time troubles Wister's words by exposing Molly's erotically charged physical presence and amplifying the fungible, performative nature of gendered identity. So I have drawn attention to how, during the novel's interlude detailing the Virginian's rescue and convalescence, a talismanic miniature heirloom organizes Molly's cabin interior along the lines of the enchanted "noble household of the soul," whose informing warrior ethos emerges as an alternative to the modern rationalized economy that fully incorporates the Virginian by novel's end.

The two Keller illustrations to which I have given extended critical attention in this essay clearly represent stages of the masochistic paradigm attending the western hero's overall passage through abjection to mastery. Yet by means of Keller's visual art, these illustrations also bring into the light an "underside, a double edge, or residue" that can be seen to extend, complicate, and at times – as I have suggested with regard to Keller's visual rhetoric of layering and the magical objects on display in the warrior's noble household – even surpass the apparent aims and intentions of Wister's verbal discourse. Taken together, all the illustrations that Keller contributes to the 1902 edition reveal the textual space of Wister's popular novel to be a complex terrain, a force field of competing as well as complementary ideological frames. More specifically, the two pictures that I have discussed at some length here vividly remind us of Jane Tompkins's claim that the popular western tradition that Wister's novel inaugurates "owes its essential character to the dominance of a women's culture in the nineteenth century and to the women's invasion of the public sphere between 1880 and 1920."[22] If one is willing to accept this claim, then such dominance and such an invasion surely get registered before readers' eyes in the form of Keller's illustrations embedded within and facing the pages of Wister's words.

NOTES

1. Owen Wister to George Brett, 11 November 1901.

2. Wister, *The Virginian* (1988), 3. Page numbers for subsequent quotations will be given in the text.

3. Owen Wister to George Brett, 2 April 1902.

4. Wister's correspondence with Brett during the preparation of Wister's novel *Lady Baltimore* indicates not only that Wister gave his hands-on attention to the matter of the novel's illustrations, their placement in the text, and the selection of a frontispiece picture. It also indicates that he met with the illustrator, Lester Ralph, and "coached him as to type and atmosphere" (Owen Wister to George Brett, 9 September 1905).

5. See Dykes, *Fifty Great Western Illustrators*, 181–88; and McCracken, *Portrait of the Old West*, 223.

6. Relevant illustrations by Keller are those of Jane Austen's Jane Eyre and Rochester, George Eliot's Dorothea Brooke, Charles Kingsley's Hypatia, and Anthony Trollope's Lucy Robarts. Although several illustrators provided the numerous pictures included in Howells's study, Keller and Howard Chandler Christy receive top billing.

7. The fact is, however, that Wister was probably being overly cautious in this instance. As Vorpahl (*My Dear Wister*, 288–306) has documented, the Wister-Remington friendship in the first years of the new century had already begun to cool for a variety of reasons. For his part, in addition to paying increased attention to his sculpture, Remington wanted now to produce oil paintings that would establish his reputation as an artist, not a mere illustrator of books. So in March or April 1902, at the very moment when Wister was completing his manuscript and negotiating the details of its publication with Brett, Remington wrote Wister that he was behind in his painting schedule for the year and thus must "suspend all illustrations for awhile" in order to make his usual late-May trip to Ingleneuk, the island in the Saint Lawrence River to which he and his wife retreated every summer (Splete and Splete, eds., *Frederic Remington – Selected Letters*, 299). Wister for his part was increasingly restive about being pigeonholed by the reading public and his writer peers as only a "western" local color sort of writer. For another guide to this episode, see Payne, *Owen Wister*, 188–95.

8. Owen Wister to George Brett, 16 May 1902.

9. My approach to these questions is informed throughout by Miller, *Illustration*, esp. 61–111.

10. My discussion of this aspect of Keller's style has been influenced by the essays on fashion and the body in Gilbert-Rolfe, *Beyond Piety*, esp. 255–304.

11. See Best, *American Popular Illustration*; and Meyer, *America's Great Illustrators*.

12. For an instructive overview of the New Woman, see Rudnick, "New Woman," 71. Rudnick identifies a first and second generation of New Women. Jane Addams and Charlotte Perkins Gilman are exemplars of the first generation of (often) college-educated women who both entered professional fields such as

social work, progressive education, and day care and became involved in various civic endeavors, such as establishing libraries.

13. My understanding of the function of the heirloom is generally indebted to Stewart's (see her *On Longing*, 132–51).

14. This metonymic logic works along similar lines in Willa Cather's *A Lost Lady*, where Niel Herbert associates Marian Forrester with her dead husband, who helped, via the railroad industry, pioneer the West: "It was as Captain Forrester's wife that she most interested Neil, and it was in her relation to her husband that he most admired her. Given her other charming attributes, her comprehension of a man like the railroad-builder, her loyalty to him, stamped her more than anything else" (Cather, *A Lost Lady*, 74).

15. Wister, "The Evolution of the Cow-Puncher" (1895), 604.

16. See Pecora, *Households of the Soul*, esp. chaps. 1 and 3. Although not specifically addressing Wister's works, Pecora's observation about adventure narratives is pertinent. Such narratives should be regarded, not mainly as exercises in nostalgia, but as efforts to construct a politically compelling ethos in contradistinction to the bearings of a modernizing political economy. The project of adventure narratives is to reconstruct a seemingly threatened warrior ethos for its predominantly male readership and to construct through words an imaginative, epical "household of the soul" that values freely chosen, not wage-driven, labor; patronage; autarky; landed estates. Like Wister's concept of "quality," the imagined homecoming to the noble oikos inhabited by noble souls supposedly transcends class divisions. The heirloom and "trophies of the frontier" circulate as gifts within a familial circuit of exchange and encode the magical force of a patriarchal warrior ancestry, not the commercial marketplace.

17. Radway, "The Utopian Impulse in Popular Literature," 248. White's *The Eastern Establishment and the Western Experience* represents in part what is perhaps the first critical examination of the ideology of gender with regard to Wister's life and work. More recently, the work of Jane Tompkins (*West of Everything*) and Lee Clark Mitchell (*Westerns*) on Wister and the western genre provides significant insights into the shaping influence of gender concerns.

18. Hickey, *Air Guitar*, 140.

19. "Orthodox structuring code" from Smith, *Clint Eastwood*, 156.

20. Hickey, *Air Guitar*, 141.

21. Smith, *Clint Eastwood*, 167.

22. Tompkins, *West of Everything*, 44.

2   WISTER'S OMNISCIENCE AND OMISSIONS

William R. Handley

Like Stephen Tatum, who concludes that the "textual space of Wister's popular novel [is] a complex terrain," William Handley finds "a narrative far more complicated in its formal methods and thematic effects than most critics have recognized." Tatum focuses on the "formal methods" of layering and concealment, in text and illustration, while Handley explores the narrative omissions produced in part by Wister's use of a narrator with an unfocused gender identity. While Tatum examines the novel's "dialectical interplay of erotic passion and violence," revealed both in illustrations and in Wister's portrayal of the relationship between the Virginian and Molly Wood, Handley looks closely at the submerged role of homoerotic desire, finding Wister's imposition of a "marriage plot" "overly sentimental" and "unsatisfying." Yet he argues, the "happily ever after" marriage plot is essential to Wister's understanding of nation building and its racial components. Later writers in this collection will return to both themes. Victoria Lamont, for instance, argues that the marriage plot is "crucial to the signification of property and class" in both The Virginian *and Frances McElrath's* The Rustler *(1902), while Louis Owens and Jennifer Tuttle explore how Wister's West and its preoccupation with gendered identity depends on the appropriation and erasure of American Indians.*

The nomadic, bachelor West is over, the housed, married West is established.

OWEN WISTER, Members of the Family

If men and women do not marry, and if there are not sufficient children to a marriage, the race will in a short time vanish – surely any one can see this. . . . [T]here is no form of happiness on the earth, no form of success of any kind, that in any way approaches the happiness of the husband and wife who are married lovers and the father and mother of plenty of healthy children.

THEODORE ROOSEVELT, "Race Decadence"

Nothing would have induced me to unite him to the little Vermont person. . . . I wouldn't have let him live & be happy; I should have made him perish in his flower & in some splendid and somber way.

HENRY JAMES TO OWEN WISTER, RESPONDING TO THE ENDING OF *The Virginian*

Owen Wister was not a very happy man. Yet his most famous novel, *The Virginian*, has a happy ending: the nomadic, bachelor cowboy known as the Virginian gets married to his sweetheart from Vermont, Molly. Wister wrote to his mother on 5 August 1902, shortly after *The Virginian* appeared, that the novel's "whole raison d'être" was its "nationality."[1] With this sense of national consequence, the novel is plot driven to the altar of marriage. Regionally identified with New England and the South, Molly Stark and the Virginian marry out West in Wyoming, and their union caps, among other things, the novel's extended polemic about the state of democracy in the American Union. It is specifically in the marriage plot of *The Virginian*, in which the hero must make difficult choices both to prove his character and ultimately to be made suitable and irresistible to Molly – with her implicit threat to traditional marriage as a single New Woman trying to make it alone on the frontier – that Wister formulates or, rather, reformulates the meaning of democracy and American character.[2] In Wister's view, men are created unequally at birth, and those of "quality" (among a restricted category of Anglo-Saxons) have a democratic opportunity to prove their superiority over those born without it, those he dismissively calls "the equality" or the masses clamoring for artificial rights. As Richard Slotkin argues, "Wister's 'democracy' thus provides a biosocial rationale for class privilege." The Virginian's courtship of Molly "is played out as an ideological dialogue" in which the Virginian tries to persuade her to alter her belief in equality and to see democracy, like her classroom of unequally talented students, as "the means through which a naturally qualified ruling class can make its way to the top."[3]

In a chapter that follows the Virginian's ventriloquizing the same views in his argument with Molly, Wister's narrator argues that with the Declaration of Independence, "we Americans acknowledged the *eternal inequality* of man. . . . By this very decree we acknowledged and gave freedom to true aristocracy, saying, 'Let the best man win, whoever he is.'"[4]

Wister omits his belief that only Anglo-Saxon men need sign up for the contest.

The depression and "neurasthenia" that this progenitor of the western suffered much of his life, preventing him from being "husband, father, or author with any persistence," arguably suggest the personal cost that Wister paid for living with incompatible beliefs, desires, and responsibilities.[5] What prevented Wister from fulfilling these responsibilities with consistency was, in part, his extended periods of seclusion in order to recuperate: "I must have this sort of thing periodically as I suffer in some spiritual way," he wrote his wife in 1904.[6] The deep resentment that he bore against those social and economic groups that deprived his class of its former preeminence also bears an informing relation to a pervading sense of dissatisfaction in his life that was as idiosyncratically psychological and emotional as it was bluntly political. Such powerful emotions, of nostalgia for past happiness and of bitter reaction against the present, emerge in Wister's most famous novel in a series of affective divides among sentimentalized romance, angry polemic, and withheld scenes of violence. These disjunctions produce a narrative far more complicated in its formal methods and thematic effects than most critics have recognized.

While the novel is at the most basic level the story of the cowboy hero's courtship of Molly and his defeat of his enemies, three unnamed figures play an important role in the narrative structure: the authorial voice; the first-person narrator; and the reader, whom the author addresses. Only the first-person narrator is a character. The author's intermittent addresses to the reader remind us why this hero has a national importance. *The Virginian* figures the reader implicitly as feminine – as one who, like Molly, cannot see how democracy is about natural, born quality as opposed to equality and who is courted to fall in love with the cowboy hero. For the novel to work on both a polemical and an emotional level, the feminized reader must effectively consent to her own inferiority. Yet the polemicizing narrator who courts us is also suggestively feminized by his attraction to the Virginian. To the extent that he is aligned with Wister himself, this bachelor narrator reveals how ambivalent Wister was about fulfilling the heterosexual marriage plot. While the frontier purportedly produced its greatest character traits precisely without women, *The Virginian* needs feminized figures – both Molly and the reader it addresses – to consent to the romance and perpetuate its hero's values. There is, thus, a telling paradox in Wister's figuration both of the reader and of the Virginian's masculinity. Wister's social ideology stands against majority views, those of the "bystanders" or the equality, yet his narrative depends on bystanders – the narrator, but especially the readers he courts – in order to form a consensus about the Virginian's heroism. The Virginian's quality, in other words, is like the tree falling in the forest: it needs ears (and hearts) to sound its virile heroism. Indeed, his "independent" value depends on Molly's, the narrator's, and the reader's romantic attraction to him and deference to his authority. Yet deference to feminine sensibility is one reason the narrator selectively withholds vision of the violence involved in building the Virginian's character, particularly in a scene in which the narrator is present but refuses to watch the lynching of Steve, instead giving us a vision of the honeymoon, a scene in which the narrator as character is entirely absent. The novel caters to a sensibility figured as feminine while denigrating it at the same time.

After seeking the Virginian's approval and intimate confidence throughout the novel, the narrator is left to play voyeur on the Virginian's honeymoon in the form of an omniscient narrator. On the honeymoon, the Virginian sees a small animal (a beaver) and imagines that it asks him, "What's the gain in being a man?" He adds, "But . . . the trouble is, I am responsible. If that could only be forgot forever by you and me!" (425). Addressed to Molly, the Virginian's words are curious since she does not have to assume the responsibilities of being a man. They might as well be addressed, as so many of his most intimate confidences elsewhere are, to the second person missing from the scene, the narrator. It is as if Molly has taken the narrator's place at the moment when the Virginian questions the masculine aims that the novel everywhere else supports. Once he is married, that is, the Virginian calls into question the gendered difference that otherwise drives this marriage plot. At one brief but key culminating moment, Wister seems to doubt the gendered grounds on which his novel stands, as if he would take the formula out of the western genre that he was ineluctably to shape.

Why would Wister give his novel an ending that its masculine ethos does not require? Wister's antidemocratic sentiments were as much a reaction against his bitter nostalgia for a romantic life that he could not claim for himself as they were a reaction against his class's loss of power; his longings for the nomadic, bachelor West were in conflict with the national imperative of marriage. The imperatives of convention are transmitted, according to Wister, by "bystanders," which include those reading masses who made him a success. Soon after the novel was published in 1902, writes Darwin Payne, Wister's biographer, the author "was the idol of the popular crowd which he so disdained."[7] Yet insofar as his bachelor narrator speaks for him, Wister was also such a bystander, courting and denigrating himself at the same time in order to marry his notions of Anglo-Saxon superiority to heterosexuality for the sake of American democracy.

Wister's wish to perpetuate his racial beliefs informs the novel's ending as much as the conventional sentimental reconciliation that, as Christine Bold argues, authors of popular westerns exploited after Cooper.[8] If the honeymoon scene reveals the price of being a (national) hero, that price, for this novel, is the affective gulf between marrying for love and marrying for race and nation. While the Virginian's marriage would seem to domesticate him, it is more accurate to say that domesticity allows the masculine individual to fulfill imperial imperatives – and at the expense of personal longing. Wister married off his hero not because he romanticized marriage in any private sense – his parents' marriage alone gave him little reason to – but because there would be a diminished national significance to what the frontier produced if it could not be reproduced.[9] Wister nostalgically wants his imaginary frontier in *The Virginian* to undo the transforming effects of Emancipation on the meaning of democracy and racial equality. *The Virginian* is Wister's response to the leveling implications of the Gettysburg Address, his emancipation of the Anglo-Saxon from Lincoln's racially more inclusive sense of the equality of men.

The "bachelor" West that Owen Wister celebrated and literarily memorialized was for him a double-edged sword. It created the true American and represented the greatest happiness that he had personally known, yet the brief era of the cowpuncher was ineluctably supplanted by the national imperatives of family and civilization, the very responsibilities that Wister's literary hero momentarily longs to escape on his honeymoon and that Theodore Roosevelt – to whom Wister dedicated *The Virginian* while Roosevelt was president – considered the subject on which any other subject's importance absolutely depended.[10] "Wilful sterility" in marriage was for Roosevelt "the capital sin, the cardinal sin, against the race and against civilization," one that he ranked as "not one whit better than polygamy" because marriage not only had no virtue without reproduction but also corrupted the meaning of both marriage and the civilization of which it was the cornerstone.[11] It is in regard to the assured perpetuation of racial traits that, on the last page of the novel, Molly's great-aunt, the Yankee matriarch, tells Molly and the Virginian that she will have the nursery ready for their next visit: "And so it happened that before she left this world, the great-aunt was able to hold in her arms the first of their many children" (434). By this ending, Wister intended to perpetuate, through marriage and procreation for the sake of his version of American democracy, that which was born on the all-male, individualistic frontier – instilling in the right families, in other words, the sense of innate and individual superiority that he discovered out West and that he instilled in the Virginian.

This essay looks at how Wister's retrospective longings and conflicted points of view affected his narrative methods. The divide between a romanticized "nomadic, bachelor" West and the responsibilities of the "housed, married West" was never emotionally (or even literarily) bridged by Wister, and in *The Virginian* it shows: not only is the most sustained romantic devotion in the novel the eastern tenderfoot narrator's toward the Virginian but the most genuine, poignant emotion is reserved for the Virginian's feelings for his fellow nomad (gone bad) Steve, whom, in the name of honor, he hangs for stealing cattle. His honeymoon with Molly, in contrast, has the feeling of a hypertrophied sentimentalism. Molly functions in a political endgame in which the personal is sacrificed and violently silenced. That the novel's ending questions the masculinist aims that undergird the novel's nationalism is not surprising when one considers that there is a divorce throughout the novel between private affect and national imperative – or between the personal and the political. This divorce mirrors the formal division of the novel between first-person narrative and forms of omniscience. Wister's ideology – his subordination of the lower classes, women, and non–Anglo Saxons to a select, naturally aristocratic class of Anglo-Saxon men – is most broadly understood as a reactionary response to the decline of his class and the rise of labor, immigrant classes, and the newly wealthy. What has not been given sufficient critical attention are the affective disjunctions and formal narrative problems regarding point of view that result when he translates his ideology into fiction. *Point of view,* understood narratively and politically, is key to understanding how the narrative structure of the novel works in consort with Wister's ideological beliefs. Even though the novel's narrative structure is the result of Wister's botched attempt to make his previous short stories cohere into a novel, and even if he had succeeded in creating a more consistent narrative voice, the narrator-author's intrusions in the text – when he addresses the reader not only in the preface but also at critical junctures in the novel – yet make narrative fiction serve fictionalized polemic.[12] Wister's narrative methods enact by proxy the presumptuousness of his elsewhere more explicitly racial ideas, ideas that propel the marriage plot and turn that plot into national allegory. The inconsistency of those methods exacts an aesthetic cost from the novel's formal and affective integrity, and a personal cost from Wister himself, related to the social costs of his ideology.

The greatest paradox of *The Virginian*'s fate in literary history and popular culture is that, even more than is the case with Frederick Jackson Turner's "frontier," it should be so embraced in a democratic society as if in inverse proportion to the narrowness of its author's racial ideology. Wister's Anglo-Saxon racism is not, as Jane Tompkins writes, "spelled out in capital letters" in the novel.[13] It is spelled out, however, in his earlier essay "The Evolution of the Cow-Puncher" (1895) and in his subsequent novel *Lady Baltimore* (1906), which drove Theodore Roosevelt to write a scathing fourteen-page response to Wister on White House stationery.[14] That novel romanticized the southern aristocracy and denigrated the innate intelligence of African Americans (both aspects drawing attack from Roosevelt) after Wister grew disenchanted with the West because he saw it as a seedbed for populism. Even by the time *The Virginian* appeared, its author had moved on: having romanticized the West because it had nothing to do with his upbringing in the eastern establishment against which he briefly rebelled, he now romanticized the South of his slaveholding ancestors.[15]

In part because the marriage plot serves the novel's underlying polemic, the ending has struck many readers and critics as forced and overly sentimental – even as a "betrayal" of the myth of the bachelor cowboy hero that the Virginian otherwise embodies.[16] Henry James told Wister in 1902 that his one, perhaps "perverse" reservation about the novel was the happy ending: "Nothing would have induced me to unite him to the little Vermont person. . . . I wouldn't have let him live & be happy; I should have made him perish in his flower & in some splendid way."[17] In addition to thinking the heroine a failure, Wister's mother complained that the last chapter about the couple's honeymoon and future married life was "superfluous."[18] Wister agreed with her in part on both counts but, writing her on 5 July 1902, insisted, "I should write it the same way over again."[19] While Tompkins argues that the Western excludes everything domestic from its worldview, she reads *The Virginian* as a complicated case that "states so openly the counterargument to its own point of view" when the Virginian, on his honeymoon, questions the purpose of masculinity.[20]

At the beginning of the novel, the Virginian asks another question related to his last one: "What's the use o' being married?" (6). This question, in the opening chapter, "Enter the Man," is to be expected of the bachelor cowboy, yet the scene actually ridicules not marriage per se but marriage for such unsuitables as Uncle Hughey. The scene effectively points to the superior suitability, when the time will come, of the Virginian's own marriage. The novel is, thus, framed by the Virginian's two questions, one that would seem to question marriage and the other that calls into question the aims of masculinity, those aims that make the Virginian's marriage socially valuable, as he goes on to become a member of the corporate class.[21] One way to answer the novel's framing questions is to look beyond the man to the future nation that Wister wants him to figure: the personal sacrifices to be made in assuming the responsibilities of being a man and of marrying are justified, for Wister, by their capacity to reframe the meaning of democracy through the ascendancy (continued through descendants) of a new, naturally aristocratic class.

Metaphors of germination and birth mark Wister's view of how quality finds expression over against the equality. What is key for Wister about the West's relation to natural, born quality is that as a laboratory for shaping and testing character, only those born with the right qualities will benefit from the environment. While the natural aristocrat can adapt to changing conditions, his ability to adapt is innate, not acquired. In the year *The Virginian* appeared, Wister made this point explicitly in his essay "The Open-Air Education," in which he cites the case of a farmer's boy "from good rustic stock" who is sent away from home for "a little cowboy life in the healing air of the West" but who, unlike the wellborn Wister, quickly cries for home and leaves: "Open-air education could not make a man of this luckless weakling, because there was no man in him to make. I am afraid that men, like poets, must be born so. . . . We may be sure that nothing ever comes out of a person save that which was originally in him. . . . Books, travel, open air, all these things are merely fertilizers and if there is no seed in the field no sprouts will appear."[22]

One sign of the Virginian's innate superiority is his ability to adapt to the new conditions of the West to which he has migrated. It is essential not only that he has come from somewhere else but also that he derives from a state associated, as Slotkin points out, with a natural aristocracy.[23] To be equal to any situation, in other words, is to prove one's quality over the equality – the urban masses but also the eastern establishment that is, precisely, *too* established in its ways. In this sense, the narrator as tenderfoot at the novel's beginning is Wister's self-indictment of his eastern self before he learned to shoot a bear or sleep under the stars. Arguably, however, the Virginian's most significant adaptation, especially as it separates him from the bachelor narrator, is his final willingness to marry. A fore-shadowing of the novel's marriage plot constitutes the first chapter of the novel, in which the Virginian's first words, as he teases Uncle Hughey for his repeated marriages, are an interdiction against such a plot and set the stage for his final adaptation to new conditions: "Off to get married *again?* Oh, don't!" "It ain't again," says Uncle Hughey. "Who says it's again? Who told you anyway?" The Virginian replies, "Why, your Sunday clothes told me, Uncle Hughey. They are speakin' mighty loud o' nuptials. . . . Ain't them gloves the same yu' wore to your last weddin'" (3). At this point, the narrator steps out to the rail platform to see the man whom he overhears and whose story he will narrate. It is the narrator's first act of courtship, serving as mediator between the reader's and (later) Molly's desires for the irresistible Virginian. In this mediation, the narrator's attraction feminizes him when translated heterosexually:

Lounging there at ease against the wall was a slim young giant, more beautiful than pictures. . . . Had I been the bride, I should have taken the giant, dust and all.

He had by no means done with the old man.

"Why, yu've hung weddin' gyarments on every limb!" he now drawled, with admiration. "Who is the lucky lady this trip?"

The old man seemed to vibrate. "Tell you there ain't been no other! Call me a Mormon, would you? . . . Then name some of my wives. Name two. Name one. Dare you!" (4)

The Virginian then demonstrates his adroitness at humiliating an old man of legendary unsuitability for marriage by raising a litany of tall tales about canceled engagements: to a woman whose doctor ordered a southern climate; to one who got hanged; to one who got married to someone else the day before Hughey was to wed her; to one who claimed to have lost her memory. Uncle Hughey can defend himself only by saying, "Where's the wives in all this? Show the wives!" In another attempt to defend his failure to make it to the altar, he reverses the national argument for procreation and grumbles, "This country's getting full of kids. . . . It's doomed" (5). The Virginian finally urges him,

"Oh, don't get married again, Uncle Hughey! What's the use o' being married?"

"What's the use?" echoed the bridegroom, with scorn. "Hm! When you grow up you'll think different."

"Course I expect to think different when my age is different." (6)

The Virginian, who warns Trampas in the next chapter to smile when Trampas insults him, knows how to leaven his jibes with humor. More important, he knows how he will change his own mind about marriage, as a man who adapts to new conditions. Tucked into this dialogue is the surest evidence that he will: the narrator's profession of seduction by this giant "more beautiful than pictures." *Had I been the bride*: by this claim, the narrator seduces the feminized reader as the Virginian will seduce Molly. Contrasted with the litany of women who found it all too easy to resist Uncle Hughey, the narrator's assertion of a helplessness saved only by his gender situates the Virginian's marriage to Molly as something beyond free choice, in the realm of an imperative. It will constitute a forced choice in the manner that Wister's evolutionary model for the cowpuncher is, in the socially Darwinian sense, inevitably foreordained by that which "slumbers" in the Anglo-Saxon.

As author, Wister not only orchestrates the nationally symbolic union between his characters but also carries the affective investment in the novel's marriage plot as the eastern, tenderfoot narrator he so closely resembles. The narrator is more memorable than the Virginian's love interest precisely because he is won over by the Virginian from the beginning. He is the affective gauge telling us that Molly is next. Much of the novel involves the narrator's gradual coming to equality with this man of quality, proving his worth to the Virginian over time, by learning when to speak and when not to, for example, or how not to show fear. The narrator is not so much the eastern, aristocratic arbiter of superiority, as Slotkin suggests, as he is the Virginian's tutee in naturally aristocratic behavior.[24] Yet the elision of author and narrator makes that distinction moot: more and more, as the narrator omnisciently narrates the Virginian's story and as the Virginian ventriloquizes the narrator/Wister's views, the bearer of innate superiority and the tutee of that superiority mutually constitute each other and become ideologically indistinguishable.

The narrator provides erotic descriptions of the Virginian that have no equivalent in his descriptions of Molly. For this reason, Forrest Robinson has called the narrator "Molly's leading, if unannounced, competitor in love."[25] Many critics have commented on these passages in which the narrator compares the cowboy's movement to "the undulations of a tiger, smooth and easy, as if his muscles flowed beneath the skin" (2) and in which he says that he has "never seen a creature more irresistibly handsome" (212). Indeed, the romantic ardor that he feels for the Virginian is translated in heterosexual terms: "Had I been a woman, it would have made me his to do what he pleased with on the spot" (215–16). The narrator twice reminds the reader that he is not a woman. Robinson argues that the narrator "envies Molly her triumph, and . . . his envy, in turn, flows into and informs the management and tone of his narrative."[26] Indeed, his envy sends him voyeuristically on the couple's honeymoon, in abrogation of his fictional self: narrator bleeds into author in an excess of vision.

As we have seen, during the honeymoon, which is mandated by a heterosexual plot, the Virginian questions the very imperatives that sent him there: "What's the gain in being a man?" The Virginian's unexpected question and desires on the honeymoon have been interpreted as a wish to return to innocence or to an earth mother, a wish that verges toward oblivion as the Virginian desires "to become the ground, become the water, become the trees, mix with the whole thing. Not know myself from it. Never unmix again." Looking at Molly, he demands: "Why is that?" (425–26). What he questions, tellingly, is the gendered structure of human identity and relations. The passage reveals more than just the price of being a hero or the desire to become a little boy again: having finally acceded to marriage, the Virginian expresses a wish to lose *all* human and sexual identity in his wish "never [to] unmix again" from an undifferentiated natural world. The natural order, however, is the model for the Virginian's socially Darwinian evolution as a cowpuncher who has had his Anglo-Saxon blood awakened in him on the frontier. Having finally mated with his suitable counterpart, then, the Virginian seems to relinquish the evolutionary fight, much like Edna Pontellier at the end of Kate Chopin's *The Awakening.* And like Chopin's heroine, the Virginian seems to want to escape the imperatives of gender roles, domesticity, and civilization. But whereas Edna's escape is from marriage, the Virginian's is into it. The innate ability to adapt to the imperatives of civilization, the honeymoon suggests, has its (natural) limits.

While on the level of plot Wister succeeds in wedding the North and the South after the Virginian's courtship of Molly, the emotional believability of that marriage depends on the success of the narrator's courtship of the reader. Slotkin argues that the courtship structure defines the hero's relations with the male narrator: he must be won over by the Virginian's superiority.[27] Yet the crucial courtship that supersedes even that one in importance is that between the narrator and the reader. The reader is an explicit figure whom the narrator often addresses, breaking away from his role as a character. What interests me is not so much the fact that the Virginian courts Molly to share what is essentially Wister's point of view as Wister's attempt to court the reader, a reader whom he simultaneously figures as someone too unthinking to see things as they are: "Forgive my asking you to use your mind. It is a thing which no novelist should expect of his reader" (372), he interjects at one point. Since Wister situates himself as first-person narrator, as third-person limited and omniscient narrator, and as author, the reader is oriented to points of view that feel authoritative individually but that collectively undermine the novel's persuasiveness and produce telling elisions and blind spots, especially regarding the moments of violence that Wister's ideology ultimately makes recourse to, as Lee Mitchell has explored.[28] While, like any novel, *The Virginian* depends on imaginative energy and a capacity to bring things to vision, Wister presumes that most of his readers naturally do not have the vision to see; the novel's values can be seen as true, in a self-reinforcing way, only by those with the natural eyes to see them as true. Yet the novel vies for the reader's consent as few novels do.

Wister did not just admire Roosevelt; he desired his presidential powers. While in *The Virginian* omniscience is incompatible with first-person narration, it acts as the wishful literary equivalent of executive power or of the presidential bully pulpit. "Let the best man win! That is America's word. That is true democracy. And true democracy and true aristocracy are one and the same thing. If anybody cannot see this, so much worse for his eyesight" (125), the narrator polemically explicates for the author, with a force like that of Roosevelt (who writes, "Surely any one can see this").[29] "If anybody cannot see this": the political presumption here is inseparable from the narrative presumption involved in a first-person narrator who often reports on things that he cannot have seen or heard in his role as a character. It is that overtly polemical nature of the novel – with the voices of narrator and author blending indistinguishably into each other – that both damages the literary quality of the novel and authorizes its national allegory, rededicated as it was in 1911 "to the greatest benefactor we people have known since Lincoln," Theodore Roosevelt. In his concluding assertion that "we people will prove ourselves equal to the severest test to which political man has yet subjected himself – the test of Democracy" (vii), Wister omits mentioning the narrowness of the "we" whose point of view he assumes.

Wister's lack of self-consciousness about the distinction between his role as author and his role as narrator is evident in his address "To the Reader" before the novel, in which he describes his relationship to his fictional creation with a paternal simile that suggests just how personal this fiction is: "Sometimes readers inquire, Did I know the Virginian? As well, I hope, as a father should know his son" (xi). The simile is apt: Wister transformed his bachelor days into literary offspring, a transformation not unlike that of the Virginian's transition between his former love for his best friend, Steve, and his subsequent devotion to Molly, with whom he will have "many children." The author's giving birth to his literary creation fulfills in a different form Roosevelt's imperative to perpetuate the race and its civilized values. In the same year that Roosevelt published "Race Decadence," in which he praises the happiness of marriage and family, Wister published a collection of his Western tales that he titled *Members of the Family* – the family, that is, of his western offspring.

Wister's use of a procreative simile to describe his relationship to the real-life figure of the Virginian publicly heterosexualizes a same-sex friendship characterized by romantic ardor. The depth and quality of the author's affections for other men – and of one man's affections for Wister – are apparent in his biography. The likelihood of this unconventional and deep emotional core in Wister's life helps explain how his fiction works narratively and why his ideology splits the differences among love, responsibility, justice, and violence in the cause of national and heterosexual imperatives. As Krista Comer has argued, if *The Virginian* "consolidates the new twentieth-century heterosexual imperative, it also consolidates the struggle *against* that imperative," or at least suggests such a struggle.[30] The unsatisfying, sentimental resolution of *The Virginian* resolves things both personally and politically for Wister. While the Virginian commits acts of violence explicitly against Molly's wishes, she is only the ostensible, and heterosexualized, figure of capitulation before the hero's sense of moral imperative. The others are Wister himself and the reader whom he figures. Seeming archetypically to support the cause of patriarchal honor and marriage, violence between men and conflict between a man and a woman in this novel serve alike to keep from view love between men, that which falls outside of heterosexual marriage and the national cause of reproduction, as the Virginian on his honeymoon by implication longs to escape.

Wister reveals the "hidden" and more genuine emotions to characters who are bystanders and hides the most sentimental emotions from every character but the Virginian and Molly while presenting them in full view to the reading masses, as if he were capitulating to them, through a thinly veiled version of himself who could not be standing by as the narrator-character. Wister weds marriage and nation in his novel and beliefs only insofar as he keeps from readers' immediate view what he sacrifices on the altar of Western marriage for the sake of national significance. For Wister, such sacrifice likely involved the repression of something between homo-social desire and same-sex love, the suggestive evidence of which is made especially ambiguous by the silence surrounding it in Wister's time. It is unlikely that even if Wister had not killed off these feelings but "gotten to know himself," as Tompkins wryly puts it, either in Europe studying mu-sic or among his fellow nomadic, bachelor cowboys, he would have ulti-mately avoided the "housed, married" life that he came to know.[31] Evi-dence for Wister's deep affections toward the same sex has primarily been located in those textual moments when the narrator, with whom the au-thor aligns himself, describes the Virginian's beauty or imagines himself as a woman easily seduced by him. Jane Tompkins and Blake Allmen-dinger also read this possibility into the special relationship between the Virginian and his friend Steve, who is the only one to call him "Jeff" and who knew the Virginian "awful well" (343).[32] I would add to these sugges-tive passages other suggestive facts and silences in Wister's life and in Dar-win Payne's biography of the writer.

The biographical moments mostly involve the aptly named George West, who was the original inspiration for the Virginian. Wister met West in 1887, on his second trip to Wyoming, when West was one of his guides. A correspondence immediately sprang up between them. In his first let-ter to Wister shortly after Wister returned to Cambridge for law school, West described in detail how he went hunting for horse thieves who had stolen thirteen head from him and more from neighbors. One of the ag-grieved parties persuaded West that stern measures must be taken and that they must capture them and return them for vigilante execution. The result of this search is not known, but it stirred Wister's imagination. Wister's biographer writes, "If Wister had been captivated by West's mas-tery of the outdoors, so had West obviously been captivated by the charm of this cultured Easterner." West thanked Wister for a quilt with which he had presented him, and he hoped that the report was untrue that said that the other guide, Jules Mason, was to receive an even greater gift of a six-shooter. "It irritated West," writes Payne, "that Mason already was claiming full credit for the success of their hunting expedition." West vied not only for Wister's affections but also for his continued financial support, and over the next few years, that support came in a series of large loans to help West build a cabin and develop his ranch. West, how-ever, had persistent financial troubles, and his letters to Wister requesting more aid were laced with longing: "Well it won't be long before we will be out in *our mountains* again," he wrote in 1890.[33] After a visit in 1891, Wister wrote his first western story, "Hank's Woman," to which I will return at greater length below, in which Wister based the main character, Lin Maclean, on George West. The eastern tenderfoot describes him in the first version of the story as the one "whom among all cowpunchers I love most."[34] In the 1900 version of the story, after Wister had married his wife, Molly, this line is omitted, and the Virginian replaces Lin McLean as the central character. Thus began the erasure of George West from the public record about the personal sources for the Virginian.

Shortly after the Johnson County War of 1892, which found Wister siding with the large cattle ranchers and which served as inspiration for the vigilante justice in *The Virginian,* Wister decided not to go through with a planned hunting expedition with West. The time was not propitious since Wister was also an outspoken friend of imprisoned vigilantes and could not "easily resume his relationships with common cowboys and noted badmen." Although the precise reason for canceling the trip is not clear, Payne writes,

Curiously, however, instead of writing a letter, he made a round trip of some five thousand miles to tell West in person. His friends were puzzled that he would take such a journey only to turn around and come back, and indeed a hint of mystery exists as to why he did. . . . On July 11, Wister's train rolled into Cinnabar, Montana, and there on the platform stood an expectant George West. Wister was reluctant to admit that he was cancelling the hunting trip and returning East that very afternoon. But as they walked up and down the platform, he at last managed to tell West. They drank beer and talked for the rest of the afternoon, and at 6:15 P.M. Wister boarded the East-bound train for the return trip.

While some have suggested that the trip was an act of bravado to prove that he was not afraid to go West in the midst of the Johnson County War, Payne offers another explanation – that Wister insisted on paying West the $75 fee for his services for the hunting trip and that "he may have wanted to do so in person" since West had already arranged to take time off and was "as usual in financial difficulty." Yet especially given the fact that Wister described this nine-day round-trip as one of "almost unalloyed pleasure and content," it seems that something much more personal and self-interested was involved. West's letters to Wister following this trip mixed financial with emotional need and offered expressions of love. West complained that his part of the country seemed less and less important to Wister and that, as Payne describes it, "if his friend no longer were to spend summers there, West was not certain he cared to stay himself," reminding Wister that at one time they had discussed becoming partners. The constant requests for money did begin to annoy Wister, who asked West, like a father to a son (although they were the same age), to account for what had happened to the money. West responded that were it not for Wister's advice, "he would have left cowboy life two years earlier to work on the railroad. Wister was so swayed that he cancelled all West's debts." Overwhelmed, West wrote to Wister that his letter "sent a chill" over him: "You are good, Wister and a Christian if there are any on earth. . . . Yes, you are a friend to me & the best I have ever had or will ever have I know. I never thought one man could love another as I have grown to love you."[35] Still, the requests for money continued, and eventually Wister refused.

Why should a man, one whose politics did not support handouts to the incompetent, be so eager to respond to and to see, so briefly at the cost of nine days' travel, a man who continually asked for money he never repaid? Moreover, the same man who inspired the Virginian wrote to Wister in 1900, as if he were the model for Steve also, "I was arrested for cattle stealing, and gave bond." That year, West married a refined Massachusetts woman who had studied at the Boston Conservatory of Music. Wister served as best man, and the Wests visited Wister and his new wife, Molly, in Philadelphia. On returning to the cabin that Wister financed for them, West wrote, "I do wish you could see me in my new house. . . . When evening comes and Mrs. West [is] at the piano singing some sweet soft air while I am lying on an easy couch dressed in some of the nice clothes that you have sent me[,] I cannot help thinking that life is sweeter to me than to any other man." West's own good fortune, he declared, was largely due to Wister. "I love you for it," he wrote. It was at this time that Wister composed "the best pages I have ever written," the honeymoon scene in *The Virginian.* Years later, Wister acknowledged some of the actual individuals who had inspired the Virginian, although none of them, as Payne observes, was from Wyoming and all of them had been met after the character was created. "The one cowboy to whom Wister obviously owed the greatest debt he never mentioned. . . . Wister's omission of the man who was his first and most impressionable western hero is striking," writes Wister's biographer. Payne offers two explanations for this omission: to tie the Virginian too closely to an individual would detract from the character's imaginative power; and Wister had become disenchanted with West because of his never-ending requests for help. I would offer a third: too

closely for Wister's own comfort, the eastern tenderfoot's ardor for the
Virginian resembled Wister's devotion to West or, perhaps more point-
edly, West's devotion to Wister: "When I clearly see what you have done
for me I must acknowledge you as my God, for I know that *you* have saved
me."[36]

In the next thirty years, West wrote Wister two letters; there is no evidence that Wister reciprocated. After sixteen years of not writing, West
wrote in 1918, "Wister: I want you to remember this, that with all my faults
I love you as I did long years ago, and shall always want to see you when you
come to Seattle." (West had left Wyoming after having been warned by
his cattle associates that if he did not he would be shot.) Then in 1934
came the last letter: "I think of you every day, . . . when I go about my work
as a janitor in an apartment house." Payne writes, "As far as West was concerned, there was no question about it – he himself was the Virginian.
Ironically, this man, whose supposed lack of self-control had brought a
breach in the relationship with Wister, never publicly claimed the honor.
Only his close friends and relatives heard the story."[37] West died in 1951,
at the age of ninety. He and his wife had no children.

Although the case of West does not demonstrate conclusively that he
and Wister shared "forbidden" feelings, it certainly does demonstrate
that Wister's approach toward this real-life Virginian, who, like Steve,
stole cattle and squandered others' property, is quite different from the
way in which the Virginian metes out unforgiving justice to his own best
friend in the novel. Another curious episode in 1917 suggests Wister's
softness toward a handsome young man who was accused of theft – and of
borrowing, like a talented Tom Ripley, Wister's very identity:

Wister's young French valet disappeared in Wyoming with many of Wister's
possessions. The valet, a French Army veteran named Charles Bret, packed
about one thousand dollars worth of Wister's clothes in his employers' luggage
and fled to Boston, where he rented a suite of rooms at the Hotel Savoy and
posed alternately as a count and as Wister himself. . . . Finally, though, his bad
checks caught up with him, and he was arrested one day. . . . Wister suggested
that charges against the handsome young man be dropped if he would reenter
the French Army. Bret preferred to stand trial. Wister urged in court that the
punishment not be unduly severe, and Bret was sentenced to prison for one
year.[38]

Wister's biographer does not stop here to speculate why the writer who
has his hero lynch his best friend should have been so lenient toward a
thief. Was Wister trying to make sure that the young man was not asked

to testify in the first place about their relationship? Omitted from Wister's biography is what the novel itself barely conceals: a type of love not legitimated by law that makes the execution of justice awfully hard to bear. When the Virginian is recuperating from the attack against him by Indians, he cries out "Steve!" "in poignant appeal," and in the presence of Molly and other women: "'Steve!' To the women it was a name unknown, – unknown as was also this deep inward tide of feeling which he could no longer conceal, being himself no longer. 'No, Steve,' he said next, and muttering followed. 'It ain't so!' he shouted; and then cunningly in a lowered voice, 'Steve, I have lied for you' (289). The Virginian unwittingly reveals a "name unknown" that calls up an otherwise hidden "deep inward tide of feeling." The cunning claim, "I have lied for you," suggests the Virginian's desire to break even his code of honor to spare his friend's life in the execution of extralegal justice. But if the Virginian was modeled on George West, the fictional character literally lies for Wister's friend by displacing onto Steve the figure of the cattle thief and bachelor who knew "Jeff," as the Virginian says to the narrator with a sob while "utterly overcome," "awful well" (343). Lying in the name of love is what the Virginian secretly longs to do. What is so telling about this bedside scene is that it is women as bystanders who hear this poignant appeal. And like the women, the reader is in on the secret: we know more than "Jeff" seems to know himself about the costs of being a hero.

Wister seems to have understood both the liberties worth killing for and the liberties worth dying for – as Steve does when he resigns himself calmly to his death – when he wrote in 1911, "All government, all liberty, reduces itself to one man saying to another: You may do *this*; but if you do *that*, I will kill you."[39] Although Molly threatens the Virginian by saying that if he kills Trampas, "there can be no to-morrow for you and me," Wister has her marry the Virginian anyway after the fatal shoot-out, not only because the man must be master to the woman but also because the Virginians of the world must kill the Steves and Trampases and will neither achieve their nobility nor perpetuate their kind without doing so. In this sense, the convention of marriage is acceptable – to Wister, as to the Virginian – only if the Virginian is not blackmailed into accepting the conventional morality that Molly represents. On the honeymoon, the Virginian reveals the "secrets of his heart" to Molly as he begins to resemble a boy of nineteen: "What I did not know at all . . . was the way a man can be pining for – for this – and never guess what is the matter with him" (426). The Virginian's brief hesitancy in naming what he has longed for, without having guessed before what was the matter with him, gives the admission the quality of a false confession and the marriage of this otherwise farseeing individual the quality of a conversion. While in the end the novel seems to support Roosevelt's idea that no happiness is greater than the happiness of a husband and wife who have children, Wister suggested otherwise when writing to one Mr. Hancock in 1933, toward the end of his life: "No, I don't want to see any of that country again. Too much nostalgia for past happiness. I have never enjoyed anything more than those camping days in Wyoming."[40] Once again, Wister, who could otherwise see things "objectively" and without the aid of bystanders, could not bear to look – to the past, to the place where he was most happy and free.

In 1902 when his novel appeared, Wister wrote, "Oh, the blackmail that we pay to convention! the petty, cowardly tons of blackmail! . . . The bystanders are always with us; whenever we take an unusual step we peep and squint to see how the bystanders are looking. In fact, it is chiefly through the eyes of bystanders, and not our own, that we look at life."[41] While the Virginian would seem to kick against convention and the gaze of bystanders, curiously enough it is because of the eyes of others that he feels compelled to fight Trampas: "If folks came to think I was a coward. . . . My friends would be sorry and ashamed, and my enemies would walk around saying they had always said so. I could not hold up my head again among enemies or friends" (409). This contradiction can be explained simply: the masculine gaze sees things objectively; women see things personally and subjectively. Wister continues, "Let nobody suppose that I suppose convention is an unmitigated evil. We all of us know that it is an imperative necessity; but I do not purpose to let it bleed me of my principles, my pleasures or my purse, or in any way whatever rub me out. . . . How, then to get rid of the bystanders? How to see things as they are and not as somebody else sees them?"[42] *We all of us know that it is an imperative necessity*: Wister's admission describes the imperative of his novel's ending when, even though he has bucked female convention about violence and equality, the Virginian marries conventionally. To "see things as they are" is to see them through the eyes of other men who measure masculine honor. Wister's answer to his question about gaining independent and objective eyesight is for young men to go to the open air of the West and be tested, as he himself did in acquiring some semblance of independence from his parents and their conventional imperatives. To consider Wister's views about "things as they are" apart from the bystanders' perspective, together with the fact of the Virginian's concern about how he will be regarded by other men, is to see how a presumedly objective point of view in *The Virginian* is purchased only by denigrating female subjectivity – and at the cost of Wister's most personal feelings. Since the novel depends on a feminized subjectivity – the reader's and the narrator's as well as Molly's – to grant the Virginian his qualities, it is the narrator, suggestively, who is denigrated by the very structures and aims of masculinity that the novel supports.

In 1885 as he was struggling with his decision not to study music in Europe, Wister wrote, "Were I surer of my powers, – or rather were my powers sure – I think I should not now be in America, but wandering with musicians and other disreputable people – having kicked over all traces. [But] a fortunate grain of common sense self knowledge . . . says 'You're too nearly like other people to do more than appreciate & sympathize with revolution' – thus I remain conventional."[43] Even Wister's decision to marry came through the persistence of others. Still single in 1895 at the age of thirty-five, Wister attended a birthday party for Winthrop Chanler, who, seeing Wister's large belly, recommended some "boudoir gymnastics." As Wister's biographer recounts it, "It was past time, he said, for Wister to take a bride. A few days later, Elizabeth Chanler raised the subject again, and Wister discussed it with enthusiasm, confiding with her 'more than I've ever told to any one.' " Payne adds without elaboration or explanation that, up to this point in his life, Wister "had purposefully decided against marriage. Now, however, he had concluded that he should marry."[44] To the extent that Wister's sense of calling to write about the West served a deeply personal need, including his need to serve the national purpose through the literary birth of a racial type, it may be that it provided a sense of romantic transition where there may otherwise have been only an affective rupture: when, in 1898 on the day the United States declared war against Spain, Wister assumed the responsibilities, as his family and era thought imperative, of marriage and family and wedded and raised children with Molly, the daughter of his second cousin, once removed.

This about-face is reflected literarily in dichotomous representations of marriage written before and after Wister's own. The last chapter of *The Virginian* figures as the marital Eden to the marital hell of Wister's first published western story, "Hank's Woman" (1892). Yet in both the story and the novel's honeymoon scene, what follows marriage is a drive toward oblivion, a desire for the swallowing up of sexual difference either in death or in an elemental return to prehuman nature. The story depicts, in grisly form, precisely the racial and cultural *unadaptability* of its characters to marriage out West: the no-good frontiersman Hank and his new, religious bride, an Austrian woman. As revised in 1900 to include the Virginian, "Hank's Woman" inspired the dialogue in the first chapter of *The Virginian*, where the hero mocks marriage, and is alluded to in the novel. The 1900 story is framed, significantly, like *The Virginian*: in his first literary appearance, the Virginian tells Hank's story to an eastern narrator. But while the Virginian knows the characters he talks about, he, like the reader, the narrator, and everyone else in the camp, does not witness the story's culmination in marital violence when Hank shoots his wife's crucifix – a sign of European civilization and of religious devotion completely alien to him – and out of rage and despair at her ill choice in marriage, his wife smashes his skull in with an ax. In not representing the violence that follows marriage, the story mirrors the withheld scenes of violence that precede marriage in *The Virginian*. The story is seen through a group of men's voyeurism and dismay in witnessing the misery of the only married couple in the camp but in not (fore)seeing the outcome. Indeed, the story's main events are presented in a relentlessly subjective fashion. As Lee Mitchell describes similar moments in *The Virginian*, "It is as if the very possibility of objective description were being denied."[45] If in Wister's beliefs masculinity is aligned with the ability to see things objectively, "as they are," and women are associated with subjectivity, then the men in "Hank's Woman" are suggestively feminized when faced with this mismatched marriage, as if their unmarried status limits their ability to see things objectively.

The Virginian's inexperience in marriage is aligned early on with the narrator's: "Have yu' studied much about marriage?" he asks the narrator. "'Not much,' I said; 'not very much.'" This exchange is immediately followed by a reversion to childlike play: "Let's swim," the Virginian says. "Forthwith we shook off our boots and dropped our few clothes."[46] After the swim, the narrator writes,

We dried before the fire, without haste. To need no clothes is better than purple and fine linen. Then he tossed the flap-jacks, and I served the trout, and after this we lay on our backs upon a buffalo-hide to smoke and watch the Tetons grow more solemn, as the large stars opened out over the sky.

"I don't care if I never go home," said I. (7)

While rejecting the domesticity of "home" and preferring relaxed nudity (in the company of men) to "fine linen," the narrator and the Virginian re-create domesticity in sharing the cooking responsibilities. The scene is a more natural version of the Virginian's and Molly's honeymoon, when the newlyweds lie by the water and the Virginian longs to swim like a little wild animal. In both the story and the novel, nature takes on the clothes of domesticity before the responsibilities of marriage and reproduction take over; this substitution naturalizes domesticity between men as a pleasant contrast to the later, unnatural violence in Hank's marriage, a soothingly subliminal substitute for the "real" (heterosexual) thing. In "Hank's Woman," such naturalized domestic motifs are seen when the narrator says that "glazed laps" of snowfields shone "like handkerchiefs laid out to dry" (3) and when the Virginian says that the waters by Pitchstone Canyon are "green as the stuff that gets on brass" and trickle "along over soft cream-colored formation, like pie" (21).

Contrasted with these descriptions of a naturalized, all-male domesticity are the images that surround Hank and his wife, Willomene, which are anything but soothing. Mismatched by Willomene's desperate circumstances and religion and Hank's lust and drunkenness, the couple represent the clash between a European woman and a "little black" (16) man who, unlike the Virginian, does not know better than to take advantage of a blind but "good" (11) woman. Marriage was "but a little thing to Hank – agaynst such a heap of advantages" (12), surmises the Virginian. Berating her for her ignorance of horses, Hank takes her on a trail along Pitchstone Canyon, which emits a "queer steam" (20) from its cavernous depths, down in which, the Virginian explains, "is caves that yu' cannot see. Tis them that coughs up the steam now and agayn. . . . And when it comes that-a-way risin' upon yu' with that fluffy kind of sigh, yu' feel might lonesome" (21). Although the Virginian knows how unhappy this marriage is – "when he'd come home and see her prayin' to that crucifix he'd always get riled up" (23), he says – the reader never hears a word from Willomene. What is key is that the voyeur-bachelor knows more than the married protagonists ever tell – yet he is not given to see things as they are or as they happen. The story ends when, on returning from a hunt and having left Hank and Willomene alone, the men of the camp see – at first with difficulty – the visible signs of what finally explodes between the married couple, leaving both of them dead. At this point in the story, the marriage is just about all the men think or talk about – or look at. They share field glasses as they look at the now lonely camp and newlyweds' cabin from afar, in a passage filled with as much detailed information as ambiguous appearance and guesswork:

The Virginian took the glasses. "*I reckon* – yes, that's Hank. . . . he's comin' in out o' the brush."

Each of us took the glasses in turn; and I watched the figure go up the hill to the door of the cabin. It *seemed* to pause and diverge to the window. . . . It was *too far to discern*, even through the glasses, what the figure was doing. *Whether* the door was locked, *whether* he was knocking or fumbling with a key, or *whether* he spoke through the door to the person within – *I cannot tell.* . . . I was handing the glasses to the Virginian for him to see when the figure opened the door and *disappeared in the dark interior.* As I watched the *square of darkness* which the door's opening made, *something seemed to happen there* – *or else* it was a spark, a flash, in my own *straining eyes.*

But at that same instant the Virginian dashed forward upon his horse, leaving the glasses in my hand. (32–33; emphasis added)

All the men follow, as now a woman's figure appears, committing unknown acts. When they arrive at the cabin, the fait accompli is visible through a series of clues:

There hung the crucifix, with a round hole through the middle of it. . . . The cabin was but a single room, and *every object that it contained could be seen at a glance; nor was there hiding-room for anything.* On the floor lay the axe from the wood- pile; *but I will not tell of its appearance.* So he had shot her crucifix, her Rock of Ages, the thing which enabled her to bear her life, and that lifted her above life; and she – but there was the axe to show what she had done then. (35; emphasis added)

Wister's style of narration by elision when the crucial, plot-turning acts of violence occur is here apparent: what we do not know, are not given to see ("I will not tell of its appearance"), is the violence that had simmered under the surface of this marriage, worrying every man in camp, and that has already erupted. It carries both the sense of inevitability and the inscrutability of the working out of a natural law. One cannot see, up close, the natural causes at work, only their effects.

As they follow the trail of a woman's footsteps that leaves the cabin, they come on the scene that "tells" the story and that yet leaves much to guesswork. As they approach Pitchstone Cañon, the narrator writes,

At first *I failed to make out* what had set us all running.

"*Is he* looking down into the hole himself?" some one asked; and then I did see a figure . . . leaning strangely over the edge of Pitchstone Cañon, *as if* indeed he was peering to watch what *might be* in the bottom.

We came near. But those eyes *were sightless*, and in the skull the story of the axe was carved. (37–38; emphasis added)

The figure that is not easily made out seems to be looking "as if" he was "peering to watch what might be in the bottom," but its eyes are "sightless," imitating the characters' obscured vision and the scene's opacity. But "the story of the axe" – indeed, the story of this marriage – is carved in violence that we do not witness as it occurs. What the figure seems, finally, to be looking at is the figure of Willomene below; the narrator "staggered at the sight" of "Hank's woman, brought from Austria to the New World. The vision of that brown bundle lying in the water will never leave me, I think. She had carried this body to this point; but had she intended this end? Or was some part of it an accident? Had she meant to take him with her? Had she meant to stay behind herself?" There is no answer from the dead, but from the canyon "a giant puff of breath rose up," a sigh that seems to ventriloquize Hank for McLean, who points at his body: "He's talkin' to her! . . . See him lean over! He's sayin', 'I have yu' beat after all'" (38).

The husband's right to proclaim such final victory over his betrothed is repeated in *The Virginian*, comedically rather than tragically, and with an excess rather than a dearth of objective description, as if the triumph of the heterosexual imperative marks the mastery of objective reality and the turning away from the feminized subjectivity (and feeling) of the bachelor cowboy's life. In this formative story, the landscape naturalizes and swallows up the bottomless violence, along with its precise contours of intent and motive, that terminates this marriage plot. At once subliminally, sublimely domestic and the sign of domesticity's demise, nature has a prescience beyond that of any character's capacity to know, as silent as Willomene and as unpredictable. While Hank's body is brought to burial by the men, Willomene's unreachable body is "left in such a vault of doom, with . . . no heap of kind earth to hide it. But whether the place is deadly or not, man dares not venture into it" (39). Neither do the Virginian or the narrator, in this story, dare to enter into marriage. Since the story naturalizes homosocial domesticity, fear of marriage in "Hank's Woman" is a fear of a different "natural law," that of heterosexuality, and of female sexuality. When marriage triumphs at the end of *The Virginian*, the Virginian tellingly longs for a nature anterior to heterosexual difference.

"Hank's Woman" can be read to represent Wister's misogynistic fear, not only of the female body but also of a feminized landscape that is marked, like the woman's body, by death. But in the light of the novel that it anticipates in its characters and concerns about marriage, the story can also be read as a corollary allegory to the one that Wister makes in *The Virginian* about marriage between racially suitable types. While, as Slotkin argues, the novel suggests that violence is a right reserved for a particular class of Anglo-Saxons on the national domestic scene against the laboring masses, violence erupts in "Hank's Woman" in the scene of domesticity when the married couple come from unsuitable and incompatible classes or racial types. In other words, while Willomene's violence is a logical extension of her marriage's unsuitability, is irrational and unsuccessful, and gives evidence of the need for social order, the Virginian's violence – against Steve and Trampas – is rational, successful, and enforces social order. Moreoever, the Virginian's violence is the prelude to his marriage or, more precisely, to Molly's submission to him in their ideological debate, while Willomene's violence is the postscript to a marriage doomed by the clash of cultures and types. In both cases, the narrative structure places one or more men, but always the eastern narrator, in the voyeuristic position of witnessing and interpreting these almost-laboratory-like experiments in social order. At the end of the 1900 version of "Hank's Woman," the Virginian "corrects" the moral of the story that Lin McLean draws from it:

"Well," [McLean] said, taking an offish, man-of-the-world tone, "all this fuss just because a woman believed in God."

"You have put it down wrong," said the Virginian; "it's just because a man didn't." (40)

In this early story, revised shortly before the publication of *The Virginian*, Wister has the Virginian espouse something associated with women – religion – precisely as a curb and a corrective to male lawlessness and desire; this is the conventional way he resolves the matter. Religion is that which sanctions the law that sanctions marriage, according to the values of Wister's civilization; to reject it, as Hank does, is to open up marriage to a violence that knows no bounds. Haunted by Willomene's unburied, and thus unsanctified, body, and feeling, as one might expect of him, no desire to attend Hank's burial, the narrator comes to Pitchstone Canyon, where he finds the Virginian, who "had set up the crucifix as near the dead tree" (39) above Willomene's body as it could be planted. In *The Virginian*, in contrast, masculine honor legitimates the violence that precedes the marriage – and the Virginian and Molly stand as far apart in their view of such violence as Hank and Willomene do in their view of religion.

Wister's work thus holds two contradictory ideas together. On the one hand, certain universal values enacted in the religious rituals of marriage and burial are upheld. On the other, the naturally aristocratic cowboy's sense of justice requires no universal consensus or practice to be valid – it is, if not extrareligious, extralegal. This contradiction between grounds for conduct and value is, however, resolved in an illustration that the narrator offers the reader late in *The Virginian* in order to explain how the Virginian's lynching of his best friend, Steve – outside legal jurisdiction – is not, as Molly would have it, immoral. (This passage precedes her submission to the Virginian in marriage.) In this illustration, Wister as author usurps the role of first-person narrator to ventriloquize Judge Henry in his effort to persuade Molly that the lynching was justified and right. The awkward narrative means used to advance this view enact, in other words, the view that they advance: the author is aligned in his sense of right, not only against one of his characters but against, he presumes, his reluctant readers as well. Yet this propounder of "objective reality" depends on the contingencies of perspective to make his case.

The paragraph begins with third-person omniscient narration that orients the reader to the Judge's argument against a view of the lynching as a crime, a view that the narrator assumes the reader shares with Molly: "Judge Henry sat thinking. . . . He did not relish what lay before him. . . . He had been a stanch servant of the law. And now he was invited to defend that which, at first sight, nay, even at second and third sight, must always seem a defiance of the law more injurious than crime itself" (370). Admitting everything that the reader or Molly might think she sees clearly at first, second, and third sight – that lynching "must always seem a defiance of the law more injurious than crime itself" – the paragraph then shifts into first-person and then, at the end, authorial voice. What occurs narratively is, in other words, the exposition of a subjective view – Judge Henry's – as, gradually, an objective or authoritative one beyond the contraints of character, including the narrator's. These are the aesthetic costs involved as Wister expounds a minority viewpoint precisely against a majority that includes his sense of the reader: we begin with a situated individual within the text ("Judge Henry sat thinking") and conclude with a polemical call to the politics of Wister's day. As the third-person omniscient voice describes a man's moral dilemmas, the narratorial "I" and then the authorial "I" step in to solve Judge Henry's dilemmas:

There come to him certain junctures, crises, when life, like a highwayman, springs upon him, demanding that he stand and deliver his convictions in the name of some righteous cause, bidding him do evil that good may come. I cannot say that I believe in doing evil that good may come. I do not. I think that any man who honestly justifies such a course deceives himself. But this I can say: to call any act evil, instantly begs the question. Many an act that man does is right or wrong according to the time and place which form, so to speak, its context; strip it of its particular circumstances, and you tear away its meaning. Gentleman reformers, beware of this common practice of yours! Beware of calling an act evil on Tuesday because that same act was evil on Monday! (371)

This passage is one of the rare instances when Wister addresses readers figured as men, yet his association throughout the novel of reformism with women's suffrage, and his deriding of the female reformers in the misogynist parable of Em'ly the Hen, would seem to emasculate these "gentlemen." That concluding admonition covers over the moral divagations that precede it, as Wister moves from authoritative declamation ("There come to him"), to subjective doubt ("I cannot say"), to an assertion about the relativity of context. In this passage, the moral or contextual difference between Monday and Tuesday echoes the geographic difference that Wister invokes at the beginning of the novel in "To the Reader": "Had you left New York or San Francisco at ten o'clock this morning, by noon the day after tomorrow you could step out at Cheyenne" (x). It also recalls the relativity of place in Wister's admission, when he chose not to study music in Europe, that were he surer of his powers, "I should not now be in America but wandering with . . . disreputable people, having kicked over all traces" and acting in revolutionary ways. The different world of the West is, like the world of Europe, one in which, as context changes, morality must change also. But while Wister seems to be arguing for the specificity of times and places and the relativity of moral contexts, his own sense of right here narratively transcends the specificity of his fictional settting, as the "I" becomes that of an author-polemicist's and not a narrator's, situated in 1902 and not 1874. While he views morality as dependent on context, he puts his fiction's context aside – thus reminding his readers that this argument is a fiction of his own making. While most good novelists and playwrights depend on a suspension of disbelief through the unresolved clash of worldviews and values that seems to imitate the clash of values in the actual social order, Wister presumes the need, because he feels that he knows precisely why the social order is misguided, for authorial intervention in making his fiction make sense.

Having shifted the narrative "I," Wister introduces the second person to/as the reader: "Do you fail to follow my meaning? Then here is an illustration," he writes, as he cites the instance of a man walking across his neighbor's lawn on a Monday and then walking across it the next day when there is a "no trespassing" sign. "Do you begin to see my point? Or are you inclined to object to the illustration because the walking on Tuesday was not *wrong*, but merely *illegal*? Then here is another illustration which you will find a trifle more embarassing to answer" (371). Wister reveals here not so much the limits of a legal code as his presumption of an absolute moral code in marriage that supersedes even the different contingencies of western context and that we can all, presumably, "see." In this illustration, setting is universal, and the consensus about the absolutely sanctifying act of marriage enables – in Wister's mind at least – the author to persuade his readers of the relativity of all other moral codes. Indeed, by the end of this authorial intrusion of shifting "I's" and "you's," there is a consensus of "we."

Consider carefully, let me beg you, the case of a young man and young woman who walk out of a door on Tuesday, pronounced man and wife by a third party inside the door. It matters not that on Monday they were, in their own hearts, sacredly vowed to each other. If they had omitted stepping inside that door, if they had dispensed with that third party, and gone away on Monday sacredly vowed to each other *in their own hearts*, you would have scarcely found their conduct moral. Consider these things carefully, – the sign-post and the third party, – and the difference they make. . . . Forgive my asking you to use your mind. It is a thing which no novelist should expect of his reader, and we will go back at once to Judge Henry and his meditations about lynching. (371–73)

The moral code regarding pre- and postmarital sex is the one code, significantly, beyond question, that is, the one by which he can assume that all his readers would grant his argument logic. Yet that code is dependent on a bystander: that figure that Wister bemoaned in its conventionality and yet here the one figure on which his argument rests. The status of "the third party" is not only legally critical in the act of marriage, and rhetorically critical in Wister's defense of extralegal justice, but also structured into the novel's narration. The eastern narrator performs this function of third party, extending all the way to the honeymoon. When that narrator becomes author addressing reader, the third party becomes two parties rolled into one: both judge and jury. While many have noted that *The Virginian* celebrates an individualistic hero so self-determined that he can say no to even the pleas of a sweetheart who threatens not to marry him, few have taken stock of the fact that, narratively speaking, the Virginian is not allowed a single act of significance without the narrator peering, at the least, from offstage. He is the one whose values Judge Henry and the Virginian speak in concert with. Yet in the end, the narrator falls out of the marriage plot and has no role to play. The marriage legitimates the Virginian's national importance and completes the novel's national allegory in part by divorcing the Virginian from the narrator's affections. For it ultimately does not matter what is "really" in the narrator's heart: it matters what he would do if he were the bride.

The law of marriage cannot, thus, be subsumed under the laws of popular government – or of the reformers – that Wister feels free to disavow. It is a law in line, rather, with those immutable values that will save democracy. The Virginian is, then, seen as obeying a law of the land, not in formally marrying his bride, but in following a law of his own second nature, after he has demonstrated his exemption from existing presumptions about legal justice. In the conversation between Judge Henry and Molly, which will help woo her to the altar, the "civilized" nature of the lynching of Steve is identified with the West as a region determined to avoid the barbarism of the South. This "son of the South" will thus redeem the nation from southern barbarism by exercising lynching in a different form out West and, ultimately, by winning over his northern bride. Judge Henry makes the following distinction: "I see no likeness in principle whatever between burning Southern Negroes in public and hanging Wyoming horse-thieves in private. I consider the burning a proof that the South is semi-barbarous, and the hanging a proof that Wyoming is determined to become civilized. We do not torture our criminals when we lynch them. We do not invite spectators to enjoy their death agony. We put no such hideous disgrace upon the United States. We execute our criminals by the swiftest means, and in the quietest way" (374). The South's barbarism lies, not in the fact that all-white juries take the law into their own hands – the criminality of blacks put to death is here assumed – but in the nonaristocratic way in which black suffering is displayed, as Slotkin has pointed out; hence the "genteel" way in which the lynching of Steve is related through the narrator, who cannot bear to watch more than the preparations. It is one more curious paradox, then, that in a novel that everywhere else seems to exceed the limitations of the first-person narrative point of view that it establishes at the start, the sign of the Virginian's civility is that his violence is not given to public view. In that sense, the narrator is linked to the reader as among those "not man enough" to watch. Tompkins reads the lynching of Steve as representing the necessity of killing off that which the western hero must abjure, such as femininity, emotion, and transgressive behavior – all in the name of the social order and his marriage into it.[47] When one of the men who are about to hang him urge Steve to drink some coffee, the narrator writes, "These words almost made it seem like my own execution. My whole body turned cold in company with the prisoner's. . . . I put the blanket over my head" (334). If femininity is being killed off, the narrator as a feminized figure would be lucky to escape his own execution: it is as if he survives by not looking, especially at the costs of becoming a man who marries and is severed from the other man he loves.

At once feminine and the denigrator of femininity, limited in what he can (bear to) see but omniscient, disdainful of third parties yet acting as one, Wister's narrator suggests more than just the author's own fractured sensibility as a man who subjected himself to the imperatives of a civilization that he was born to uphold but who longed to escape civilization, arguably because of something inborn. The novel's narrative structure, with its disjunctions of affect and perspective, suggests that the epistemological means by which "justice" is measured and meted out for the sake of a national imperative depend on the eyes of those to which such justice is blind: the democratic majority. What is remarkable about the world of *The Virginian* is that so much violence serves as the prelude to marriage and, hence, that so many other codes of morality and feeling – including not only Molly's against lynchings and shoot-outs but also the Virginian's "inward tide of feeling" for Steve – should be subordinated before the altar of marriage for the sake of a nation's racial future out West.

NOTES

1. Quoted in Payne, *Owen Wister*, 204.

2. For the argument that the novel is a reaction against the politics of suffragism in "the Equality State," as Wyoming was called for being the first to give women the vote, see Mitchell, *Westerns*, 113–16.

3. Slotkin, *Gunfighter Nation*, 177, 178.

4. Wister, *The Virginian* (1955), 125. Page numbers for subsequent quotations will be given in the text.

5. Bell, *Major Butler's Legacy*, 471. For a discussion of Wister's neurasthenia and the "West cure" that the family friend Dr. Weir Mitchell prescribed for him, see Will, "The Nervous Origins of the Western."

6. Quoted in Payne, *Owen Wister*, 227.

7. Payne, *Owen Wister*, 209.

8. Bold, "How the Western Ends," 123. Bold argues that the ending of *The Virginian* does not, however, successfully fulfill the imperatives of the sentimental reconciliation.

9. What drove both Wister and Frederic Remington, Christine Bold argues, "was a desire to create, in stylized fiction, an alternative to the pattern of Western history. They struggled to present the Western archetypes in ways which would protect their own versions of the West from the changes happening on the real frontier" (*Selling the Wild West* [1987], xv).

10. "The importance of all other subjects depends absolutely upon treating this subject as of far more importance," Roosevelt (*Works*, 158) wrote about reproduction in marriage.

11. Roosevelt, *Works*, 151, 160.

12. Darwin Payne notes Wister's difficulty with the incompatibility of narrative styles but adds that Wister chose to let those incompatible styles remain (*Owen Wister*, 193). Lee Mitchell argues that Wister's "very lack of success in integrating stories and points of view only contributed to the novel's appeal" by encouraging "a series of imitations that strained to clarify Wister's materials but ended reinforcing generic tendencies that allowed mutually contradictory possibilities to coexist." Mitchell is the only critic to have addressed the novel's structural incoherence. He does so in order to make sense of "the strange oscillation in our view of the Virginian as at once decidedly verbal and yet somehow inarticulate." Chiefly contributing to this effect is "the overinvested narrative perspective. The narrator's delight in the Virginian's verbal shenanigans and resentment at his restrained silence are both the result of a distantly third-person perspective, of standing self-consciously apart from the figure he is also so clearly drawn to know. Compounding this paradoxical effect is the structural incoherence of the novel, which alternates between first- and third-person perspectives as a result of Wister's incomplete consolidation of eight earlier stories. Midway through the novel, an omniscient view of the Virginian is established that gives a more intimate insight into his sensibility and makes it clear how much his silence is a matter of intentional self-restraint" (*Westerns*, 97, 101).

13. Tompkins, *West of Everything*, 147.

14. Wister quoted this letter in full in his memoir (*Roosevelt*, 248–56).

15. See Bell's *Major Butler's Legacy*, a study of the Butler family. Wister's great-

great-grandfather on his mother's side was the slaveholder Pierce Butler of South Carolina, delegate to the U.S. Constitutional Convention, who introduced the motion that became the fugitive slave clause in the Constitution. His grandson, Pierce Butler, was notorious for having squandered his inherited fortune and for having to sell 450 slaves as a result in order to keep his plantation. In an undated manuscript, Wister wrote, "I was brought up to revere my Grandfather. . . . Only since I have been past middle life have I gradually made out that on the whole he couldn't have been a good person. . . . Butler was cold. Never forgave" (quoted in Bell, *Major Butler's Legacy*, 476).

16. Forrest G. Robinson makes this point on the grounds that "it is part and parcel of the cowboy's culture to be suspicious of marriage. He regards matrimony as all that is artificial, constraining, corrupting and hypocritical in civilization" (*Having It Both Ways*, 43).

17. Quoted in Payne, *Owen Wister*, 201.

18. See Wister, ed., *Owen Wister Out West*, 17.

19. Quoted in Wister, ed., *Owen Wister Out West*, 18.

20. Tompkins, *West of Everything*, 155. Robinson (*Having It Both Ways*, 42) also gives attention to this passage.

21. Given the Virginian's future as a corporate manager, Alan Trachtenberg (*The Incorporation of America*, 24) reads the novel as the cultural equivalent of an economically incorporated America. Richard Slotkin (*Gunfighter Nation*, 173–74) also reads the Virginian as embodying the privileged classes' rights of aggression against the laboring classes.

22. Davis, ed., *Owen Wister's West*, 106–7.

23. See esp. Taylor, *Cavalier and Yankee*.

24. Slotkin, *Gunfighter Nation*, 176.

25. Robinson, *Having It Both Ways*, 45.

26. Robinson, *Having It Both Ways*, 45.

27. Slotkin, *Gunfighter Nation*, 176.

28. Describing the narrative as "curiously uneventful," Mitchell points out that "the Western's most distinctive stock features are never actually shown: the Indian attack, roundup, and lynching each forms instead a narrative lacuna, alluded to proleptically and after the fact but never represented directly." The novel thus "raised expectations for a genre it did not actually quite define, prompting readers to exceed the text in their own reconstructions" (*Westerns*, 96).

29. Roosevelt, *Works*, 158.

30. Comer "Literature, Gender, and the New Western History," 112. For an analysis of how this imperative was consolidated – at just the historical moment that *The Virginian* appeared – see Sedgwick, *Epistemology of the Closet*, 1–63.

31. Tompkins, *West of Everything*, 151.

32. See Allmendinger, *Ten Most Wanted*, 158.

33. Payne, *Owen Wister*, 104, 116.

34. Wister, "Hank's Woman" (1892), 821.

35. Payne, *Owen Wister*, 127–28, 133, 134.

36. Payne, *Owen Wister*, 197, 203, 196.

37. Payne, *Owen Wister*, 299, 328–29.

38. Payne, *Owen Wister*, 297–98.

39. Davis, ed., *Owen Wister's West*, 144.

40. Quoted in Rush, *Fifty Years of "The Virginian,"* 2–3.

41. Davis, ed., *Owen Wister's West*, 115.

42. Davis, ed., *Owen Wister's West*, 115.

43. Payne, *Owen Wister*, 78.

44. Payne, *Owen Wister*, 162.

45. Mitchell, *Westerns*, 102.

46. Wister, "Hank's Woman" (1900/1972), 6. Page numbers for subsequent citations will be given in the text.

47. Tompkins, *West of Everything*, 151.

3   WHITE FOR A HUNDRED YEARS   *Louis Owens*

Both William Handley and Stephen Tatum read through and beyond the manifest text of The Virginian *to suggest that its silences, tensions, distortions, and fairy-tale ending disclose the central questions and anxieties underlying the novel. They discover at its center symptoms of real sociocultural and biographical problems that Wister displaces through plots of romance and adventure. By examining the novel's formal and thematic contradictions and disjunctures, then, their essays show how gender identity and the related issue of homoerotic desire both constitute the novel's central, structuring absence and explain its overall dis-ease. The next several essays in the volume will similarly explore the evasions or silences in the visible text of* The Virginian *but focus on racial and class tensions evident in Wister's historical moment, with ongoing significance today.*

Louis Owens exposes the novel's historical erasure of American Indians and their long history in the West. Since, "in contrast to the drama of Wister's fiction, Indians were very much a part of the real Wyoming picture during this period," Owens examines how the novel's narrative organization of spaces reflects colonization. The dominant culture's cartographic impulse — evident in the surveying and mapping that produced bounded reservation lands and national parks in Wyoming — provides a metaphor for Wister's commodified tourist spectacle. For Owens, then, the novel's preoccupation with images of mobility and distinct boundaries points out how the West ought to be regarded as a "profit-making enterprise for establishment America, a capitalist resource in which stability is a highly desired commodity." Developing a theoretical insight from Gerald Vizenor to argue that "motion is a natural human right that is not bound by borders," Owens himself moves across the borders of Wister's text, in the process restoring some of its forgotten history and also claiming, for himself and for other American Indians, the privileged "American Dream" of mobility.

In August 1877 a handful of surprised tourists camping in Yellowstone
National Park awoke to find themselves staring into the faces of angry Nez
Perce warriors. Taken captive, the shocked sight-seers were plunged into
the violent midst of the Nez Perce War, the tribe's desperate attempt to
fight its way northward across the "Medicine Line" into Canada. This col-
lision of catastrophically different realities illuminates antithetical constructions of the West in America's imagination. For the tourists, Yellowstone was a national park, a bounded and strictly defined area of both
geography and culture created just five years earlier in 1872. At a time of
extraordinarily rapid and frequently violent change in the American
West, a historical period dominated west of the hundredth meridian by
the U.S. government's brutal, final campaign to neutralize indigenous
nations forever as obstacles to European expansion in North America,
the park's borders were meant to keep history and the chaos that history
embodies safely outside and thus to preserve a changeless portion of
mythic America. Parks are fixed spaces within which the imagination of
the dominant culture can play; they are not meant to be interstitial frontiers where cultures or worlds collide and Vanishing Americans reappear
suddenly like ghosts in war paint.

A reservation is a portion of land *reserved* for the disempowered, a concentration space designed to get the *indigenes* out of the way and keep
them out of the way while the rest of what had been their homeland is up
for grabs. The Nez Perce warriors, who had refused to be confined within
already overcrowded reservation boundaries, did not recognize such
lines of demarcation, and by capturing and removing the tourists beyond
the borders of the national park, they refused to allow any portion of their
world to be excluded from historical process.[1]

Eight years after this amazing encounter in Yellowstone, an Ivy League
graduate suffering from neurasthenia was sent West by his doctor, to Wyoming and Yellowstone, in search of health. The West that Owen Wister
found and eternalized in the most famous western novel of all time, *The
Virginian*, is not the West of Chief Joseph and the Nez Perce, not the un-
bounded world where native people moved freely. The West of *The Virginian* is a reality in which boundaries such as those surrounding Yellowstone
National Park have been carefully constructed by men in power, where Indians have agents but not agency. As much as it is about anything, Wister's
novel is about the questions of who fixes boundaries, for whom such
boundaries are permeable, and what lies in the vague, liminal margins of
such borders; the Indian, largely invisible, embodies these issues in *The
Virginian*.

Lines of demarcation have been established in Wister's West to control historical, cultural, and social chaos. The most obvious of these lines are the reservation boundaries meant to keep Indians in place and out of the way, and Wister makes much of the phenomenon of "permitted" and "unpermitted" Indians, those natives allowed by their white custodians to cross reservation lines and those who cross such lines in violation of white rule. As definite as the offstage reservation boundaries are in the novel, however, the reservation lines extend symbolically well beyond the scraps of America left for Indians and are mirrored and replicated in other boundaries the collective aim of which is to control and determine the privilege of mobility in America. Finally, the ultimate hegemony lies in the novel itself: Who defines the West and its constituent element? Whose novel is the West, and who gets to tell the story? For whom are all Indians "chiefs," all small cattlemen and homesteaders "rustlers" and "thieves"? For whom is the West a region of extractable resources, and for whom is it home? To define (from *definir*, "to limit"; *finis*, or "boundary, limit, end"), we should remember, is to fix, prescribe, control; in *The Virginian*, Owen Wister defines the West. At issue in *The Virginian* is who has the last word about the West, who defines, and who, therefore, controls. At issue is also what the Native American writer Gerald Vizenor has termed the *sovereignty of transmotion*. Vizenor argues that "motion is never granted by a government. Motion is a natural human right that is not bound by borders."[2] Mobility – geographic, cultural, social – defines the American Dream, and those in power are those who possess this mobility to the fullest degree. Covered wagons heading west, Huck Finn lighting out for the Territory, Ishmael shipping out on a whaling vessel, or frenetic hipsters on Route 66 all imitate this privilege, but their motion is a pale and insufficient simulation of the privileged motion belonging only to the dominant caste of America. When the Nez Perce fought to maintain their sovereign right to move, to be in motion rather than concentrated on a reservation, the U.S. military converged to brutally deny that right just as it had done and would continue to do for other native peoples.

Owen Wister, pampered Harvard graduate, family friend of Henry James and Theodore Roosevelt, and fervent admirer of Kipling, like all his class possessed this kind of privileged motion. Like the unnamed narrator of his novel, Wister can move West for recuperation on a ranch in Wyoming or hunting in the Cascade Mountains and then move East again on a whim, shuttling back and forth as he desires with all doors open to him. Just as they can access all geography, Americans of Wister's social class and economic power have privilege of entry into all social strata, hobnobbing with presidents and cowboys alike, joining both exclusive college fraternities and the campfires of frontier hunters. Those who do not have such access, those who are, in fact, denied the privilege of mobility, are not only Indians but also cowboys. Just as they have been frozen together in American mythic time, both cowboys and Indians are expected to remain where they are put in Wister's West. Cowboys are, in the economy of *The Virginian*, not far removed from Indians. Like Indians, when perceived as threats to the economic system, cowboys can be killed and their killings justified in eloquent paeans to "democracy." Wister declared, it should be remembered, that he liked cowboys because "they work hard, they play hard, and *they don't go on strike*" (emphasis added).[3]

Wister defined his novel as a "colonial romance" that "faithfully" presents Wyoming between 1874 and 1890.[4] These dates span a period that saw what has been called the *Great Sioux War*, the defeat of federal troops at the Little Bighorn, the Nez Perce flight toward Canada, the Ghost Dance movement culminating with the brutal massacre at Wounded Knee in 1890, and a great deal more violent history arising from the government's final push to shatter the resistance of Native Americans. At the end of this time, Native America was no longer in motion, the tribes that formerly ranged across mountains and plains now fixed forever in place. America east of the Mississippi had already been secured with the destruction and/or removal of indigenous peoples. In the South and Southeast, the major tribes had been removed to Indian Territory half a century earlier in America's most obvious example of what today is called *ethnic cleansing*. Indians had been contained by the final decades of the nineteenth century and were expected to stay where they had been put, as Wister's novel makes clear.

Although, by the time the action in *The Virginian* takes place, the power of the native cultures in Wyoming Territory had been effectively crushed, with the tribes decimated and enclosed on reservations, Wister's Powder River country had very recently been the setting for a great deal of conflict between the European American invader and indigenous tribes. In 1875 when Johnson County was created, the great Lakota leader Red Cloud still held sway in the region. However, virtually no trace or echo of this conflicted history finds its way into *The Virginian*'s supposedly faithful presentation of Wyoming. In *Imperial Eyes*, Mary Louise Pratt says, "There is never an excuse for this dehumanizing western habit of representing other parts of the world as having no history."[5] In the West of Owen Wister's novel, there is no Native American history, no history at all to be found in the western landscape prior to the coming of the European settler. Wister's Wyoming is a new land, a clean slate on which white ranchers will write their history and build their fences. In the rare moments when Native Americans appear in the novel, they are not merely dehistoricized but carefully and fully dehumanized.

The West was already an idea when the Nez Perce attempted to flee to safety in Canada, where Sitting Bull had taken temporary refuge with his Lakota followers. The idea of the West contained Indians, but only as a romantic residue of the past and a neutralized and fully contained component of the present, one doomed, according to popular thought, to vanish quickly. Indians were not supposed to have agency, and they were not supposed to be able to move across the boundaries established for them both literally and figuratively.

Owen Wister came West in 1885 at the suggestion of his doctor, the family friend S. Weir Mitchell, in an attempt to cure the young man's neurasthenia. It is worth noting that this same famed doctor/author treated Charlotte Perkins Gilman and looms large behind her best-known story, "The Yellow Wallpaper," a work in which a doctor's prescription for a young mother suffering from neurasthenia, or "nerves," is imprisonment in a kind of solipsistic nightmare in which the woman is not to write or to read or to converse. Chains and shackles on the walls of her nursery-room prison, bars on the windows, and a bed nailed to the floor symbolize the noted doctor's prescription for women in Gilman's story. S. Weir Mitchell sends a privileged young man on a wild western journey as a cure for the same illness for which Gilman's fictional version of Mitchell prescribes total isolation and immobilization for a woman. Both Wister and Gilman were treated by Mitchell, both were writers, and each responded very differently, although Gilman rewrote the doctor's prescription and took herself west to California. Like Indians, women were not supposed to have agency, and they were not expected to wander or cross certain boundaries, rhetorical or otherwise.[6]

The lesson would seem to be that for ideal "health" men are meant to be mobile, women immobile; European Americans are meant to explore and settle the continent, Native Americans to be confined in controlled, static enclosures. In *The Virginian* everyone comes West, but not everyone has free range of motion. The cowboys have all come from somewhere else, the way Scipio Le Moyne has come from Ohio and Shorty, destined to die for his weak mind, from New York. The novel's protagonist and par-

adigmatic western hero has, as his title indicates, come from the Old
South, the genteel world of cavaliers and tidewater aristocrats. The name-
less narrator is thoroughly an Easterner, and he comes West to vacation
on the ranch of an eastern friend who has settled in Wyoming; by the end
of the novel the narrator roams the wilderness of the Northwest alone
and confident, just as he returns to the East at will. The hero's love interest, Molly, is another Easterner come West, and her role – with one significant exception – is to remain in her cabin while the hero comes and
goes in the process of cementing his ownership of her. While some might
argue that by journeying so far West Molly demonstrates her own mobility, it takes only a quick glance to see that once in the West Molly becomes
a largely stationary feminine icon around which the Virginian will circle
as he makes the frontier safe for profit venture.

Members of the ruling class in Wister's Wyoming, characters such as
Judge Henry, have come from the privileged circles of the East, just as the
historical ranch owners in Wyoming of this time were often corporate
ranchers from New York, Boston, London, or Edinburgh.[7] The West of
Wyoming in this novel is a landscape settled by the East and used both
for extractable profit and as a vacation resort for big-game hunting, fly-
fishing, and rejuvenation just as Wister himself used it.

Before a landscape can be fully occupied, both literally and symbolically, of course, it must be emptied. An Edenic garden in which man will
define himself and name his world cannot be a landscape with a history
and preexisting names. Wister thus effectively cleanses Wyoming of a native history. In the "Rededication and Preface" to the 1911 edition of the
novel, Wister writes: "If this book be anything more than an American
story, it is an expression of American faith." In "To the Reader," his preface written in 1902, he says, "It is a vanished world. . . . The mountains are
there, far and shining, and the sunlight, and the infinite earth, and the air
that seems forever the true fountain of youth – but where is the buffalo,
and the wild antelope, and where the horseman with his pasturing thousands?" (ix). The Indian, the indigenous inhabitant, is neither a part of
this extant world along with mountains and sunlight and earth nor a note-
worthy part of what has vanished; nor does he participate, apparently, in
the American faith that Wister has in mind. The native is simply erased in
this paean to a mythic West. At the same time, Wister eulogizes the vanished cowboy: "What is become of the horseman, the cowpuncher, the
last romantic figure upon our soil?" (x). Elsewhere, he wrote that the
landscape of the West was "much more than my most romantic dream

could have hoped" and described the sudden appearance of horsemen and cattle as like "Genesis."[8] Judge Henry, the narrator's host in the novel, describes his new home as "the newest part of a new world" (139). On riding out of Medicine Bow into the Wyoming plains, the narrator comments on the trash heaps and towns spread out "like soiled packs of cards" but says nonetheless, "Yet serene above their foulness swam a pure and quiet light, such as the East never sees; they might be bathing in the air of creation's first morning. Beneath sun and stars their days and nights were immaculate and wonderful." He describes the prairie as "a land without end, . . . a space across which Noah and Adam might come straight from Genesis" (8). The land is not populated; on the first evening of his 263-mile journey from Medicine Bow to his host's ranch, the narrator says: "We never passed a human being this day." He and the Virginian, riding toward Judge Henry's ranch, are "swallowed in a vast solitude" (33).

Obviously, this is, on the one hand, the American Eden once more, that worn-out stock-in-trade of American literature and America's self-production. Before this New World Garden can be occupied and named, it must be emptied, and Wister reenacts the familiar mythic cleansing with his "creation's first morning," "immaculate" landscape, and evocation of Genesis. In the beginning was the novelist's word, all before it inchoate. However, Wister's pairing and reversal of Noah and Adam – with the Bible's first man coming after the Flood's chosen survivor – complicate the familiar trope by suggesting first a cleansing of the earth through violence – the genocidal war on Native Americans figuring as a kind of biblical flood necessary to prepare for a new beginning – and only then a new start in a new Garden. Rhetorically, Wister is acknowledging a preexisting reality, or history, and simultaneously erasing that history. It would be difficult to imagine a world that is "immaculate" and bathed "in the air of creation's first morning" (8) if one had also to imagine the slaughter, starvation, and displacement of prior inhabitants of that same world. The fact that with his first appearance in the novel the story's hero whips his rope out "like a sudden snake" (2) might even suggest that, at least on the subliminal level, Wister understands where the serpent in his fictional New World Garden truly lurks, but this is a knowledge that he will keep carefully suppressed throughout the book.

The first mention of Indians occurs more than fifty pages into the novel, simultaneous with our introduction to Molly through a letter she has written. The narrator says, "Now, it is not usual for young ladies of twenty to contemplate a journey of nearly two thousand miles to a country where Indians and wild animals live unchained" (56). A few pages later he adds, "The wives of Bear Creek were few as yet, and the homes scattered; the schoolhouse was only a sprig on the vast face of a world of elk, bear and uncertain Indians" (61). Thus far in the novel we have hints of uncontrolled and dangerous Indians present in the region, on an equal standing with "wild animals" – creatures that by implication should be chained. Not too long afterward, however, the same narrator says of a vanished restaurant, "It is gone the way of the Indian and the buffalo, for the West is growing old" (92). Natives described as "Indian chiefs" turn up at a train stop to offer tourists "painted bows and arrows and shiny horns" (115), and "Indian chiefs" come "in their show war bonnets and blankets" (123) to pay homage to the Virginian's storytelling skills at the same train station as he gets the better of Trampas in tall-tale spinning. The narrator explains that the "Crow agent has let his Indians come over from the reservation" (116) and that the Indians "naturally understood nothing of it, yet magnetically knew that the Virginian was the great man. And they watched him with approval" (123). A couple of pages later the narrator adds, "[T]he Indian chiefs came, saying, 'How!' because they followed their feelings without understanding" (125). To condescendingly make all Indians into "chiefs" is, of course, a way of not merely denigrating but neutralizing any native system of hierarchy that codifies stature or respect. The result is to diminish all Indians through these representative specimens who feel rather than think, naturally intuit rather than understand. Lacking agency both rational and spatial, these Indians are – far from being "unchained" – presented as property of the Crow agent, "*his Indians*" whom he may "*let*" off the reservation as he determines.

Indians are used on rare occasions to add color to the novel, but they are used falsely and in unmistakably contradictory ways. Although at times he raises the specter of Indian violence to titillate the reader, Wister knows, and conveys clearly to the reader, that the native has been neutralized, removed, and contained safely on reservations, vanished from a meaningful place in the world just like the buffalo. He writes, "But although Indians and bears, and mavericks, make worthy themes for song, these are not the only songs in the world" (158). The extended analogy between Indians and animals that runs through the book is particularly intensified when we see the trophies on Molly's wall surrounding her ancestor's photograph: "Till yesterday a Crow Indian war-bonnet had hung next to it [the photograph], a sumptuous cascade of feathers; on the other side a bow with arrows had dangled; opposite had been the skin of a fox; over the door had spread the antlers of a blacktail deer; a bearskin stretched beneath it. Thus had the whole cosey [*sic*] log cabin been upholstered, lavish with trophies of the frontier" (200). Descendant of New England colonizers, Molly, we are told, "was inclined to think under glass and to live underdone – when there were no Indians to shoot!" (217). Not only, however, have Indians been neutralized and safely contained but also, like the hides and horns of the big-game animals that men such as Wister came West to bag, the remains of Indians serve to signify white conquest. Rhetorically, the Indian is unmanned on Molly's wall, the warrior reduced to a "cascade of feathers" and weapons that "dangle" impotently among a white woman's trophies. The underlying terror of miscegenation that haunts earlier American fiction about natives is displaced, and since we cannot assume that Molly herself has killed the animals or collected the warriors' possessions, we must assume that white men have brought the spoils to adorn the woman's nest about which the hero hovers. The Virginian, who sings a virulently ugly racist ditty about a "big Car-'lina nigger" just after quoting Shakespeare at length, finds the tragedy of *Othello* highly distasteful, declaring to Molly, "No man should write down such a thing" (174). It is possible that in the self-made Othello the hero sees a reflection of himself, and his own potential, and that he is, therefore, profoundly disturbed by finding his reflection in the Moor's dark, miscegenistic mirror. Indians, Jews, "niggers," and all non–Anglo Saxon sorts are not celebrated in this novel. The prize cowboy Scipio Le Moyne even feels compelled to insist, "I've been white for a hundred years," to which the Virginian replies reassuringly, "You're certainly white" (101).

Natives as actual affective elements in the drama that Wister produces are for the most part simply outside the frame of *The Virginian*. In a letter to Molly, the Virginian says, "Do not believe reports about Indians. . . . Indians do not come to settled parts like Bear Creek is" (174). The horse-abusing rancher, Balaam, complains of Indians: "What business have they got off the reservation, I'd like to know?" (180). Given this neutralizing and erasing of the native presence, it is fascinating to examine the one episode in which the Indian figures in the novel's plot.

In the vaguely defined mountains beyond Judge Henry's ranch, the Virginian and Balaam – the latter having just been beaten by the hero for mistreating a horse – are searching for runaway horses as evening approaches. The setting becomes increasingly shadowy and ominous as a buzzard wheels above them on its "black pinions" and owl calls begin to sound in the darkening forest. Wister writes, "The spell of evil which the sight of the wheeling buzzard had begun, deepened as evening grew, while ever and again along the creek the singular call and answer of the owls wandered among the darkness of the trees not far away" (196). Balaam and the hero separate, with the Virginian going deeper into the forest, and we remain with the older rancher as he suddenly comprehends "the destruction that lurked in the interior of the wood" (197), undoubtedly in the form of Indians. Balaam flees from the "ominous wood" and invisible natives, and we ride to safety with him, leaving the Virginian behind in the dark forest. No Indians have appeared. We have only the calls of owls, the deepening atmosphere of foreboding, and Balaam's terror. Indians per se are not even named in the episode, only suggested in the destruction that lurks in the interior of the dark forest. That is all that we experience of the Indians who send the hero home with a near-mortal wound. It is as if the Virginian has strayed into Hawthorne's forest – that dangerously liminal zone on the edge of community – where disembodied forces of evil lurk, the serpent ready to test America's Adamic resolve. The "Indian" manifests the uncertain and ominous threat of a kind of psychic disintegration concealed in the undefined wilderness. The Virginian has just enforced his code on Balaam through violence, asserting an order that demands, among other laws, that one does not thoughtlessly abuse an animal. He rides away from Balaam into the night wood as the embodiment of that same civilizing order and runs afoul of the liminal space resistant to his defining presence. When he returns from that dark zone, that undefined space marking the edges of the Judge's civilized and civilizing ranch, he is found by Molly lying partly immersed in the purifying water of a spring, and it is Molly, the representative of eastern civilization, who must bring him home and cure him of his contact with such vague and lethal Indianness.

Molly does not participate in the dark possibilities of the dangerously liminal zone that the hero has penetrated. When she rides out instinctively to save him, she stops just within the margin of the settled and fenced ranch land, and her world is described as the antithesis of the ominous realm that has wounded her lover: "In this cuplike spread of the ravine the sun shone warmly down, the tall red cliff was warm, the pines were a warm film and filter of green; outside the shade across Bear Creek rose the steep, soft, open yellow hill, warm and high to the blue, and Bear Creek tumbled upon its sun-sparkling stones" (205).

In this warm, womb-like space, shadows serve merely to heighten the warm and nurturing sunlight, while the pines that were so dark and fore-boding for the Virginian become a luminous filter suggestive of rich life. The dark stream in the former scene has become a sun-sparkled creek in the heart of sylvan nature. Clearly, for Molly nature holds no threat of In-dians or any other violence; she brings the safely circumscribed Garden world with her.

For a moment, disoriented between worlds, the hero is unmanned in his lover's presence. In his delirium, he tells Molly, "It is mighty strange where I have been. No. Mighty natural" (206). Too natural, one might add, too "Indian," and, therefore, mighty strange. And he follows this statement with an exhortation to her: "You have got to be the man all through this mess," a strange giving over of power in the masculine world of the novel that both the narrative and Molly quickly correct as first the narrator, looking through Molly's eyes, describes the Virginian as "her lord" and then Molly herself restores power to the him, at least in his own comprehension, by saying, "You must take me home. . . . I am afraid of the Indians" (208). Finally, Wister nullifies any possibility that the actual Indians who supposedly shot the hero represent a real threat or active agency when he writes that the culprits had "come unpermitted from a southern reservation" and dismisses them as merely "five Indians in a guard-house waiting for punishment" (212). Compared to the power-fully disintegrative and sinister implications of the forest into which the hero vanished, the actual Indians in the guardhouse are made to seem en-tirely insignificant.

It is only in the Virginian's brief but starkly meaningful dark night jour-ney into a vague, liminal space that the Indian figures actively, if invisibly, in the novel. In this single episode Indians are shown to act of their own volition, although they do so as invisible presences speaking in the voices of owls. It is as if Wister has posited the disembodied Indian threat as a right of passage that takes the hero from one world – the isolate, shadowy world of the questing American hero, the world of a Huck Finn or an Ish-mael – to another, the latter being the purely civilized reality represented by Molly. In Molly's world Indians provide decorations for one's wall but do not threaten civilized values or cross certain boundaries. Later, when the narrator rides West alone to meet the Virginian in a remote wilder-ness, the former tenderfoot who is intimidated by Medicine Bow in the opening pages of the novel now roams the mountains fearlessly, appar-ently never concerned about any threat from the Indians whose former homeland he traverses. He appears to be in an uninhabited paradise:

"Far in front the foothills rose through the rain, indefinite and mystic. I wanted no speech with any one, nor to be near human beings at all. I was steeped in a revery [*sic*] as of the primal earth; even thoughts themselves had almost ceased motion. To lie down with wild animals, with elk and deer, would have made my waking dream complete" (235).

Despite the hero's ominous interlude in the mountains, European Americans have taken full possession of the West in *The Virginian*, lock, stock, and barrel. The Indian is no longer permitted free entry into this West, and when a handful of "unpermitted" Indians break out of a reservation, they are quickly apprehended and incarcerated with no obvious difficulty. When the Virginian takes Molly into the mountains on a honeymoon, it is as if they have reentered Eden. Within the paradise of the wilderness, "For thirty days by the light of the sun and the campfire light they saw no faces except their own; and when they were silent it was all stillness, unless the wind passed among the pines" (311–12). As the Virginian, a gentleman fly-fisherman when not lynching or shooting bad men who endanger the large ranchers' profits, casts his "brown hackle" (312) for trout, Molly watches him with eyes full of love. Not for a single moment does either bride or groom think of resentful Indians or fear molestation in this New World Garden. There are no natives any longer; the land has been purged clean for the new man and woman in their American bower.

It is interesting to contrast this honeymoon interlude in *The Virginian* with another, different sort of honeymoon in another novel set in the same corner of the continent at nearly the same time. In the Blackfeet writer James Welch's 1986 novel *Fools Crow*, the hero, a traditional Blackfeet warrior and holy man named Fools Crow, takes his new wife, Red Paint, on a very similar trip into the mountains where they can be alone in the splendor of nature. Set approximately a decade before the time of *The Virginian*'s action, Welch's novel is presented through Indian eyes and Indian consciousness. And Welch's couple have a far different experience, for their paradise has been penetrated by an extraordinarily evil and destructive white man who is bent on slaughtering every living thing in the wilderness, killing and leaving his prey to rot. Fools Crow must slay this monster to protect the life around him, but even when he succeeds in defeating the white man the message is clear: there is no place where the white man cannot penetrate, no place in the Indian world safe from the invader. The native paradise sought by Fools Crow and Red Paint for their marriage idyll is infinitely permeable to the European, and therefore vulnerable. The white man's sylvan paradise found by the Virginian and

Molly is, in sharp contrast, safe from any penetration by the native. Indians are just not "permitted" entry.

Despite repeatedly dismissing any threat posed by Indians and determinedly erasing any significant native presence in the world of the novel, when Wister needs an Indian to provide titillation in the woods and the western hero's requisite flesh wound, he trots a few invisible Indians into the margins of his text. However, he gives them no more palpable presence than he gives to Trampas's ghostly bullet in the novel's climax.

In 1924 in his *History of the American Frontier*, Frederic Paxson wrote, "The searching pen of Owen Wister has preserved the picture of Wyoming of this period. His Virginian (1902) is among the most real of American heroes, and is one of the most accurate of our historical portraitures."[9] Obviously, far from being historically accurate, the picture of Wyoming that Wister has preserved is one of his own imagination. In contrast to the drama of Wister's fiction, Indians were very much a part of the real Wyoming picture during this period. In 1881 the Crow agent, Henry Armstrong, decried white attitudes toward the natives in Wyoming and Montana, declaring, "It is deemed no crime to kill an Indian but rather an act of heroism." A year later he wrote, "There is no doubt . . . that the whites have committed greater depredations on those Indians than the Indians have on the whites," and he noted that whites had recently stolen two hundred horses from the Crow chief Crazy Head and shot and killed Round Iron, Crazy Head's brother, while shaking hands with him.[10] By 1887 at the same time that the head of the Wyoming Stock Growers Association was complaining bitterly about Indians leaving the reservation and killing cattle for food and state politicians were insisting loudly that the government "confine these Indians to their reservation[s]," cattlemen were being prosecuted by the federal government for illegally grazing cattle on reservation lands. With the range disastrously overgrazed elsewhere throughout the state and the cattle bubble bursting in the disastrous winter of 1886–87, Wyoming cattlemen and politicians began lobbying vehemently to open reservation lands for grazing.[11]

Reservation boundaries were meant to contain Indians, to keep them safely inside, just as the boundaries of Yellowstone National Park were meant to keep them outside. And just as the park's boundaries were meant to be permeable for European Americans, reservation boundaries were obviously expected to be penetrable for white ranchers, who thought that they could move in and out at will for the extractable resource of grazing rights. And while demanding access to reservations, the large ranchers constructed fences across public land, a process akin to the enclosure of commons in England. Even as the enormous cattle empires overgrazed and destroyed the range lands, a cattle boom had exploded in Wyoming. According to the historian Richard White, "New stock companies multiplied; 20 new companies with a capitalization of $12 million were organized in Wyoming alone in 1883."[12] In 1885 under Grover Cleveland, Congress passed the Enclosure Act, designed to prevent the large stock companies from fencing public lands and therefore freezing out the small rancher. The federal government even sent marshals "riding over the Plains to cut fences, but as soon as the marshals had turned away the wires went back."[13] Clearly, reservation boundaries and fences were meant to be manipulated by those who created them.

That those in power felt themselves possessed of a unique privilege of motion is demonstrated ironically in the infamous Johnson County War. As most people know, this "war" consisted of an invasion of Johnson County by large ranchers and their hired Texas gunmen with the goal of killing those they considered a hindrance to profit making, whether the targets were small ranchers labeled *rustlers* or the townsmen, journalists, and lawmen who supported the small-time cattlemen. The invaders, however, were surprised to learn that the small ranchers and townsmen, too, possessed mobility and were capable of moving quickly enough to surround the invading army. Lead by Wister's friend and host Major Frank Wolcott, the would-be army of extermination had to be rescued by the U.S. cavalry, who, even more ironically, "had just come that evening from chasing a band of marauding Crow back to the reservation." Wister, who modeled Judge Henry of the novel on Wolcott, wrote of one of the "regulators" indicted for the lynching of a man and woman accused of rustling: "He seemed a good solid citizen, and I hope he'll get off."[14] Judge Henry, a "good solid citizen," delivers a resounding defense of lynching in *The Virginian.*

Owen Wister's West is not the frontier. It is a profit-making enterprise for establishment America, a capitalist resource in which stability is a highly desired commodity. In the interstitial zone of frontier, where cultures come together and deal with one another, what Pratt calls *transculturation* occurs. In describing the frontier as "the meeting point between savagery and civilization," Frederick Jackson Turner anticipated a form of this transculturation when he pronounced the frontier to be a space of "perennial rebirth" where "the wilderness masters the colonist.... It strips off his garments of civilization and arrays him in the hunting shirt

and the moccasin. . . . [H]e fits himself into the Indian clearings and follows the Indian trails. . . . [H]ere is a new product that is American."[15]
Turner dated the closing of the American frontier at approximately the
same time that Wister concludes his fictional vision of Wyoming, 1890.
However, it is the privileged East that masters the wilderness in Wister's
novel. The Virginian is not "Indianized." On the contrary, the novel's
hero comes from the South and is in the course of the novel molded into
a good Easterner, complete with an education including Shakespeare,
George Eliot, Victorian poetry, and Russian novels. While being canoni-
cally educated, he serves as a very effective tool for the corporate ranchers
in controlling the cowboy working class.

In real Wyoming, the Stock Growers Association passed a rule in 1883
forbidding its members "to employ any man who owned a brand or cattle."[16] For a time in the 1880s, the time of *The Virginian,* cowboys who
owned land or cattle were blacklisted in Wyoming, meaning effectively
that the quintessentially American faith in upward mobility was denied
the working cowboy and that the wealthy owners were thereby assured of
a permanent peasant class to work their ranches for them. The Virginian,
in contrast, not only has his own land and "savings in bank" (171) but as
a good middle-management tool is willing to hang his best friend, Steve,
when his employer's interests are threatened. After all, Steve's only crime
has been to steal cattle and thereby diminish profit; otherwise he seems a
highly decent individual. When Trampas attempts to convince other cowboys to jump train and light out for the gold rush, the Virginian labels the
prospective action a *mutiny* and prevails over Trampas to prevent the cowboys' flight. In a free world, of course, what Trampas proposes is utterly
reasonable, just as the Nez Perces' journey to Canada was reasonable.
Why shouldn't the cowboys have the freedom to go where they like and do
the kind of work they prefer, even if it is prospecting for gold instead of
herding cattle? Unlike their employers, who can head for New York or
London or Edinburgh or Paris as the urge strikes them, the cowboys simply do not have the privilege of mobility. Just as the Indians are expected
to remain on their reservations and out of the way, the cowboys are supposed to remain on the range or in the bunkhouse as a stable workforce.
While a superficial reader might argue that the cowboys have the freedom to go where they like – at least in theory – a careful reading shows
that the Virginian intervenes as a tool for corporate ranching to deny
them that freedom, a denial that the label *mutiny* clearly underscores. The

Stock Growers Association had in 1883 similarly attempted to disempower its own cowboy vassals.

Like the more privileged caste of the novel, the Virginian rises to the level of geographic, social, and intellectual mobility. He is in almost constant motion throughout the story as he virtually orbits around Molly in her static cabin space, traveling by train and horse, and venturing far out into the mountains to bring itinerant rustlers to justice. He travels East with Molly and triumphs in his exchanges with her aristocratic family, and by the end of the book he is an important man, a coal baron, because he had the foresight to stake his claim to extractable resources. Even the hero's ultimate wealth and political stature depend on his association with mobility in the form of the railroad, which assures a market for his product.

In *Imperial Eyes*, Pratt asks, "How has travel and exploration writing *produced* 'the rest of the world' for European readerships at particular points in Europe's expansionist trajectory?" We can extend Pratt's notion to the literature of the American West, which was – and remains significantly today – a kind of travel writing in which the educated Easterner comes West and reports back on his discoveries in language that produces the reality that it purports to describe and produces it strictly in terms the audience in the East is prepared to comprehend. In discussing Camus's "The Adulterous Woman," Pratt cites what she calls "the momentary permeation of the colonialist boundaries."[17]

In *The Virginian*'s white world, the definitive world of the fictional West for a century now, these boundaries are not permeated. Not only does the Virginian not turn native but the woman who is deposited in this frontier zone is never threatened, never attracted to the colonized "other." Indians are kept at a safe distance, and the West is claimed as a productive dominion of the East. Better smile when you call this novel historically accurate – an Indian smile.

NOTES

1. For an account of this incident, see McWhorter, *Yellow Wolf*, 170–78.

2. Vizenor, *Fugitive Poses*, 188–89.

3. Davis, ed., *Owen Wister's West*, 10.

4. Wister, *The Virginian* (Signet, 1979), ix. Page numbers for subsequent quotations will be given in the text.

5. Pratt, *Imperial Eyes*, 205.

6. See Gilman, "Why I Wrote 'The Yellow Wallpaper.'"

7. For a history of the West during this period, see Merk, *History of the Westward Movement*; Paxson, *History of the American Frontier*; and Smith, *The War on Powder River*.

8. Davis, ed., *Owen Wister's West*, 1.

9. Paxson, *History of the American Frontier*, 558.

10. Hoxie, *Parading through History*, 111, 113.

11. Hoxie, *Parading through History*, 154.

12. White, *"It's Your Misfortune and None of My Own,"* 223.

13. Merk, *History of the Westward Movement*, 463.

14. Smith, *The War on Powder River*, 225, 134.

15. Turner, "The Significance of the Frontier in American History" (1941), 662–63.

16. Smith, *The War on Powder River*, 27.

17. Pratt, *Imperial Eyes*, 5, 224.

4 INDIGENOUS WHITENESS AND WISTER'S INVISIBLE INDIANS

Jennifer S. Tuttle

Louis Owens concludes his essay with the assertion that "the Virginian is not 'Indianized'" but rather "molded into a good Easterner." In her essay, Jennifer Tuttle introduces a different perspective, arguing that Indians, "although 'unseen,' . . . 'haunt' the text." She suggests that instead of keeping the Virginian from being contaminated by the Indian's presence, Wister marks his cowboy character with "savage" and "dark" qualities or traits in order to claim an "authentic" and "indigenous" white ethnicity "on behalf of America's ruling class," who are anxious about the viability of white manhood during "a time of post-Reconstruction racial tensions, increased immigration, and falling birthrates among native-born whites." While both Owens and Tuttle examine what Tuttle calls "Wister's appropriation of Native American culture and identity" by looking closely at such details as the decor of Molly's cabin, Tuttle reads Wister's photographs, journals, and magazine pieces – emphasizing particularly that Wister expunges from The Virginian *the influence of his Shoshone guide, Tigie – to show how Indians' absence from the text in fact speaks to how significantly their ongoing historical presence determines the novel's presiding ideology about race and gender.*

Since Owen Wister's *The Virginian* first appeared in 1902, readers have remarked on the cultural import of its eponymous hero. He is an invocation, many agree, of an emerging ideal of white masculinity that underwrote American expansionist ideology in the Progressive Era. Wister's cowboy has been understood by critics as an attempt to reinvigorate white American manhood in response to perceived threats to elite men's cultural and economic dominance.[1] The Virginian's unique qualities as a hero are symbolized in the photograph that he gives to his love interest, the blue-blooded eastern schoolmarm Molly Stark Wood. It "display[ed] him in all his cow-boy trappings, – the leathern chaps, the belt and pistol, and in his hand a coil of rope." Stammering that the Virginian is "not a bit like" and yet "exactly like" a "savage," Molly anxiously presents her paramour's photograph for her great-aunt's approval. Despite his rough appearance, the great-aunt resolves to accept him, understanding that Molly "wants a man that is a man." Significantly, she also reassures Molly of her confidence that the Virginian is "worthy of the Starks."[2] Molly's perceptive relative discerns, then, the Virginian's heroic combination of qualities that has been so widely remarked among critics: he is both virile and genteel, both wild and civilized.[3] A hero in terms of both gender and race, he is "a man that is a man" with the pure white bloodline that makes him "worthy of the Starks." In his prolific marriage with Molly in the Edenic West, he promises a white racial rejuvenation at a time of post-Reconstruction racial tensions, increased immigration, and falling birthrates among native-born whites. As an embodiment of "balanced modern masculinity," he combines the strenuosity and authenticity associated with the West with the imperial and capitalist ethos associated with the East.[4]

If indeed the Virginian embodies this heroic white manliness, and I would agree that he does, what are we to make of the "savage" qualities that so unsettle Molly as she contemplates his photograph? While such descriptions of the Virginian generally are taken as references to his association with the violence and hypermasculinity of the so-called wild West, Wister's choice of a word that was commonly used during his time to refer to Native Americans demands further scrutiny. Combined with other textual clues, it signals, in fact, that the Virginian's character is more complex than the novel's overt references to Anglo-Saxon ancestry would suggest. In this essay, I will explore Wister's invocations of Native American culture and identity in order more fully to explain his heroic constructions of manliness and whiteness in *The Virginian*. Wister's recuperation of white manhood in his novel involves an attempt to usurp the entitlement to dominance that comes with native status from those who have a more authentic claim to it. On the surface, of course, "Indians" are all but absent from the plot and landscape of *The Virginian*. Yet a manifestation of idealized Indianness – dark, untamed, and potent – flows beneath Wister's cowboy drama and takes bodily form in its hero. Wister's antidote to the "hordes of encroaching alien vermin" that, he believed, so threatened America's white bloodlines, then, is a claim to indigenous status on behalf of America's ruling class.[5] Wister's novel attempts to construct an "indigenous" white identity – an authentic American whiteness entitled to dominance on all fronts – through an appropriation of the "native." In doing so, he articulates a pattern that is still strikingly familiar to readers one hundred years later, for Wister's struggles with Indians illuminate a long-standing tradition in American modernist thought and twentieth-century popular culture more generally. A deeper understanding of these struggles may cast some light on the broader implications of Wister's race and gender politics for American writing in the twenty-first century as well.

HUNTING FOR MATERIAL: OWEN WISTER OUT WEST

It has long been understood that, like much of Wister's other fiction, *The Virginian* is based to a great degree on his own experiences in the American West. His constructions of heroic manliness and whiteness have their origins in many biographical and literary endeavors in which Wister sought to "master" Western material, including the "wild Indian." Like many eastern white men of his social class, Wister made numerous trips to the West in the late nineteenth century, averaging nearly one a year between 1885 and 1900. The travel journals, letters, writing notebooks, and photographs from these western journeys provide a genealogy for the heroic notions of manliness and whiteness that would take shape in *The Virginian* in 1902. Central to both these notions in Wister's early western travels is the attempt to master and appropriate the West's purported authenticity and wildness, traits that Wister often associated with Native Americans. In his hunting and camping expeditions into the wilds of Wyoming and the Southwest, Wister had a variety of encounters with indigenous peoples, and his constructions of them formed an integral part of his dual mission: to heal his own manhood and to capture the "wild West" for his eastern reading audience.

As Wister enthusiasts are well aware, Wister first went West on the advice of a physician. In using the West as the setting in which to revitalize his ailing manliness, Wister partook of an impulse widespread among the elite of his time. Scholars have examined a variety of phenomena articulating such "strenuous masculinity," from the popularity of dude ranches, hunting excursions, and wilderness-based fraternal organizations to the broad appeal of literature and performance eulogizing the frontier. In these endeavors, middle- and upper-class white men attempted to appropriate what they saw as the "savagery" and "barbarism" of racial others and working-class men in order to claim a superior manliness and racial supremacy.[6] Wister's "West cure," prescribed by the neurologist S. Weir Mitchell, was certainly part of this trend.[7] "The surest remedy for the ills of civilized life," wrote Mitchell, "is to be found in some form of return to barbarism," a journey that involved, not only living "the out-door life of the camp" and wielding the rod and gun but also imitating "the guides, woodmen and trappers, and the simple-minded, manly folk who live on the outposts of civilization."[8] That is, the eastern "man of business," exhausted and feminized by the demands of the marketplace, could relieve his resulting nervous collapse by emulating those to whom strenuous masculinity supposedly came naturally.[9] Wister's first West cure in 1885 brought him to Major Frank Wolcott's Wyoming cattle ranch. Through roundups, horseback rides, and hunting and fishing excursions, Wister interacted with working-class men who inspired his imagination. His admiration of the "cowpunchers," above all, for their virility and redemptive possibilities is widely known. In an early essay called "Among the Cow-Boys," he confirmed that "their life face to face with nature brings out their manhood."[10] Through emulating the cowboys, this tenderfoot reclaimed his own manhood: as his biographer reports, after a mere three weeks of "ranch life," in which he "was spending as many as six hours a day in the saddle" and pulling his weight on "frequent hunting expeditions away from the ranch," Wister's "health had virtually recovered."[11]

Despite Wister's valorization of the cowpuncher in this essay and in his better-known writings, however, he modeled his own revived masculinity on a variety of men, including his white cooks and packers and his Native American guides. He sums up a typical West cure in 1936 while looking back on his "old Yellowstone days." On his second trip to the Yellowstone area, made in 1887, he writes, he was accompanied by two eastern friends of his own class, a white packer and cook, and a Shoshone guide and hunter named Tigie. He recalls that his party proved a "spectacle" for tourists, who screamed at the sight of them and craned their "tame citified necks" in order to immortalize the men in snapshots. Although he recognizes that the tourists were "credulous to the point of distortion" to be so alarmed by the group, Wister opines nevertheless that the men's "wild and predatory aspect" was "justif[ied]" by the "trophies, heads and pelts" piled on their packs.[12] No longer himself a "tame citified" tourist, the Wister represented here has become, however temporarily, part of the "wild and predatory" West in his fellowship with his hunting party.

Wister's representation of his relationships with Native American guides illuminates his acquisition of this "wild and predatory" manliness. Although he employed several throughout the years, his relationship with Tigie is most telling. A "famous hunter and tracker of big game," Tigie is described by Wister as hardworking, "grave," and laconic (speaking when he does in the requisite broken English that for Wister is a mark of authentic, "full-blooded" Indianness).[13] While Wister's other Indian guides serve as escorts into the wild, it is Tigie who truly initiates Wister into predatory manliness. This is made clear in an extended journal account in which, with Tigie's guidance, Wister stalks and kills a grizzly bear. "Follow[ing] Tigie like his shadow," Wister attempted to match his guide's stealth and agility through the wild terrain. When they spotted the bear, Wister "jumped on the bare rump of his horse and sat there behind Tigie, my rifle in one hand, the other on his shoulder," afraid that at any moment he would "slide off . . . with a crash and ruin the whole thing." As they neared the bear, Tigie directed Wister toward the spot, crawling with him, until they were within range. "'Shoot! shoot!' said Tigie, running out from his tree, and he worked his arms as if he held the lever of the Winchester himself." "I felt like a murderer," Wister confesses, "as I pumped the bullets into" the bear, to which he refers as a "poor old gentleman" (*owow*, 53–56). Having shadowed his Indian guide and mimicked his predatory manliness, Wister seems aware that his own gentlemanly qualities must temporarily be "murdered" if his masculinity is to be affirmed.

After this rite of passage, Wister's biographer confirms: "The friendships between the eastern hunters, the two hired white men, and the Indian guide flourished amid such intimacy."[14] Their camaraderie is represented eloquently in a photograph, in which Wister, ammunition belt around his hips, pours a drink for Tigie (ironically, a very gentlemanly gesture) while the others strike carefree poses. Yet we are reminded of the temporary and site-specific nature of this fellowship, especially between Indian and white man, when, on a subsequent trip to Wyoming, Wister mentions that Tigie visits his campsite to see another Indian guide and offers no greeting to the white men. Indeed, Wister did not know that Tigie had visited until his former guide and hunter had already gone (*owow*, 85–86). To use Philip Deloria's formulation, perhaps Wister has been merely "playing Indian": as an apprentice hunter, he valued Tigie, not so much as a living, breathing subject, but as an embodiment of a romanticized and masculinized Indianness.[15] Tigie is merely a mediator through whom Wister attempts to reinvigorate his own white identity and perhaps his "authentic" Americanness.

Wister's embrace of predatory masculinity, crystallized so eloquently in his discussion of Tigie, took new form, however, as his sights became focused less on wild game than on the "Old West" itself. In 1893, Wister received a commission from *Harper's Monthly* to write a series of tales about the West. In response to the magazine's request for "thrilling stor[ies] . . . [that] portray certain features of Western life which are now rapidly disappearing with the progress of civilization,"[16] Wister assumed a new "duty": "to hunt material of adventure voraciously" (*OWOW*, 168). He fulfilled this duty by favoring the camera and the pen over the rifle, a choice befitting the elegaic task ahead.[17] "Once domination is complete," after all, "conservation is urgent."[18] Using these new tools of the hunt, Wister sought to tell the story of the vanishing West for the consumption of his eastern audience.[19] This story depended, of course, on the Old West and its inhabitants' willingness to vanish, for they were appropriable only if they remained pliant to the story that Wister wished to tell. Viewed in this light, Wister's hunt for material resembles a form of taxidermy that both effects and represents the American conquest of the West and the dominance of strenuous white manhood. It is a gesture that is well expressed by Donna Haraway in her analysis of taxidermy in the American Museum of Natural History, where the symbolic redemption of American manhood is "made possible only by [the animals'] death and literal re-presentation. . . . Only then could the hygiene of nature cure the sick vision of civilized man."[20] Viewed in this context, Wister's camera seems an ideal weapon indeed, for it identified him not only with the fast-growing phenomenon of amateur tourist photography, sparked by the invention of the portable Kodak in 1888, but also with the older tradition of survey photography. Both used the camera toward "a distinct mode of seeing, knowing, and possessing" that was explicitly implicated in the conquest of the American West.[21] As Haraway has aptly put it, "the camera" is "ultimately . . . superior to the gun for the possession, production, preservation, consumption, surveillance, appreciation, and control of nature."[22]

Not surprisingly, then, while many of Wister's photographs feature natural landscape scenes, a large number express an ethnographic impulse in recording images of Native Americans.[23] In several of his pictures, Wister seems to be seeking an idealized Indianness that will help him memorialize the closed frontier. One photograph taken on the Shoshone Reservation at Fort Washakie, Wyoming, for example, records a ceremony in which the Indians wear traditional dress. He takes both candid and posed photographs in this quest, capturing various moments in Indians' lives, from children playing, to men on horseback, to women resting after obtaining provisions. Yet his photographs suggest an increasing realization of his inability to represent abstract Indianness without the intrusion of living, breathing Indians, whose lives on the reservation disrupt the narrative that he would like to be able to tell. This is represented poignantly in the cluster of photographs that he took documenting issue day at the San Carlos Indian Agency in Arizona, the day on which the Apaches received their rations from the U.S. government. It is here that the abject, flesh-and-blood, alive-in-the-present Indian becomes truly impossible for Wister to ignore, and his detailed descriptions of the long lines and the sad countenances confirm that he could not help but note their despair and degradation.[24] His comments on the Apaches' attitudes toward photography suggest this refusal to conform to the myth and to submit to its taxidermic impulse, for they all manifest resistance to the objectification inherent in Wister's project: "The Indians took being photographed variously," he wrote in his notebook. "Most did not like it – some ran away, or hid their faces. . . . Some requested to be taken, and one old squaw sat on the ground screaming and throwing stones at me."[25]

An image of the Shoshone Chief Washakie, one of Wister's willing objects, is a telling example of such resistance. Describing him as "ninety-odd years old – tall, splendid, a wonderful figure of a man," Wister seems to perceive Chief Washakie as a representative of the "authentic" Indianness that he has been seeking. Yet Washakie's image disrupts this attempt to capture such free and "splendid" Indianness. Wister writes that, in the photograph, he "stood [Washakie] stark straight with one hand lifted" (*owow*, 175) – a pose that, by its very stereotypical nature, undermines any claim to authenticity. Beyond that, however, is Chief Washakie's own self-presentation, for while he wears what appears to be native dress, he has nearly covered it with a hat, coat, and necktie. His "Indianness" is thus in tension with these markers of assimilation.[26] Years later, in an extraordinarily self-referential story, Wister would reflect on this failure of the camera to capture the "wild Indian." In "Bad Medicine" (1928), he revisits his photograph of Chief Washakie and dubs the camera "the evil eye of civilization." The story dramatizes the camera's deadly effect on "authentic" Indianness through the sad tale of Washakie's grandson, Sun Road. His vanity seduced by the "evil eye," Sun Road loses his nobility as he learns no longer to run from the camera but to "dramatiz[e] himself" for Kodak-wielding tourists in Yellowstone Park. He dies when, frightened by a gunpowder flash, he flees into Old Faithful and drowns.[27] Although it is Sun Road's vanity and superstition, not photography, that incurs the narrator's disgust, Wister seems to offer an underlying recognition that the camera cannot capture the "wild Indian" and is indeed deadly to him.

In his "hunt" for this mythic Indian, Wister's pen and notebook were somewhat more successful weapons than his camera was. Wister wrote in his journal of his desire to "find out all about" the "details of . . . life" in the West "and master it – theoretically" (*owow*, 35). These details included all sorts of items, from descriptions of the natural scenery, to cowboy exploits, to regional slang and dialect. His western journals and notebooks are, however, also punctuated by references to Indians, many of which seem designed to add authenticity and nostalgia to his portrait of the Old West. In addition to his frequent discussion of the Native American laborers whom he has hired, he records visits to his camp by other Indians, including, on one occasion, a Shoshone medicine man; he retells a story of an Indian funeral and quirky tales about Chief Washakie's life; and he records Indian legends (*owow*, 73, 175–76, 178). With equal enthusiasm, however, he also remarks on tales of Custer and Indian fighting (*owow*, 177). In some cases, it is his own commentary on the details that he observes that most fully expresses this impulse to preserve Indianness over living Indians. Although in Arizona he frequently passes Apache huts and buys Apache baskets, for instance, his description of what he calls an Apache "Devil Dance" belies the Apaches' existence in the present: it was, he says, "a wild sight of remoteness from our day" (*owow*, 190–91). Indeed, although he witnesses a regiment of Indian soldiers at Fort Washakie, he is skeptical of their capacity to fulfill their duties, noting that "an Indian's brain is remote from hours and drills" that regulate soldiers' lives (*owow*, 121).

It is the "remoteness" of the Indians, it seems, that assures their authenticity. Wister reflects on his struggle to maintain this distance in 1894: "The frontier has yielded," he laments, "to a merely commonplace society which lacks at once picturesqueness and civilization. When I heard that the Apache squaws now give their babies condensed milk, my sympathy for them chilled" (*owow*, 210). Neither "picturesque," on the one hand, nor "civilized," on the other, Wister's Indians ultimately refuse to be "mastered" by his pen, just as they had resisted his attempts to photograph them on his terms. And Wister, repelled by the reality of their de-

Wister with his hunting party, Jackson, Wyoming, 1887. Standing (*left to right*):
Tigie (guide and hunter) and Wister. Seated (*left to right*): George Norman,
Copley Amory, George West (cook), and Jules Mason (packer). Courtesy
University of Wyoming, American Heritage Center, Owen Wister Collection,
negative 5736.

based, abject state, loses all sympathy. Unable to capture the remote "wild
Indian" in the crosshair of his camera or in the documentary record of his
journal, then, it remained for Wister to perform this taxidermic function
where his mastery was assured: in his fiction.[28]

OWEN WISTER'S NATIVE COWBOY: *THE VIRGINIAN*

Wister made no secret of the fact that his fiction lifted characters, anec-
dotes, and citations from his travel journals. Aspects of his photographs
can also be seen translated into his stories and novels. Native Americans
figure in several stories published before *The Virginian* as well as in those

published later in his career. Familiar with Wister's paternalistic attitude toward Native Americans, however, scholars have registered no surprise at their portrayals there, which range from the noble and "full-blooded" to, more often, the depraved, drunken, anarchic, and bloodthirsty.[29] Given the attention that Native Americans are shown in Wister's early fiction, it seems curious that in *The Virginian*, the culmination of not only his earlier fiction but also his personal experiences discussed above, they would be nearly absent. Although Native Americans are marginal to the plot of this western, however, as they are to the West cures that inspired it, their presence is crucial to the dramas of recovered white manhood and redeemed American culture that unfold there.

Scholars have established that *The Virginian* links an individual man's attempts to recover his health and manliness with the nation's recuperation from supposed racial and cultural decadence.[30] Written at a time of great anxiety among Anglo-Americans about ailing manhood among the eastern elite and about "tainted" bloodlines and "race suicide," the novel is meant by Wister, himself a fierce advocate of Anglo-Saxon racial superiority, to be a healing narrative for the nation: it ends with the potent promise of national and (white) racial rejuvenation in an Edenic West. In his relationships with the novel's narrator and the New England schoolmarm Molly Wood, the Virginian links these two healing plots of manhood and nationhood. For it is the Virginian whom the tenderfoot narrator attempts to emulate in his Wyoming West cures, and it is the Virginian's prolific marriage with Molly that promises to regenerate the nation's white bloodlines. There is little doubt that these healing narratives are articulated through a whitewashing of the West and of its hero, the cowpuncher whose rough veneer, Wister suggests, disguises a true, Anglo-Saxon gentility. Although Native Americans have, however, received little attention in scholarly analyses of this white-centered plot – a fact that is due largely, no doubt, to their virtual invisibility in the text – it is precisely their necessary invisibility that makes them such a potent ingredient in the whiteness valorized in the novel. Recall that in his West cures and his search for material Wister sought a primal, authentic Indianness that he found could represent this native authenticity only so long as it remained invisible to the "evil eye of civilization" or somehow removed from the present day. Inhabiting the present, of course, were those abject, demoralized, flesh-and-blood natives who intruded so insistently into Wister's mythmaking. His attempts to transform these individuals – the Indians he *could* see – into manifestations of mythic Indianness re-

Chief Washakie, 1893. Courtesy University of Wyoming, American Heritage
Center, Owen Wister Collection, accession number 290.

sulted, as the photograph of Chief Washakie so poignantly demonstrates,
in failure. In *The Virginian,* however, Wister captures such elusive Indianness indirectly, through its figurative embodiment in his "Anglo-
Saxon" hero. Having dispensed with the true natives of the American
soil, then, he revitalizes elite American whiteness with an infusion of the

"native," granting this whiteness an indigenous status that justifies its renewed claims to dominance in American culture.

Although their presence in the West is all but erased in *The Virginian*, Native Americans are not entirely absent from the landscape, for they do appear in the flesh in one scene. Their brief presence, however, serves, in fact, to represent their absence from the West and to deprive them of any claim to authenticity, for the only Indians the book's characters actually see are Crows who have left their reservation, with the permission of the Indian agent, to sell the spectacle of Indianness. Appearing outside a stranded train in Rawhide, Montana, "Indian chiefs," wearing "show war bonnets and blankets," attempt to sell the white passengers their "painted bows and arrows and shiny horns" (133, 125). Like those Indians who performed in the wild West shows flourishing at the time, these "chiefs" are, in fact, powerless, reduced to pawning a commodified Indianness that denies their own subjectivity. Their arrows dulled and their warbonnets a mere costume, they are visible only as representatives of their own impotence, of their own erasure from their homeland.

To say that Indians are otherwise invisible, however, is not to say that they are not present elsewhere in the text. Untamed, potent, supposedly more "authentic" Indians haunt the narrative and stalk its characters. They are unseen, skulking in the forests, exceeding the borders of their reservation and refusing to be contained by U.S. government authority, their power and danger amplified in myth. Following reports that a group of Indians has left the reservation for the Bow Leg Mountains, the Virginian, Shorty, and Balaam muse: "Somewhere over there were the red men, ranging in unfrequented depths of rock and pine – their forbidden ground." Their conversation soon turns to the red-shirted trapper who "ain't been heard from" (190) and whose horse came home without him; his fate is later confirmed when, on a journey through the mountains, the Virginian and Balaam see a buzzard drop an ominous piece of red flannel. As the travelers come on the remains of an Indian camp, hear the hoots of "owls" and sense "evil" (206) coming from the forest, their sense of foreboding grows. Balaam, we are told, "needed no interpreter for the voices of the seeming owls that had haunted the latter hour of their journey." "'Peaceable' Indians," he concludes, "were still in these mountains, and some few of them had for the past hour been skirting his journey unseen, and now waited for him in the wood" (207–8). It is these same Indians who will shortly injure the Virginian, although the assault must be imagined by the reader: the narrative reports only the result, the bleeding Virginian being described after the fact. Although "unseen," then, these Indians "haunt" the text, inspiring fear in and drawing blood from the characters. It would seem that the very fact of their invisibility contributes to their wildness and potency, for they cannot be captured by the "evil eye of civilization." "Ranging" into "forbidden ground," exceeding the boundaries of so-called civilized behavior, they embody the barbarism and untamed authenticity of the mythic Indian.

It is the task of the novel to harness the potency of these invisible "savages," not only to contain its threat to emerging "civilization" in the West but also, perhaps more important, to garner its mythic Indianness, putting it in service of reinvigorating whiteness. The unseen Indians await, in short, the inevitable taxidermic gesture. The former feat is accomplished with relative simplicity: the Indians in question, the narrator soon reveals, "were now in military custody," the story of their exploits publicized in the papers. "Editors immediately reared a tall war out of it; but from five Indians in a guard-house waiting punishment not even an editor can supply war for more than two editions" (222–23). Their mythical status owed more to the conjurings of editors than to fact, it seems. Like the Crow Indians who sold their wares to the train passengers, these Indians become commodified, bolstering the editors' profits; although invisible, they, too, are made into a sort of spectacle, this time in the medium of print. Although such containment after the fact cannot – and perhaps is not designed to – negate the novel's considerable emphasis on the fear that they inspired as they tracked the white men, it does assert, in what is likely a self-referential gesture, the power of the written word to "master" them and defuse their threat.

The other, and perhaps more significant, manifestation of "wild" Indianness in the novel takes shape in the Virginian himself. Such a claim invites explanation, of course, because scholars have long concurred that the Virginian's heroism lay precisely in his whiteness. Certainly, Wister's own views and statements support this interpretation. Not only was he, as I have noted, a staunch supporter of white supremacy but much of his writing also explicitly marks *the* cowboy as homogeneously white (despite his having seen with his own eyes evidence to the contrary): "the knight and the cowboy," he insists, "are nothing but the same Saxon of different environments."[31] Equally, scholars have made convincing arguments supporting the Virginian's heroic whiteness, noting everything from his southern, aristocratic heritage to his likeness to Thomas Jefferson, George Washington, and Theodore Roosevelt.[32] What are readers to

make, then, of the fact that Wister emphasizes the Virginian's racial indeterminacy and dark coloring in some two dozen references spread
throughout the novel? When she first sees the Virginian in Bear Creek,
for example, Molly asks, "Who is that black man?" (81). While the other
cowhands were as white as the young men in Danbury, Connecticut, the
narrator notes, "The Virginian did not, to be sure, look like Danbury, and
his frame and his features showed out of the mass" (159). Such descriptions of the Virginian's difference in features and coloring from the obviously "white" settlers of the West are enhanced by the narrator's repeated
references to his, not just dark, but black hair. He not only assigns the Virginian the epithet of "the black-headed guy" (28) but punctuates this frequent refrain with more extended commentary, such as the observation
that the Virginian "certainly had a very black head of hair. It was the first
thing to notice now, if one glanced generally at the table where he sat at
cards" (31).

It is at the precise moment when the Virginian seems to proclaim his
Anglo-Saxon purity, in fact, that he reveals the likely source of this racial
indeterminacy, suggesting that the dominant referent of his dark features
is a distant – indeed, "remote" – Native American heritage. Attempting
to assure his fiancée's relations of his worthiness to wed the blue-blooded
Molly Wood, the Virginian boasts that he is "of old stock in Virginia English" (243).[33] This Virginian "stock," especially those prominent families such as the Bollings and the Randolphs, has made no secret of its own
roots in the mixing of "English" and "Indian" blood, for it proudly locates its origins in the marriage between John Rolfe and Pocahontas.[34]
The Virginian's suggested descent from Pocahontas invokes, then, the
appropriation of Indianness toward an indigenous whiteness entitled to
conquest. Indeed, such a reading of the Virginian is not incompatible
with others that emphasize his Anglo-Saxon roots and his resemblance to
revolutionary heroes, for his Indianness is less a literal marker of mixed
race (which Wister would have abhorred) than a symbolic infusion into
his "pure" whiteness of mythic "native" power and status.

This Native American referent of the Virginian's darkness helps explain certain aspects of his role in the narrator's West cures, for he is a
composite of the various representatives of "barbarous" masculinity that
Wister met on his own journeys West, just as the narrator is a transparent
double for Wister himself. Functioning as the narrator's "escort," the
"untamed soul," "proud of his wild calling," mediates between the eastern "tenderfoot" (52–53) and the dangers and mysteries of the frontier.

He guides the narrator on hunting expeditions and models the strenuous masculinity that the sickly tenderfoot attempts, never with complete success, to emulate. That the subtle strain of Indianness underlying the Virginian's masculinity contributes to his status as an exemplar of New Western manhood is suggested in an early scene of trickery. He shows his ability to achieve mastery over other men when, in attempting to prevent a traveling salesman from sharing his bed in Medicine Bow (itself a setting that suggests Native American culture and healing), he warns, "Just don't let your arm or your laig touch me if I go jumpin' around. I'm dreamin' of Indians when I do that. And if anything touches me then, I'm liable to grab my knife right in my sleep" (34). Although one implication of this statement is that his instinct is to draw his knife against an imagined Indian attack, the passage could equally be read as a reference to his own "savagery": he may, in fact, be signaling that his Indianness would cause him to draw his knife on a white man. Although the narrator is justly impressed and intimidated by this show of barbarous masculinity, he eventually establishes a rapport with his "escort." "It must be a poor thing to be sick," writes the Virginian to the narrator, who has returned home. "You will be well if you give over city life and take a hunt with me. . . . It would be pleasure not business for me to show you plenty elk and get you strong" (63). While this letter bears a striking resemblance to correspondence between Wister and his white cook, George West, it is also inflected with the choppy English syntax that Wister used to mark Indian speech. The narrator's health-giving embrace of the Virginian's barbarous masculinity is articulated most eloquently, however, in a passage late in the narrative, where he describes a journey with the Virginian, now his "friend," as "like living back in ages gone." To "leave behind all noise and mechanisms, and set out . . . into the wilderness, made me feel that the ancient earth was indeed my mother and that I had found her again after being lost among houses, customs, and restraints" (246). Noting the narrator's progress in his "education" since their first acquaintance, the Virginian tellingly remarks, "You'll equal an Injun if you keep on" (266).

While his pairing with the narrator echoes the healing of white manhood enacted in the West cure, the Virginian's pairing with Molly is significant on an even greater scale, for it provides a scenario for recuperating white racial dominance at a time when, as mentioned above, such privilege was imagined to be in doubt. Wister suggests in a variety of ways that Indianness informs the Virginian's suitability as a mate for Molly in a coupling that matches his hero's new, indigenous American manhood with Molly's blue bloodline. All in Molly's proper eastern family discern the Indianness that informs the Virginian's nature, yet as mentioned above, only her wise great-aunt is able to comprehend its significance, to see that far from threatening the Virginian's whiteness, it in fact confirms its power. Although Molly's own mother would later protest her engagement to the Virginian with the outburst, "A savage with knives and pistols!" (242), her great-aunt knows better, understanding that the Virginian's "savagery" is a source of both his manliness and his "indigenous" whiteness. Significantly, it is the Virginian's photograph that reveals so much about his nature. Whereas photography degrades the authenticity of Native Americans in Wister's mythology, it seems to have the opposite effect on the Virginian, for it makes his "savage" nature visible, marking him as a "real" man, his masculinity both authentic and indigenous.[35]

The Indianness underwriting the novel's promise of dominant whiteness is further suggested as a powerful subtext of the chapter in which the Virginian and Molly enact their mutual seduction and secure the engagement necessary for Wister's racial and national recuperation. The seduction begins when Molly, healing the ailing Virginian in her cabin, throws "around his shoulders" her "scarlet and black Navajo blanket, striped with its splendid zigzags of barbarity. Thus he half sat, half leaned, languid but at ease" (231). In his "languid," half-sitting pose, "at ease" under "splendid zigzags of barbarity," the Virginian is clearly orientalized: this supposedly white hero of the American western is pictured as a racial other, literally and symbolically embodying the native cultures that were conquered in the making of America. Such an interpretation is buttressed by Wister's use of setting, for Molly's cabin – the domain of the paradigmatic domesticator, the eastern schoolmarm in the West – symbolizes the sexual, racial, cultural, and geographic appropriations of the novel. The "whole cosey log cabin [had] been upholstered," we are told, "lavish with trophies of the frontier": over her mantle, Molly hung "a Crow Indian war-bonnet" with "a sumptuous cascade of feathers"; "a bow with arrows"; and "the skin of a silver fox." "Over the door had spread the antlers of a blacktail deer; a bearskin stretched beneath it" (210). This literal and symbolic taxidermy of the native species of the West – of the "savages" and the animals with whom they were grouped – suggests that Wister's national cure was to be effected precisely through the violent death and consequent reanimation of the native cultures and peoples of the West to serve a strengthened race of white Americans. Significantly, it is under the same Navajo blanket that the lovers finally "plight their troth," "the fair head nestling in the great arms, and the black head laid against it" (232–33). Using seduction and figurative taxidermy, Molly, the novel's representative of eastern "civilization," has captured the Indianness within the Virginian.[36] Such Indianness is a "trophy": it is valuable only for the abstract qualities that it symbolizes, for the "native," authentic American status, so coveted by Anglo-Americans at the turn of the century, that it will grant their plentiful offspring.

In *The Virginian*, then, Wister completes with fiction the process that he began with his camera. Having made his living Indians visible to the "evil eye of civilization," he is able to deprive them of any claim to savagery, nobility, and authenticity – to what he views as the privileges of "native" status. This he has claimed for his Anglo-Saxon hero, who is thus both a vehicle for redeeming white manhood and an emblem of the taxidermic gesture of conquest. Indeed, by 1902 white mastery over Native Americans in the United States had been firmly established, the violent echoes of the massacre at Wounded Knee more than a decade gone. In response to perceived threats to white hegemony by groups such as African Americans and new immigrants, Wister's vision of "native" whiteness is poised to renew its dominance. Fittingly, Wister's own reputation as an authority on American identity and nativism was greatly enhanced by his novel, leading Edward Clark Marsh to write in 1908: "It can quite safely be said that no living American writer of fiction is more completely indigenous than Mr. Wister." *The Virginian*, then, earned Wister the status of "indigenous," which he reinforced himself with the declaration, "They say my writings are very American. . . . They ought to be. I have been on this soil, ancestrally speaking, since the Merion settlement in Pennsylvania, more than two hundred years."[37] Through penning this early western, Wister claims, for himself and for his hero, an authentic American identity, a "native," "indigenous" status that belies not only white genocide of flesh-and-blood Native Americans and their culture but also his own appropriation of "Indian" bodies and symbolism.

BECOMING NATIVE: THE NEXT HUNDRED YEARS

Since its publication one hundred years ago, *The Virginian* has had a profound influence on American literature and culture. Much has been made of its effect on the development of the western genre throughout the twentieth century, not only in literature but also in film and popular culture more generally.[38] Certainly, Wister's appropriation of "Indianness" (in service of his claims to white Americans' indigenous status and to revitalized manliness for white men) is a pattern that has been repeated often in the past one hundred years. Although the United States has undergone great changes over this period, and although we arrive at the beginning of the twenty-first century with social and cultural contexts that are quite different from those that informed Wister's anxieties about whiteness and manhood, lingering traces of his ethos of "playing Indian" exist to this day, and they cast uncertain shadows on the future of western writing in America.

Two of the more familiar literary echoes of Wister's Indian ethos are formulated in the work of the twentieth-century writers Ernest Hemingway and Mary Austin, whom I will consider very briefly here. Tellingly, although they invoked native cultures in very dissimilar ways and for quite divergent purposes, a central part of both Hemingway's and Austin's writerly identities was a claim to *being* Indian, although this took a different form from Wister's own declaration of indigenous status. For Hemingway, Indianness is an important element in the construction of white manhood, for his characters as well as for his public persona.[39] Like Wister's, Hemingway's writing – both public and private – is shot through with references to Indianness, "not as a major element, but perhaps as a trace element essential to psychic health."[40] Scholars have read such invocations as attempts to achieve a sense of authenticity supposedly lost amid disillusionment with modern American civilization felt by Hemingway and his contemporaries.[41] Like Wister's, therefore, Hemingway's Indians are not major characters but rather foils for white heroes; they are "part of the landscape, . . . appropriate to the scene and symbolic within it," but not subjects in their own right.[42] This objectification of Native Americans is part and parcel of the white male protagonist's developing subjectivity and recovery of "psychic health," a process mirrored in Hemingway's own self-construction. His claim to having "Indian blood" is well known, as are his boasts of Indian mistresses and offspring and his penchant for imitating stereotypically "Indian" speech.[43] In his writing as well as his personal affectations, then, Hemingway's appropriations of Indianness serve to define and revitalize white manliness, a gesture whose genealogy can be traced, at least in part, to his western antecedent.

Like Hemingway, Mary Austin associated Indianness with authenticity and health, echoing also Wister's desire to infuse white American identity with "native" status; yet although her invocation of indigenous peoples and cultures is in some ways problematic, it nevertheless undergirded a multicultural, antipatriarchal, egalitarian worldview. As Lois Rudnick has argued, Austin was one of a host of "Anglo expatriate" women, including Alice Corbin Henderson and Mabel Dodge Luhan, who migrated West after the turn of the century, touting the region and its native inhabitants as "a model of ecological, spiritual, and artistic integration" that "could teach modern Anglo-Americans how to overcome the psychological fragmentation and alienating isolation of their modern, industrial society." They proposed building a new, revitalized American culture that was "grounded in indigenous myths and symbols."[44] Finding her "muse" in Native American prayer and song,[45] Austin employed a mimetic technique in her creative process in order to become "native" herself. She explains, for example, that if she "wished to know what went into the patterns of the basket makers" whom she intended to represent in writing, she would make a basket herself in the traditional Indian way. "When I say that I am not, have never been, nor offered myself, as an authority on things Amerindian," she insists, "I do not wish to have it understood that I may not, at times, have succeeded in being an Indian."[46] Austin's claim to "be an Indian," as well as her appropriation of native cultures toward an authentic American identity for Anglos like herself, is not, of course, without its problems, sharing a great deal with both Hemingway and Wister in their attempts at "playing Indian."[47] Yet it must be understood that these gestures on Austin's part were made, however naively, as part of an attempt to grant native peoples the subjectivity and self-determination that they had so long been denied. Like her fellow Anglo expatriates, Austin worked tirelessly during her life to promote Indian rights in a variety of contexts, leaving most of her estate to the cause at her death. In this, as well as in her notable rejection of assimilationism and masculinist primitivism, she gestures toward a more promising vision of "becoming native."

Beyond modernist literary formulations represented by Hemingway and Austin, the phenomenon of "playing Indian" articulated in *The Virginian* has taken many other forms in twentieth-century American culture. The pattern has been evident in everything from scouting and camping organizations early in the century to communalism and environmentalism in the later periods. It has been demonstrated graphically in the powwows of white Indian lore hobbyists, which center around a fascination with Indian artifacts and costume and sometimes with "unmediated personal contact with native people," the object being "white appropriation and self-discovery." Like Wister, the twentieth-century practitioners of "playing Indian" find "redemptive value," not, for the most part, in flesh-and-blood Native Americans alive today, "but in the artifacts they had once produced in a [supposedly] more authentic stage of existence." The most striking example is perhaps the recent New Age men's movement: focusing on "healing a wounded Self," it promotes vision quest experiences and pipe ceremonies "in Indian-tinged settings." Passing a "talking-stick," designating personal totem animals, and reading manifestos such as Robert Bly's *Iron John* and Sam Keen's *Fire in the Belly*, men's movement participants attempt to recover an authentic American manliness supposedly threatened by the vagaries of postmodern society.[48] These vagaries include, of course, cultural movements like feminism and multiculturalism (perhaps the present-day equivalents of Wister's nemeses, New Womanhood and immigration). On a wider scale, it surely is no accident that at precisely the time when "authentic" Indianness has functioned as such a valuable commodity for followers of the men's movement and other white Americans, Indians' own access to traditional culture and identity has been under dire threat. From turn-of-the-century boarding schools, to relocation and termination policies at mid-century, to the continued social and economic discrimination perpetuated both on and off reservations, Native Americans have had to struggle to maintain their traditional languages, culture, and spiritual practices. Indeed, attempts by the American Indian Movement and others to retain such connections have been criminalized and often violently subdued. At the dawn of the twenty-first century, the appropriable artifacts of Indianness are still valuable commodities – yet living, breathing Indians are still refusing to submit to the taxidermic gesture. Although the perceived threats to "authentic" American identity, as well as to "authentic" manliness (and its accompanying privileges), may have shifted somewhat from what they were in Wister's time, then, the appropriation of Indianness still serves a purpose for many Americans today.

What the *next* hundred years hold for these issues in western writing and American society will depend, perhaps, on the interplay between literature and culture in movements for social change. As long as the focus remains on healing and revitalizing the dominant culture, and as long as Native Americans are valued less for their complex and diverse subjectivities than for their recognizably "Indian" products, the pattern is sure to continue. Yet if we look at the variety of ways in which the literature of the New West is transforming ancestral texts such as *The Virginian* so as to serve the cultural, ideological, and aesthetic interests of the new century, it may be possible to imagine more positive trajectories for the phenomenon. Perhaps, for example, the next *Virginian* will be an ironic subversion of the old paradigm: if we look at the existing works of native writers such as Sherman Alexie or Louise Erdrich, we might argue that such a novel has already been written. Just as literary critics are beginning to envision diverse, hybrid, decentralized literary traditions – many of them long established yet made visible only through these antihierarchical critical practices – so American writers are constructing new formulations of national and cultural identity, formulations that invite subversion, transformation, possibly even rejection of the paradigms of the Old West.

NOTES

1. A recent review of the relevant scholarship can be found in Bederman, *Manliness and Civilization*, 10–15.

2. Wister, *The Virginian* (1998), 171–72. Page numbers for subsequent quotations will be given in the text.

3. See esp. Leverenz, "The Last Real Man in America," 34; and Will, "The Nervous Origins of the American Western."

4. Will, "Nervous Origins," 310.

5. Wister, "The Evolution of the Cowpuncher" (1998), 331.

6. See esp. Bederman, *Manliness and Civilization*; Deloria, *Playing Indian*; Kimmel, *Manhood in America*; Lutz, *American Nervousness*; and Rotundo, *American Manhood*.

7. For detailed analyses of Mitchell's West cure, see Tuttle, "Rewriting the West Cure"; and Will, "Nervous Origins."

8. Mitchell, *Nurse and Patient, and Camp Cure*, 45, 47, 57.

9. Mitchell, *Wear and Tear*, 74.

10. Wister, "Among the Cow-Boys," 65.

11. Payne, *Owen Wister*, 87. It is important to note that this narrative of manliness regained was underwritten by the very "civilization" and privilege that it seemed to reject. Not only would such a journey have been prohibitively expensive for all but the most wealthy in American society but Wolcott's ranch was also anything but rustic. Indeed, the need to deny the trappings of its Persian rugs, excellent piano, white linen, and Chinese serving staff may have underlaid Wister's de-

cision, after his first night there, to sleep in a tent on the grounds. These sleeping arrangements may also have had something to do with the fact that Wister was chaperoned on this trip by two spinsters in their forties who were friends of his mother's. See Payne, *Owen Wister,* 82–83.

12. Wister, "Old Yellowstone Days," 471, 473.

13. Wister quoted in Wister, ed., *Owen Wister Out West* (hereafter OWOW), 43, 48–49.

14. Payne, *Owen Wister,* 101.

15. Deloria, *Playing Indian.*

16. Quoted in Payne, *Owen Wister,* 138.

17. Mark Gardner ("The Western Photography of Owen Wister," 14–15) has argued that Wister's camera was most likely a No. 4 Kodak Junior, which weighed, with film, approximately four and one half pounds and "would fit in a saddle bag." Gardner offers a detailed discussion of Wister's photographs. See also Dorst, "Owen Wister and Emergent Discourse of the American West," and *Looking West,* 40–74.

18. Haraway, "Teddy Bear Patriarchy," 34.

19. Wister had already begun to document his West cures in both photographs and written and published accounts. Tellingly, however, his 1891 trip, when he first undertook to write such a tale, was also the first journey on which he brought his camera (see Gardner, "The Western Photography of Owen Wister," 7; and Payne, *Owen Wister,* 116–17).

20. Haraway, "Teddy Bear Patriarchy," 30.

21. Trachtenberg, *Reading American Photographs,* 154. For a detailed discussion of photographs of Native Americans during this period, see Sandweiss, "Views and Reviews," 186.

22. Haraway, "Teddy Bear Patriarchy," 45.

23. Deloria (*Playing Indian,* esp. 71–94) examines the significance of these and other ethnographic tendencies expressed in those practices that he labels *playing Indian.*

24. For a detailed discussion of Wister's issue day photographs, see Gardner, "The Western Photography of Owen Wister," 76–83.

25. Quoted in Gardner, "The Western Photography of Owen Wister," 76.

26. This stark reality certainly would have hit home for Wister when he met other chiefs at Fort Washakie, for "many of them gave Wister gold-edged calling cards: 'North Axe, Chief of Pregan-Blackfeet,' 'Red Crow, Chief of Blood-Blackfeet,' and 'Bull Head, Chief of Sarcis-Blackfeet'" (Payne, *Owen Wister,* 140).

27. Wister, "Bad Medicine," 40–41.

28. An important study has yet to be done of Wister's portrayal of Mexicans in his photographs and journals, a portrayal that shares much with his vision of Native Americans, particularly in his writings on the Southwest.

29. See Cobbs, *Owen Wister.*

30. See esp. Vorpahl, "Roosevelt, Wister, Turner, and Remington," 289; and Will, "Nervous Origins."

31. Wister, "The Evolution of the Cowpuncher," 333.

32. See, e.g., Marovitz, "Testament of a Patriot"; Scharnhorst, "The Virginian as a Founding Father"; Vorpahl, "Roosevelt, Wister, Turner, and Remington," 288; and Westbrook, "Bazarov, Prince Hal, and the Virginian."

33. Alternative referents for this darkness are many; e.g., the Virginian also reveals that he has Scotch-Irish ancestry. For a study of the relation of this darkness to homoeroticism in the novel, see Allmendinger, *Ten Most Wanted,* 153–70.

34. See Abrams, "National Paintings and American Character."

35. Although it is meant to indicate the Virginian's authenticity, this photograph is also a "highly constructed simulation": like Wister's Yellowstone hunting party, it is a spectacle of wild and predatory masculinity. As Amy Kaplan ("Romancing the Empire," 665) has argued, such spectacles, appearing in *The Virginian* and in society at large, underwrote both Manifest Destiny and American imperialism at the turn of the century.

36. Certainly, this seduction scene and subsequent events in the novel narrate a simultaneous "taming" of Molly, a New Woman and representative of neurasthenic and linguistic excess, by the Virginian. Although a consideration of this issue is beyond the scope of this essay, it is addressed nicely in Mitchell, "'When You Call Me That . . .'"; and Will, "Nervous Origins," 305–8.

37. Both Marsh's and Wister's statements are quoted in White, *The Eastern Establishment and the Western Experience,* 196, 199.

38. See, e.g., Cawelti, *Adventure, Mystery, and Romance,* 215, and *The Six-Gun Mystique,* 2, 34; Cobbs, *Owen Wister,* 1; French, *Westerns,* 26; Milton, *The Novel of the American West;* and Whipp, "Owen Wister," 250.

39. See Hays, "Hemingway's Use of a Natural Resource," 51; and Strong, "Screaming through Silence," 30–31, 42 n. 4.

40. See Robert W. Lewis, "'Long Time Ago Good,'" 212.

41. See, e.g., Cowley, introduction to *Hemingway,* xx.

42. Hays, "Hemingway's Use of a Natural Resource," 45–46.

43. See Lewis, "'Long Time Ago Good," 201, 481 n. 4; and Meyers, "Hemingway's Primitivism and 'Indian Camp,'" 215.

44. See Rudnick, "Re-Naming the Land," 10, 19, 22. For a discussion of such

Native American elements in Austin's writing, see Dilworth, *Imagining Indians*, 183–84; and Graulich, introduction to *Western Trails*, 4.

45. Graulich, introduction to *Western Trails*, 21.

46. Austin, *The American Rhythm*, 40–41.

47. See Dilworth, *Imagining Indians*, 208; and Rudnick, "Re-Naming the Land," 25.

48. See Deloria, *Playing Indian*, 129, 137, 141, 173–74.

5   WISTER AND THE GREAT RAILWAY STRIKE OF 1894

Gary Scharnhorst

As both Louis Owens and Jennifer Tuttle suggest through their historical research, the building of the transcontinental railroads brought destructive changes to the lives of American Indians in the West; the Yellowstone tourists who invade the Nez Perce homelands and the Crow "chiefs" "allowed" off the reservation to sell their wares to stranded tourists are two examples in The Virginian *of expanding capital's transformation of the West. Indeed, both the "privileged mobility" of the tourist or traveler and the "West cure" — along with Judge Henry's cattle operation — depended on the railroad. While novels contemporaneous with* The Virginian *like Frank Norris's* The Octopus *explicitly explored the role of the railroads and the rail barons in the West's settlement, the predominant critical focus on* The Virginian *as a paean to cowboy culture has obscured Wister's insights about technological and political changes taking place in the West and the United States. In his essay, Gary Scharnhorst builds on an earlier essay in which he argued that Wister's novel displaced the Revolutionary War to Wyoming, where the Virginian assumes the symbolic role of the nation's founding father. Scharnhorst here continues to regard the novel as a political and social allegory, focusing more closely on one of its most analyzed scenes, the four-chapter "The Game and the Nation" sequence. Reading these chapters as a veiled allegory of the 1894 Pullman strike, Scharnhorst recovers the novel's keen investment in class issues through its specific references to labor disputes, "markets," "capital," "cheap foreigners," and scabs, all critical in the revisionist historical view of the West. Whereas an earlier generation of critics typically argued that Wister's novel was popularly received because it was politically neutral or even apolitical, Scharnhorst brings into view how the novel relates to a specific historical context and simultaneously stages an ideologically loaded version of that history.*

She is just one o' them parables.

OWEN WISTER, The Virginian

Rarely are westerns only about the West. From the beginning, western narratives have been vehicles for topical commentary. From Fenimore Cooper to Gary Cooper and beyond, that is, westerns have functioned as symbolic melodramas or social and political allegories. As Philip French remarks, "The Western is a great grab bag, a hungry cuckoo of a genre, a voracious bastard of a form, open equally to visionaries and opportunists, ready to seize anything that's in the air from juvenile delinquency to ecology."[1] The various sagas about the Earps in Tombstone may begin to illustrate the point: In such movies and books as *My Darling Clementine* (1946), *Gunfight at the O.K. Corral* (1957), Frank Waters's *The Earp Brothers of Tombstone* (1960), *Hour of the Gun* (1967), *Doc* (1971), *Tombstone* (1993), and *Wyatt Earp* (1994), there has been no clear consensus about the roles that the brothers and their allies played in their confrontation with the Clantons. They have been portrayed as everything from avenging angels in a Manichaean conflict of good versus evil to pathological hired gunmen, dissipated defenders of the cattle companies.

To be sure, the allegorical function of westerns has been especially apparent in novels and films over the past sixty years. "From World War II through the troubled Cold War years," as Gerald Nash notes, westerns "accommodated a variety of issues and ideas that echoed feelings of . . . alienation and disillusionment."[2] Walter Van Tilburg Clark explained, for example, how he conceived his novel *The Ox-Bow Incident* (1940) as an anti-Nazi allegory: "The book was written in 1937 and '38, when the whole world was getting increasingly worried about Hitler and the Nazis, and emotionally it stemmed from my part of this worrying." The story became something of "an allegory of the unscrupulous and brutal Nazi methods."[3] More commonly, of course, such westering epics as *Men of Texas* (1942) and *The Great Man's Lady* (1942) subtly endorsed the war effort by celebrating patriotic virtues. John Cawelti has, in fact, noted the "similarity between the pattern of justifying rhetoric used to defend American military policy and the Western drama."[4]

Predictably, in the late 1940s and the 1950s westerns often mirrored the politics of the cold war. As Richard Slotkin remarks, the "cavalry western," epitomized by John Ford's *Fort Apache* (1948), *She Wore a Yellow Ribbon* (1949), and *Rio Grande* (1950), "provided a way to treat the concerns" of the cold war – for example, preparedness, "peaceful coexistence" with the Soviets, whether to negotiate, attack, or defend – "in the language of the western."[5] By no mean coincidence did Audie Murphy, the most decorated U.S. soldier of World War II, star in over thirty western movies between 1950 and 1971, including such cold war classics as *Posse from Hell* (1961). In contrast, *High Noon* (1952), based on John Cunningham's short story "The Tin Star" (1947), was a transparent parable or "allegory about existential man standing alone in the McCarthy era."[6] As Harry Schein adds, "The little community seems to be crippled with fear before the approaching villains; seems to be timid, neutral, and half-hearted like the United Nations before the Soviet Union, China, and North Korea; moral courage is apparent only in the very American sheriff," Will Kane.[7] The screenwriter of *High Noon*, Carl Foreman, was subsequently blacklisted in Hollywood. Indeed, there were a number of well-known directors and actors in western movies in the 1950s who suffered the humiliation and ostracism of the blacklist, among them Edward Dmytryk (*Warlock* and *Broken Lance*), Victor Kilian (*The Ox-Bow Incident*), and Will Geer (*Blood Brothers*), a detail that alone ought to suggest the political significance of the genre.

The western formula continued to evolve in the 1960s, 1970s, and 1980s in response to a variety of social and political issues. For example, John Ford's *Sergeant Rutledge* (1960), featuring an African American hero, was among the first "civil rights westerns." As James Maguire has observed, moreover, "Many Westerners saw in [the Vietnam War] parallels with our westering experience, marked as it was by our nearly genocidal treatment of Native Americans and by our oppression and exploitation of minorities and women."[8] In dramatizing American soldiers as aggressors, not rescuers, Thomas Berger's *Little Big Man* (1964) was one of the first anti-Vietnam westerns, whereas such John Wayne movies as *El Dorado* (1967), *Rio Lobo* (1970), and *The Cowboys* (1972), as well as the *Magnificent Seven* (1960) and *100 Rifles* (1968), were "counterinsurgency westerns" that commended military intervention in the Third World. As Slotkin concludes, "It was the western, and the western alone, which bore the cultural burden of providing or withholding mythological sanction for the [Vietnam] war."[9] Over the years, too, westerns have satirized corporate oligarchy, as in Edmund Naughton's *McCabe* (1970), and promoted sexual liberation, as in *The Cheyenne Social Club* (1970). More recently, John Nichols in *The Milagro Beanfield War* (1974) and Edward Abbey in *The Monkey Wrench Gang* (1975) have inaugurated a tradition of "environmental westerns," and Maxine Hong Kingston in *Woman Warrior*

(1976) and Sandra Cisneros in *Woman Hollering Creek* (1991) have helped invent a type of "feminist western." The formula has morphed, too, into other forms of popular narrative, particularly science fiction. ("Space – the final frontier.") Not only the Lone Ranger and Tonto but Captain Kirk and Mr. Spock as well are lineal descendants of Natty Bumppo and Chingachgook.

Owen Wister may have inherited a western romantic literary tradition of allegory and melodrama, but more than any other pioneer of the genre he also turned the western into a form of social and political commentary. His story "Em'ly" (1893), later revised for inclusion in *The Virginian*, was recognized from the first as a type of (anti)feminist parable, and as I have argued elsewhere, the novel as a whole becomes a "fable of renewal" by reenacting the Revolutionary War in Wyoming with the Virginian, the archetypal cowboy, in the role of founding father.[10] I now believe that Wister subtly commented on at least one other topical political issue in the novel. In chapters 13–16 ("The Game and the Nation"), I will argue, he re-created, or reenacted, or dramatized, the Great Railway Strike of 1894, led by Eugene V. Debs, which virtually closed all rail travel and transport in the West. In the western hero's defeat of the labor leader, typified by Trampas, that is, Wister decisively sided with capital and against strike organizers such as Debs.

In his essay "The Evolution of the Cow-Puncher" (1895), Wister infamously decried the "encroaching alien vermin" that infested the country and threatened to "degrade our commonwealth from a nation into something half pawn-shop, half broker's office."[11] Fortunately, or so goes the argument, Wister muted such extremist views when he wrote *The Virginian* (1902), whose composite hero synthesized a number of cultural types. As Neal Lambert remarks, in his archetypal western hero "Wister pulled together into one character successful affirmations of essentially contradictory systems of values."[12] John Cawelti echoes the point: Wister "combined in the Virginian several conflicting images of American life."[13] Just as the Virginian was the avatar of a civilized West equally at home in the effete and sophisticated East, *The Virginian* seemed to be a neutral text onto which reformers and conservatives alike could project their positions, in which both progressives and reactionaries could find support for their views. In a word, the novel was free of the knee-jerk agenda that marred his next book, his racial and unapologetically racist novel *Lady Baltimore* (1906). As Louis Tanner contends, "*The Virginian* was the most 'liberal' thing Wister ever wrote, strikingly free of the right-wing polemics that dominated his nonwestern writings thereafter. . . . Had Wister written *The Virginian* as a political document full of hatred for 'alien vermin,' had he identified the hero's virtues with one party or faction over another, the book's popularity would have been greatly diminished. . . . But Wister suppressed his prejudices and kept the cowboy in the middle of the political spectrum or perhaps outside of politics altogether."[14] Put another way, neither the hero nor the villain, Trampas, offers an opinion on a topical political issue (with the exception of the Virginian's derisive comments about feminism in the "Em'ly" chapter), so the novel gives offense to neither Democrat nor Republican, Jeffersonian nor Federalist, worker nor capitalist, immigrant nor native. The Virginian and Trampas are apparently divided by no issue more nuanced than the (im)morality of cattle rustling, or so goes the argument.

Not so, however, if we may construe chapters 13–16 of the novel as Wister's veiled attack on labor unions. But first some background.

In an effort to redress falling wages in the Pullman factory and exorbitant rents in the company town of Pullman, Illinois, among other grievances, the American Railway Union (ARU), headed by Debs, voted to authorize a boycott or strike against the Pullman Company on 26 June 1894. The strike quickly spread among railroad employees throughout the West. On 2 July the U.S. attorney general, Richard Olney, obtained an injunction forbidding the strike in federal court in Chicago. Debs and the other ARU leaders chose to defy the injunction, whereupon President Cleveland, citing the threat to railroad property, sent federal troops to Chicago on 4 July and soon to other western cities. While some pockets of railworkers held out until September, the strike was largely crushed by the National Guard by August. Debs was arrested and charged with conspiracy to obstruct a mail train and with contempt of court for ignoring the injunction against the strike. He was sentenced to six months in the federal prison in Woodstock, Illinois. That is, the strike ended disastrously for the union, which was effectively broken.

Traveling in the Southwest and California in July 1894, Wister suffered the effects of the strike at firsthand. As he later remembered, "Vaguely I had heard something about a strike at the town of Pullman, where the company had its works; vaguely I had noticed here and there the name of Eugene Debs. One day I got on the Sunset Express at a junction called Benson, and I expected to get out of that train at Oakland in two days." Instead, the next day in Los Angeles the passengers "were informed that

our Pullman would go no farther, because it was a strike against the Pullman company; and we were advised to get into the day coaches. We
crowded into the day coaches and sat in them till it grew dark. Nobody
told us anything." He booked passage aboard the steamer San Pedro for
San Francisco and "found my first-class ticket gave me the privilege of
sleeping on any portion of the vessel that I could find unoccupied."[15] As
he wrote a friend in late August, after his return to the East, "I was caught
in the strike. My train reached Los Angeles and there expired. Quite a
combination of discomforts and uncertainties followed, ending in my
travelling by sea, sleeping on the floor with 55 other cabinless wretches,
and for two nights twisting about in order to dodge the adjacent feet of
passengers who seemed bent on plunging the said feet into my hair. It was
a thoroughly unsavory journey, and I reached San Francisco with a bad
cold and greatly disgusted."[16]

At first he sympathized with the strikers. In his journal for July 1894 he
noted that several "rioters" had been shot and millions of dollars worth of
"property burned or otherwise destroyed." "Yet still I am glad" because
"the cause and root of this present evil is that money has grown too powerful in our republic." The strikers' "protest and grievance is against the
Jay Goulds, the Carnegies, the Huntingtons, the Sugar Trust, and they'll
go on protesting till they've reduced those abuses to unrecognizable powder – if the thing is not corrected. So far as that, I'm on their side."[17]

Yet within days he had reversed his field. Because he was personally inconvenienced by the Pullman strike, Wister recoiled from the cause of labor much as, in another context, Thoreau "saw yet more distinctly the
State in which [he] lived" after spending a night in the Concord jail.[18]
"What set me against [Debs], what lodged this very grave event in my
thoughts," Wister later explained, "was my own inconvenience in the
strike, shared by a legion of other absolutely innocent citizens who were
in no manner whatever to blame for the grievance of Debs."[19] As soon as
"travel became reasonably reliable" again, he hurried back to Philadelphia, "stopping at Cheyenne a much shorter time than had been my original plan."[20]

His animus against the strikers is obvious in the first article that he
wrote on his return, a piece entitled "The National Guard of Pennsylvania" that appeared in Harper's Weekly for 1 September 1894. In 1877, during the last major rail strike, he declared, "we saw how a horde of vermin [the same term that Wister used the next year to describe the threat
to American democracy in "The Evolution of the Cow-Puncher"] had

swarmed over our body-social, and how we had been driven to ask outside help to knock the rats back into their holes." At the Homestead steel plant outside Pittsburgh in July 1892, "the rats came out of their holes again," and the state militia was needed to quell the violence of the "contemptible mutineers." "I have had a recent experience in California – not relevant here, save for comparison," he added, "and Sacramento in '94 was worse than Pittsburg in '77."[21] Wister concluded that labor violence "has schooled Pennsylvania to a sane and sound idea about militia; men have acted on that idea. Calamity in Chicago, California, and elsewhere has lately cured many diseased opinions concerning our regular army." Lest he be misunderstood, Wister asserted his belief that the only buffer between striking labor and political chaos was the American military: "It remains to be seen if, like Pennsylvania in a small way, the United States in a large way has had a sufficiently severe lesson to place a correct value upon the soldier. If not, may we have one soon – before, what with the Debses" and others of the same ilk, "we are become altogether rotten."[22]

A year later, in an interview with Arthur Stedman of the *New York Journal*, a piece subsequently reprinted in the *San Francisco Examiner*, Wister was still venting on the subject of Debs and the Pullman strike. "A year ago, you remember," he told Stedman, "we had those railroad strikes that Debs inaugurated in Chicago; there was a much worse one at the time in California. The reason that most people did not know much about it was because Chicago rose between and blotted out what lay behind. But when I tell you that on the 15th day of July, in 1894, in San Francisco, the latest New York paper that we could get was of date June 23rd, you will realize what the strike was like. It was like a blockade – a blockade by a foreign country. Of course I could tell you many more things about it. I came back here to the East and alluded to it among my friends, and my hearers were utterly unaware that such a thing had occurred."[23] As Wister later explained, his eastern friends "had been placidly passing those June and July days at Bar Harbor, or Newport, or pursuing their holiday or their business as usual."[24] In brief, the Pullman strike of the summer of 1894 left a vivid impression on Wister during the years he was writing some of the stories folded into *The Virginian*.

From its original preface and first chapter, in which the narrator arrives in Medicine Bow aboard a train, to its final chapter, in which the narrator reports that "the railroad came and built a branch" to land owned by the hero "where the coal was," *The Virginian* celebrates the railroad as a progressive civilizing force.[25] As Tanner observes, "Wister almost always wrote about a narrow time frame from roughly 1870 to 1890, a period when railroads rapidly civilized an earlier and wilder frontier."[26] Wister repeatedly referred in his letters and diaries to rail travel, particularly in Pullman cars.[27] For example, he wrote the story "Twenty Minutes for Refreshments" (1900) as a series of diary entries by a Pullman car passenger as he crosses the continent to Los Angeles, a technique reminiscent of W. D. Howells's one-act plays *The Parlor Car* (1876) and *The Albany Depot* (1891). In other words, Wister's decision to set the four-chapter "The Game and the Nation" sequence, first published in *Harper's Monthly* the same year as "Twenty Minutes for Refreshments," against a backdrop of railway locations was entirely in character. The narrator repeatedly alludes in these chapters to the railroad, from the initial reference to Colonel Cyrus Jones's eating palace near the railyards in Omaha in chapter 13 to the caboose that "trundled on to Billings along the shingly cotton-wooded Yellowstone [River]" (126) at the close of chapter 16.

At the outset of "The Game and the Nation," Wister asserted in his own voice that "every man should . . . have equal liberty to find his own level. . . . Let the best man win, whoever he is"; this promise, he declared, epitomizes the American Dream. "That is true democracy. And true democracy and true aristocracy are one and the same thing. If anybody cannot see this, so much the worse for his eyesight" (91). In a word, these four chapters silhouette a contest between the Virginian and Trampas, a conflict between the "quality" and the "equality" (91), with the Virginian the natural aristocrat of virtue and talent and Trampas clearly the social leveler or advocate of a false and unmerited "equality." Put another way, Trampas functions in these chapters allegorically as a labor leader à la Debs and the Virginian as a type of strikebreaker.

Their conflict is joined in these chapters because Judge Henry of the Sunk Creek Ranch has sent the Virginian on a mission: first to sell twenty railcars of cattle in Chicago, then to negotiate with the directors of the Northern Pacific for "especially cheap rates" in the future, and finally "to lead his six highly unoccupied brethren . . . back in peace to the ranch. . . . These things sometimes go wrong in a land where they say you are all born equal" (95–96). Gold has been discovered near Rawhide, however, and the cowboys employed by Judge Henry must decide whether to remain with the Virginian and return to Sunk Creek or mutiny with Trampas and strike for the goldfields. (Wister plays in these chapters with the term *strike* as either a gold strike or a labor strike, as when the Virginian declares that he "had the boys plumb contented. . . . Away along as far as Saynt Paul I had them reconciled to my authority. Then this news about gold had to strike us" [103].) The "mutineers" (114) – the same word that Wister had used to describe strikers in his essay "The National Guard of Pennsylvania" – have been "drugged by their satanically aroused hopes of gold" (123). The cowboys are also described as "enthusiasts" (112) and, most tellingly, as "trainhands" (106), and they occupy the caboose where Pullman employees were normally quartered. The Virginian is forced to dismiss one of them, Schoffner, the cook, the only mutineer other than Trampas given a name – and, significantly, an ethnic German and so a "foreigner." (In an aside, the Virginian also confuses Chinese coolies with "I-talians" and complains that "[w]ithout cheap foreigners they couldn't afford all this hyeh new gradin'" [113]. For the record, Wister would later become a vice president of the Immigration Restriction League.) Not that Wister indicts all the worker-cowboys per se: "[T]he rest of that young humanity was average rough male blood, merely needing to be told the proper things at the right time" (108). Wister suggests that the gullible workers have simply been misled by the false promises of labor leaders like Trampas/Debs, who cynically dangle dreams of higher wages before them: "Fact and falsehood blended with such perfect art" (112), as the narrator allows. Lest there be any doubt, in this scene Wister intends Trampas to be a type of labor leader; he refers to him and his "herd" of men (118), to "Trampas and his followers" (119), and to "the Trampas faction" (121).

At the Rawhide station, the train is halted behind "four stalled expresses" and "several freights" because of a washed-out bridge. Trampas, the Virginian, and the "mutineers" are stranded, much as Wister had been stranded in Los Angeles by the Pullman strike in July 1894, although to be sure the train is not stalled through Trampas's agency. Still, the passengers on the trains are hostages, no less than the innocent passengers inconvenienced by the 1894 strike, and the stage is set for a "show-down" between Trampas and the Virginian "before the caboose gets off the bridge" (117). The mutineers choose to "grub first" at the expense of the Sunk Creek Ranch before heading for the mines. As the narrator reports, the "dark bubble of mutiny swelled hourly beneath my eyes" (141) in this "undercurrent of war" (109). (Wister later used the same term to describe the 1894 Pullman strike: "Debs was beaten in this war – for civil war is the only name for it – and went to prison.")[28] On balance, moreover, Trampas enjoys a tactical advantage in the war: his "great strength" was that "he need make no move" but "lie low for the immediate temptation to front and waylay [the workers] and win his battle over the deputy foreman" (109).

At this point in the narrative, Wister envisions a nonviolent resolution of the conflict in which the workers forsake their threatened strike to heed the authority and superior intellect of the Virginian, the deputy foreman of the crew. When "the Trampas faction" threatens gunplay, Scipio Le Moyne, hired to replace Schoffner, disarms Shorty, and the Virginian defuses the threat by noting, "This hyeh question has been discussed peaceable by civilized citizens" (115). He spins a tall tale of frog ranching in Tulare County, California, where wages are high but the work risky. Even the frogs are shipped East by rail – "clear to New York afteh the Southern Pacific was through" (120), "frawg trains tearing acrosst Arizona – big glass tanks with wire over 'em – through to New York, an' the frawgs starin' out" (122). ("I wish we had gone to Bar Harbor as usual," declares one of the bored passengers before "she returned to her Pullman" [123]. Wister here evokes a trace of his eastern friends who were indifferent to, or unaware of, or apathetic to the strike.) The market for frogs is ruined (much as the labor market for rail workers might be undermined, the Virginian implies) when two leading chefs, "Saint Augustine" and "Lorenzo Delmonico," collude to wipe "frawgs off the slate of fashion" (125). Completely fooled by the tall story, Trampas is humiliated in this "final pitched battle of wits," which endears the Virginian to the "reconstructed mutineers"[29] and makes them "his captives and admirers" (126, 127). As Scipio explains, "[A]s boss of the outfit he beat Trampas, who was settin' up for opposition boss. And the outfit is better than satisfied it come out that way, and they're stayin' with him; and he'll hand them all back in good condition, barrin' that lost cook" (129). Or as one of Judge Henry's friends realizes back at Sunk Creek, the deputy foreman "cajoled them into a bout of tall stories, and told the tallest himself. . . . I couldn't be a serious mutineer after that" (142).

In all, the episode illustrates nothing less than the triumph of benevolent capital over labor, exactly what had occurred (from Wister's perspective) in the "Debs strike" of 1894. Why else are these chapters set against the backdrop of stalled trains? Could the Virginian not have outwitted Trampas just as easily aboard a moving train or in a saloon? While a damaged bridge, not a labor action directed by Trampas, has stalled the trains, there might just as well have been a causal relation between the blockade and his temptation of the "railworkers." As if by miracle, the blockade is lifted, restoring rail traffic, and Trampas outwitted on the same page. As the narrator notes, "Possibly the supreme – the most American – moment of all was when word came that the bridge was open, and the Pullman trains, with noise and triumph, began to move westward at last" (126).[30] The image evokes the end of the Pullman strike in 1894, with employees pacified and back on board. At Sunk Creek, Judge Henry praises his deputy foreman's "management of the expedition" (145), while Trampas soon quits for a "better job" (171). In short, what seems on the surface merely a battle of wits between the Virginian and Trampas subtly allegorizes or restages the Pullman strike of 1894. In his "Rededication and Preface" to the 1911 edition of *The Virginian*, in fact, Wister made explicit his opposition to organized labor: "Our Democracy has many enemies, both in Wall Street and in the Labor Unions" (vii). He was far more critical of labor leaders like Debs (and Trampas) than he ever was of any robber baron, however.

One other point: His foreign-sounding name notwithstanding, Scipio Le Moyne is a native-born descendant of French immigrants, an American family of long-standing. As he declares, "I've been white for a hundred years" (101). More to the point, because he is hired by the Virginian to replace Schoffner, he is technically a scab, which is altogether to his credit, according to the author. As Wister argued in "The Land of the Free," an essay originally entitled "The Scab" and published two years after *The Virginian*, "Let us clearly understand the significance of the scab. He is the man who needs our backing now. He stands for liberty, the right to live, the right to work, every right that we have all inherited in the land of the free."[31] Tanner fairly concludes that "Wister's glorification of the scab was part of a broader conservative attack upon all forms of collective bargaining, particularly those forms that worked."[32]

Wister described his experiences during the 1894 Pullman strike most fully in his last book, *Roosevelt* (1930). There he recalled how "one evening in New Mexico or Arizona" in the summer of 1893 he had watched some marchers in "Coxey's army of the unemployed . . . out of a Pullman window." The next summer, en route to Los Angeles after a visit "with army and ranch friends in the Southwest, . . . Eugene Debs became a very definite reality" to him. His experience in the West that summer "sank rather deeper than seeing Coxey's army out of the car window the preceding November." The "Debs strike sank into my mind rather deep," he allowed. "It had been driven home to me not by hearsay, not by reading of it in the morning paper while I went on living in my tame security," but at firsthand: "I had felt the consequences, and I did not forget."[33] As I have contended in this essay, Wister recast his experience in the West in 1894 in "The Game and the Nation" six years later, with Trampas, the villain, understudying the role of Eugene V. Debs. Tanner has correctly argued that Trampas "is not a Populist, not a Jew, immigrant, or other ethnic type, not a Robber Baron or corrupt politician."[34] Trouble is, however, he is a type of labor leader à la Debs, reason enough for Wister to have consigned him to eternal damnation in the hellfire of his imagination.

The western formula, like a resilient species of antediluvian reptile, has survived by adapting to changes in political climate and social environment. No doubt the genre will continue to evolve in response to topical issues. I would not be surprised to discover one day an "anti-OPEC western," or an "anti–World Bank western," or a "war-on-drugs western," or even an "animal rights western," although, on second thought, Wister may already have invented the latter form in the "Balaam and Pedro" chapter of *The Virginian.* A distinctively, although not uniquely, American genre, the western, like the novel itself, is as robust as ever: all reports of its demise are premature. With a sort of ragged genius, Owen Wister helped devise a literary form set in an allegorical or symbolic West that has not merely survived but flourished. So long as the mythological West inspires (screen)writers, moreover, the western will remain a popular vehicle for topical commentary and so will continue to engage our critical attention.

NOTES

1. French, *Westerns*, 24.

2. Nash, *Creating the West*, 249.

3. Quoted in Webb, afterword to *The Ox-Bow Incident*, 223–24.

4. Cawelti, *The Six-Gun Mystique*, 84.

5. Slotkin, "The Movie Western," 878.

6. French, *Westerns*, 34.

7. Schein, "The Olympian Cowboy," 309.

8. Maguire, "Fiction in the West," 453.

9. Slotkin, "The Movie Western," 880.

10. Scharnhorst, "The Virginian as a Founding Father."

11. Davis, ed., *Owen Wister's West*, 37.

12. Lambert, "Owen Wister's Virginian," 100.

13. Cawelti, *Adventure, Mystery, and Romance*, 229.

14. Tanner, "Owen Wister," 30.

15. Wister, *Roosevelt*, 200–201.

16. Wister, ed., "Letters of Owen Wister," 24–25. See also Payne, *Owen Wister*, 151.

17. Quoted in Tanner, "Owen Wister," 75–76.

18. Thoreau, *Walden and Resistance to Civil Government*, 240.

19. Wister, *Roosevelt*, 203.

20. Wister, ed., "Letters of Owen Wister," 25.

21. "Soldiers of the regular army next appeared at various points – at Sacramento, for example, where they protected the station and had a cannon or two ready for the mob, and finally escorted the first local which the Southern Pacific attempted to run from Sacramento to Oakland" (Wister, *Roosevelt*, 203).

22. Owen Wister, "The National Guard of Pennsylvania." Theodore Roosevelt later wrote Wister that his essay had suggested his own essay "True American Ideals" (Wister, *Roosevelt*, 39).

23. Stedman, "A Talk with Owen Wister." This interview is new to Wister scholarship. Both the *Journal* and the *Examiner* were Hearst newspapers.

24. Wister, *Roosevelt*, 204.

25. Wister, *The Virginian* (1979), 316. Page numbers for subsequent quotations will be given in the text.

26. Tanner, "Owen Wister," 16.

27. Wister, ed., *Owen Wister Out West*, 45, 98, 118, 133, 228–29.

28. Wister, *Roosevelt*, 203.

29. In the original publication of the story, Wister referred to them as "recent" mutineers (see Wister, "The Game and the Nation," 905).

30. In the original publication of the story, Wister wrote that this was "possibly the most *beautiful* – the most American – moment of all" (Wister, "The Game and the Nation," 905; emphasis added). Wister's revision of *beautiful* to *supreme* – from an adjective describing an aesthetic experience to one connoting might or power – reinforces my argument that the entire episode should be read in the light of the contest between triumphant capital and defeated labor in the Pullman strike of 1894.

31. Wister, "The Land of the Free," 7.

32. Tanner, "Owen Wister," 83.

33. Wister, *Roosevelt*, 198–204.

34. Tanner, "Owen Wister," 29.

6   EARLY FILM VERSIONS OF *THE VIRGINIAN*

Richard Hutson

By beginning his essay on the early film versions of The Virginian *with the question, "What is an author?" Richard Hutson highlights what every essay in this collection assumes: that Wister's novel is not a coherent, harmoniously unified text entered with authorial intention but rather a verbal and visual construct where the confrontation of several discourses – some explicit, some implicit or absent – produces a multiplicity of meanings. Like other writers in the collection, he explores the way in which masculinity is "performed" in the text, but he does so by discussing the novel's evolution into the long-running stage production and then into various early film adaptions leading to the 1929 "talking" film starring Gary Cooper. His discussion of the acting styles and physical presences of the various actors playing the Virginian, Trampas, Molly, and Steve clarifies how indebted our understanding of masculinity and femininity is to particular historical contexts, a theme explored by other writers such as Melody Graulich. Thus, while one film version minimizes Molly's role, another establishes "a near reciprocity in the relations between the Virginian and Molly, as they dish out critiques of each other's behavior." Hutson's readings of the three film versions of the novel produced during the so-called Roaring Twenties reveal how film directors and screenwriters staged the novel in relation to leading "cultural anxieties" of their historical moment, such as women's suffrage and the problems of adolescence. Hutson also implicitly reminds us that now, a century after the novel's release, the dissemination of* The Virginian's *character types, imagery, and plots into American culture through film and television and later literary westerns means that Wister's novel is an intertextual cultural production not bounded by the book's covers.*

What is an author? This question has been asked again and again by students of cultural production in recent years. What we consumers of culture tend to idolize as an author might rather be thought of as a "secretary" or amanuensis of society, the scriptor of society's discourse. Especially when thinking of the afterlife of a famous text, itself the weaving of multiple strands of cultural themes, a question about the true nature and scope of the sovereignty of the author might well arise.

For instance, consider the information that Owen Wister's biographer Darwin Payne recounts about events relating to Wister in 1894: *"Harper's Monthly* desired to publish a series of articles on the West, and their first choice to write it, Rudyard Kipling, had declined." Wister, who had published a couple of favorably received stories, was then recommended for the job, and he was informed that the editor wanted him "to write a series of eight western sketches to be published in consecutive issues of *Harper's Monthly.*" In a letter to Wister, the editor further outlined some desired features of the sketches: "Each must be a thrilling story, having its ground in a real incident, though you are left free scope for imaginative treatment. . . . We wish in this series to portray certain features of Western life which are now rapidly disappearing with the progress of civilization. Not the least striking of these is that of the appeal to lynch law, which ought to give capital subject for one of your stories."[1] Who is responsible for the demands, the topics, the themes that appear in writing? As the magazine editor's demands illustrate, an author is, at the very least, multifaced. Within the specific requirements of editorial stipulation, there is ample room for "imaginative treatment," but these kinds of demands already diffuse the concept of an autonomous, self-sufficient author. Certain features of Wister's stories that we might identify as offering the signs of his individual authorial vision and style were dictated by the magazine's editor. Roland Barthes might have been greatly exaggerating the news of the "death of the author," but in this view when "writing begins" "the author enters into his own death." Such is the hazard of writing: at best any "author" has limited mastery over his writing. And, as Barthes suggests, a text is truly "a multi-dimensional space in which a variety of writings, none of them original, blend and clash. The text is a tissue of quotations drawn from innumerable centres of culture."[2]

Owen Wister's *The Virginian* has had a prolonged afterlife from the time of its publication in 1902 to 2002, in stage versions, in later textual editions (especially those published during Wister's life – in 1911, 1923, and 1928), in numerous film and television productions. I wish to limit the range of my references to the novel, the stageplay that Wister wrote in collaboration with Kirk La Shelle, and especially the three earliest film versions (1914, 1923, and 1929) of Wister's story of the famous Wyoming cowboy. These films are, in my view, the most interesting and vital translations of Wister's cowboy story, in part because they are closest to Wister's and his culture's authorial and ideological interests, and in part because, with the 1929 version, the western established itself as a coherent and distinctive genre in its own right.

The diffusion of any narrative into a recognizable genre – the collaborative labor of a culture's discourse with the stylistic touches of individual scriptors – may well be thought of as a dissolution, if not exactly the death, of the author. In Wister's case, he appropriated several strands of his culture's popular medievalist discourse and wove them around the developing figure of the cowboy. The cowboy's cavalier or Virginian heritage, in this view, extended back into the mists of King Arthur's knights of the round table. For a number of reasons, this "medievalist impulse" in late-nineteenth-century American culture served, and has continued to serve, as a counterdiscourse to the inexorable modernizings of the United States – against commercialization, against immigration, against multiculturalism, against the American liberal tradition in general.[3] Owen Wister certainly played an important role in this configuration of the chivalrous and militant knight of the Great Plains. What scholars recently have regarded as a symptomatic anxiety about masculinity was for Wister and his like-minded contemporaries a commitment to certain imagined "medieval" virtues – honorable behavior, especially to women but also to one's fellow man; courage; integrity; responsibility for one's words and deeds; loyalty; and so forth. Since Wister refashioned and bequeathed this discourse back to the culture at large, it is no mystery that other, later culture producers would revise the narrative tapestry that Wister had woven. In the end – in fact, from the beginning – American popular culture would reclaim and rework the themes that Wister had selected so perspicaciously for his novel – which is no doubt what Wister would have wanted.

When Wister was urged to write a stageplay from his successful novel, he realized that he had to adapt his story to the requirements of another genre. According to Darwin Payne, Wister initially believed "that the book could not hold material for a theatrical production," but "under the allure of Broadway," he struggled with the need to construct a lucid narrative that would be entertaining for a theater audience. Since the novel was a relaxed, meditative series of stories sketching a coherent sequence of events, Wister felt challenged by the new and different demands of a stageplay. Still, he became convinced that the novel's popularity would contribute to the success of a stageplay, whether good or bad, and that eventually a stageplay would in turn contribute to the ongoing sales of the novel. The two versions would thus be advertisements for each other. Once Kirk La Shelle, a theater producer and writer, took over Wister's play, the two worked together toward a satisfactory script that they would take to the stage. According to Payne, La Shelle " 'picked the novel to the bones' and preserved much more of it than Wister had been able to."[4] La Shelle worked primarily on plot, while Wister worked on dialogue and details of set design "to preserve the color of a vanished world."[5]

From the evidence available, it seems that the two writers gravitated toward a narrative structure of melodrama, a plot based on the clash of oppositional figures, implicit from the beginning in the novel, the polarized opposition of the Virginian versus Trampas, for instance, from the moment of the famous saying, "When you call me that, *smile.*" This melodramatic narrative structure, somewhat recessive behind the novel's philosophical and political musings, would be foregounded by the stageplay. Writing against the popular culture of the dime novel tradition, Wister moved his fiction beyond mere action by successfully weaving dialogue and ideological statements around the armature of his plots.[6] Now, however, he needed to return to highlighting the action. At first, he found it difficult to separate his meditative writing from the action, but he found in the novel enough continuity of action to help the more theatrically experienced Kirk La Shelle collect his themes into a coherent plot. And, just as he wrote against the dime novel in his fiction, for the stage he also wrote against what an early reviewer of the play referred to as "Buffalo Bill drama."[7] The first reviewers of the play identified it as "melo-drama," although some still thought the play "fragmentary."[8]

For Wister the main problem to solve was how to get his conservative political and cultural views across to an audience in the action and dialogue of a plot. In jettisoning the philosophical interpretations for the stageplay, he risked losing the novel's political design. With the help of different stage professionals and producers, however, Wister was willing to run the risk. Perhaps he kept insisting on the necessity of the hanging scene, against La Shelle's and his mother's objections, because he felt that this event would convey at least an aura of his political conservatism.[9] Of course, the transposition of the novel's action sequences, minus the accompanying Wister commentary, into the stageplay and then into the film versions made the the original narrative vulnerable to different interpretations than those orginally intended by Wister in the novel. In fact, from the evidence that Payne and Rush present, Wister appears to have become interested simply in getting a good play on the stage, one that would hold an audience's attention through all four acts.[10] He wanted as much of the action from his novel as could be plausibly incorporated, but he also seems to have been willing to sacrifice whatever could not be made to fit. Wister's willingness to revise, rearrange events, and, in general, rethink his story for different media could serve as a model for the later filmmakers working on his materials. The selection of actions for a plot was reworked in the three early screenplays based on the novel. The novel's story would be manipulated to accommodate the changing and various cultural/historical contexts for the three early screenplays.

Cecil B. DeMille was interested in bringing stageplays to the screen as a way of promoting the cinema to a higher, genteel status of entertainment, overcoming the view that movies were principally targeted toward the working class, children, and immigrants.[11] Once De Mille joined the Jesse Lasky Feature Play Company in 1913, the company's announced policy was to "film adaptations of 'familiar novels and plays for presentation on the screen'" as a "strategy to upgrade cinema for respectable middle-class audiences."[12] The Lasky Company even brought the original star of the stage version of the novel, Dustin Farnum, to the screen in the first film version of *The Virginian*. This version may be closer to the spirit of the original stageplay as conceived by Wister and La Shelle than the actual stageplay that is extant, the one found in London.[13] Certainly, DeMille's 1914 screenplay is closer to the spirit of Wister's novel than is the 1929 screen version, a masterpiece of the western genre and a brilliant screenplay in its own right. Like stage producers, film producers feel free to revise basic events from the stageplay or the novel to suit their sense of the significance of the materials. The presence or absence of events from the novel or stageplay and the mixing or condensing of these events can generate subtle changes in the significance of the plays or the films.[14]

In his 1914 version of the film, DeMille had the advantage of the popular stageplay and the novel behind him. He apparently tried to translate the stage version to the screen as literally as possible, dependent on what Sumiko Higashi calls DeMille's sense of *intertextuality*. That is, DeMille presumed that audiences would view the film after having already read the novel and seen the play. One important sign that DeMille relied on his audiences' intertextual knowledge is his relative lack of interest in depicting plausible motivation for the Virginian's actions. His various actions seem to arise spontaneously, as if referring to familiar incidents in the novel rather than expressing a convincingly developed and psychologized character. For instance, we do not know why the hero mixes up the babies. After saying something to Steve about "bachelors" and "parents," he simply enters a bedroom and begins changing the babies' clothing. The overall result is that for a later viewer the different actions of DeMille's Virginian proceed on the assumption that audiences know who this character is and what his actions signify, without the need for further explanation or motive. No doubt, early spectators would have been prepared to understand and laugh at the Virginian's prank as a vaudeville joke.

DeMille's film is distinctive in its parallel editing or crosscutting and in its impressive outdoor scenery. The prospect of placing this drama in an actual western landscape may have been the temptation to bring the stageplay to the screen. As DeMille wrote in 1914, "The scope of the photoplay is so much wider than that of the legitimate drama. In the first place we DO things instead of acting them."[15] And, with his background in legitimate theater, DeMille was what Higashi calls a *quick learner* in the different possibilities of constructing film drama. Whereas the film opens with the notorious card game between the Virginian and Trampas, its most impressive opening feature is what were called at the time "flashes" or "cutbacks" – the alternating scenes of the Virginian in Wyoming and of Molly both in Vermont and during her train travel to Wyoming – to suggest roughly the simultaneity of the two different actions in different places. This crosscutting continues until the Virginian rescues Molly from the stage bogged down in a Wyoming river. The point of this technique is to keep "the two apparently distinct stories running at the same time and not allowing them to converge until the time is ripe for them being dovetailed," in this case, the first encounter between the Virginian and Molly, her rescue, and his punishment of the drunken stage driver.[16]

DeMille's *The Virginian* depicts a number of incidents from the novel that do not appear in the play or the other film versions. There is the scene in Medicine Bow in which the Virginian rousts a salesman from his bed, in a much less subtle and more cruel manner than he does in the novel, gouging his bed partner with his spurs. The timely rescue of Molly is given prominence here (as it is in the 1923 version), unlike the comic rescue of Molly from a tame cow in the 1929 version. The heavyset Farnum plays the Virginian as someone who seems always confident in his ability to throw his weight around and master any situation. In the baby-swapping episode, the Virginian first blames Steve, and, then, to the mothers who have righted the mix-up, he boldly confesses that he is the perpetrator, confident that the mothers will understand his prank as a harmless joke. He displays little sentiment in the hanging of Steve, even as Steve reminisces about their friendship in a scene of their earlier relationship presented in double exposure. Yet because the film assumes that audiences will know the motives underlying the Virginian's actions, he tends, to a later viewer outside the 1914 context, to look more like a bully than Trampas (William Elmer), whose black, "killer" mustache signifies his bad-guy status. Dustin Farnum is playing a role that a year later Douglas Fairbanks would play in a number of popular films: the Anglo-Saxon, "red-blooded," masculine hero. A contemporary description of Fairbanks in his early westerns could apply to Farnum in *The Virginian*: "He is athletically rugged and distinctly masculine. When he talks you get the impression of a boy who hasn't grown up. He seems to be charged with a sort of restless energy."[17] To a post–Gary Cooper viewer of these early films, the similarity in body and acting styles between Farnum and Fairbanks suggests that different historical contexts generate different styles of male cultural icons. In DeMille's film, the male hero expresses a cruel form of masculine energy.

Trampas, of course, is the leader of a gang of cattle rustlers, and after his escape from the posse, he induces Indians to chase the Virginian and shoot him. It is especially important that DeMille has the Virginian get shot and subsequently rescued by Molly, but he leaves out the convalescent scene that is important for the novel and for the 1923 and 1929 film versions. Such scenes, with the concerned Molly watching over the hero, belong to a convention of the period of taming the hero's strong, "wild" masculinity, domesticating him prior to marriage. Ellen Garvey refers to "the formula of the injured man rescued into marriage" as already a subject for parody in late-nineteenth-century magazines.[18] In this rescue scene, Molly comes on the wounded hero with his face down in a stream, in danger of drowning, a scene reminiscent of the Virginian's earlier rescue of Molly in the middle of a stream, suggesting now a reciprocity between the hero and the heroine that bodes well for the success of their marriage. But DeMille's Virginian does not undergo a serious "taming." Farnum's portrayal is of a physical and mental expression of single-minded resoluteness, an elementary virtue that will not be tamed or compromised. Perhaps he has convinced Molly that he has overcome what she earlier refers to as his "uncouthness" for his role in the baby mix-up. The final scene is of their honeymoon encampment in the wilderness. The male rules.

The release of *The Virginian* in September 1914, after DeMille's other two 1914 "westerns," *The Squaw Man* and *The Call of the North,* concided with a changing, apparently more conservative political mood in the country. As Theodore Roosevelt, a former Progressive president, noted after the 1914 elections, "The fundamental trouble was that the country was sick and tired of reform," referring to the earlier "Progressive" era of middle-class reform movements and the heyday of muckraking writings.[19] As Higashi notes, the two DeMille brothers, Cecil and William, "shared a belief in the didactic function of art," but unlike the "liberal" William, a successful playwright and screenwriter, "Cecil was conservative and retained toward the public a stance of cultural stewardship that he shared with the elite classes of the Progressive Era."[20] DeMille's early-career conservatism would roughly coincide with Owen Wister's; consequently, this first screen version of Wister's story captured, as well as could be expected, something of Wister's own sense of the meaning of the actions of the novel.

Perhaps because it was an independently produced film rather than a studio film, the 1923 Tom Harmon–directed film has tended to be ignored by film historians and critics.[21] And it seems to have gotten lost in what was referred to as a "market glutted with westerns" in 1922 and 1923, as it was released between two popular western "epics," *The Covered Wagon* in 1923 and *The Iron Horse* in 1924.[22] But Harmon's version is an excellent film in its own right, with impressive acting and spectacular cinematography. It captures an emotional aura around the characters that, in fact, is in keeping with the spirit of Wister's novel. Apparently, the film's screenwriters turned to Wister's novel rather than to the stageplay or to the earlier film for their inspiration. The town of Medicine Bow has the depressing look of a settlement just barely hanging on against the immensity of the landscape. The Taylor ranch, where we see Molly hanging stockings on a clothesline outside her "renovated bunkhouse," looks as if it offers only the most primitive accommodations for the elegant and dignified woman of Vermont, a glimpse of a character who seems not to belong in this setting. Harmon and his writers are able to capture an emotional seriousness, a sense of tragedy and loss that gives the story a dignity throughout. There is, in addition, a near reciprocity in the relations between the Virginian and Molly, as they dish out critiques of each other's behavior. When the Virginian makes his claim that "I'm going to make you love me," Molly looks archly skeptical, and later she challenges, "How are you going to make me love you?" She adds, "You men think that all you have to do is look strong and make chests at a girl," even as she confesses that she has come to "like" the Virginian. He had, after all, rescued her from danger in the stagecoach bogged down in the middle of a river, and he had also stood up to Trampas in defending her honor. In this version, the character of Molly is given a much more prominent role in the narrative. She is not the wallflower that she is in DeMille's version. Whereas she may concede that the Virginian has acted chivalrously, she is able to maintain her independence and skepticism. Obviously, the filmmakers are responding to a new sense of the prominence of women as relevant and autonomous figures in the culture of postwar America and the success of the women's suffrage movement in 1920.

The film was intended to be as much a character study as an action narrative. Also, the screenplay indicates, again and again, a serious concern with the smoothness and coherence of the story. The filmmaker meshes parallel narratives, as when the Virginian is seriously courting Molly and at the same time learns that his friend Steve is illegally branding one of Judge Henry's yearlings, a conjoining of the themes of love and duty that will be repeated and expanded in the 1929 version and that expresses the complexity of the character of the Virginian. There is an apparent supposition by 1923 that the novel and the stageplay can no longer be taken for granted as the intertextual background for the spectators. The story would now have to stand on its own, even as it is loyal to the novel, as it would also in the 1929 version, and the excellence of the 1923 narrative will no doubt be a factor in the brilliance of the later version, which credits Wister's and La Shelle's stageplay.

Harmon seems to be struggling, as was DeMille in a different context, against the sense of the "low status of most silent Westerns."[23] Richard Abel's study of an earlier era of filmmaking is still pertinent to the later production of silent westerns: "As the genre grew ever more popular during 1909, . . . an important difference began to emerge between one 'school' of films that valued action above all else and another 'school' that valued acting and logical plotting."[24] In Jean-Louis Leutrat's account of 1920s westerns, what historians would eventually refer to as a genre, the *western*, had to break its alliances to burlesque, melodrama, and other genres or quasi genres of popular entertainment.[25] Obviously, the baby-swapping scene is crucial for the alliance with the burlesque, as well as pointing to the youthful playfulness of the hero, and Fleming's 1929 version expands on this element, making it the most comic version of the three films. Also, in the 1923 film, Shorty is given a burlesque role; his resolute focus is not, as in Wister's novel, his horse but the dream of owning an accordian for which he has been saving for eight years. In frustration, he has to resort to his harmonica, which he is playing when Trampas shoots him in cold blood, a shocking move from burlesque to pathos. Besides being identified typically with "action," in Leutrat's view, westerns of the early 1920s and before were generically "heterogeneous," in contemporary viewers' eyes always allied with some other recognizable mode or genre. As Abel demonstrates, producers of early westerns could always easily fall back on the dime novel traditions in order to get "the true Western snap and go" of thrilling action in "authentic" American scenery, "themes 'racy of the soil.' "[26] DeMille, Harmon, and Fleming obviously wanted to transcend this popular "school" of filmmaking in their use of Wister's material while still incorporating the features that had made westerns so popular with audiences.

In an extended analysis of the 1923 version of *The Virginian*, Virginia Wright Wexman argues that it depicts the central themes of a number of important westerns in the period (and later, no doubt). Especially relevant to her thesis are films made from Wister's materials. In her view, such westerns offer "competing visions" of approaches to the land. On the one hand, there is the Anglo-Saxon rancher with a patriarchal, imperialist appropriation of the land, who can think of himself as the master of all he surveys in the expansive landscapes of the frontier West. On the other hand, westerns depict the family farmer's democratic sense of the land with "the ideal of the imagined community of equals." In this view, "nationalist discourse involves . . . a 'hierarchy of group identities,' in which a dominant segment of the population is designated as the repositors of the national language and appearance. . . . Americans look to the image of one particular national type who can represent the amalgamation of the wide diversity of groups that make up the American citizenry. As a myth of national origin, the Western focuses on this contradiction in

American nationalist discourse." And this nationalist ideology, in Wexman's view, is "portrayed in Westerns [as] wedded to the ideal of the romantic couple," especially, one might add, when the couple represent different cultural regions as "rival models" of culture.[27] The 1929 version of *The Virginian*, especially, is able to make these themes explicit in arguments between the characters, in the scene in which Mrs. Taylor chastises Molly for her objection to the Virginian hanging Steve as well as in the scene in which the Virginian proposes to Molly and explains his intentions about making more United States out of the frontier. Wexman describes a nationalist ideology that clearly hearkens back to Wister and a number of his contemporaries and that will stimulate the production of early westerns, as Richard Abel has demonstrated.

Fenin and Everson note that in the advertisements for Victor Fleming's 1929 version of *The Virginian* the emphasis was on the film as "TALKING," the name of the film in a secondary position and the names of the stars in a tertiary position.[28] At this time, despite the fact that he had already been in a number of silent films, Gary Cooper, playing the Virginian, was relatively unknown. The emphasis is on talking, with credits going to dialogue creators. There is a snappy vernacular language throughout, intended for humor, even when the narrative turns deadly serious. Much of the language is designed to suggest western folk talk, and it is not to be found in Wister's novel or stageplay, although it must have been intended as capturing the spirit of the novel's dialogue. After all, as Lee Clark Mitchell has observed, readers of Wister's novel have to "acknowledge how fully the novel celebrates language at the expense of actions it describes," with the result that a talking-film version would appear to be reaching back to the novel.[29] In fact, as one of the early instances of an "all-talking" film, it displays a certain anxiety about whether audiences will find talking boring rather than natural or realistic. Fenin and Everson observe that "recognizing that its appeal lay still primarily in its clean-cut action," the western "made small attempt to let dialogue dominate."[30] But Fleming and the producers obviously strove to find a language for their film that would be congruous with the action. In this respect, the dialogue writers took on a burden that Wister had successfully accepted for the novel, creating dialogue with special attention to language as comic, economical, and performative, demanding personal responsibility for the words that one speaks. Paramount studio's choice to make *The Virgin-*

ian was a good one to test the idea of making dialogue as exciting as action and of highlighting the moral implications of talk.

But Fleming's film is an important historical achievement because it modernized the genre of the western under the pressure of the cultural anxieties that developed in America in the 1920s. If the problem of adolescence was invented in the 1890s (and Wister especially emphasized the youthfulness of his Western heroes like Lin McLean and the Virginian), it became a central cultural theme in the post–World War I period. Paula Fass has noted that in the 1920s the "young had become one way for adults to demonstrate their own conscious adjustment to change." "The young had come to represent modernity, the impulse toward adjustment, and even the promise of twentieth-century life."[31]

What gives this film its coherence is the focus on the adolescent peer group, consisting initially of the Virginian and Steve, with Molly joining in shortly. Trampas does not exactly belong to the group. As played by Walter Huston, he is older than the others and acts more like a bully trying to influence the younger men with his cynical views. In an important respect, the film is about the struggle of youth at the threshold of adulthood, for the young adults have, in effect, been left to themselves to work out their lives without much interference from a more adult world. In the argument between Molly and Mrs. Taylor over lynching Steve, Molly is given the final, if hysterical, word. And Mrs. Taylor interprets the differences in their views as regional rather than generational. In his marriage proposal to Molly, the Virginian invokes Judge Henry as his model for his own plans: "I don't aim to stay here, not if you'll be my partner. I'm pushin' west and do what the Judge did, make more United States out of prairie land." The ease with which he incorporates the adult model indicates that there is no hint of generational conflict.

The one time that we see serious conflict in the Virginian is over the issue of hanging the rustlers. He seems merely to be going along with the judge, playing the role of the judge's foreman rather than acting as the true leader of the hunting party. Otherwise, there is no intrusive presence of adult authorities in the film. The impulse for the adolescents to develop seems to be an organic inevitability, although this mysterious inevitability can malfunction. The Virginian and Molly are able to progress in a drama of self-overcoming, as they develop an attachment to each other and plan to get married. By contrast, Steve seems unable to get over the barrier of adolescence and move into adulthood. In the novel, Molly

is always writing home to her Vermont family. In the film, the young people seem completely uprooted from family. This emphasis on the peer
group, thoroughly consistent with social developments in the 1920s, contributes to the overall gentleness of this version of the film, despite Steve's
lynching, by omitting the suggestion of generational conflict. In a conversation with Molly, the Virginian interprets *Romeo and Juliet* as a story about
a young man and woman who have to work out a relationship with each
other as isolated, abstract individuals. He reduces what René Girard has
called *the first great saga of the generation gap* to a drama about young lovers
completely disassociated from familial or historical realities.[32] Obviously,
this interpretation is an important self-characterization for the Virginian
and for the film. If the popular western developed out of the Walter Scott
border romances at the beginning of the nineteenth century, the film version of *The Virginian* offers the new interpretation of the border romance
for the twentieth century: the eternal borderland between adolescence
and adulthood.

Wister's novel is about serious male competition. The dynamic of a
Darwinian cosmos, pristinely active in the as-yet-unspoiled West, generates a perpetual competition that brings genuine character, the fittest,
into visibility. The novel affirms the innate superiority of the Virginian, as
he undergoes a series of trials, and the innate inferiority of other males
who come in contact with the Virginian or with the pure and merciless
testing environment of the West. In Fleming's film, however, the basic relationship between individuals is a peer rivalry that looks like adolescent
playfulness, at least at first. And it is not a Darwinian cosmos that stands
behind this relationship but a much more benign pastoral nature, represented by the quail call that Steve and the Virginian use to signal each
other and that is repeated by an actual quail as Steve is being hanged. This
final call of the quail and Steve's acknowledgment of the call remind us of
the youthful innocence that lies at the heart of Steve's and the Virginian's
friendship, an innocence of nature that has to be overcome and yet preserved in the adulthood of the Virginian himself.

The role of Steve is enlarged in the film so that he becomes a major figure, almost a rival brother to the Virginian, a friendly but disturbing foil.
After their initial greetings, which take the form of verbal insults and attempts to catch up on their lives from the last time they were together
(the Virginian recalls, "It's been about four years since we burned up
the border down in Texas"), their friendship turns to playful ritual adolescent rivalries, as they compete to buy the Mexican bar girl a drink

and then to win recognition from the newly arrived young schoolteacher from the East. The wooing of Molly Wood begins as an adolescent male prank. In the beginning, she is clearly no threat to their friendship but simply the means of regressing to their old games of rivalry. Steve loses the contest over the Mexican girl, then seems to win again as he gets to escort Molly from the train, only to be outdone by the Virginian with his mock-heroic rescue of Molly, only to win again when he shows just how mocking the Virginian's rescue has been. Steve also wins the first dance with Molly and the promise to walk her home after the dance, only to be outmaneuvered once again by the Virginian, who actually does get to walk Molly home after the dance.

Although Steve and the Virginian appear to be two of a kind, their rivalry is not exactly synonymous despite the opening rhythm of playful winning and losing. For we come to see that their sameness is branching into different directions that will bring them eventually into a mortal contest, one that Steve stands no chance of winning. Steve makes fun of the Virginian for his promotion to foreman of the Box H ranch, as if he had caught the Virginian in an embarrassing social gaffe. On the other hand, the Virginian establishes that Steve has not changed in the four years that they have been apart. "I'm goin' to have my fun," Steve says. "I'm not goin' to waste my time with workin'." Clearly, the two attitudes are diverging and will be incompatible with their friendship. And whereas the Virginian is willing to hold onto the friendship, Steve's commitment to a life of moral or, rather, of premoral drift rather than resoluteness creates a problem for their ongoing friendship. At the party welcoming Molly, for instance, Steve has arrived with Trampas instead of waiting for the Virginian. As the Virginian chides him for not being very "choosy about your company," we see that Steve is not capable of making the kinds of distinctions that the Virginian keeps imposing on him. And although he will work for the Virginian for a while, he drifts into rustling cattle for Trampas, as if that held out the promise of getting by in the world without having to work.

The ideological showdown in this divergence of the two friends comes when the Virginian catches Steve putting Trampas's brand on one of Judge Henry's yearlings. The Virginian presents the most ardent expression of the theme at the heart of the film when he lectures Steve: "You and I done a lot of loco things, but there are some things more than loco; they're wrong." The film is about the rise of the need to differentiate, in this case, the need and the ability to distinguish, between *loco* and *wrong.*

Steve seems not to grasp the difference. Instead, he interprets the distinction as the difference between *fun* and *the solemn*, concepts that are not wrong, exactly, but that diverge significantly from the Virginian's concepts since they eliminate the ethical.

The Virginian himself, along with Steve, has been willing to enter into the loco transgressions of the community by swapping the babies. But this humorous loco event will be echoed shortly in another event that the community places in the category *wrong*, rustling cattle. Swapping babies as they are about to be christened belongs to a kind of misrule, an acceptable transgression that can, in this instance, be easily corrected.[33] But why is mixing up "baby" cattle before they are branded so much more wrong than mixing up baby human beings before they are christened? In doing something loco, the community may join forces to denounce you as an "ornry polecat" and run after you to impress on you their collective frustrations. But if you do something wrong, such as put the wrong brand on cattle, the community will join forces to hang you. As Molly asks in the stageplay, "What is the difference – in principle?"[34] Branding calves, like christening children, is an institutional supplement to nature since property is nothing but an institution and a wrong brand has no natural form of self-correction. Children can readily be identified by their parents in case of a mix-up, so why do babies have to be "branded," christened? It seems that human beings have to validate their childrens' identities transcendentally as well as naturally. In this view, a lack of differentiation always seems to threaten the foundations of society. Even human beings, merely as natural, have to be certified by culture. Without culture, there presumably would arise no such distinction as that between the loco and the wrong.

In both these events, Steve is the loser or, rather, the scapegoat. He takes the rap for the baby-swapping episode initiated by the Virginian and for the cattle rustling initiated by Trampas. Steve is a classic random victim, except that his participation in these episodes is always a sign of his drifting nature. Because of his desire to have fun and never take responsibility, because of his cynicism, he is not a purely arbitrary victim. He has to be differentiated from the Virginian in a definitive way because his values are too close for comfort to what many observers in the 1920s thought had become the dominant values of the postwar era. Richard Arlen's portrayal of Steve is very convincing.[35] He is consistent in his commitment to play, to truancy, to such an extent that for him the loco reaches into the wrong. But this movement may be the 1920s' guise for justifying Steve's death, for criminalizing his loyalty to adolescent play and a spirit of truancy that runs deep in the history of American culture and that must have seemed to be getting out of hand as the United States was transforming values toward a new consumer capitalism. If this film has a liberal look of popular culture, the conservatism implicit in the role of Steve may be an echo of Wister's novel. The need for a difference between Steve and the Virginian is so serious that the exorcism of Steve is carried out by the violence of his hanging.

Now, with the loss of Steve, the difference between Steve and the Virginian is transferred to the hostility between the Virginian and Trampas, a melodramatic clarification of values. If Steve was a threat, Trampas is even more of a threat, but at least he makes the moral stakes legible. Steve had wanted the world to stay in its eternal, playful, pastoral state. While he is alive, the film is full of humor and fun. With his death, the West, as he had already complained, becomes very solemn, as does the film. Even at the moment of his death, he displays the courage of adolescent bravado. His death has the style of youth, and so it is consistent with his refusal to move across the threshold into adulthood. Consent combines with violence in what might look like a liberal political reinterpretation of the meaning of the West for the nation. When Steve returns the quail's call at the moment of his death and the Virginian remains silent, the gentle pastoral world now belongs only to Steve and has been overcome. It has been the landscape of the nonaspiring, nondeveloping mind. Steve can only wake up now, as Honey Wiggins says to one of Trampas's cronies, and "find himself seriously dead." The Virginian is committed to something quite different – to Molly and domesticity, revenge for Steve's death, economic and patriotic goals.

For the Virginian, the name of the law by which Steve and his fellow rustlers are hanged and the move into adulthood emerge at one and the same time, and this moment of inner betrayal to the Virginian's adolescent outlook is revealed in the expression of anguish on the Virginian's face as Steve is hanged. All the oppositions of the narrative – the loco and the wrong, the fun and the solemn, nature and culture – are present and resolved in the moment of lynching. The Virginian is not just killing a friend; he is, in effect, killing at least a part of his own youthful self. In this interpretation of the lynching, the filmmakers may have had Wister's and La Shelle's stageplay in mind. In the play, Molly's and the Virginian's Shakespeare discussion is about Falstaff and Prince Hal, not Romeo and Juliet, as in the film.[36] I would suggest that Steve's death in this film version alludes to Prince Hal's rejection of Falstaff, in effect painfully shedding his own adolescence before entering the responsibilities of adulthood. Youth must die so that the adult may live. Falstaff must be rejected so that the prince can maintain the social order. The solemn must take over and reject the playful.

Of course, films of different genres took on the problem of youth, which seemed so urgent in the late 1920s that writers from every political persuasion took up the issue, as Paula Fass recounts. For instance, a 1928 film, *Our Dancing Daughters*, with a young Joan Crawford and a future star of westerns, John Mack Brown, shows that privileged middle-class adolescents who drink and dance and kiss are actually perfectly moral and stable. Those youths who claim to hold themselves aloof from such activities and publicly take the moral high ground are, at heart, hypocritical and self-destructive. Ann, the hypocritical good girl, drunkenly falls downstairs to her death in the end. Here, as in Fleming's *The Virginian*, the adolescent problem seems to be able to take care of itself, without intervention from an older, more conservative generation. In a more profound film, King Vidor's *The Crowd* (1928), the young male hero, John Sims, enters New York with anxiety and aspirations and with the spirit of energetic youthfulness. He gets a job, marries, has two children. But the narrative of his adult life emphasizes that he is always an adolescent, that American culture is organized in such a way that wives and children have to adjust to this fact and support and protect the eternal male adolescent, especially in a time of tragedy. For such an eponymous American, crossing the threshold into adulthood is difficult, if not impossible.

Moreover, despite the many historians of the 1920s who have taken F. Scott Fitzgerald's writings as key insights into the decade, Fitzgerald offers a view that is not the usual one. Amory Blaine, in *This Side of Paradise*, at first detects a "real moral letdown" in the country, so widespread that "he saw the cities between New York and Chicago as one vast juvenile intrigue." But Amory also offers a theory that his generation is the end of youth, a youth that extends back for a couple of hundred years: "What we leave here [they are graduating seniors from Princeton University] is more than this class; it's the whole heritage of youth."[37] This is an expression of the notion that the United States was an adolescent nation until some time in the early twentieth century. Amory is claiming that this terminus to youth coincides with his graduation and his entrance into the military during World War I. In these different views about the fate of American youths as a cultural ideal or problem, we can see the difference in national and cultural self-consciousness between Wister's early sense that the nation needs the youthfulness that he identifies with the ranching West after the Civil War and Fitzgerald's sense that America as "the whole heritage of youth" is now disappearing. In my view, Fleming's version of Wister's story suggests that the adolescent problem, or the problem that it symbolized for the 1920s, solves itself in the West, in the purity of God's own and the nation's landscape, by being left to itself. In this view, the true myth of the pristine West, correcting what was Huckleberry Finn's sense of the meaning of the "Territory," is the story of overcoming a perpetual adolescence and irresponsibility. For as Horkheimer and Adorno would claim, "Immaturity is then the inability to survive."[38]

Given a narrative complex such as Wister devised, however buried or disguised some of its elements might be, we can recognize the structure of his narrative in whatever medium we encounter it. Wister had, in the success of his novel, provided the elements on which subsequent interpreters could base a number of varying interpretations without those elements losing their identity. Stage versions and film versions could change the elements around, eliminate some, add others, in order to build a coherent drama that would reflect the different historical contexts and poach on different generic traditions. The elements of the novel could take on different interpretations in their cultural dissemination. But Wister had captured themes no doubt characteristic or elementary in American culture, features that could tempt screenwriters even as late as 2000 for a television version of the novel.

In his story of a displaced Southerner with a cavalier and Arthurian heritage, the virile cowboy who can meet the challenges of a new and "wild country," Wister set in motion elements of a story that has seduced readers and viewers from 1902 to our own time. But it is next to impossible to pin down the story's meaning as it is translated from era to era. The risk of bringing the narrative to mass entertainment was a risk, for one thing, of democratizing the story and losing its racist Anglo-Saxon ideology. Sumiko Higashi claims that not just Wister but DeMille as well faced this dilemma. In DeMille's attempt to raise the cultural stature of film, there was also something like a cultural lowering into film that was an inescapably democratic art.[39] The dilemma could be quickly overcome since, for Wister and DeMille, there were satisfactions in understanding that their work had an effect on mass culture, that they were still the elite in charge of culture, giving direction to culture. The question remains what was driving what – whether Wister was driving the direction of popular culture or whether the democratic tendencies within popular culture were driving the adaptations. Given the culmination of the cultural workings toward the establishment of an "archetypal" western in Victor Fleming's *The Virginian*, that is, given what Jean-Louis Leutrat claims was the establishment of the western as a genre, during which it worked a separation from its earlier "alliances" in spectators' minds, Wister's effect on popular culture has had an extremely long run. For the most part, westerns in the decade after Fleming's sophisticated film moved toward the boys' "B" western. But the Wister model of making serious adult drama out of western materials was only dormant. With the reemergence of westerns as serious cultural commentary in 1939, the genre would once again attain popular appeal for at least the next thirty years.

Wister may have thought that he was working with myth. His essay "The Evolution of the Cow-Puncher" argues that the cowboy as he sees him in Wyoming is a figure with a long history that can be traced back to King Arthur and the knights of the round table.[40] And he might have believed that the historical background behind this figure is so long as to transcend history, that it would thus have the force of myth as a story created in eternity. But in fact, Wister presented to his readers materials and narratives that would eventually coalesce loosely into genre, a gathering of cultural narrative strands that take on a certain illusory monumentalization but that never transcend history. These strands are what a historical period has for improvising a stable narrative and a set of characters in order to construct a counterfactual insight for its own self-understanding. If Wister could successfully attribute meaning and the force of truth in 1895 or 1902 to his cowboys and events, then at least some of these elements could be reiterated in different historical contexts and take on different meanings while holding onto a core of meaning. Stephen Tatum is undoubtedly correct in suggesting that there is a "conservative impulse at the core of the classic Western."[41] As a cultural conservative, Wister is not totally responsible for this feature, but he was certainly a major contributor. A reviewer of Wister's novel in 1902 remarked that Wister had "driven into the soil of Wyoming a stake which seems likely to remain for a long time to come."[42] If *Wyoming* could be translated as *United States*, the reviewer's remarks were prescient. In the cultural work of constructing a genre, Wister's contributions would be transformed and inscribed in various forms of American popular culture for a hundred years. Not only is that the power of "myth," what Richard Slotkin has referred to as "the primary language of historical memory,"[43] it is also the power of genre, a culturally specific quasi myth that, in effect, has no origin or author. An author's name, let us say Owen Wister, is "situated among the discontinuities [of multiple cultural strands, themes, motifs], and gives rise to new groups of discourse and their singular mode of existence." "The function of an author is to characterize the existence, circulation and operation of certain discourses within a society."[44] And so, in this case, it is the power of Wister's imagination in composing a narrative with the philosophical supports that could provide the materials for its variations. Wister or, rather, his tenderfoot narrator noted that after his first confrontation with Trampas, in which Trampas backed down from a challenge, the Virginian would never be "rated a novice at the cool art of self-preservation."[45] Wister perhaps could not have foreseen at the moment of composing these lines that his hero's self-preservation would be able to sustain so many avatars of his appearance in the course of twentieth-century American popular culture.

NOTES

1. Payne, *Owen Wister,* 138.

2. Barthes, "The Death of the Author," 142, 146.

3. See Moreland, *The Medievalist Impulse in American Literature*, esp. chap. 1. See also Lears, *No Place of Grace*, esp. chap. 4.

4. Payne, *Owen Wister,* 213, 216.

5. Herron, "Owen Wister as Playwright," vii.

6. See Payne, *Owen Wister,* 179–80.

7. Rush, *The Diversions of a Westerner,* 103.

8. Rush, introduction and notes to *The Virginian*, iv.

9. Wister also told his mother that his model was Oedipus's self-blinding, what Aristotle (*Poetics*, 37) referred to as "pathos." See also Payne, *Owen Wister,* 213.

10. Rush, *The Diversions of a Westerner,* 111–17.

11. A number of film historians have noted the importance of DeMille's innovations in "the ways in which cinema was legitimated as art" (Higashi, *Cecil B. DeMille,* 5; see also Burch, *Life to Those Shadows*, 59 and passim).

12. Higashi, *Cecil B. DeMille,* 10.

13. Rush, introduction and notes to *The Virginian*, i, v.

14. Rush's quotations from letters (see, e.g., *The Diversions of a Westerner,* 112) show Wister condensing characters for the stageplay, e.g., Lin and Shorty into Steve.

15. Higashi, *Cecil B. DeMille*, 27.

16. Bowser, *The Transformation of Cinema*, 59.

17. Studlar, "Wider Horizons," 63. Also, Payne (*Owen Wister*, 313–14) relates the story of Douglas Fairbanks's "dismay" that he had not been chosen to play the Virginian in the 1923 film version.

18. Garvey, *The Adman in the Parlor*, 129.

19. Cooper, *Pivotal Decades*, 213.

20. Higashi, *Cecil B. DeMille*, 28.

21. It is not mentioned in, e.g., Fenin and Everson, *The Western*. It has been "restored" by Blackhawk Films, but the quality is poor.

22. Leutrat, *L'Alliance brisée*, 20.

23. Koszarski, *An Evening's Entertainment*, 183.

24. Abel, *The Red Rooster Scare*, 156.

25. For a list of possible linkages or alliances for westerns in the 1920s – western biographical drama, western burlesque, western comedy, western farce, western melodrama, and so forth – see Leutrat, *L'Alliance brisée*, 157. Peter Stanfield ("The Western," 997) suggests that because there was a standard cast of villains in westerns by 1909, the genre was already in place. But demonizing Indians and Mexicans does not exactly add up to the clarity of a genre.

26. Abel, *The Red Rooster Scare*, 156, 164.

27. Wexman, "The Family on the Land," 142, 132, 130, 130, 151.

28. Fenin and Everson, *The Western*, 177.

29. Mitchell, *Westerns*, 98.

30. Fenin and Everson, *The Western*, 173.

31. Fass, *The Damned and the Beautiful*, 129, 128.

32. Girard, "Lévi-Strauss, Frye, Derrida, and Shakespearean Criticism," 37.

33. In Wister's novel the baby-swapping episode is considered a much more serious attack on domesticated Westerners than it is in the stageplay or the three film versions, although the Virginian confesses to the crime and is forgiven even by the mothers (see Wister, *The Virginian* [1988], 94–99).

34. Wister and La Shelle, *The Virginian*, 69.

35. Paramount had the wisdom to balance the established star, Arlen, with the relative newcomer, Gary Cooper. Whereas Arlen's career was declining, Cooper's role as the Virginian precipitated him into stardom. See Tatum, "The Classic Westerner."

36. See Wister and La Shelle, *The Virginian*, 40.

37. Fitzgerald, *This Side of Paradise*, 59, 144.

38. Horkheimer and Adorno, *Dialectic of Enlightenment*, 83.

39. Higashi, *Cecil B. DeMille*, 29–33.

40. Owen Wister, "The Evolution of the Cow-Puncher," (1987), 39.

41. Tatum, "The Classic Westerner," 73.

42. Quoted in Payne, *Owen Wister,* 199.

43. Slotkin, "Myth and the Production of History," 70.

44. Foucault, "What Is an Author?" 123, 124.

45. Wister, *The Virginian* (1988), 23.

7 HISTORY, GENDER, AND THE ORIGINS OF THE "CLASSIC" WESTERN *Victoria Lamont*

"Why is mixing up 'baby' cattle before they are branded so much more wrong than mixing up baby human beings before they are christened?" asks Richard Hutson in his essay. In her essay, Victoria Lamont provides an answer, based on historical research into the legal issues associated with property rights and the "maverick question." Lamont revisits familiar territory in Wister scholarship – he has long been recognized as a supporter of the big ranchers, not the homesteaders, during the Johnson County Range War – but she adds two new historical pieces, a little-read 1902 novel, Frances McElrath's The Rustler, *and Wyoming's 1884 "Maverick Law." By closely reading* The Virginian *and* The Rustler *within and against each other and the legal issues raised by the Maverick Law, Lamont furthers the discussion of gender and class themes launched by several of the previous essays. By focusing on how the novel's recuperation of manhood takes place "in response to a social environment in which the gender of citizenship was vigorously contested," Lamont's reading contrasts with the recent critical discussion of gender and the popular western that assumes the absence or insignificance of women writers. Lamont's comparativist approach discloses how at the very moment of its generic origin the popular western was "a field that admitted not only women writers but also feminist positionings." Her essay illustrates the continued importance of the feminist recovery project; in the next essay, one also employing a comparativist approach, Zeese Papanikolas will demonstrate the importance of ranging far afield to recover texts by other marginalized authors.*

There was once a man living on the southern range, Maverick by name, who accumulated a large herd of cattle by the simple method of branding as his own all stock which in the great general roundups of the olden days had escaped the branding-iron. . . . Maverick-branding became a recognized feature of the cattle industry.

FRANCES MCELRATH, *The Rustler*

It was quite common for herd owners to pay the boys from \$2.50 to \$5 per head for all the "mavericks" they could put the company's brand on, and "rustling for mavericks" in the spring was in order all over the range country. . . . This practice taught the cowboy to look upon the unbranded, motherless calf as common, or public property, to be gathered in by the lucky finder.

A. S. MERCER, *The Banditti of the Plains*

You leave other folks' cattle alone, or you take the consequences, and it was all known to Steve from the start. . . . He knew well enough the only thing that would have let him off would have been a regular jury. For the thieves have got hold of the juries in Johnson County.

OWEN WISTER, *The Virginian*

Frances McElrath's little-known novel *The Rustler* raises intriguing questions about the origins of the generic formula that we now recognize as the western. Like Owen Wister, Frances McElrath was an eastern writer who traveled in the West. Like Wister's *The Virginian, The Rustler* first appeared in the spring of 1902, inspired by the Johnson County Range War of 1892, a crisis with roots in the ongoing tensions between large cattle companies and the local cowboy population. Although these "coincidences" certainly invite speculation about possible contact between the two authors, I am more interested in two intriguing and related differences between the two novels – differences that yield important insights about the sexual politics underlining the cultural production of the western novel as a "masculine" genre at the turn of the last century. The first has to do with the ways in which each novel interprets the history of the Johnson County War, particularly their representation of the so-called maverick question. While *The Virginian* makes only passing reference to this debate, its centrality to the plot of *The Rustler* is linked to a feminist politics in the novel. This relation brings us to the second difference between the two texts, one that concerns the fate of the cowboy hero. By successfully winning battles on moral, sexual, and economic fronts, the Virginian shows America how to sustain its frontier values in a postfrontier economy; in *The Rustler*, it is ultimately the heroine who performs this cultural work, and McElrath makes this so by taking up the discourse of what has been called *domestic feminism*, drawing various links between the frontier landscape and the public sphere that suggest that frontier closure requires forms of management associated with "women's work." Meanwhile, the uncanny resemblance between *The Rustler* and *The Virginian* suggests that whether or not Wister had ever read McElrath's work, and vice versa, these novels occupied opposing positions in a common debate. Perhaps the genre that we now recognize as the western became insistently masculine precisely because it, like so many other traditionally masculine spheres in turn-of-the-century American culture and society, had become subject to feminist occupation.

The Virginian and *The Rustler* respond in different ways to the Johnson County War of 1892, but the most intriguing difference lies in the ways in which *The Virginian* suggestively displaces the very figure most central to the crisis: the motherless calf, or maverick. Calves of unknown origin posed a unique problem for the cattle trade throughout the period of open-range ranching, which prevailed in Texas and the Great Plains from about 1870 until the close of the nineteenth century. During the great roundups, when ranchers banded together to sort, count, and brand their herds, orphaned calves became objects of explosive tension because of the way in which they disrupted the discourses of class and property on the free range: cowboys hired to manage the roundups were usually ordered to turn mavericks over to their employers, but some considered these animals part of the public domain and established their own small herds by branding mavericks as their own. Although maverick cattle constituted a relatively small proportion of industry profit, the ideological stakes were high enough to start a war. Beginning in Johnson County, Wyoming, in the spring of 1892, when two accused cattle rustlers, Nate Champion and Nick Ray, were murdered by a group of fifty vigilante stockmen, this war played out anxieties over class and property ownership in a particularly unstable and difficult-to-control social space.

The Johnson County War supplied Owen Wister with material for his paradigmatic tale of the West, *The Virginian*, credited with rescuing the western from the dissipation of the pulp magazine and making it into a respectable genre fit for the discriminating reader.[1] It has since been recognized by scholars of the genre as the foundational text of twentieth-century popular western mythology, inspiring generations of novelists, from Zane Grey to Louis L'Amour, to reproduce Wister's paradigm in endless permutations. Given that Wister had lived for a time in Johnson County and was likely familiar with the nuances of the maverick debate,

his evasion of the maverick question in his fictionalized version of the rustler wars suggests that this debate was somehow incompatible with his
own desire to read the conflict as a straightforward contest between thieving rustlers and honest, hardworking ranchers.

Wister's hero, known only as the Virginian, is the foreman of a large
Wyoming ranch who must break with his cowboy brethren in order to fulfill his duties to his employer. Hanging rustlers – including his best friend,
Steve – is among the Virginian's more unsavory duties. Such is his loyalty
to his employer, however, that the Virginian steadily climbs the ladder of
ranch society. Meanwhile, his romance with the refined Easterner Molly
Stark Wood supplements his increasing salary with the cultural capital
necessary to make him a true gentleman. At the novel's climax, the Virginian jeopardizes his social achievements by accepting an invitation
from the rustler Trampas to settle their differences in a gunfight, knowing full well that Molly despises violence. But when her fiancé returns victorious, it is Molly who renounces her sentimental principles in thankful
surrender to the Virginian's embrace. Marriage to Molly and a partnership in his employer's cattle business are the rewards for our hero's stead-
fast loyalty and unyielding principles.

The Virginian embodies Wister's ideal democratic citizen – a "natural
aristocrat" who rises to the top of the socioeconomic hierarchy without
posing a threat to those already there. In order to sustain itself, however,
Wister's ideological apparatus depends on distinguishing the cowboy
hero, who earns his wealth, from the rustlers, who steal theirs. This distinction was by no means easily achieved in Johnson County, where cattle
rustling was an ambiguously defined practice and where any cowboy who
owned cattle was vulnerable to rustling charges no matter how his herd
had been acquired. Wister's fictionalized version of the rustler wars thus
achieves a degree of moral clarity lacking in the historical record, where
the ambiguous status of the maverick calf made cattle theft an ideological
problem rather than a moral one.

Maverick cattle are significantly present in McElrath's *The Rustler*,
which invokes the rustler wars as the setting for the romance between a
rugged cowboy and a haughty eastern gentlewoman, assembling through
this now-classic plot device a host of dialectical relations – East and West,
civilization and wilderness, social and natural, aristocrat and commoner,
woman and man – all of which in some way speak to the exceptional conditions under which American nationhood is constituted. *The Rustler*'s di-
vergences from Wister's paradigm are equally suggestive: McElrath's nar-

rative takes a direction antithetical to that of *The Virginian* when, rejected by his disdainful sweetheart, its silent and sinewy cowboy hero becomes a notorious rustler.[2]

Although *The Rustler* received relatively little attention when first published in comparison to the enormous publicity secured by *The Virginian*, the novel is important with respect to contemporary scholarship about the popular western, not simply because it poses a challenge to the assumption that the genre has emerged without the participation of women writers, but also because it illuminates how the very emergence of the "classic" western novel engaged citizenship debates in which gender was a key site of struggle. Implicated in the articulation of America's exceptional status as a frontier nation and, therefore, the exceptional character of its "pioneering" citizens, the cultural production of western images during the Progressive Era was a process necessarily caught up in the struggle to define American citizenship. If *The Virginian*'s central priority is to guarantee the virility of its male hero – who rises through the ranks to become the model American citizen – it is precisely in response to a social environment in which the gender of citizenship was vigorously contested, as Jane Tompkins has argued.[3] Given both the contingency of the gendered status of American citizenship and the stake of western narratives in this debate, the cultural production of this mythology was a field that admitted not only women writers but also feminist positionings.

My argument departs from recent discussions of women and the western: Jane Tompkins has argued, for example, that "when women wrote about the West, the stories they told did not look anything like what we know as the Western."[4] More recently, Norris Yates has initiated a recovery of popular westerns by women, but he uses models of recovery – specifically those developed by Elaine Showalter, Sandra M. Gilbert, and Susan Gubar – in a way that reinscribes the assumption that the popular western is an inherently masculine discourse in which "authentic" female voices are manifest only in "palimpsestic" form: "By writing from within the male camp in this 'gender war' and using the double-voiced strategy, intentionally or otherwise, women authors could bore from within, still get published, and to some degree resolve the conflict between the demands of the macho Western and their feminist leanings."[5] Yates's argument, like Tompkins's, implies that the misogyny commonly associated with the popular western is an uncontested characteristic of this "macho" genre, which somehow prevents women from speaking in their own voices. My findings, on the contrary, suggest that popular westerns are produced through debate in which the place of women in the mythological West is a crucial point of contention and that this very debate has authorized female as well as male voices. Mobilizing a very effective strategic feminist discourse, McElrath targets specific sites of social antagonism and discord in order to challenge the exclusion of women from American citizenship. Like "social feminists" who argued, as Steven Buechler has shown, that the vote would enable women to clean up the various socio-economic "messes" made by men in the public sphere, McElrath authorizes her frontier heroine by exposing a similar "mess" in the very region that was supposed to guarantee America's exceptional status as a classless society.[6] In order to map out the terrain of this debate, it is necessary first to return to the historical materials used by Wister and McElrath to ground their novels.

"THE MAVERICK IS A MOTHERLESS CALF": CLASS, PROPERTY, AND THE RUSTLER WARS

In 1884 the Wyoming government attempted to put an end to ongoing disputes involving maverick cattle by passing the controversial Maverick Law, giving control of calves of unknown origin to the Wyoming Stock Growers Association (WSGA), an elite society of stock owners, many of whom were investors from the eastern states and from overseas. Under this legislation, mavericks were to be turned over to the WSGA, who would be responsible for distributing them at regular auctions.[7] Opponents of the WSGA – including cattle-owning cowboys and homesteaders – bitterly resented the legislation as yet another step in the monopolization of the Wyoming cattle industry by the "cattle lords," an elite inner circle of wealthy aristocrats.

The Maverick Law was supposed to put to rest a problem that had existed for as long as the industry itself but that had become particularly pressing as the cattle industry in Wyoming became more fiercely competitive. Although the practice of grazing cattle on the open range was appealing to the entrepreneurial fantasy of limitless economic expansion, it made the task of determining property ownership problematic. Inevitably, a few animals would escape branding at the yearly roundup, and once they were separated from their mothers, their origin became impossible to determine. This unmarked property was not so much a material as a discursive problem: the orderly distribution of maverick calves required an ideological framework for determining who could legitimately own them. To many cowboys, the maverick calf was the just reward for their skill and resourcefulness. Their claims to the animals, however, were regularly challenged by the owners of large cattle companies, known locally as *lords* or *barons*, who claimed title to mavericks found on their property or roped by one of their employees. It was common practice for larger operations to offer salary bonuses to cowboys who turned mavericks over to their bosses and to prosecute cowboys who "mavericked" for themselves. The issue, however, had as much to do with what was implied ideologically by the availability of such animals in the public domain as it did with their formal economic value. The cattleman Granville Stuart averred, "It was only a step from 'mavericking' to branding any calf without a brand, and from that to changing brands."[8] To define mavericks as part of the public domain and concede to their more or less arbitrary distribution had implications for the stability of the institution of property itself.

Contrary to popular fantasies of the West as a timeless refuge from the afflictions of modernity, then, the consolidation of huge economic power blocs and the emergence of a highly vulnerable wage-earning class implicated the cattle industry in debates that were violently engaged in urban settings. Indeed, there are significant correspondences between labor disturbances in Johnson County and those in Chicago, such as the Haymarket massacre of 1886 and the Pullman strike of 1894. The Wyoming cattle trade was not immune to the pattern of boom-and-bust economics, labor unrest, and violent class antagonism that underlined these crises. The boom began in the late 1870s, when the industry began to attract major investors – hailing from such far-flung locations as New York, Philadelphia, Boston, England, and Scotland – who saw in open-range cattle ranching the seemingly ideal realization of laissez-faire capitalism on a corporate scale. These investors purchased huge herds, left them to graze on the open range, and reaped the profits in the spring. Publicity material such as General James S. Brisbin's *The Beef Bonanza; or, How to Get Rich on the Plains* (1881) contributed to the popular belief that raising cattle on the open range amounted to a license to print money for those with enough capital to make the initial investment. This and other promotional material, used to attract investors to the cattle frontier, claimed that open-range cattle ranching delivered high dividends with little expense aside from the initial capital investment and that the only skills required were those that came naturally to the well-rounded businessman who enjoyed the vigorous, outdoor life – "merely a form of outdoor sport that paid dividends."[9] The imaginary dimension of the industry infected even its accounting procedures: entire herds were bought and sold on the basis of the "book count," determined through crude (and wishful) calculations meant to save the expense of actually rounding up and counting the herd. More often than not, the numbers on the books were not borne out when the herds were finally tallied before going to market. Many stock owners went bankrupt this way.

Poor management and harsh weather took their toll, profits dwindled, and in many cases labor was asked to absorb the losses. In 1886, the year of the Haymarket massacre, Wyoming stockmen attempted to implement a significant wage cut, which was successfully resisted through a cowboy strike. Relations between cowboys and their employers deteriorated rapidly in the ensuing years, as did the stability of the industry itself. The crushing blow was delivered when the disastrous winter of 1887 decimated herds and bankrupted ranchers, reducing community morale to an all-time low.

Class struggle in Johnson County was both articulated and enacted through the discourse and practice of cattle rustling. "Men ordinarily honest," writes the Johnson County historian J. Elmer Brock, "stole cattle from the big outfits and did not consider it dishonest but an act justifiable in a war of classes."[10] The WSGA drew up blacklists of cowboys barred from employment, using the term *rustler* in its pejorative sense to label strikers and thieves as well as cowboys who ran their own small herds. Jack Flagg, among the most notorious rustlers of the time, had been blacklisted by the WSGA for his part in the 1886 strike. In 1888, he and a group of other blacklisted cowboys formed the HAT brand, sealing their reputations as cattle thieves through this challenge to the WSGA monopoly. With its local newspaper advertisement appearing in brazen proximity to those of established outfits, the prosperous HAT brand signified to many that the rustlers had indeed got hold of Johnson County.

Wyoming courtrooms were bogged down with rustling cases in the late 1880s, including various charges against the HAT partners, but popular opinion weighed so heavily against larger cattle companies that, as Smith points out, most juries refused to convict rustlers, no matter how convincing the evidence. When legal channels failed, some stockmen apparently resorted to vigilante justice. In 1889, suspected rustlers Ella "Cattle Kate" Watson and James Averell were hanged. Eyewitnesses named a well-known cattle lord as the leader of the lynching. In October 1891, Nate Champion, another well-known cowboy activist and reputed rustler, was attacked in his bed by four men, one of whom Champion identified as a detective working for the WSGA. On separate occasions in December of that same year, two men with connections to the HAT brand were murdered, both under similar circumstances. Hindsight has prompted historians of Johnson County to look on these events as precursors to the "war" that broke out in April 1892, when a group of vigilante stockmen invaded Johnson County in order to exterminate every suspected rustler in the county, apparently with the blessing of Wyoming governor Amos Barber.[11]

Lurking in the immediate vicinity of this violent confrontation was the figure of the maverick calf. The proceeds from mavericking figured insignificantly in the income of the large cattle companies and can hardly account for the energy spent to prevent cowboys from accessing them. Given the way in which the branded bodies of cattle functioned as representations of property, however, a reading of their structural place in the discourse of free-range capitalism is more likely to account for the way in which the maverick calf was almost always implicated in property disputes between cowboys and cattle companies.

Within the discourse of property on the open range, the cow's branded body occupied the structural place of what theorist Slavoj Žižek calls the *sublime object* of ideology, a term borrowed from Lacanian psychoanalysis. The sublime object is an ordinary, everyday object that finds itself occupying the place of the impossible/real object of desire. Such objects appear to transcend the insurmountable gap between signifier and signified – the gap on which the symbolic order is constituted – but in fact they only mask the absence of the impossible/real object within the symbolic. Žižek explains this principle using money as an example: "In the social *effectivity* of the market we . . . *treat* coins as if they consist 'of an immutable substance, a substance over which time has no power, and which stands in antithetic contrast to any matter found in nature.'" Žižek's emphasis here is on the behavioral rather than the intellectual dimension of the illusion: "What [individuals] 'do not know,' what they misrecognize, is the fact that in their social reality itself, in their social activity – in the act of commodity exchange – they are guided by [a] fetishistic illusion."[12] Ideology is, therefore, manifest in social behavior: the social effect of capitalism is such that subjects behave as though money were a sublime object.

The orderly flow of capital within the free-range cattle industry depended on all participants behaving as though cattle were born branded with the transcendental mark of their owner. As Blake Allmendinger has shown in his study of cowboy culture, the brand filled the place of the absent owner – or, rather, masked the owner's absence:

Before fencing transformed the public space of the open range into a series of privately controlled segments of land, cattlemen let their livestock graze with other ranchers' wandering herds; hence animals could easily mix and become confused with one another in promiscuous groups that roamed the unfenced frontier. Ranchers used brands to distinguish their stock from that of other cattlemen and to protect their possessions from outlaws who could rustle and sell unbranded mavericks. Ranchers invented hieroglyphic economic inscriptions, or forms of language, to inform readers that no one could take ranchers' cattle or mistake their bulls, heifers, calves, and castrated steers for other men's real estate.[13]

The discourse of private property on the free range required its subjects to treat the brand as though it embodied the transcendent, sublime presence of the owner watching over his or her property. Maverick cattle disrupted this illusion by exposing the absence masked by the brand, requiring the industry to confront regularly the arbitrary naming that underpinned the institution of private property.

The fact that rustling convictions were rare was read by cattle companies and their supporters as evidence of a legal-judicial system controlled by rustlers, but most property disputes were grounded in the difficulty of distinguishing between theft and purchase on the open range. Individuals accused of altering or removing existing brands or of driving calves away from their mothers could always legitimate their claim by insisting that the animal in question was found a maverick. The fundamental illegibility of the brand made it possible for competing fantasies of ownership to vie for legitimacy. The social effect was not, however, a general breakdown in the institution of private property; rather, the struggle was articulated as an antagonism between two distinct classes: the wealthy cattle companies, which controlled the range and most of its resources, and an alliance of cowboys, homesteaders, and small-business owners. As the historian Helena Huntington Smith observes, the conflict focalized around the figure of the maverick: "To the big stockman the maverick is a symbol of property and the property is mine, not thine. To the little stockmen who came along later, the maverick is a symbol of his own rights on the public domain. The maverick is a source of hatred and strife. The maverick is a boil on the neck of the body politic. The maverick is a motherless calf."[14]

In keeping with the class-based underpinnings of the dispute, mavericking was considered a problem only when it disrupted the subordinate status of certain groups, especially cowboys, whose expertise in managing cattle gave them an edge over their tenderfoot employers. Attempts to regulate the distribution of maverick cattle throughout the 1880s affected particularly the access of cowboys to mavericks. The 1884 Maverick Law required all mavericks to be turned over to the wsga for auction but deliberately made no provision for how the auctions were to be carried out, enabling the wsga to exclude cowboys by demanding expensive bonds and by auctioning the animals in large lots that no cowboy could afford.

Rustling became a crisis in Wyoming in the years following this particular piece of legislation: cowboys refused to turn mavericks over for auction and were branded rustlers; others deliberately plagiarized cattle from large stock companies in retaliation against their monopoly. Juries increasingly preferred the claims of the little stockmen over those of the cattle barons. Histories of the Johnson County War tend to dwell on the difficulty of distinguishing the real rustlers from the honest cowboys and attempt to settle the vexed question of which side of the dispute stood on the moral high ground.[15] Such questions are unanswerable because the conflict was, in fact, engendered by a structural fracture in the discourse of property itself. Maverick legislation served only to call attention to the arbitrary naming that underpinned the institution of property, infecting virtually every property dispute with the maverick's scandalous ambiguity.

The crisis exploded in violence when, after months of planning and preparation, a number of wealthy ranchers, frustrated by the difficulty of securing rustling convictions, decided to take the law into their own hands. On 6 April 1892, at 4:00 A.M., a party of fify-two men, including hired mercenaries, eastern tenderfoots who had come to help defend their western interests (and no doubt to indulge their heroic fantasies), local cattlemen, and two journalists, arrived via train in Casper, Wyoming. On Saturday, 9 April, the "invaders" surrounded the ranch house where Nate Champion and Nick Ray were staying. Both men were well-known members of the rustlers' side, but Champion was a particularly desirable target. A blacklisted cowboy who now ran his own herd of allegedly rustled cattle, Champion had become a local celebrity because of his open defiance of Johnson County's most powerful cattlemen. At dawn, an unsuspecting Ray emerged from the ranch house and was shot and mortally wounded. Champion managed to drag him back to safety, and the two remained under siege for several hours, with Champion firing at every opportunity, until the impatient invaders finally forced him out by setting fire to the ranch house: "In his sock feet he burst out on a dead run. There are all kinds of reports about how many bullet holes were in his body."[16]

The invasion went no further, thanks to the timely arrival of Jack Flagg, who stumbled on the scene en route to, of all places, a Democratic state convention in Douglas, Wyoming. Flagg had no difficulty mobilizing more than enough armed men to stop the invaders, who were eventually forced to retreat to a ranch house just outside the town of Buffalo, remaining under siege for several days while a huge and menacing crowd gathered around their precarious refuge. Friends of the invaders, meanwhile, were for a time unable to telegraph for help because the invaders themselves had cut the telegraph lines.

Although reluctant to deliver his allies into the hands of the authorities, Governor Barber had no choice but to telegraph President Benjamin Harrison for military assistance, which he was finally able to do on Tuesday, 12 April 1892.[17] Federal troops arrived the following day and took custody of the invaders, who were subsequently held in various facilities until, in August 1892, they were released on bail. When, after numerous delays, the invaders were finally brought to trial in January 1893, every single case was dismissed because of legal technicalities – an outcome facilitated, no doubt, by the invaders' many influential supporters.

THE RUSTLER, THE RANCHER, HIS CALF, AND HER MOTHER: DOMESTIC POLITICS AND FRANCES MCELRATH'S WESTERN HEROINE

Owen Wister's interest in the Johnson County War is no surprise given his immediate involvement with many of its key players, places, and events. His first western journey took him to Wyoming in 1885, one year after the Maverick Law was passed. His host in Wyoming was Major Frank Wolcott, the manager of the VR ranch and a key participant in the invasion. And of course, Wister was part of a famous inner circle of men – also including Roosevelt, Remington, and Turner – who collectively orchestrated a number of reorientations in the meanings and politics of hegemonic frontier

discourse during the late nineteenth century. Clearly, the Johnson
County War was also of interest to Wister because industrial expansion
and class conflict in the West spoke to his interest in articulating the national importance of western American culture and history.

But Wister was not alone in recognizing the implications of the Johnson County War with respect to the national cultural imaginary. In the
spring of 1902, Frances McElrath's *The Rustler* was published – a "coincidence" made all the more intriguing because of the implied relation
between the two novels: so closely do they resemble each other, some
critics have commented, that "the two authors of the two books could
have been accused of collaboration."[18] *The Rustler* raises questions about
the relation between gender and genre with respect to the emergence of
the "classic" western. Representing rustling as a form of class antagonism constituted by the indeterminate status of the maverick calf, McElrath makes explicit the authorizing function of the maverick's (absent)
mother.

Because this novel is neither widely read nor readily available, some detailed plot description is useful here. In the opening chapter of *The Rustler*, the heroine, Hazel, refuses an offer of marriage from the English
ranch owner Horace Carew. "You do wrong in thinking that in settling
down you would be giving up your entire freedom," he tells her in the
novel's opening line.[19] While Horace is absorbed in his proposal, Hazel
"[chances] to look over the edge of the cut-bank along which her horse
was slowly walking and she [sees] Jim [the foreman of the ranch belonging to Hazel's cousin]. . . . Their eyes met, and that was the beginning of
all things" (9–10). Although Hazel is a regular guest at the great houses
of Newport, the recent death of her father, whose affairs are in some disar-
ray, has forced her to economize by staying at the Wyoming ranch until it
can be discovered whether she has been left "an heiress or a pauper"
(51). As in *The Virginian*, a love relationship evolves between the silent,
virile cowboy (a self-proclaimed woman hater) and the well-bred lady tenderfoot, but with highly suggestive differences in outcome.

Jim is at first indifferent to Hazel, who considers him beneath her but
nevertheless expects him to admire her refined looks and manners.
When he does not, Hazel hatches a plan "to make Jim know that I've been
on the ranch before I leave it" (49). To this end, "Hazel stoops to con-
quer" (57), ridding herself of her expensive dress and demeanor and se-
ducing Jim through various performances that make her appear humble
and vulnerable. Her strategy works too well. For Jim, "Miss Clifford rich

and cared for would have been somebody altogether outside the pale of possibility. But the simple young woman earning a scanty subsistence by teaching – poor, proud, and alone – was some one whom he dared offer his protecting arm to support" (113). Yet Hazel takes no pleasure in her triumph. Sensing the shift in Jim's feelings for her, Hazel is overcome with panic: "The strong spirit of the man looked out at her for once and she quailed before it. . . . In her sudden revulsion of feeling she hated the vulgar and trivial impulse that had prompted her all winter. She was sanely herself again" (106–8).

Unfortunately, Hazel's awakening comes too late for Jim, who, devastated and disillusioned by her rejection, becomes the most notorious rustler in the county. Over a period of time, he becomes the leader of a highly organized gang of rustlers whose ЯOB brand flaunts both their crimes and their imperviousness to the law. A vigilante army, led by Hazel's spurned suitor, Horace Carew, is organized to stop Jim's gang. The two plots converge when Jim abducts Hazel and takes her to his rustlers' hideout in an attempt to force her to acknowledge his wealth and power.

While Hazel is in captivity, the rustler war breaks out in a way that closely follows the historical record of Johnson County. McElrath's romantic plot is intertwined with these events. A secondary romance also develops when Horace Carew conducts a covert investigation of local rustler activity. Suspecting the involvement of a man named Nathan Grimes, Horace cultivates a relationship with Grimes's adopted daughter, suggestively named Mavvy (short for Maverick), in order to learn details about the rustlers. Mavvy, who falls in love with Horace, learns of a plot by the rustlers to kill him and risks her life to prevent the murder: she first warns Horace of the danger and then, by disguising herself as Horace, takes a bullet meant for him. Mavvy narrowly survives; meanwhile, Horace and his "gentlemen army" kill Nathan Grimes and Nick Lowry, clearly modeled after Nate Champion and Nick Ray, after a prolonged siege at their cabin. Jim stumbles on the spectacle, escapes under gunfire, and rides through the county warning its inhabitants of the invasion – a deed carried out in Johnson County by Jack Flagg. McElrath closes the rustler war in a way that is similarly consistent with the historical record: the vigilantes are arrested by the local law enforcement with the assistance of enraged citizens, who did not know "that practically the stockmen's interests were their own" (248). Later, "through the exertion of considerable money and outside influence, the stockmen were let out of jail on heavy bail with the understanding that the case would never after be brought to trial, and the forty gentlemen, with the charge of murder still against them, were set at liberty" (258).

Jim comes through the crisis, his rustling operation for the most part unscathed, and focuses his attention on flaunting his power and wealth before Hazel's captive gaze. Unimpressed by Jim, Hazel is deeply moved by the hard life of the rustlers, especially their children, who are uneducated, in poor health, and in need of moral guidance. Among these children is Jim's adopted son, Tips, whose parents were killed in an Indian raid. When Tips dies of a fever epidemic that has swept the rustler colony, Hazel blames herself for exposing him to the unhealthy environment of the rustlers' hideaway (since she blames herself for Jim's turn to rustling). She does her penance by taking responsibility for the welfare of the rustler families, teaching the children to read and offering their mothers advice on parenting and other domestic matters. Jim is also stirred by the death of Tips, but his repentance comes too late; while he is busy returning stolen cattle to their appropriate ranges, he is shot and fatally wounded by an unseen assailant. He manages to make his way back to the rustlers' hideout, where he spends his last days under Hazel's care. Jim's death marks the end of the reign of the rustlers and helps determine Hazel's decision to continue her work with the former rustlers' families rather than marry Horace. That role is reserved for Mavvy, who finally manages to win Horace over with her self-sacrificing devotion.

Like *The Virginian, The Rustler* constructs the East/West split through its composition of gender relations and marriage. It negotiates a very different resolution, however, on behalf of its heroine, who manages successfully to evade the marriage that looms over her in the novel's opening paragraph. This evasion, moreover, is the novel's central project and is explicitly tied to McElrath's reading of the rustler war as an event that deconstructs the economics of both class and gender. Whereas *The Virginian* articulates the clear distinction between good and evil (and erases the class content) in the rustler wars by, among other ways, evading the maverick issue, McElrath explains the nuances of the debate in the chapter following Jim's turn to rustling. She represents the rustler wars as a phase of class antagonism marking the transition from "baronial conditions" to a more "commercial condition. . . . The cowpuncher was beginning to feel dissatisfied with the mere romance of his occupation, and was whispering to himself that the profits on the range were rather more one-sided than need be" (164). The maverick, according to McElrath, was pivotal in this "evolution of the *rancher*" (165). In considerable detail,

McElrath explains that "maverick-branding became a recognized feature of the cattle industry," eventually encouraging the cowboy to compete with his employer: "If his employer could make thirty or forty dollars out of the maverick which *he* found and branded, the cowpuncher argued, why should not he himself have that large profit instead of the paltry sum paid him?" (165, 167). This in turn leads to "quasi-honest" branding practices: "Then the cowpuncher who had used to go out and 'rustle' mavericks for his employer became on his own account a 'rustler'" (167).

McElrath's account of mavericking makes clear how the uncertain status of mavericks exposes the discourse of property to alternative readings, which are manifest by means of the cowboys' subversive labor. This is precisely what *The Virginian*'s moralized version of class struggle, founded on the transcendental signification of private property, disallows. The latter text recuperates the ideological fantasy of Wister's "natural aristocracy" – which rationalizes his "democratic" class system – through its depiction of the Virginian's social mobility, founded on his "naturally" conceived aristocratic status. The transcendental signification of property supplies the linchpin of this narrative: the salient difference between the Virginian and his former friend, the rustler Steve, is that Steve steals cattle and the Virginian does not. This construction rewrites the economic distinction between the cowboy and his employer as a moral distinction between the cowboy and the rustler in order to represent a sameness of interest between two competing classes: the Virginian is both a cowboy and an aristocrat and, therefore, embodies the fantasy of unequal equality.

The marriage narrative is crucial to the signification of property and class in both novels. The historian Nancy F. Cott supplies a model for reading these marriage plots: "The differentiation of public from private [in the late nineteenth century] was incomprehensible without marriage, which created couples who made homes and families that amassed and transmitted property. Because marriage bears a formative relation to both private property and domestic intimacy, it not only inhabits but undergirds the domain of privacy."[20] As Cott argues, the cultural work of marriage in constructing the public/private distinction meant that it was read as a matter of both public and private interest. Because the intelligibility of the boundary was maintained through the denial of citizenship to women and their containment within the private sphere, the signification of private property and the social status of women were inextricably linked. Women political activists, therefore, enjoyed more cultural legitimacy when advocating on behalf of the moral and economic stability of the family; they figured prominently, for example, in efforts to ban the sale of alcohol because of its effect on the family, particularly the women and children who were victimized by alcohol-related violence and unemployment. Women's abolitionist groups, similarly, highlighted those aspects of slavery that corrupted the institution of the family: the sale of children from their mothers; the sexual domination of enslaved women by their masters; and the corruption of slave-owning families caused by the master's infidelity. Women's political activism met with far more resistance when it advocated empowering women as an end in itself rather than as an extension of women's domestic duty.[21]

In both *The Virginian* and *The Rustler,* the marriageability of male heroes denotes their social status, which in turn formulates a particular epistemology of social organization: Molly Stark signifies the power and status to which the Virginian is "naturally" entitled because of his inherent physical and moral virtues. To subordinate herself to him, as she finally does on the eve of their marriage, is to signify the Virginian's natural entitlement to the status that she represents. On the other hand, Hazel's rejection of Jim marks his "awakening" from this ideological fantasy: he too possesses all the right virtues and is seduced by Hazel into believing that he can therefore aspire to a higher status; however, the novel stops short of representing a social reality in which this dream can be realized. Jim is thus stunned by "the absurdity of his thinking for a moment that a refined lady would love him – and marry him – and that he should have children of his own and a home, and live a respected man in some good community" (137).

These two novels, then, are in agreement with respect to the national orientation of their western narratives and to their engagement with an entire apparatus of assumptions about class, gender, and social organization. The crucial difference between them has to do with their arrangement of the gender hierarchy and its link to a way of processing certain contradictions inherent in American democratic ideology. In *The Virginian,* Wister argues that democracy is a social reality despite the stratification of American society because the latter is the effect of a natural hierarchy formed through a social-Darwinian process of struggle. *The Rustler* bases its feminist strategy on a refusal of this rationalization, arguing that class stratification and antagonism are socially constituted processes that undermine the achievement of real democracy – that is, democracy at the level of social reality (equal equality) rather than ideological fantasy (unequal equality).[22]

The distinction between social reality and ideological fantasy is articulated through the Jim-Hazel courtship: Hazel's pretense of making herself available to Jim is the dream, while her return to her former self marks Jim's awakening. The novel endorses Jim's aspirations. They are a sign that by cultivating the capacity to recognize Hazel's attractions he has "simply come to his own, to his better self" (111). The problem is that he does not yet inhabit a social reality in which these dreams can be realized. Hence, Hazel ends her performance on recognizing that she is not prepared to become, in her own social reality, the poor, proud governess with whom Jim had fallen in love: "The play was at an end. The sudden revelation of the soul of the man had been too much for Hazel. It had stirred her into a deeper comprehension of him and of what she had been doing, and she had dropped the rôle she had assumed. . . . She was sanely herself again" (108).

The narrative does not simply return to the status quo (a Hazel-Horace marriage), however, because it is the marriage myth that is itself at stake: as the crucial naturalized social relation – differentiating classes on the basis of female desire – the marriage myth must be deconstructed in order to make democracy a social reality. This procedure is entwined with the novel's feminist project. The maverick dispute – specifically the way in which the ambiguous status of the maverick calf disrupts the articulation of private property – supplies the basis for generating the more radical feminism embraced by Hazel once the limitations of her earlier performance are exposed. A clear homology is drawn, first of all, between the status of women in classic patriarchy and the status of calves as property. Most explicitly, the link is embodied by the character of Mavvy, whose symbolic name invokes a reading of gender and property as mutually implicating discourses. Mavvy is introduced in a chapter that follows directly Hazel's successful evasion of advances from both Jim and Horace. Seeking distraction from Hazel's rebuffs, the dejected Horace attends a nearby ball, where, during an illustrative square dance, the (male) dancers are instructed to "lock horns with your own heifers, and rassle 'em to their places" and to "corral the fillies, rope your own, and back to your claim with her!" (144). Whereas Hazel has just escaped the marriage "roundup," the less fortunate orphan Mavvy is brought to the dance, apparently to be prostituted by her adoptive father, who forces her to accept the crude advances of another rustler. She is rescued by Horace, who is glad for the opportunity to restore his recently bruised masculinity.

Just as the ambiguous status of the maverick upsets the symbolic economy through which private property is articulated, so it also raises questions about the status of women, who are treated within the marriage market just like cattle. To recognize the status of women/property as the effect of a symbolic economy is one step toward upsetting the apparatus of social relations through which this status is determined. Hence, McElrath explores the enabling potential of the women/cattle analogy as well as its more disturbing implications. On the one hand, for example, Hazel's situation is as precariously contingent as that of the calf whose brand can easily be altered or plagiarized: if her social identity is constituted through symbolic processes, then what is there to distinguish her from the destitute Mavvy, especially given Hazel's eroding income? The possibility of marriage to Jim is, thus, "an impending avalanche" (108) threatening to subsume Hazel's identity. But when Hazel becomes aware of her place in the marriage market, she is able to behave in a way that effects substantive changes to her social situation. By refusing marriage, she disrupts the gender economy that commodifies women in order to constitute the fundamental privilege of citizenship – the right to own property – as masculine.

Hazel awakens to the social reality of the marriage economy after her seduction generates an unanticipated outcome. Her initial plan is simply to make herself desirable in an economy in which her highly refined manners, dress, and accomplishments are not valuable. Jim, the only remotely eligible bachelor in the novel, is initially "as insensible to her charms as a post" (45). Hazel decides that because Jim is "too independent to allow himself to be taken up by people socially" (64), it is up to her to go, like Mohammed, to the mountain. Her plan, however, is based on a fundamental misrecognition of her status within the marriage market. Her adaptability, we are told, is "true to [Hazel's American] breeding and nationality," which gives her the "capacity of 'fitting in' in any environment" (60). Accordingly, she adapts to the local marriage economy, inspiring Jim to dream of what a life with her could mean: "I might get to be a partner some day," he muses. "With Hazel beside him he could strive for any glory" (114). However noble these aspirations may be, they are fundamentally antidemocratic because they merely replace one form of inequality (based on class) with another (based on gender). Hazel is repulsed by Jim precisely because his awakened desire exposes her transformation as nothing more than crude adaptation to an economy in which her fundamental status as marital property remains unchanged.

On the basis of this rupture between two ideological fantasies – both of which are at some level consistent with democratic ideology but neither of which constitutes democracy as a social reality – *The Rustler* formulates a radical feminist position, advanced as a step toward realizing democracy as social practice. McElrath argues that the subordination of the subject to the arbitrary forces of the market economy is effected specifically by the mother's negated authority, for the brand both marks the subject as property and subordinates the authority of the mother to that of the market. The authority of the mother, then, is the necessary alternative to the symbolic violence of the branding iron. Jim's turn to rustling is the symptom of social trauma originating specifically in the objectification of women and the consequential neutralization of their moral authority as mothers. Immersed entirely in the world of work, Jim and his adopted son, Tips, inhabit a motherless, misogynist landscape: "*Women*," observed Tips, "may be all very well in their place, but their place ain't on the range nor anywheres near it!" (21). The role of Tips's mother in this landscape has fallen to Jim: "Can't see what a feller'd want of a mother when he'd got Jim" (27), Tips belligerently informs Hazel. Jim is himself the product of a motherless, dysfunctional, and impoverished home: his father was an outlaw, and his mother "was always too hard-worked" (75) to have time for him.

Having inscribed Jim's fall in terms of a seduction plot that exposes both the myth of the classless society and the commodification of women within marriage, McElrath undoes the negation underlining these fantasies in order to repair the social damage that they cause. Hazel's maternal consciousness is awakened by the death of Tips, which Hazel blames on her own "vulgar" behavior. Accepting the blame for this and virtually every other crisis in the novel, Hazel recognizes her own power to effect change in the social world and atones for past wrongs through acts of social mothering: "She had set one discordant note jarring through the world; now she wanted to atone by bringing others into harmony" (325). She opens a school for the rustler children, tends to the sick, and advises the rustlers' wives on domestic matters. Jim's ЯOB brand eventually dominates the local cattle industry, but his power has no effect on Hazel, nor can he compete with her growing popularity in the rustler community: "Her gentle measures were designed to frustrate the very work he was carrying on. He had brought her to the camp to witness with her own eyes his supremacy, and instead of bowing before it like the rest, she had quietly gone to work to undermine his power" (340–41). In her new role as a prototypical social worker, Hazel repairs the trauma that Jim had experi-

enced when his earlier fantasies had been shattered. At first seduced by
Hazel and the democratic fantasy that she performs in order to mislead
him, Jim is ultimately redeemed by the example of her newly realized maternal authority: "Witness the little weeping child beneath the mesquite
bush vowing to bear an honest name. Witness his years of faithful labor as
foreman of the K cattle company and the first worthiness of his love for Hazel. It had sent him widely astray, that love, but it had come from an intrin-
sically true source and it had finally brought him back to the right" (353).

Hazel's domestic feminism places *The Rustler* in the tradition of feminist discourse closely associated with the progressive reform movement of
the late nineteenth century. Feminist reformers argued that with respect
to issues such as poverty, disease, unemployment, crime, and exploitation, "cleaning up" the Republic was the task for which women were best
qualified because their moral authority supplied an antidote to the cor-
ruptive impulses of unbridled individualism, associated with male domination in business and politics, as Steven Buechler has argued.[23] The
disappearing frontier was also an occasion for publicly authorizing the
domestic woman because the growth of various forms of social antagonism and discord was widely attributed to the disappearance of the
western "safety valve," announced in the census of 1890. Without frontier land reserves, there were not the resources available to guarantee the
social reality of democracy in America;[24] American democracy, consequently, had to be reinvented in a way that addressed the now undeniable
reality of scarcity. The matrix of approaches to this issue cut across the political spectrum, from the emphasis on rational management of popula-
tions and resources to the development of imperialist policies – such as
those embodied in Roosevelt's Rough Riders – that extended the American frontier beyond national boundaries by constructing other nations
as frontiers ripe for "civilization." *The Virginian* too can be situated
within this vector of "frontier anxiety."[25] In contrast to the rugged individualism privileged by frontier imperialism, feminist reformers situated
their approach domestically: they focused on specific social effects of scarcity – poverty, disease, unemployment, child labor – figuring these issues
as domestic ones best handled by the experts in domestic matters, women
who, in the course of home management, dealt with the problem of scarcity on an everyday basis.

Domestic feminists unsettled the very basis for a gendered distinction
between public and private space in American society at the turn of the

century. By arguing that the public sphere was, in practice, an extension of the domicile, they simultaneously reinvented the domicile as a public space, fundamentally enmeshed in the political and economic worlds rather than eternally isolated from them. The difference between this and earlier-nineteenth-century forms of women's political mobilization was that the idea of women's suffrage gradually lost its radical edge as the public sphere was reconceptualized as a place that women could inhabit and still remain "women." Predicated as it was on conventional representations of gender, domestic feminism nevertheless created more opportunities for women than had existed for them previously. Hence the progression in Hazel's range of choices in *The Rustler.* At the beginning of the novel, Hazel's choices are circumscribed by the seeming inevitability that she will marry – the only question is, Will she marry Horace? In the end, however, the successful suitor proves to be her profession, for Hazel chooses to remain unmarried so that she can continue to oversee the reformation of the rustlers' children. By advancing this progression within the framework of a western novel, McElrath anticipates an important outcome of feminist activity at the turn of the century: the achievement of national women's suffrage in 1920. Eighteen years before women's suffrage recognized women as equal participants in American democracy, McElrath embodied the democratizing force of frontier individualism in the figure of the maternal woman rather than the rugged frontiersman. Given that *The Rustler* appeared during a period in which women's increasing participation in the public sphere made this traditionally masculine terrain increasingly subject to occupation by women, this text offers us an example of how this process engaged mythological as well as material spaces. Indeed, the cultural work of authors such as McElrath was as crucial to the women's movement as the work of domestic feminists in the formal political arena because the former enabled Americans to imagine the public woman as a social possibility.

GENDER AND THE FIELD OF THE WESTERN NOVEL

In addition to offering a detailed historical reading of a forgotten woman's text, I suggest that incorporating women writers into the debate about the popular western tradition requires that we rethink the terms in which this tradition is understood. *The Rustler* cannot in and of itself bear the burden of this argument, but it does indicate how our understanding of the genre changes when we seriously engage the possibility that women write westerns. The theorist Pierre Bourdieu has shown that the work of marginal or "dominated" writers is not necessarily trivial because it too determines the conditions structuring the work of all subjects in a given cultural field.[26] The way in which *The Rustler* and *The Virginian* address one another at every turn indicates that both novels were engaged in a struggle over the gendered status of the archetypal American, producing diametrically opposed positions on the issue, yet clearly sharing a common generic vocabulary. Wister's literary practice was thus situated within a broader cultural field also occupied by women writers who vied for literary enfranchisement.

Bourdieu's theory of the field of cultural production as a set of positions encompassing both mainstream and minority subjects might also explain why the western is so often defined in ways that explicitly exclude women writers. Bourdieu argues that such exclusions mark a presence in a given field; indeed, it is this presence that produces the exclusion. Tania Modleski's observations of critical responses to Maggie Greenwald's 1993 western film *The Ballad of Little Jo* are consistent with this model. Modleski contends that critics perpetually resist new developments in the genre, singling out "good" westerns as those that "it turns out, have white men as protagonists."[27] Films that challenge this paradigm are either dismissed as conventional and derivative or considered guilty of cheap Hollywood gimmickry. While Modleski assumes that Greenwald represents a relatively recent development in the genre, she is, in fact, only the most recent in a long line of women authors whose incursions into the western have been overlooked for one reason or another or have been situated in a subcategory that obscures the complexity of the western's genealogy.

The publication of *The Rustler* is a case in point: whereas Wister was well supported by his publisher, receiving funds for his western journeys and a prestigious illustrator to accompany him, *The Rustler* was marked as an ephemeral text from the very moment of its production, receiving little attention either from its own publisher, Funk and Wagnalls, or from the broader publishing community. Its debut was announced in *Publishers' Weekly* on 15 March 1902, along with Funk and Wagnalls's other spring titles, but it was not singled out for special promotion.[28] Funk and Wagnalls allotted two novels, Israel Putnam's historical novel *Daniel Everton, Volunteer Regular* and Michael Davitt's history *The Boer Fight for Freedom*, full-page advertisements in *Publishers' Weekly*, on 3 and 24 May 1902, respectively.[29] *The Rustler* was among a list of titles publicized on 31 May as "Novels for the Vacation Outfit." The copy constructs the novel as light reading:

A STORY OF LIFE AMONG COWBOYS.

Every reader who delights in a tale full of dash and adventure, love, and breathless suspense will revel in this story of the adventures of a spirited Eastern girl in the recent "Rustler" uprising of outlaw cattlemen in Wyoming.[30]

The novel received no further publicity in *Publishers' Weekly*, and no additional editions were produced. Funk and Wagnalls's advertising economy positioned the novel, then, as recreational reading, the value of which did not transcend its commodity function or fundamentally distinguish it from other offerings in this category. The legacy of *The Rustler* in American literary history fulfilled the ephemeral status originally assigned by its publisher.

McElrath's literary reputation followed a trajectory common to women western writers. Lydia Maria Child's *Hobomok* (1824) preceded and influenced Cooper's *Last of the Mohicans* (1826), yet unlike Cooper, Child is not considered a formative participant in the popular western tradition. Ann S. Stephens's influence on the dime novel western is less well-known than that of Cooper, despite the fact that Stephens's novel *Malaeska* was used to launch Beadle and Adams's dime novel series in 1860 and was one of its most often reprinted works. Owen Wister takes most of the credit for the literary "rebirth" of the western, yet he considered Mary Hallock Foote the first author to "honor the cattle country and not to libel it."[31] Perhaps most telling among the invisible contributions that women have made to the western literary tradition is the example of Wallace Stegner's Pulitzer Prize–winning *Angle of Repose* (1971), which, as Mary Ellen Williams Walsh has shown, relies heavily on Foote's autobiography, *A Victorian Gentlewoman in the Far West*, but does not acknowledge – except in a very roundabout way – its debt to that text.

In *The Land before Her* (1984), Annette Kolodny reconstructs a woman-authored tradition to which these authors may be added, for they, like the authors in Kolodny's study, challenge the "classic" western paradigm epitomized in the work of Cooper, Wister, and others: Child's *Hobomok* represents a marriage between a Native American man and an Anglo-American woman, a possibility shut down by Cooper in *The Last of the Mohicans*. While Stephens's *Malaeska* reinscribes the offspring of miscegenation as a tragic figure, her novel departs from the public discourse of the period because it does not advocate the expansion of white settlement. Mary Hallock Foote criticizes the doctrine of frontier exceptionalism in novels such as *The Led-Horse Claim* (1882) and *The Chosen Valley* (1892). These are just a few examples of how women writers have contested prevailing myths of the frontier as a masculine proving ground. But drawing polarities between masculine and feminine literary traditions sometimes obscures both the complex relations between men's and women's writing and the broader implications of what we might call *the woman's western*. In her analysis of *Little Jo*, Modleski contends that "the very border between male and female worlds of popular culture shifts when a woman is working on what has hitherto been exclusively masculine territory."[32] The work of women writers requires that we conceptualize gender as the very contested terrain on which the genre is constituted rather than as a boundary defining what does and does not count as a western, a struggle with high stakes insofar as the representation of American nationhood determines who is and who is not included in its body politic. Behind just about any western American hero one can think of is the shadowy figure of a woman – and that woman represents more than a character type included to advance the plot or enhance the male hero. She represents both the trace of a voice and the attendant possibilities articulated by that voice. As Tompkins has shown, the alternative form of frontier individualism represented by Molly Stark Wood was a very real possibility in American society at the turn of the last century – a possibility that, eighteen years after the publication of *The Virginian*, would be enshrined in law when American women were recognized as autonomous voting citizens.[33] Historians sometimes puzzle over the relative ease with which the Nineteenth Amendment was passed, given the duration of the struggle for women's suffrage. But if women's suffrage was by 1920 no longer such a radical idea, it is because feminist culture had done its work.

NOTES

1. Aquila, "The Pop Culture West," 9.

2. The Rustler is not unique in this regard. Frederic Remington's *John Ermine of the Yellowstone* (1902) also depicts the demoralization of a Western hero rejected by an upper-class eastern woman. For a discussion, see Bold, *Selling the Wild West,* 46–47.

3. Tompkins, *West of Everything,* 43.

4. Tompkins, *West of Everything*, 41–42.

5. Yates, *Gender and Genre*, 4.

6. Buechler, *Women's Movements in the United States*, 52.

7. Histories of the Johnson County War consulted to formulate this sketch of the maverick dispute include Baber, *The Longest Rope*; Flagg, *A Review of the Cattle Business in Johnson County*; Gage, *The Johnson County War*; Mercer, *The Banditti of the Plains*; and Smith, *The War on Powder River*. Much of this history is conflicting, and the exact details of many key incidents are in dispute. I have found Smith's book especially helpful for sorting through this material because hers is the only text to supply thorough documentation and more rigorous critical analysis of the social conditions underlining the dispute.

8. Quoted in Smith, *The War on Powder River*, 57.

9. Smith, *The War on Powder River*, 11.

10. Quoted in Smith, *The War on Powder River*, 115.

11. For a full discussion of court cases and vigilantism, see Smith, *The War on Powder River*, 116–68. Suspicion of Barber's involvement is based on an order that he issued shortly before the invasion that effectively prevented the sheriff of Johnson County from summoning the militia to intervene. See Smith, *The War on Powder River*, 193; and Mercer, *The Banditti of the Plains*, 40–45.

12. Žižek, *The Sublime Object of Ideology*, 18, 31; Žižek's definition of the sublime object can be found on p. 19.

13. Allmendinger, *The Cowboy*, 4.

14. Smith, *The War on Powder River*, 86.

15. An especially intriguing example of this tendency in Johnson County historiography is Gage's *The Johnson County War*.

16. Gage, *The Johnson County War*, 58.

17. Barber's telegraph did not mention the murders of Champion and Ray or the premeditated invasion, again suggesting that Barber had been involved in the plot and was now protecting his colleagues. The telegraph correspondence between Barber, the president, and the military has been collected in Heald, ed., *Wyoming Flames of '92*.

18. Frantz and Choate, *The American Cowboy*, 160–61.

19. McElrath, *The Rustler*, 9. Page numbers for subsequent citations will be given in the text.

20. Cott, "Giving Character to Our Whole Civil Polity," 110.

21. Baker, "The Domestication of Politics," 90–93; Buechler, *Women's Movements in the United States*, 51–53; Dubois, *Feminism and Suffrage*, 40–52; and Riley, *Inventing the American Woman*, 47.

22. McElrath's version of equality is, of course, invested in ideological fantasies

of its own. Hazel's independence is authorized on the basis of Jim's failed "revolution," on the one hand, and Mavvy's marriage to Horace, on the other. A similar politics was engaged in by middle-class women reformers and suffragists, who tended in their paternalism to infantalize the working class and to exclude African American and immigrant women from active participation in their organizations.

23. Buechler, *Women's Movements in the United States*, 95–97.

24. It is important to distinguish between the ideological implications of frontier land reserves and their material effects. It was the perception that land was available to all, not the realization of its distribution, that made all the difference, as the journalist Charles Nordhoff observed in 1875: "It is plain that the knowledge that any one may [take up land in the public domain] makes those who do not more contented with their lot, which they thus feel to be one of choice and not of compulsion" (quoted in Wrobel, *The End of American Exceptionalism*, 10). Indeed, the entire discourse of frontier exceptionalism depended on repressing the very antidemocratic way in which aboriginal people were displaced in order to make the frontier "available" for settlement.

25. On the relation between frontier anxiety and imperialism, see Wrobel, *The End of American Exceptionalism*, 53–68; Bold, "The Rough Riders at Home and Abroad"; and Kaplan, "Romancing the Empire," 682–84.

26. Wacquant, "Towards a Reflexive Sociology," 36.

27. Modleski, "A Woman's Gotta Do . . . ," 519.

28. Funk & Wagnalls, "Spring Publications."

29. Funk & Wagnalls, "Daniel Everton," and "The Boer Fight for Freedom."

30. Funk & Wagnalls, "Novels for the Vacation Outfit."

31. Quoted in Johnson, *Mary Hallock Foote*, 157.

32. Modleski, "A Woman's Gotta Do . . . ," 521.

33. Tompkins, *West of Everything*, 44.

8   THE COWBOY AND THE GAUCHO   *Zeese Papanikolas*

For the most part the essays in this collection study Wister and the production of The Virginian *as anything but immune from what Victoria Lamont terms the* afflictions of modernity, *however those afflictions might specifically be defined. Beginning and ending with an interpretive reading of the Chicago World's Fair, Wister's presence there, and its cultural contexts, Zeese Papanikolas develops a hemispheric comparativist approach by contrasting* The Virginian *to the nineteenth-century mythologizing of the gaucho figure in two Argentinian epic poems by José Hernández. The world's fair leads Papanikolas to a meditation on empire building and the icons and spectacles that are tributes to it across continents and time, its simulacra, facades, and performances of identities and cultures anticipating postmodernity.*

Like others in this volume, Papanikolas discusses the ideological function of violence and the perennial nostalgia for primitivism to argue that Wister's novel represents "a sort of foundation myth of a new America, an America where the natural aristocrats will tame the chaotic social violence of rustlers" with "the morally superior violence" at their command. Such violence intends to reduce the hemisphere to order just as Edison and Tesla were taming the violence of nature in the machinery displayed at the fair. Whereas in The Virginian *the function of violence seems to be to "obscure" Wyoming politics, in Hernández's two poems about the demise of the gaucho and his way of life the violent code guiding Martín Fierro "is shown to be what it is, fragile, brutal, insufficient against the greater brutality of the* estanciero, *the judge, the army, the government."*

THE FAIR

At the end of June 1893, the not-yet-famous writer Owen Wister and his ever-difficult mother left Philadelphia for the Chicago World's Fair. Wister has provided an image of their arrival at Grand Crossing. As they traveled the few paces to the Illinois Central train, there is Wister, carrying his mother's bags, his mother marching with his hunting rifle over her shoulder, looking like, as he put it, "the Janissaries or something." The image captures a good deal of their relationship, a relationship that Wister spent much of a lifetime trying to unwind. (Somewhere in the rear of the procession was the man with the rest of the luggage and Molly Moss, a member of Wister's piano quartet.)[1]

You could say that Owen Wister had gone West eight years earlier to escape the genteel prison of the East: his father's expectations that he give up music for a proper career; his literary mother's hypochondria and endless exactions on her only child.[2] The West that he came back with was a territory of the imagination formed out of what he had seen and experienced in a few months in Wyoming, but more important, it was the theater for the working out of his own psychological and political drama.

Wister toured the exhibition halls of the fair, watched the fireworks at night, bumped into friends, listened to the classical music that he loved. Finding the need to write, he repaired to the Hunter's Cabin on the Wooded Isle, an ersatz shanty that a couple of weeks earlier he and a few other members of the Boone and Crockett Club had christened with a celebratory dinner. In keeping with the surroundings, Teddy Roosevelt had wanted the drinks to be whiskey and beer, but Wister and the others had outvoted him: seated under the melancholy glass eyes of dead quadrupeds, the party drank champagne.[3]

It is significant that Owen Wister brought with him to Chicago that summer pieces of what nine years later would become *The Virginian*. Chicago, that overnight metropolis of skyscrapers and factories, was the city that, for Americans and for the world at the end of the nineteenth century, represented the future. And Chicago was the gateway to the great West. But it was a new West, one of railroads and vast mining enterprises and industrialized farms.

The West was very much on the mind of another visitor to the fair that week. At the meeting of the American Historical Association held at the fair, a young professor from Wisconsin named Frederick Jackson Turner presented a paper that would become central to American historical thought. In Turner's analysis, the frontier, by which he meant the line of European settlement, became a shifting geographic space that, in his racial mythology, was the site of the creation of what was most powerful in the national character: "Stand at Cumberland Gap and watch the procession of civilization, marching single file – the buffalo following the trail to the salt springs, the Indian, the fur-trader and hunter, the cattle-raiser, the pioneer farmer – and the frontier has passed by. Stand at South Pass in the Rockies a century later and see the same procession with wider intervals between."[4]

That conquest was all but over. Turner had begun his paper by observing that the superintendent of the census for 1890 had declared in a recent bulletin that the frontier had closed. In that same year General Miles, grand marshal of the exposition's opening parade, had directed operations against the Ghost Dancers of the Dakotas from Chicago's Pullman Building. The ghosts of which the dancers had dreamed had not come to drive the white men from the land. Sitting Bull had been murdered at his cabin door. At Wounded Knee the ghost shirts had not protected Big Foot and the Miniconjous from the Springfields and the Hotchkiss cannons of the Seventh Cavalry. The Indian resistance was gone, but so was the "free land" – Turner's phrase – that had drawn the white settlers. The first phase of American history had ended, Turner concluded, but he was confident that American energy would continually demand "a wider field for its exercise."[5] Turner was not able to see over the ridgeline of the future to San Juan Hill and Manila Bay and could not know, of course, how portentously, in retrospect, that phrase would ring.

Two days after Turner presented his paper, while Wister was still wandering about the precincts of the fair, there was another talk given on life on the frontier, but this frontier was far to the south. Like the cowboys of Wyoming, whom Wister was trying to capture on the page, the impoverished gauchos of Paul Groussac's Argentina were anachronisms: civilization was killing them, and their way of life, just as they had supplanted the Indians. It was something that Groussac welcomed, as he welcomed the massive European immigration that he hoped would purify the mestizo population and put an end to the gauchos, those centaur-like drovers, with their skill with *lazo* and bolas, their knife fights and their fatalism and their poetry, as a kind of separate people:

The tribes are to-day driven back and scattered in the desert, where they gradually die out; and the gauchos have taken their place, giving way in their turn to the European immigration, or transmuting themselves by contact and blood mixture. . . . Stables take the place of the old *corral*. From the next railroad station, the enriched landlord drives to his *estancia*. The old farm house has become a fine country dwelling, sometimes a castle with gardens and park. There are large farms at one hundred leagues from Buenos Ayres, formerly in the power of the Indians, where now English teams cross the plains, and where you go to dinner in a dress coat. The European breeders have thus thrust away the gaucho towards the old style farms, in the desert. It is there he is yet to be found, but weakened and impoverished by the contact with civilization, whenever he did not blend with the urban people.[6]

The gaucho was becoming, for Groussac, a kind of relic, like those curious tomes stored in the Biblioteca Nacional whose librarian he had the honor to be. The gaucho's racial distinction was, it turns out, only the faintest tinge: "The gaucho himself, tall and elegant, of Arabic type and often fine-looking, has in his veins but little Indian blood, diminished each generation by added European elements. The first cross-breeding with an immigrant girl completes the purifying. . . . In some years, the gaucho of the plains will be no more than a legend and a memory."[7]

A legend and a memory. Well enough. But a legend and a memory that would continue to haunt Argentina, and not just in the salons of the literati and the volumes gathering dust on shelves of Groussac's library.

We will go back sixty years.

PRIMITIVES AND ARISTOCRATS

This is Charles Darwin, writing in 1832, off on what would be the great adventure of his youth and the great intellectual adventure of his age:

At night we stopped at a pulperia, or drinking-shop. During the evening a great number of Gauchos came in to drink spirits and smoke cigars: their appearance is very striking; they are generally tall and handsome, but with a proud and dissolute expression of countenance. They frequently wear their moustaches, and long black hair curling down their backs. With their brightly colored garments, great spurs clanking about their heels, and knives stuck as daggers (and often so-used) at their waists, they look a very different race of men from what might be expected from their name of Gauchos, or simple countrymen. Their politeness is excessive: they never drink their spirits without expecting you to taste it; but whilst making their exceedingly graceful bow, they seem quite as ready, if occasion offered, to cut your throat.[8]

For six months Darwin rode with the gauchos, hunted with them, boondoggled himself with a pair of bolas, and dined on *ñandu* ("ostrich"). (Indeed, Darwin verified a new species of the American rhea, subsequently named after him, only when he had almost finished eating it.)

The gauchos with whom Darwin lived and hunted were in transition from independent seminomadic existence to feudal vassalage. The pampas, where once anyone with a *lazo* and a set of bolas and mounted on a good *pingo* (saddle horse) could eat for nothing from the flocks of ostriches and the droves of wild cattle, were now being cut up into huge feudal estates. Soon the pressures of modern economy and liberal leadership would force the gauchos into even greater servitude. Thirteen years hence the liberal politician and writer Domingo Sarmiento would find the very source of his country's evils, its incessant civil wars, its violence, and its backwardness in the gaucho.[9] But Darwin would never forget the first night that he had ever spent under the open sky, the "deathlike stillness of the plain, the dogs keeping watch, the gipsy-group of Gauchos making their beds round the fire," and the high enjoyment and independence of these men, who needed only pasture for their horses, a muddy puddle of water, meat, and firewood to live in luxury.[10]

Aristocrats (and, of course, artists, who frequently imagine themselves aristocrats) have always been fascinated by a certain kind of primitive. Byron's Greek and Albanian mountaineers, Baudelaire's and Chataubriand's imaginary North American Indians, Delecroix's Arabs: what these primitives have in common with the nobility is a natural sense of superiority, a dandyesque vanity, martial courage. Like their European admirers, they are epicures and erotic adventurers. But more important, their societies are seen as prior to history, antedating the social changes of industrial life and its democratic leveling – in short, all that threatens the superiority of the aristocrat and his supposedly "timeless" values. The code of the savage, like the code of the aristocrat, is seen as simple, inflexible, and impervious to the battering rams of economic and historical change. Let us not forget that the youthful Darwin and his scientific objectivity with him were born to the gentry, and for all Darwin's willingness to sleep under a greasy poncho, he had taken a manservant to attend him when he boarded the *Beagle.* Of course the twenty-three-year-old Darwin admired the gauchos. Of course he admired General Juan Manuel Rosas, who outgauchoed the gaucho, who had been so unfailingly courteous to him, and who, he accurately foresaw, would soon become dictator of Argentina, although Darwin could not have predicted the oceans of blood that would flow over Rosas's boots.

Darwin came back from that young man's voyage, as we know, haunted with paradoxes of creation that would one day find their solution in a powerful vision of all life as a vast and unending struggle for existence. But thirty years after *The Origin of Species* arrived with a distressing noise in the parlors of Victorian consciousness the world had grown thoroughly comfortable with the struggle for existence. Riding up there on the Ferris wheel at the World's Columbian Exposition, Henry Adams, who had visited Chicago a few months before Owen Wister, Frederick Jackson Turner, and Paul Grousac (he would be named president in absentia at the same meeting of the American Historical Association that heard Turner's paper), had pondered the chaos of the fair with horror and delight. He would later observe that there had been no need for the movers and shakers of the world to worry about Darwinism after all: "It was the very best substitute for religion; a safe, conservative, practical, thoroughly Common-law deity."[11]

To an astute observer, the fair might have spread out in a kind of Darwinian map that relegated the losers in the game of history to the fantasy reservation of the Midway, where camels and sword swallowers jostled the crowds on the streets of Cairo (Egypt without the flies and the dirt), belly dancers jiggled, and the recently conquered Dahomeans danced fiercely in their thatched village. As for our own tribes, they were represented by Indian school exhibits, some sadly ineffectual and unnoted protests, and tasteful birch-bark souvenirs. In front of Sitting Bull's cabin, which entrepreneurs had dragged from the Grand River, some wag had propped up a sign: "War Dances Daily." With its Arabs and Indians and Dahomeans safely roped off in little reservations under the power of the industrial world, the fair was almost a textbook on the survival of the fittest. To an America still groggy with Puritanism's long hangover, Calvin's vengeful God separating the sheep from the goats in visible manifestations of his pleasure merged nicely with the tenets of social Darwinism. How convenient it was for science to offer up a secular prop to what they always knew was their moral superiority, these "Easy Winners" in the cakewalk of mankind. Playing itself out amid the palaces and lagoons and the allegorical statuary was a frozen war whose terms had been translated into horsepower and kilowatts. It was as if Von Clausewitz's dictum that the decision by arms was what cash payment was in commerce had simply been reversed.[12] The fittest would survive, had survived. And should anyone miss the point, there was a full-size concrete mock-up of the battleship *Illinois* over at the Naval Pier, while, presiding over all, rose the Krupp pavilion with its monster cannon. (But, one could ask, looking at the hodgepodge of grace and banality and instruments of naked power that the fair presented, fittest for what?)

THE USES OF NOSTALGIA

Twenty-some years before Paul Groussac declared the gaucho dead in his Chicago talk, a ten-peso pamphlet appeared in Buenos Aires that would enshrine this figure in Argentine national mythology. The title of the poem that the pamphlet printed was *El gaucho Martín Fierro.*

The story that serves as the background to both *The Virginian* and Hernández's *Martín Fierro* is the same story told in brief by Groussac. We see a vast prairie, home of mounted Indians, who, pushed back, give way to the horseback cattle herders of an alien civilization, who themselves are doomed to annihilation by the driving forces of the modern world. But Hernández and Wister come from different stock, and their positions on this process are different. There is much cruelty in the frontier of *Martín Fierro,* as much racism and violence and xenophobia and exploitation as one could wish, but it is a frontier mercifully free of John Calvin.

Hernandez's story begins with an idyll, the primitive Eden of freedom and sexual happiness of the old days on the pampas:

> I knew this land
> when the gaucho lived free
> and had his little house
> and his woman and kids . . . .
> That was a delight – to see
> how he spent his days.

The passage presents the gauchos waking at dawn to gather around the fire, passing the gourd of maté while the "chinas" – their women – still lie rolled in their ponchos asleep. When daybreak comes, the gauchos strap on their spurs, collect lassos and whips as their mounts whinny and stamp at the hitching rail, and a horse breaker rides a pitching colt out of the corral:

> Those were the days!
> It made you proud
> To see a bronc-buster ride.[13]

The poem establishes a myth, the myth of the times that are gone: its whole meaning will be played off against this secular gaucho Eden and the fall from its grace. In *Martín Fierro* nostalgia has a good deal of the original Greek sense, "return pain" (from *nostos,* "return," and *algos,* "pain"). The pain held up against return, the pain of never being able to return. That past, for Fierro's creator, was personal as well as historical. If Owen Wister suffered from having had too much of mama, Hernández seems to have suffered from not having had enough. Shunted from relative to relative in the dangerous days he found himself born into in 1834, his mother's death when he was nine sent him to live with his father, who was managing a huge ranch. As with Wister, the ranching frontier was a site of recuperation, for as a child Hernández suffered from a lung condition. The ranch, the gauchos Hernández lived with and, it is claimed, fought Indians alongside, marked him for life. The idyll of the early passages of the poem stands for a world without time, a world without history. For if Hernández lacked enough mothering, he had far too much history. In 1852 the dictator Rosas was defeated at the Battle of Caseros. Hernández was eighteen. He joined the Federalist cause against the victorious city-based Unitarios and for nine years fought in major battles until his side was finally defeated at Pavon. Against the dream of the past is the reality of history – a personal history of orphanhood, loss, war, defeat, and exile. Amnestied, Hernández returned to Argentina, continued his journalistic polemics, and, of course, wrote his poem.

The Virginian, too, is a work of nostalgia. Published in 1902, Wister was well aware that the West that it represented was no longer there (if it ever was is another matter); but the nostalgia of Wister's novel is a more subtle tool than Hernández's. It is a sort of emotional subterfuge to hide and distort the violent elements of a history of which the Virginian himself is a mover. The idyll of sexual renewal in nature – the Virginian's honeymoon – will become a reward for his violent victory over the frontier as civilization bringer. That victory may have represented a victory that Wister had to win over himself: the frontiers of America were like the frontiers of music, and both cowboying and composing respected only talent. The musical world was one in which a young patrician like Wister might be thrown together, higgledy-piggledy, with anyone. In that genteel bohemia, as in the saloons and shabby eating houses of Medicine Bow, one might find oneself sharing (metaphorically or not) a table or a bed with what the Virginian called "I-talians." Or even, God help us, Jews: if Wister could not civilize music, he could civilize his fictional hero and his fictional frontier.

THE USES OF VIOLENCE

For Frederick Jackson Turner – just three years after Wounded Knee, he curiously omits all but the most oblique reference to the Indian wars – the violence of the frontier was, quite literally, a footnote, a "line of scum" of vigilantes and desperadoes that "the waves of the advancing civilization bore before them."[14] But Wister, more prescient here than the Wisconsin professor, knew that violence wasn't the line of scum before the advancing civilization; it was the wave itself. The role of Wister's hero, the Virginian, is thus to turn a historical process into a mythological one, to justify, in his person, the civilizing function of violence – when it is in the right hands, of course. That is, when it is on the side of the inevitable historical cycle that will turn the West from a "lawless" frontier into a "lawful" civilization, a civilization increasingly incorporated, increasingly under the control of its elites. Recent studies of western violence have argued that far from being the sum of random acts of violent men in an untamed land, major violence was the result of wars of incorporation, where powerful interests fought among themselves for control of pasturelands and water rights, for railroads, and finally, against laboring men in an industrialized economy, just as they had earlier fought against Indians and Mexicans.[15] The Lincoln County War, which gave us Billy the Kid, was one such war; the Johnson County War, which gave us the Virginian, was another. Wister is explicit about the ideological function of his book. In his rededication of the novel to the cowboy president Theodore Roosevelt, in 1911, Wister says, "If this book be anything more than an American story, it is an expression of American faith."[16] But the "faith" that Wister means is implied by the next sentence, for this particular democracy has many enemies, both on Wall Street and among the labor unions. Thus, between what Wister sees as the anarchy of capital and the anarchy of labor comes his middle path, a democracy that can be directed only by a natural aristocrat like the Virginian, this "handsome, ungrammatical son of the soil," with his "perfect civility" (10),[17] who is, for all that, a man who "knows his business" (2), or by an aristocrat born, like Theodore Roosevelt. Roosevelt was not only a cowboy and a warrior and a president but also a member of Wister's own club at Harvard – a fact that is of no little importance to Wister, who wrote a biography of his idol and friend.[18] He was the ideal representative of a leadership based on bon ton.

Like *Martín Fierro*, and like other epics that rely on or seek to establish an ethos, Wister's book presents itself as a series of contests. Wister calls these contests *games*. And the ideological point that he is making is clear when he titles a chapter sequence "The Game and the Nation." The Virginian's superiority in contests of wit, in tall-tale telling, and in "innocent" lying show his natural superiority, a superiority that Wister directly sees as the basis of American democracy, a political system based not on equality (he once wrote his mother that the Constitution was filled with "many phrases that mean little, or nothing")[19] but on a recognition of the superiority of one man over another: "Let the best man win! That is America's word. That is true democracy. And true democracy and true aristocracy are one and the same thing. If anybody cannot see this, so much the worse for his eyesight" (125). The Virginian will beat Trampas, the fraudulent man of the West, in poker, in the fabrication of whoppers, and finally, in gunplay. He will beat Molly Wood, the woman of the East, in the contest of courtship, and he will, true to his boast, make her love him. Wister's argument is carefully constructed. The "games" in which the Virginian triumphs are initially boyish pranks, saloon heroics. Only after the Virginian's expertise is seen to harbor within it an inextricable moral superiority (in Wister, for some reason, the winner is always morally superior) is the reader's own sense of rectitude put to the test. It is done to a turn. The necessity of this civilizing force of violence is anticipated in the most famous scene in the book, where the Virginian withholds it: when you call me that, smile.

Trampas's seething need for revenge will impel the plot to its climax, the shoot-out in Medicine Bow, where we will finally learn who is the real expert. For we have seen by now that the Virginian is a brave man, a man who will measure his force. His violence will thus have a moral imperative to it; it will rid the range of cowards – rustlers, bad men – of all, in short, who stand in the way of civilization. Or to put it another way, this is, after all, a Wyoming that is remembering the 1892 Johnson County War, in which major stockmen imported a trainload of "experts" from Texas to clean out men they called rustlers[20] – all those who stand in the way of power. Thus, *The Virginian* can be read as a sort of foundation myth of a new America, an America where the natural aristocrats will tame the chaotic social violence of rustlers (or of unassimilable aliens in New York, strikers in Chicago, decadent Spaniards in Cuba and the Philippines, rebellious Filipino nationalists, and stray Central American patriots). Armed with this morally superior violence, Winchesters, Krags, and Gatling guns, this new generation of American leaders would reduce the hemisphere to order just as Edison and Tesla were taming the violence of nature in the machinery displayed at the fair.

Violence in *Martín Fierro* is of another quality. This poem is, you might say, an epic written from the bottom up. Fierro is not one of the winners of the social war. Modernity is not raising him to the top but crushing him and his brother gauchos. Fierro's natural superiority in singing games and games of violence leads only to social ruin. The free gauchos of the past, living off ostriches and wild cattle, have been pushed to the limits of survival by the conquest of the pampas by *estancieros* (ranch owners) and armies. They have become rustlers, deserters, and outlaws.[21] The poem is one long angry and finally tragic lament sung by the losers in the game of the nation.

If the function of *The Virginian* is to obscure the politics of Wyoming violence, violence in *Martín Fierro* begins with a political act. Like a good gaucho, Fierro has stayed away from the elections (a good gaucho, of course, doesn't give a damn for such things). The Judge, who already has a grudge against him, labels Fierro as one of the opposition – the poor cowboy can't even get the word right – and sends him to the frontier in a forced army draft.[22] The opening of the action of *Martín Fierro* encapsulates the differences in the method of the two works at hand: *The Virginian* mystifies power; *Martín Fierro* lays it bare.

The frontier, that far edge of European settlement, is seen in Hernández's epic, not à la Turner and Wister, as the site of those refining fires out of which character is formed, but as a swindle. Badly fed, almost unarmed (the officers have sold all the cartridges to the ostrich hunters), unpaid, making ineffectual raids against the Indians, the gaucho conscripts' real function on the frontier is to provide unpaid labor digging ditches and herding cattle on the officers' ranches. After protesting his lack of pay, Fierro is brutally staked out like a skin to dry.[23] The symbolism would not have been lost on anyone who knew the pampas in the old days. Cattle there had once been so plentiful that they could be slaughtered at need if the hides – the only thing then of value – were staked and left for their owners. What the staking punishment says is that the gaucho's "meat" – whatever he has inside him – is worthless to his "owner." His "hide" is all that matters. A switch in the rules had turned gauchos into chattel, just as it had turned poor Wyoming homesteaders and cowboys into rustlers. Living off the land on the Río de la Plata and branding mavericks on the Powder River had, with the flick of a pen, become criminal acts.[24] Fierro sees his chance and deserts.

After three years on the frontier, Fierro comes back to see his home – his *ranchito* – fallen into ruin. His cattle have been sold to pay rent; his wife has run off with a fancy man in order to survive (it is significant that Fierro does not blame her); his boys have gone off to make their way as orphans, seeking whatever work or shelter they can find. The idyll is ended.

The Gaucho Martín Fierro is, in a way *The Virginian* can never be, the story of a people. How many cowboys, after all, were there? Ten thousand or so in the heart of the range?[25] The cowboys' heyday was only a few brief decades. By 1902 Wister had declared them gone, leaving only a trail of empty sardine boxes to mark their passing. Fierro's experiences are not those of a unique figure or of the representative of a handful of backcountry laborers. The violence visited on him is experienced as irrational and amoral, but it is driven by the logic of feudalism and then, ultimately, and more disastrously, by the logic of modernity. The encroachment on the pampas by the *estancieros,* the civil wars in which the gauchos, following any scrap of a flag, found themselves caught up, the laws that proscribed their movements, the miserable wages, the internal passports that they needed to show that they were workers for one *estancia* or another, all are effects of a war waged against a free people.

Fierro's own violence, too, is an irrational response to the pain and rage of the violence visited on him. Homeless now, his family scattered, a deserter, he finds himself at a country dance. Drunk, spoiling for trouble, he insults a black cowboy and kills him in a knife fight. The very senselessness of the killing and Fierro's remorse after it tell us much about Fierro's world: it is a place where a poor man has nothing but his honor. At an isolated *pulperia* Fierro kills another man, a braggart and bully. He is an outlaw.

THE USES OF FRIENDSHIP

Surrounded by the constables who have come to arrest him, the gaucho Martín Fierro methodically takes off his spurs, cinches up his *chiripiá* (loose trousers), and prepares to fight. In the midst of the battle, one of the constables, Sergeant Cruz, changes sides. Back to back they fight until their assailants are dead or have fled in terror.

Friendship is inherently anarchic. It is a primitive thing. It is prior to law; it challenges family, social order, the state. Think of Achilles and Patrocles, who defy the Greeks. Or Gilgamesh and Enkidu, who defy a goddess. Or of David and Jonathan, who defy a father and a king. Just as the Virginian's move toward marriage will signify the triumph of civilization, so his move against friendship signifies his alliance with power. Fierro, the outsider, will stay with his friend.

When Cruz throws off his insignia and joins Fierro, there is no turning back for either of them. Henceforth to be an outlaw is to be a man. Borges – although this wasn't, I believe, his point – says this by giving Cruz his own history in his stunning little story "A Biography of Tadeo Isidoro Cruz (1829–1874)." Fierro and Cruz are, in this act of defiance, in fact, the same man. Now there is nowhere else for them to go but to a land beyond the frontier. They set off together to the realm of the Indians. As if to signal what crossing this line means, Fierro smashes his guitar: the Indians are beyond not only law – a law that has been only a tool of irrational power – but speech as well. *El gaucho Martín Fierro* is over.

The Virginian has, in fact, a number of friends. Two of them are especially significant: the unnamed dude narrator and the cowboy Steve. The narrator is in love with the Virginian (unlike the affection of the schoolmarm Molly Wood, it was love at first sight for the narrator), and ultimately, through his control of the narrative, he wins the Virginian to his side. But this victory by the narrator and his world comes at a cost. For the Virginian's other friend, the lighthearted Steve, has gone over to the other side and become a rustler.[26] The Virginian chooses power/law over friendship/anarchy and leads the posse that hangs Steve.

The hanging, which happens offstage, is meant to be a stern moral moment. But if this hanging happens off the pages of the novel, it also happens off the pages of the codes of law. A fair amount of ink is devoted in *The Virginian* to a special pleading for the necessity of such extralegal violence on the frontier. Yet the violence of the hanging and its illegitimacy are undercut by another story, the story of how men should die. Unlike his miserable fellow rustler "Poor Ed," Steve dies game to the last. He, too, is an expert. An expert at having himself stretched. And thus Steve gives a moral imprimatur to his own lynching. Later on, by way of a scrawled note on a newspaper, we learn that Steve said nothing to the Virginian during his ordeal for fear of "playing the baby." Not only has Steve's stoic behavior been an act of courage but the hanging has been ratified by an act of love. What more could any lynch mob want?

THE RETURN OF MARTÍN FIERRO

José Hernández is rich. He is a senator. He is an *estanciero*. His book is praised even by his enemies, and it is treasured by exquisites and literati in Buenos Aires salons. Amid the tinned sardines, bottles of gin, and bags of maté on the shelves of isolated *pulperias* it is the only book, and illiterate singers know whole passages by heart, as if it rose fully-formed out of the country itself. Gauchos visiting the city point Hernández out: There goes Martín Fierro, they say. Hernández's politics have undergone a shift. He makes a speech supporting Buenos Aires as the capital. He is reconciling himself to the modern world. It is time for Fierro to return from the Indians.

The final transition to modernity in Argentina had been violent. The victory of the modernizing Unitarios had only accelerated the laws hemming in the gauchos, and waves of immigrants were flooding the cities and colonizing the pampas with farms. New Year's Day, 1872, the year of *The Gaucho Martín Fierro*'s publication, was marked by a violent massacre of gringos by gauchos in Tandil. The year of the publication of Martín Fierro's sequel, *The Return of Martín Fierro*, 1879, was the year that marked the beginning of Julio Roca's "Conquest of the Desert" and the final breaking of the Indians' power.

We should consider the Indians. The Indians, who exist only at the margins of *The Virginian*,[27] become the symbolic midpoint that connects the two poems that make up the epic of Martín Fierro. In crossing the line into Indian country, Cruz and Fierro have crossed a kind of ethical boundary, where nothing contains the savage blood in men, neither law nor the code of gaucho machismo and tradition. In this land of howling wretches, where rape and torture are the norm, Fierro and Cruz are captives. A few years before the publication of *The Return*, Hernández's colleague Lucio V. Mansilla had painted a very different kind of frontier beyond the line of forts. His book – *A Visit to the Ranquel Indians*, a memoir of a diplomatic journey – is a masterpiece. Mansilla's Indians are products of a complex history, on a higher cultural level in many ways than the poor gauchos; the Ranquel camps are a home to exiled politicians and losers in the civil war, itinerant missionaries easing their way with rivers of alcohol, political schemers, outlaws. If Fierro's racism strikes one as false to history, it is true to his type, for in fact, both Indians and gauchos were doomed in Argentina and fighting for the same shrinking sliver of cultural freedom. But for all their melodramatic violence, Hernández's Indians are symbolic of another savagery. The horrors that Hernández paints beyond white civilization stand, consciously or unconsciously, for the horrors of the civil wars. The savage caciques are, after all, no more savage than the brutal caudillos Facundo, Rosas, and the Unitario commanders, whose throat slashings, tortures, and summary executions of captives – what Hernández called "the politics of the knife" – had pushed the new nation, not across a geographic and racial frontier, but across an ethical one. The "nine terrible years,"[28] as Hernández called them, of civil war were a descent into absolute savagery. If Hernández knew little of the Indians, he knew much at firsthand of the wars that had desolated Argentina. Cruz's death of the black pox in the Indian camp may stand as well for the epidemic violence of the 1850s and 1860s.

Once more Fierro escapes. He kills a savage in another of the duels that marks the book and heads off to civilization with the white woman captive he has saved. But saving a life does not lead here to the romantic bond that in *The Virginian* is the reward for a reclaimed civilization: at the first sight of the white settlements Fierro leaves the woman and heads home alone. He is, in the land of the civilized, still an outlaw.

It is now that Fierro reunites with his two boys and finds the son of Cruz. Their stories make up a large part of the return, and they are tales of orphanhood, prison, and the picaresque adventures of Cruz's son, who has lived by his wits. Tales, in other words, of education. But what the poem teaches us, its readers, is another story.

Fierro's story ends with a singing contest. After he and the boys have told their adventures, Fierro encounters a black singer, and the two face off in a battle of singers – *payadors*. This singing contest is an answer to the miserable and ordinary knife fight that has led to the killing of the black cowboy in the earlier poem and Fierro's outlaw life. It is Fierro's intemperate speech that has led to what the gauchos called, with a certain amount of laudable understatement, his *desgracia* – his "misfortune" – that is, to his becoming a murderer. Now, in *The Return* the blood violence of the duel is transmuted into the fluid truth of song.

The old frontier has ended. The poem has nowhere left to go in history. Fierro poses El Moreno – "The Dark One" – a series of riddling questions, and in answer the mysteries of nature are opened before us.

Fierro first asks El Moreno what song the heavens sing, then the earth, then the sea and the night. He asks where love is born, and squatting outside a *pulperia* all the universe becomes a song of mystery and power.

It's a dark question
you've asked me to handle . . . .

The bird who sweeps the air
wherever he likes – he loves.
And when he's finished with his run
he perches on some branch
and with his bright song
he calls to his loving mate.[29]

What is the thing men call the law? is the last question in the series. Here the tone changes: the law is a spider's web that catches only the small, a sword that does not hurt the powerful man who has its hilt in his hand. Fierro's turn to answer the riddles of El Moreno continues this line. God's universe is one: man, not God, made number, measure, and weight to measure man's sins. One more riddle, and if Fierro answers, El Moreno concedes, he wins. What is time? Fierro's answer shows that it is man who has disturbed the unity of nature; consciousness itself has divided the world: man splits time up to know how long he has to live.

Then El Moreno is put one final riddle, on *estancia* matters: a riddle far simpler and less grand than the universal questions of his first trial.[30] He cannot, will not, answer it (is he a kind of drugstore cowboy, after all?) but reveals himself to be the youngest brother of the black cowboy whom Fierro has killed in the first poem. The singing insults escalate, but the coming fight is broken up before it starts. Modernity has won the pampas. The wars between Federalists and Unitarios are over; the Indians have been massacred and driven off; the heroic age of the gaucho has ended.

Fierro leaves the three boys with some limp saws suitable to survival in a nonheroic age. He and the boys make a pact (we do not know what), change their names (we do not learn them), and separate for good. This final silence is a counterpart of Fierro smashing his guitar in the earlier book. Fierro and the boys ride off alone into the tragic dignity of art. The aristocratic singularity of the winner in *The Virginian* becomes the proud solitude of the defeated in *Martín Fierro*.

THE RETURN OF THE VIRGINIAN

Ambushed by the Indians (or was it the outlaws? – the text is unclear), the Virginian is nursed back to health by Molly Wood, goes off to hunt the rustlers, hangs his friend Steve, and returns. There remains one more task for him and the book to accomplish: the showdown with Trampas. The West must be rid of this drunken, boasting, lying inexpert. "Can't yu' see how it must be about a man?" the Virginian says. And so it is, and so Molly, who has said that she will not marry the Virginian if he goes out to fight Trampas, seeing him return alive, relents. Both the Virginian and Martín Fierro live by a code. But in Wister's novel the code is sufficient – sufficient to found a violent political philosophy on. In Hernández's poem the code is shown to be what it is, fragile, brutal, insufficient against the greater brutality of the *estanciero*, the judge, the army, the government, and perhaps the inevitable tides of history.

It is his victory over the old days that allows the Virginian to marry, at the conclusion of the book. The marriage serves an ideological function: the Virginian, the man of the West, the natural aristocrat, has triumphed over the East of inherited tradition, inconvenient moral values, and – we should never forget – money: he has won his eastern bride. But Molly Wood has won as well. She has educated the Virginian, made a present-able man of him, and allowed him to transcend class barriers. And so has Owen Wister won. Just as the Virginian has wooed Molly Wood, of the Starks of Vermont (no china rolled up in a poncho for him), Wister has wooed the Virginian, won him from his boyhood into the responsibility of maturity, from the frontier to the modern world.

For underneath his chaps, the Virginian is a gentleman. Theodore Roosevelt convinced his friend Wister to delete the brutal incident of the abused horse in the Balaam and Pedro chapter from the original story; in the novel we know that the rancher Balaam has done something horrible to his mount, but we do not know what. And just as the lynching of Steve and Ed is not witnessed by the narrator but tersely reported to him by the Virginian, so does it happen offstage in the theatrical version of the book on which Wister collaborated. Wister and Roosevelt were gentlemen, and the West that they rode to fame must be seen as a fit school for gentlemen.

To say that the Virginian could raise himself by his bootstraps and be-come as presentable in his made-to-measure tweed suit as any Philadel-phia lawyer was as much as saying that as a class Philadelphia lawyers were really all exceptionally talented cowboys under *their* made-to-measure suits. This Horatio Alger tale (without the fairy-tale coincidences) is Wis-ter's way of reconciling himself to personal defeat. The wild West of his aborted musical career has become the mild west-of-Philadelphia West of the successful popular novelist.

Is it permissible to imagine, as Henry James did, the book that Wister might have written? James praised his friend's novel but didn't care for the ending. He would not have had Molly Wood go back on her word and would have had the Virginian "perish in his flower & in some splendid way."[31] But that way, the James way, points to literature; Wister takes the trail that leads to ideology. By contrast, in the end, Martín Fierro rides off into the indeterminacy of a very different kind of work.

Two thousand years before the publication of *The Virginian*, a Roman poet received a commission to provide a synthetic foundation myth for an empire very like the one Owen Wister found himself serving. Like the United States in 1893, Augustan Rome was a new power, just coming out of civil war, its culture largely derivative, its wealth and military might ominous, hoping to make up in raw energy what it lacked in historical depth. Because he understood the contradictions of empire and how much empire cost, Virgil gave the world a work of propaganda that asked dark questions under its triumphant facade, a sort of literary Chicago World's Fair. We see the fire of Dido's funeral pyre as the fleet sails to Italy and imperial destiny, we see the noble Turnus fall into the dust in the duel that will be the end of Italy and the beginning of Rome, we see the marriage between two races that will become an empire, and we wonder if Virgil's Aeneas, like Wister's Virginian, a victor in love and in single combat, is not a hollow kind of hero after all.

SPECTACLE

Of course it was all a dream. José Hernández's pampas, Wister's Wyoming. The horseback riders. The cattle lowing. The vast sky. The Argentine pavilion in Chicago had its walls covered with tanned hides and pelts and encompassed vast exhibits of wool in the fleece. It was the pastoral industrialized. The displays of bolas and long Indian spears were confined to neat cases, relics of the past. The Indians and gauchos themselves were hung on the walls of the art gallery. If Hernández walked through these galleries, it was only as a portly ghost: he had died seven years before, attending to his senatorial duties. A living Owen Wister, however, was there to stare a very real Wyoming in the face. By the time of the fair, Wyoming, the youngest state, ranked third in the nation in area of irrigated lands and second in mileage of irrigation canals. Arranged in glass tubes were samples of grain; there were native and cultivated grasses, hay, vegetables. More impressive, perhaps, was a massive shaft of coal from the Union Pacific's mines at Rock Springs and the little glass tubes of petroleum brought by the Black Hills Oil Company. The Virginian, who had had the foresight to locate his homestead on a coal seam, had played the right side of history.[32] Trampas dead, the frontier closed, the Virginian and Molly Wood ride off into the banality of the happy ending to marry East and West and become part of a new empire of railroads and mines and barbed wire.

In his indispensable studies of the gaucho, Richard W. Slatta has traced the ideological uses to which the gauchos have been put, from the sign of all that is backward, primitive, and impossible in Argentina, to their emblematizing, when they were as good as gone and posed no threat to order, the apotheosis of Argentine identity in the nationalist literature that anticipated Juan Perón.[33] But what do you do with the residue of the dream? The shreds that still linger on waking? Borges knew at least part of the answer. The bloody history of Argentina, out of which Martín Fierro was born, the battles between half-wild armies of Unitarios and Federalists, the atrocities of Facundo and Rosas and Perón, these things were as they never had been.

But in a hotel room in eighteen-hundred sixty-something a man dreamed of a knife fight. A gaucho lifts a black man off the ground with the thrust of his knife, drops him like a bag of bones, watches him writhe in pain and die, squats down to wipe off his knife, unties his horse's bridle and swings up into the saddle slowly, so no one will think he's running away from what he's done. This thing that was once, returns again infinitely; the visible armies have gone and what is left is a common sort of knife fight; one man's dream is part of all men's memory.[34]

The final solitude of Martín Fierro becomes the tragic material of art.

And the American West? That place that Owen Wister of Philadelphia had once stepped out of a train to find? The Easterners have all gone home after a summer or two on a ranch or a hunt in the Wind Rivers or on the Yellowstone. And if the West of which they dreamed was finished – well, they had their trophies, the elk and the buffalo and the bearskin on the study floor. The cowboys they had seen and sometimes ridden with were trophies too. The dudes remembered a tall tale heard around a campfire, horseplay in a pool hall. They had seen hair-raising bronco riding, maybe seen a shot or two fired in a saloon.[35] What was left is a sense of loss. For Owen Wister's friend Theodore Roosevelt, the demise of "the great free ranches, with their barbarous, picturesque, and curiously fascinating surroundings," would inevitably give way to the "onward march" of the American people. But those who had felt the charm of that life, and had "exulted in its abounding vigor and its bold restless freedom," could only regret it for their own sakes and feel sorrow that those of the future would not have seen it.[36] As for the cowboys themselves, they were obsolescent, if not obsolete. The cowpuncher, Wister had written, was not compatible with progress. He had never made a good citizen anyway, only a good soldier.[37] Some of the old cowpunchers had amassed herds of their own and gone broke in the die-off of 1888. Some had married into power, like Teddy Blue Abbott, son-in-law of the redoubtable Granville Stuart. Some had gone to work for power, like Charlie Siringo, who became a Pinkerton detective, sabotaging strikes and battling labor men like the ex-Nevada buckaroo Bill Haywood. And some had no power at all, laid out in the back of a saloon or remembering haunting scraps of songs about the Colorado Trail like the stove-up wrangler some doctor recalled singing in a Duluth hospital ward. Laura was a pretty girl, God Almighty knows.[38] Modernity, with its railroads and meatpacking plants, had created the cowboy; now it was destroying him, as it had destroyed the Argentine gaucho.

Back in Chicago in the fall, Wister pays one last visit to the fair. Like the *Aeneid*, the Chicago World's Fair was an ideological artifact, a Roman triumph frozen into lagoons and fountains and porticos, where the spoils of a world conquered by modernity could be displayed. But the fair is unconscious of the contradictions of the victory that it celebrates. It is unconscious of the wars that the very power of its winners squabbling over the spoils will make inevitable, wars bloodier than any yet known, as modern states would employ the vast resources and technologies at their command to engulf the world. The same forces had already been turned loose in the American West in Texas and New Mexico and in that frowzy little Wyoming dustup called the Johnson County War; but these were only curtain-raisers for the real thing. The first shots of the carnage were almost beginning as the fair ended, a duel with a decaying power over the remains of its empire, and soon Wister's idol, Teddy Roosevelt, would be charging up a Cuban hill in a Brooks Brothers uniform at the head of a bunch of cowboys, would-be cowboys and society boys. It was a war whose conquests disturbed Wister, but it was fought under the terms of the manly virtues and a misappropriated Darwinism for which Wister himself had created a mythological alibi.

Night. The fair blazes with electric light. But across from the entrance to the fair there is another blaze in the darkness.

"Ladies and Gentlemen . . . ," the ringmaster cries. Fifty cents gets you into Buffalo Bill's Wild West. A Congress of Rough Riders of the World. Cowboys, Indians, Cossacks, Vaqueros, Gauchos. The frontier, which had once been a place or a process or an idea,[39] had been transformed: sitting in his seat at Buffalo Bill's, Wister saw his remembered West as spectacle, a traveling show where real Indians and real frontiersmen and cowboys acted out a fantastic script that turned all history into an entertainment.[40] And there, with his own stage version of *The Virginian*, the almost half-dozen movies, the television shows, the who-knows-how-many knockoffs, it would largely remain. Unable to incorporate the contradictions in himself and in his Wyoming into a work of art, Wister has given us an enduring entertainment – a kind of dream, like the gauchos' idyll of the pampas, like the fair, whose marble colonnades and porticos turn out to be plaster of paris and horsehair, for all the steel underpinning of a cruel ideology.

NOTES

1. Wister, ed., *Owen Wister Out West*, 169–70.

2. The Virginian represents "that last pioneer nobleman, roaming the frontier beyond the dominion of a mother culture in the East, representing both its rebellious runaway sons and its most poignant dreams of manhood and freedom" (Mogen, "Owen Wister's Cowboy Heroes," 57).

3. Wister, ed., *Owen Wister Out West*, 164. The Hunter's Cabin is described in Bancroft, *The Book of the Fair*, 449–50. See also Ward, *Boone and Crockett National Collection of Heads and Horns*.

4. Turner, "The Significance of the Frontier in American History" (1920), 12.

5. Turner, "The Significance of the Frontier in American History" (1920), 37.

6. Groussac, *Popular Customs and Beliefs of the Argentine Provinces*, 9–10.

7. Groussac, *Popular Customs and Beliefs of the Argentine Provinces*, 10–11. The racial "purity" of Groussac's gauchos is, of course, wishful thinking. See Slatta, *Comparing Cowboys and Frontiers*, 168–69.

8. Darwin, *Voyage of the Beagle*, 73–74.

9. See Sarmiento, *Facundo*.

10. Darwin, *Voyage of the Beagle*, 85–86.

11. Adams, *The Education of Henry Adams*, 926.

12. Clausewitz, *On War*, 97.

13. Hernández, *Martín Fierro* (1997), lines 133–38 (*El gaucho*), p. 51, and lines 180–81 (*El gaucho*), p. 53. My translation, with generous assistance from Horacio Tubio and Kathleen Weaver.

14. Turner, "The Significance of the Frontier in American History" (1920), 32–33n.

15. See, e.g., Brown, "Western Violence," 5–20.

16. Wister, *The Virginian* (1929/1992), xvii. Page numbers for subsequent quotations will be given in the text.

17. "The creature we call a gentleman lies deep in the hearts of thousands that are born without a chance to master the outward graces of the type" (Wister, *The Virginian*, 10).

18. See Wister, *Roosevelt*.

19. Payne, *Owen Wister*, 251.

20. And women too. Let us not forget the unfortunate Cattle Kate, mentioned *humorously* (see Wister, *The Virginian*, 4).

21. "A philosophical anarchist, the gaucho maintained his custom of free grazing on the open range even after terratenientes gained title to most of the better lands. To the gaucho rustling may have become an act of rebellion against authority and against a new pampa of foreigners and foreign ideas" (Slatta, *Gauchos and the Vanishing Frontier*, 119).

22. The word that Fierro cannot get right is *oposición*, for which he says *esposición* (Hernández, *Martín Fierro*, line 348 [*El gaucho*], p. 348).

Slatta (*Gauchos and the Vanishing Frontier*, 124) quotes an 1857 letter from Domingo Sarmiento to a friend in which Sarmiento claimed that gauchos who resisted voting for governmnent candidates were jailed, put in the stocks, or sent off to the frontier for military duty.

23. The punishment was not uncommon at both *estancias* and military camps.

24. For a good description of how an increasingly powerful ranching elite criminalized the old and well-entrenched custom of free-for-all branding of mavericks in Wyoming, see Lamont (chap. 7 in this volume).

25. Lopez ("Cowboy Strikes and Unions," 327) estimates that between 1870 and 1900 there were never many more than twenty thousand cowboys in all the United States, only about half of whom were working in the major cattle states.

26. As in the case of the transition of the gauchos from drovers to cattle thieves, the meaning of the term *rustler* depends on who is doing the defining (see n. 24 above).

27. We see the Indians in the fictitious dreams of the Virginian in chap. 3 and docily ministering to trainloads of becalmed dudes on the prairies. They are blamed for ambushing the Virginian, but have they? The Viriginian's delirious ravings seem to cast doubt on this.

28. Larraya, "José Hernández," 238.

29. Hernández, *Martín Fierro*, lines 4187–98 (*La vuelta*), p. 282.

30. The riddle translates as, "What's got to be done on an *estancia* in the months that have an *r*?" These are the months of September through April, which are warm enough to do the most important ranch work on the pampas.

31. Quoted in Payne, *Owen Wister*, 201.

32. The prediction of a glowing future for Wyoming's economy was sadly off the mark. See, e.g., Knobloch, "Creating the Cowboy State," where it is argued that the "cowboyification" of the state by commercially successful writers and artists such as Wister, Remington, and Bierstadt, with ties to the industrial centers of America, happened concurrently with, and in fact played a role in, Wyoming's persistent economic stagnation.

33. See Slatta, *Gauchos and the Vanishing Frontier,* esp. chap. 11.

34. Borges, "Martín Fierro," 312–13.

35. "This is what I came West for," says one dude, hearing the Virginian spin his cock-and-bull tale of the frog ranches, and goes off to get his wife (Wister, *The Virginian,* 166).

36. Roosevelt, *Ranch Life and the Hunting Trail,* 24.

37. Wister, "The Evolution of the Cow-Puncher" (1972), 96. Wister himself had thought of writing a novel on "the tragedy of the cowpuncher who survives his own era and cannot adjust himself to the [one] which succeeds it" (cited in White, *The Eastern Establishment and the Western Experience* [1989], 144, from a conversation that in his biography, *Roosevelt,* Wister reported having had with the president in 1912).

38. "Out of past years this rider had, Dr. Chapman's examination disclosed, 'bones of both upper and lower legs broken, fractures of collar bone on both sides, numerous fractures of both arms and wrists, and many scars from lacerations and tramplings, the bones knit any way that God and Nature let them heal'" (Sandburg, *The American Songbag,* 462).

39. "Is a frontier a place, a process, or both?" (Slatta, *Comparing Cowboys and Frontiers,* 6).

40. "While Remington hunted in New Mexico, Wister journeyed from St. Paul to Chicago, where he again visited the World's Fair, this time seeing the Wild West Show of Buffalo Bill" (Vorpahl, *My Dear Wister,* 37). For an excellent comparison of the ethos embodied by Buffalo Bill's "postmodern" verison of the history of the American West and by Turner's frontier, see White, "When Turner and Cody Both Played Chicago."

9   WHAT IF WISTER WERE A WOMAN?   *Melody Graulich*

Near the end of his essay, Zeese Papanikolas asks a series of "what ifs": What if Molly refused the Virginian and he spent the rest of his life in Jamesian irresolution and sexual unfulfillment? What if Trampas killed him, leaving poor Molly spinstering? In her essay, Melody Graulich continues to ponder the various possible Virginians, wondering, What if Wister were a woman? Focusing like others in this volume on the construction and performance of gender, her essay also questions how the gender, and the gendered assumptions, of the author and the reader help construct the text. She looks closely, if obliquely, at Wister's use of the folk tradition of the tall tale. In her reading the dialectical tension in the text is between the clothed public role, often characterized by bluffing and role-playing, by various poker faces, and the naked hidden self. Throwing some wild cards on the table, without worrying about winning the pot, she imagines a literary history characterized, not by reasoned argument, but by bluffs and bets, by "what ifs."

For the ex-colonials the declaration of an American identity meant the assumption of a mask, and it imposed not only the discipline of national self-consciousness, it gave Americans an ironic awareness of the joke that always lies between appearances and reality. . . . Masking is a play upon possibility and ours is a society in which possibilities are many. When American life is most American it is apt to be more theatrical.

RALPH ELLISON, "Change the Joke and Slip the Yoke"

ENTER THE WOMAN

In a revealing passage about book reading, the Virginian and Molly Wood talk about George Eliot's *The Mill on the Floss.* The Virginian calls it a "fine book," but he thinks that "it will keep up its talkin'. Don't let you alone."

He initially assumes that the novel was written by a man, but when Molly corrects him, his response makes perfect sense to him: "A woman [wrote that]! Well, then, o' course she talks too much."[1]

Passages like this have led many readers to conclude that this novel about the West's most beautiful spacious guy presents us with plenty of discouraging words about women, who, apparently, need to learn to stop nagging and speak more sparingly. In an influential essay, Lee Clark Mitchell claims that it "ends with a reactionary thesis of inequality between the sexes and in the process offers a model of male hegemony."[2]

Yet as Mitchell also shows, *The Virginian* itself keeps up its talking: the novel is about talk. Despite the popular perception of the Virginian as silent and violent, Wister did not write about the West in the action-packed style of earlier – and later – male western writers. The Virginian is downright chatty. In fact, if we borrow his hero's literary assessment, Wister writes like a woman.

Wister's kinship to George Eliot goes beyond style. For like *George Eliot*, *Owen Wister* is a pen name designed to hide the identity of the author from the public. As in a crucial scene Molly Wood plays the "man's part" (213), so did the author of *The Virginian* by calling herself Owen Wister. Letters recently discovered in the Wister archives at the Wyoming Historical Society in Redbluff suggest that the novel was actually written by Mary Channing Wister, Owen Wister's wife and the great-granddaughter of William Ellery Channing. Well educated, the youngest member to be appointed to the Philadelphia Board of Education, cofounder of "the socially conscious Civic Club," described by her husband as a "stirrer up and reformer of all things wrong," Molly Wister was as independent as the heroine she created and named after herself.[3] Like Molly Wood, this "New Woman" fell in love with and married a man struggling with "how it must be about a man" (298) in late-nineteenth-century America. She wrote *The Virginian* in an attempt to understand and redefine masculinity, sexual politics, and gender identities. Like many nineteenth-century women writers, she may have felt what Gilbert and Gubar called *the anxiety of authorship* and protected herself by writing from the male point of view and by obscuring her message with a troubling, ambiguous ending.[4] Or perhaps her use of a male pseudonym and a male narrator helped her claim access to the male point of view. Perhaps she thought that only from the male point of view could she convincingly explore its contradictoriness and the discrepancies between the outer and the inner man, could she enter the man's world of the West.

Yet poker-faced as Molly Wister was, *The Virginian* suddenly makes

sense when read as a woman's text. In the questions that it raises about being a western man or woman, about playing a gendered part, the woman's
point of view in the novel never lets us alone. Read as a woman's text, *The
Virginian* offers us new insights into the construction of gender in western literature.

Even before he meets Molly Wood, the Virginian knows that the
woman who signed herself "your very sincere spinster" is "not . . . awful
sincere" (38–39) at all, and Molly Wister, of course, hoped for equally astute readers; she expected to be identified as the not-always-sincere author of *The Virginian*. She always maintained that readers could not believe a woman could write so convincingly in the western tradition of the
tall tale. She was so discouraged at the obtuse reception that her novel received that she gave up writing and devoted her considerable energies to
supplying Delmonico's and the Cliff House with frog's legs from her frog
farm in Tulare, California.

And if you believe this story, do I have a frog farm for you. . . .

A RIGHT SMART OF DIFFERENCE?

"There's cert'nly a right smart o' difference between men and women"
(284), observes the Virginian. Is he right? What if Wister had been a
woman? Just how "different" would *The Virginian* read?

Male hegemony rides again? Mitchell isn't the only recent critic to ex-
pose the novel's supposedly reactionary gender politics; most writers in
this volume agree with him. And when I teach the novel every few years in
my graduate seminar on western literature, my students always bridle at
the way Molly is reined in by her new "master" at the end.[5] Indeed, it is
hard not to feel saddled with lines like, "At the last white-hot edge of ordeal, it was she who renounced, and he who had his way" (312).

But my reading of *The Virginian* is neither dominated nor mastered by
such lines. "He" may have had his way, but so does "she" in the passage
that immediately follows, a passage that celebrates male vulnerability and
the value of communication. When the Virginian shares his feelings with
Molly, she feels a "new bliss . . . to be given so much of him," and in relation to her, he experiences a kind of rebirth: "He never would have
guessed so much had been stored away in him, unexpressed till now"
(312). Sappy romantic, feminist backslider, I find his self-discovery as telling, as revealing, as Molly's momentary renunciation. I like the Virginian
(if I squirm around his racism). He's smart, funny, fast-talking, sensitive,

kind, sexy. It seems to me that the novel doesn't reinscribe male hegemony but do-si-dos with its implications.

I often teach *The Virginian* paired with Mary Hallock Foote's "The Fate
of a Voice" (1886), a story about a young woman "with a voice" who initially refuses to marry her engineer lover because his decision to live in
the West will prevent her from becoming a professional singer, will silence
her. Closely echoing Foote's own life, the story raises all the familiar questions of nineteenth-century women's texts about why a woman should
have to choose between career and marriage and about a woman's right
to "speak" in public. After temporarily losing her voice, the heroine,
Madeline, decides to marry her engineer and live in Idaho, a move that
the narrator seems to applaud, although she ironically acknowledges that
the "voice was lost." On the surface, the text appears to celebrate her capitulation and his mastery, but as we would expect, it is filled with qualifi-
ers and ironies and submerged rebellion. In my seminar, I watch as my students, well trained in feminist criticism, focus not on the story's overt text
but on its "silenced" subtext, not on its ending but on the argument
where Madeline challenges her lover's assumptions and forcefully articulates her ambitions and needs, as they suggest that the story reveals
Foote's conflicts and her efforts to challenge attitudes about women artists, as they excuse or explain away the ending as "socially constructed."

My students are generous readers, a quality I certainly hope that I encourage. But I sometimes wonder why they don't bring that same generos-
ity to their reading of *The Virginian*, why they can't or won't cut Wister
some slack. Foote exacts of Madeline far more renunciation than Wister
requires of Molly, yet contemporary feminist readers of Foote's text, female or male, attend less to the story's capitulations to "male hegemony"
than to its resistances. I suggest that if Wister were a woman, if *The Virginian* were a woman's text, we would likely read it as tied up in its own knotty
questions about masculinity, gender identity, and marriage, presenting
the kind of often-conflicted, compromised resolutions that we find in its
"sister texts," those by writers like Eliot, Foote, Louisa May Alcott, Elizabeth Stuart Phelps, and Kate Chopin. Read in the company of women
rather than as the progenitor of the western, *The Virginian* takes on a new
look. Let me develop just one example.

In the influential gunfight scene, which supposedly defined western
masculinity, the Virginian has recently been much critiqued for refusing
to accept Molly's ultimatum that she will not marry him if he fights Trampas. When the bishop reminds him, "Your life has been your own for fif-

teen years. But it is not your own now. You have given it to a woman," he responds, "Yes; I have given it to her. But my life's not the whole of me. I'd give her twice my life. . . . But I can't give her – her nor anybody in heaven or earth – I can't give my – my – we'll never get at it, seh!" (296). Uncharacteristically inarticulate, the Virginian struggles to define his most fundamental self. Is this stubborn male dominance? A mastering male self-assertion?

Let's read the passage in relation to a woman's text published only three years earlier, where the heroine says, "I would give up the unessential. . . . I would give my life for my children; but I wouldn't give myself." As the narrator says, "She thought of Leonce and the children. They were a part of her life. But they need not have thought that they could possess her, body and soul."[6]

Although some critics have pointed out Edna Pontillier's egotism, Kate Chopin's *The Awakening* has generally been celebrated for asserting that a woman has a self outside marriage and human relations, a self to which she owes her first loyalty. Like Edna, the Virginian believes that despite love and marriage, his life is still his own.

Of course, postmodernists might suggest that both the Virginian and Edna – and perhaps their authors as well – presume a fiction: that there is an independent self, apart from socially constructed roles. The Virginian can hold onto this fiction, keep his self-assertion intact, because, in the West, in "this great playground of young men" (41), he is offered a spectrum of masculine roles, from Shorty to Trampas, from the "parson" McBride to Judge Henry, from Steve to the narrator. In true Darwinian fashion, the Virginian gains power both through dominance, killing off the men he might have been, and through adaptation, learning to mimic, chameleonlike, the qualities of those with "quality." Edna, refusing to dress up in either of her two ill-fitting "unnatural" costumes, Mademoiselle or Madame, can maintain the illusion of an independent self only by self-annihilation.

Yet both texts assert that our identities are socially staged, defined by the clothes that we wear to perform: Edna strips hers off to swim off to sea, while the Virginian, although "fonder of good clothes" than his wife, exchanges his silk kerchiefs and cowboy hat for a tailored homespun suit and "usual straw hat" (313) for his trip East. While the Virginian can change his clothes, he can't get back to that naked self he imagines during his island honeymoon. As fully as Chopin, Wister sees how the clothes, the roles, construct – sometimes constrict, sometimes empower – the man. Late in the novel, Scipio's "Don't change your clothes" even becomes code for "wear your gun" (288). Throughout the novel, the Virginian desires access to a self prior to, more fundamental than, the "male role," but power is seductive, and he can dress the part. Our readings of *The Virginian* depend, then, on whether we see Wister as applauding or exposing those roles.

A PART TO PLAY: HOW IT MUST BE ABOUT A MAN

The Virginian begins with a stage direction: "Enter the Man." A few chapters later the complementary character is announced: "Enter the Woman." Medicine Bow is a set, its houses wearing "a false front . . . rearing their pitiful masquerade" (8). Wearing his own false fronts, none of them pitiful, the Virginian plays his various parts, as do that "sincere spinster" and the "Prince of Wales," only two of the misleading roles played by Molly Wood and the narrator, roles defined by wordplay and costuming. Even the horse, Buck, chooses the most "theatrical moment" (34) to bolt. In this theatrical opening, Wyoming becomes a stage, the metaphoric kind implied by the novel's most discussed author – and one of the Virginian's favorites – when he declared that all the world's a stage and that we are merely players. Reflecting Wister's fondness for Shakespeare, the theatrical trope continues throughout the novel with plays within plays, complete with audiences; chapters entitled "Between the Acts"; soliloquies and asides; and all sorts of "play-acting" (248). Wister's use of a narrator ensures an audience for the Virginian's varied performances.

On this stage, unlike the Shakespearean one, "the Man" and "the Woman" initially seem to have rigidly scripted roles, and any attempt at cross-dressing would probably seem about as successful as Huck Finn's masquerade as a girl. Yet as with so many of Shakespeare's comedies, nothing is quite what it appears in this novel where costuming, role-playing, staging, bluffing, wordplay, and masquerade reign, as they did at Elizabeth's court. Convention scripts the parts, but Wister leads us to think about what convention disguises. Like Judith Butler many years later, he leads us to think about just how much masculinity and femininity are performed according to explicit and implicit expectations, defined by public acts rather than personal inclinations.[7] (Well aware of image,

Wister's friend Roosevelt himself represented masculinity as paradoxical performance – soft words, big sticks.) This question was, as I will argue below, a deeply personal one. At various points the Man and the Woman begin to break down, to cross-dress:

Persistently refusing to be a "lady"; remaining, despite her inability to control her lover's behavior, "independent and unconventional" (86); "craving . . . the unknown" (61); able to "take care of herself, you bet" (74); having "always wanted to be a man" (83); Molly can play the "man's part" (213).

Neither stoic nor silent; relying on words before aggression; ready to read and eager to share "the secrets of his heart" (310); "never [having] guessed so much has been stored away in him, unexpressed till now" (312); sobbing on the shoulder of his friend; the Virginian is willing to question, "What's the gain in being a man?" (310).

Repeatedly and presumably playfully imagining playing a woman: "Had I been the bride, I should have taken the giant, dust and all" (3); touched when his friend "began to give [him] his real heart" (155); the narrator grows into a man through opening himself to what he would feel "had [he] been a woman" (157). (Indeed, he might be the novel's Hamlet, wondering, "To be or not to be.")

Although the novel's ending may reinforce "hegemonic" gender relations, throughout the novel Wister vacillates about "how it must be about a man." To borrow his poker conceit, we might say he hedges his bets.

Wister inherited a predilection and talent for the theater. His grandmother, Fanny Kemble, the strong-willed daughter and niece of a celebrated family of actors who ran theaters in Drury Lane and Covent Garden, debuted as Juliet and was among the most celebrated actresses of her generation. At St. Paul's he wrote a minstrel farce and played Shylock. At Harvard he joined the Dickey Club, performed in its frequent theatricals, and wrote a staged version of *Ivanhoe* (no doubt also reading Scott's *Kenilworth*, which plays such a significant role in *The Virginian*). He also served as manager and performed in plays for the Hasty Pudding Club, whose cross-dressing antics perhaps led to public masquerades such as this one: "Wister and two friends escorted to the Boston Theater a male classmate disguised as a girl, and sat primly with 'her' to see the premier performance of a play about western mining adventures. The escapade apparently fooled practically everyone."[8] He wrote widely performed operettas and aspired to spend his life composing music. (After the publication of *The Virginian*, he would of course write a successful stage version of the novel.)

Yet Wister felt pressured to give up playacting, to take on a "serious" and appropriate male role. Feeling judged by his father for his "failures" at business and law, Wister wrote a novel, *A Wise Man's Son*, "the story of a young man whose father forced him into business."[9] He sent it to the man he considered a "mentor," W. D. Howells, who recommended that Wister not show such a "rebellious" work to a publisher.[10] Wister accepted Howells's judgment, but he suffered an undefined breakdown. In 1885 he was sent to Dr. Weir Mitchell, who had treated his mother and later treated Charlotte Perkins Gilman.[11]

In Anthony Rotundo's reading of its "cultural meaning," male neurasthenia "often happened at times of vocational crisis" and "amounted to a flight from manhood": "A man who broke down was making a statement, however unconscious, of his negative feelings about middle-class work and the values and pressures surrounding it. In doing so, he made a gesture of serious opposition to manhood in his own time." The male neurasthenic, whose illness was characterized by an "utter lack of energy," "was also finding refuge in roles and behaviors marked 'female': vulnerability, dependence, passivity, invalidism." (All these are characteristics that mark Wister's narrator.) Men who traveled to recuperate pursued "the life of cultivated leisure which was associated with women."[12]

Rotundo names William and Henry James, among others, as examples of male travelers, but his conclusion is based on European travel. Mitchell prescribed "rest" to both male and female patients, but his notion of what constituted "rest" varied. He sent Wister West. His prescription: enjoy the stimulation of meeting new people, even "humble" ones, and live an active, out-of-doors life; he specifically told Wister to take along riding clothes.[13] In effect he told Wister to go play. Wister went to Wyoming at about the same time as his longtime friend Theodore Roosevelt, who also went West following a breakdown, began to publish his series of "how I became a man in the West" books. Refining Roosevelt's famous phrase, we might term Mitchell's advice *the strenuous rest cure.* Many critics, among them Jane Tompkins and Gail Bederman, have explored how writers and politicians made use of the image of the West and the development of the formula western to counter the perceived increasing effeminacy of turn-of-the-century men, whose ties to the "primitive" had been severed by urbanization and industrialization, and to construct a more "vigorous" masculinity.[14] Rather than a flight from manhood, western travel offered men like Roosevelt and Wister what David Leverenz has called a "crucible for man-making."[15]

The Virginian was forged in this constricting cultural mold. And one of the novel's theatrical motifs, *Henry IV, Part I*, provides what the Virginian himself calls "bed-rock" (217) for this story line. Max Westbrook has pointed out the parallels between Prince Hal and the Virginian: both rowdy boys who "go around town with a mighty triflin' gang" (217), they eventually model themselves on mentors named Henry, reject and abandon their closest friends, kill opponents who threaten – presumably – social order, and, in effect, inherit the kingdom.[16] Obviously in search of cultural scripts for masculinity, the Virginian rejects Eliot's Tommy Tulliver and even more emphatically Austen's Mr. Knightly. Romeo "is no man," (174), but he views the prince as a "jim-dandy." As the Virginian exclaims to Molly, "The boy showed himself a man" (217).[17]

The allusions to *Henry IV, Part I* are overt, on the table; they represent Wister's apparent acceptance of "how it must be about a man" in the 1890s. But in this hand of kings and princes, Wister keeps a card hidden under the table, a wild card that disrupts male power, authority, and inheritance, a card that signals the Virginian's primogeniture, the source of his name.

Wister's naming of the Virginian is a bluff, tantalizing critics. Does his namelessness make him a democratic everyman, climbing the ladder of equal opportunity that Wister espouses? In "The Virginian as Founding Father," Gary Scharnhorst suggests that Wister links his hero to our national architects, reinforcing the narrator's speculations about "nation." Others pick up on the single reference to a given name, Steve's calling him "Jeff," perhaps referring to Thomas Jefferson or even Jefferson Davis and underscoring textual references to gentlemen and leadership.

But in fact the real origins of the Virginian's name are absolutely clear, and they have far less to do with Wister's views on politics than with his theme of cross-dressing. The wild card is the "Virgin Queen," for whom Virginia was named: another performer, bluffer, and gender bender, the theatrical Elizabeth I.

Elizabeth enters the novel in "The Game and the Nation" section, which Wister divides into "acts." The Virginian encounters her in a book that Molly has given him, *Kenilworth*, in which Scott portrays Elizabeth as an actress, as persistently disguising her private feelings behind public roles, as wielding power through her performances.[18] Throughout the three "acts," the Virginian carries the book hidden in his pocket, drawing it out only in conversations with the narrator. Here most clearly Wister correlates power with role-playing, through the connections between theater and poker. The Virginian's own metaphors, drawn from his life experience, inflect his reading of Kenilworth. Having just developed an it's-how-you-play-your-hand metaphor to explain to Molly how men prove themselves equals, the Virginian translates Elizabeth's verbal abilities and theatricality into poker playing: he believes that she would have "played a mightly pow'ful game [of poker]" (96). In other words, she's skilled at inhabiting the border between appearance and reality, making the most of what she has, daring and bluffing, manipulating others. She clearly inspires the Virginian's inspired public performance as he cooks frog legs for stalled train passengers and bluffs Trampas and his gang into believing that they can make their fortunes off frog farming in Tulare. (With its California jumping frogs and digressive storytelling, the passage also certainly echoes a writer himself skilled at tall tales but far more skeptical of royalty, Mark Twain.) A woman who because of her sex should never have inherited the throne, Elizabeth embodies the Virginian's ideas of equality: "Equality is a great big bluff" (89). Dealt a bad hand, through skill, pretense, and intimidation she outmaneuvers her inferiors: "Well, deal Elizabeth ace high, an' she could scare Robert Dudley with a full house plumb out o' the bettin'. . . . And . . . if Essex's play got next her too near, I reckon she'd have stacked the cyards" (96). The Virginian resorts to understated poker face in describing his admiration for her: "That Queen Elizabeth must have cert'nly been a competent woman" (94).[19]

"Cert'nly" Elizabeth was much more than competent, but competence is an interesting yardstick for Wister to employ, and he uses it consistently. He concludes the section with this assessment from the narrator: "For the Virginian had been equal to the occasion; that is the only kind of equality which I recognize" (126). Initially incompetent, the narrator proves himself, not by the number of antelopes killed, but by gaining the Virginian's affection and confidence. Molly's competence as literary know-it-all and ethical arbiter – qualities monopolized by "true women" – comes into question, but I would argue that her marriage is what she looked for, "not a stooping" (58), and that we have no real reason – just because she was unable to control her spouse's actions – to question her competence as a "rebel, independent as ever" (210). After all, quite unlike Molly's mother and great-aunt, Mrs. Henry – sarcastic, unconventional, physically active, and even willing to make suggestive sexual innuendos about her attraction to the Virginian – provides her model of a competent and suitably rebellious western woman. Competence crosses genders.

At the end of "The Game and the Nation," "Last Act," when the narrator asks the Virginian, "Don't you think you could have played poker with Queen Elizabeth?" he answers, "No; I expect she'd have beat me" (126). In a tall-tale stretch, perhaps I can read that line in this way: if you can't beat them, join them. In any case, the Virginian's identity as Queen Elizabeth's symbolic bastard son oh so competently interferes with readings of *The Virginian*'s dominant misogynist ideology, as does the narrator's wishful thinking about being a woman and the evolving emotional intimacy that he and the Virginian share. Like Wister's lost first novel, *The Virginian* is a rebellious work, straining to tear the seams of the proscribed masculine dress.

WHAT'S THE GAIN IN BEING A MAN?

What's the gain? Well, one thing, if you're white, you can vote. But what if you're a woman? Wyoming's territorial government, of course, had been the first to grant equal suffrage to women in 1869, followed by an equal suffrage clause in 1890 when it applied for statehood.[20] In "'When You Call Me That . . . ,'" Mitchell suggests "that *The Virginian* offered a muted resolution to the crisis over woman's suffrage developing at the turn of the century" by representing "an independent schoolteacher who at last acccepts her social and intellectual dependency in a man's world. . . . If in 1902 the prospect of life in an 'Equality State' seemed unsettling to readers, their uncertainty would have been eased by the drama of the Virginian's courtship of Molly."[21]

I can use the same historical fact to support my argument, to argue, poker faced, that an author would naturally set a novel raising challenging questions about late-nineteenth-century gender roles in the "Equality State."[22] (In fact, Wister no doubt set *The Virginian* in Wyoming because it's what he knew, the place where he had spent most of his time in the West.) One conclusion to draw from this essay is that all literary criticism is a bluff, a tall tale featuring the teller.

But I too want to have it both ways and conclude more seriously as we look toward what role *The Virginian* might play in the next hundred years of literary history. By attempting to disrupt the dominant critical view of the novel as reifying socially constructed gender roles, I suggest that we should not cast this novel, or others, in too narrow a role in our literary dramas. In my own work I want to attend less to moments in a text where gender is "reinscribed" than to moments where it is questioned, where slippage occurs, where expectations are reversed, where we are surprised. And perhaps a text like *The Virginian*, with its mixed messages, double crosses, and bluffs, can tempt us away, sometimes, from closely argued, well-supported analyses into more speculative, performative, dialogic essays that raise more questions than they answer.

I began this essay with a tall tale, trying to place *The Virginian* in a wholly new context to surprise us out of our usual ways of thinking about the novel and its role in our literary traditions, to find it some new bedfellows. Thinking about "the Equality State" and who gets to vote, I'd like to close with another "what if" speculation. In exploring the clothes-make-the-human and cross-dressing tropes, I left out one key scene, the night at the dance when Lin and the Virginian switch the clothes and blankets of the community's babies, fooling everyone. The children are temporarily indistinguishable, but once the clothes are removed there is one significant difference: "And the other one that's been put in Christopher's new quilts is not even a bub – bub – boy!" (77), cries Lizzie Westfall. Finally, when it comes to women and men, "natural" differences do exist.

This scene, I suggest, bears the fingerprints of Mark Twain, an author whom Wister admired; indeed, those fingerprints are all over *The Virginian*. It echoes a scene with far more serious consequences from Twain's 1896 *Pudd'nhead Wilson*, a satiric exposé of socially constructed identity.[23] When Roxy, a white-skinned mulatto, switches the clothes of her enslaved son, Chambers, with those of her master's privileged heir, Thomas a Becket Driscoll, she also switches their "social positions," revealing the absurdity, in Twain's – and my – view, of defining identity by race: it is nurture, not nature, that shapes who they become.

What if Wister came to understand how social expectations skew personal inclinations, not only through personal experience but also through reading Twain? I could point out that the Virginian, a Southerner, is frequently called "the black man," that he obliquely refers to disenfranchisement when he sings – in "blackvoice" – the racist minstrel song that perhaps provided the name for the Jim Crow laws, that Judge Henry's support of lynching does not extend to "Southern Negroes" (272). Could I spin an argument out of the question, What if the Virginian were passing? I couldn't, and wouldn't, and why not? What makes such an argument perverse and ethically unacceptable? One easy answer: Wister's writings demonstrate his racism; in this one example, he reduces Twain's heavy irony to a joke. But many, recently most, have argued that they also demonstrate his misogynism. As Max Westbrook suggests, "To reject the Virginian because he is a male chauvinist with an ideologically-dictated blend of superiority, humility, idealism, and cynicism would seem to be easy; but the memory can be taught to reject any evidence which does not conform to our prejudice. A few million readers simply like this paradigmatic folk hero and refuse to register information which might diminish or corrupt his image."[24]

Mea culpa?

I can tell my feminist tall tale because I'm a woman. In essays like this, I "perform" as a woman. Not as an African American. Not as an American Indian, whose subjugation to "masters" like the Virginian cannot be playfully "unregistered."

No one talks about reader response criticism any more; has it been so thoroughly integrated into our thinking that we assume its pervasive influence? I don't think so. By and large, we still write as "objective" authorities, as if texts have meanings that we can persuade everyone to agree upon. Have I persuaded you? If so, I have a frog farm for you.

NOTES

1. Wister, *The Virginian* (NAL, 1979), 86–87. Page numbers for subsequent quotations will be given in the text.

2. Mitchell, " 'When You Call Me That . . . ,' " 74.

3. Payne, *Owen Wister*, 172, 171.

4. Gilbert and Gubar, *Madwoman in the Attic*.

5. Consider, however, this line: "But manhood had only trained, not broken, [the Virginian's] youth. It was all there, only obedient to the rein and curb" (94).

6. Chopin, *The Awakening*, 48, 114.

7. Butler, *Gender Trouble*.

8. Payne, *Owen Wister*, 31.

9. Tompkins, *West of Everything*, 136.

10. Payne, *Owen Wister*, 74.

11. While the rediscovery of Gilman's "The Yellow Wallpaper" and its rapid canonization led to an epidemic of feminist scholarship about women's health and the medical establishment, about the rest cure and its role in the lives of famous turn-of-the-century figures like Gilman, Edith Wharton, and Jane Addams, about the misogynistic cultural implications in diagnoses of "hysteria" and "neurasthenia," until recently little attention has been paid to male neurasthenics and the cultural implications of their dis-ease with their gendered roles, although Anthony Rotundo argues that neurasthenia may have been "equally common among males and females" (*American Manhood*, 189).

12. Rotundo, *American Manhood*, 190, 191, 193, 186, 191, 191.

13. See Payne, *Owen Wister*, 76.

14. Tompkins, *West of Everything*; Bederman, *Manliness and Civilization*.

15. Leverenz, "The Last Real Man in America," 273.

16. See Westbrook, "Bavarov, Prince Hall, and the Virginian," 104. Of course Westbrook discovers many more parallels than these.

17. In another passage, the Virginian asserts that "Romeo is no man" (174). With his confidence as literary critic, he would no doubt have rejected Henry James's assessment of *The Virginian*: that he would have liked the novel better had Wister cast his hero and heroine in a Romeo and Juliet drama as, in this case, class-crossed lovers, ending in the Virginian's death (see Payne, *Owen Wister*, 201).

18. In this paragraph I am indebted to the insights of my student Maya Sinha.

19. Scipio LeMoyne enters the text along with Elizabeth, and his role is far more ambiguous. His verbally outrageous performance as the long-dead Colonel Cyrus Jones at the Omaha "eating palace . . . which opened upon the world as a stage upon an audience" (92) provides the Virginian with the material for his masquerade. Equally intelligent, psychologically penetrating, and verbally dextrous, both mimics, Scipio and the Virginian "were birds many of whose feathers were the same, and the Virginian often talked to Scipio without reserve" (166). As "a library of life" (130), Scipio provides the Virginian with a wholly different kind of knowledge than does his book reading with Molly. Perhaps because Scipio represents a significant challenge to his ideology – are we to assume that if he somehow found access to Shakespeare, sexy clothes, and Judge Henry, he could become another Virginian? – Wister evades concluding Scipio's script, one of the novel's greatest failings.

20. See Mitchell, " 'When You Call Me That . . . ,' " 73.

21. Mitchell, " 'When You Call Me That . . . ,' " 73–74.

22. Mitchell does suggest generally, although not in this particular case, that "the very ability to have things both ways led to [the novel's] success" (" 'When You Call Me That . . . ,' " 74).

23. For Wister's reading of Twain, see Payne, *Owen Wister,* 19. Twain's influence is most overt in Wister's comic elements, the tall tale, complete with digressions, and the frog farm in Tulare County, but his many references to Shakespeare and "royalty" seem to be a "serious" response to the farcical exploits of the king and the duke in *Huckleberry Finn.*

24. Westbrook, "Bavarov, Prince Hall, and the Virginian," 104.

10   WISTER'S RETREAT FROM HYBRIDITY

Neil Campbell

While Melody Graulich focuses on the staged performances of gender in The Virginian, *Neil Campbell looks at the ways in which Wister stages "tentative ideas" about western hybridity and then "contains" them within preexisting ideology. Using the work of cultural geographers and James Clifford's theoretically suggestive pun of "roots and routes," he explores patterns of migration and multiculturalism in* The Virginian, *but in Campbell's reading, informed by recent postcolonial and poststructuralist theory, Wister, with his "fear of difference," "retreats" from the implications of his portrayal of the "diasporic West." He creates "dialogues between movement and stasis, nature and civilization, migration and settlement, hybridity and essentialism," but ultimately, the novel, like its heroine, capitulates to the dominance of the Anglo-Saxon. Providing the model for the "existential restlessness of the western genre,"* The Virginian *nevertheless remains entrapped in the tension between stasis and movement.*

Campbell's exploration of the importance of the theme of mobility and its centrality to the ideology of the novel was inaugurated in this volume by Louis Owens. Owens also raises the concept of "transculturation," a process in evidence throughout the volume. The essays by Victoria Lamont, Zeese Papanikolas, and Campbell might themselves be seen as characterized by critical migrations. Together, they demonstrate a cross-cultural, transnational, diasporic perspective, one that will open new critical spaces for the study of western writing.

You are mixing things – I never heard you mix things before.

OWEN WISTER, *The Virginian*

In many ways, Owen Wister's *The Virginian* is a novel of movement, understanding inherently that the West was a space constituted, not by logical design and neat frontier lines, but by dynamic and fluid "lines of flight," routes of travel, migration, and the varied interactions of people and place. The West formed by expansion, exploration, hunting and settlement trails, enforced and chosen displacements, and multiple contacts is a space that is best examined by seeing these diverse routes alongside and in dialogue with the alternative impulse to "rootedness" – that is, the impulse to settlement and to stability. The apparent contraries of these fixed and unfixed positions can and should be part of the exploration of the complex dynamics of American western history and culture that rejects one absolute interpretation, or the "monologic," in favor of a "dialogic" vision appreciating the relational, multistoried, heteroglossic West in which American identities are constructed.[1] While acknowledging and enacting many of these aspects of the West, Wister's novel has, however, a tendency to repress and contain them in order to assert and endorse another vision of identity and history formed around specific ideological values and goals. This essay will show how *The Virginian* engages dialogically with the hybrid West and yet simultaneously denies and controls it through the figure of its central, eponymous "hero without wings,"[2] leaving readers to come to terms with the consequent contradictions with which the novel inevitably presents us.

Some of these fluid formations are played out in *The Virginian* at Colonel Cyrus Jones's eating palace, since "gone the way of the Indian and the buffalo," existing "near the trains" and constructed of a mixed "shell of wood, painted with golden emblems – the steamboat, the eagle, the Yosemite, – [with] a live bear [that] ate gratuities at the entrance." This is a truly transient, heteroglot western place, "middle-aged" at ten years old, intermingling textures, materials, and lives with its natural and manmade emblems that "opened upon the world as a stage upon the audience." On this Western "stage" we find the East (the "tenderfoot" narrator) and the South (the traveled Virginian) in the presence of "rainbows of men – Chinese, Indian chiefs, Africans, General Miles, younger sons, Austrian nobility, wide females in pink. Our continent drained prismatically through Omaha once" (92). In this space, language and meaning collide as the cosmopolitan "bill-of-fare" speaks of "salmis, canapés supremes," and "Frogs' legs à la Delmonico" while the owner speaks of eggs as "white wings" and rare beef as "slaughter in the pan" (93). In this prismatic, hybrid mix, Wister captures a vision of a diasporic West forming out of encounter and contact, yet he is swift to consign it to the past, like the Indian and the buffalo, referring to the palace as only a lost, nostalgic memory of another West. The scene is part of the "vanished world" of the West that he laments in his notes "To the Reader," reached only by "journeys . . . memory can take" (ix). This is a revealing episode, demonstrating a consistent pattern in Wister's novel whereby an awareness of and fascination for ideas of cultural mixing and of a "subject in process" are tempered and retreated from by a more conventional belief in essentialized American identity as the "natural" product of a social evolution of the fittest.

Rather than a hybrid subject produced in a contact zone of exchange, Wister's version of cultural identity is embedded in a particular view of "tradition" that roots this naturally selected individual within a European, Saxon genealogy buried deeply in the American experience. Westward expansion provided, with its rigorous, masculine pursuits and its opportunities for extremes of endurance, ingenuity, and violent interaction, a laboratory for the soul to rediscover the repressed energies that Wister viewed as essential to an Anglo-Saxon "bloodline." This is exemplified in his essays, and in particular in "The Evolution of a Cow-Puncher" (1895), where he tells of an aristocratic Englishman who "smelt Texas" and found that "the slumbering untamed Saxon awoke in him" and thereby "typifie[d] the way of his race." Wister maps an American national identity rooted in the Saxon spirit and rerooted in the "cattle country" through the figure of the male "cow-puncher" who arrived as part of a "motley" "tribe," a "heap of cards shuffled from . . . various unmatched packs," a "harlequin platoon" – like the "rainbows of men" at the eating palace – and is transformed, as the Englishman in the essay, by the rediscovery of his old, essential Saxonism emboldened in the West. For Wister, these individuals cohered in the West and "soon grew into a unit," expressing the characteristics of the "race"; "pluck[ed] from the library, the haystack, and the gutter, [when] set upon . . . his horse . . . his modern guise fell away and showed once again the mediaeval man. It was no new type, no product of the frontier, but just the original kernel of the nut with the shell broken."[3]

This "original kernel" articulates Wister's version of essential, racial, and gendered identity rooted in Saxon Europe and amplified in the soil of America. Stuart Hall explains how such essentialist thinking works in relation to identity as "a sort of collective 'one true self,' hiding inside the many other, more superficial or artificially imposed 'selves,' which people with a shared history and ancestry hold in common." Such an idea provides a fixed sense of "one people" with "stable, unchanging and continuous frames of reference and meaning, beneath the shifting divisions and vicissitudes of . . . actual history," and so authorizes a sense of "oneness," "the truth, the essence" of national identity.[4] This is the "original kernel" from which the Anglo- Saxon identity emerges to redefine itself in the West. Yet it is not the environment that forms identity; it merely provides the conditions for its expression, the "soil" in which the "kernel" will root and grow. As Paul Gilroy writes, under such an essentialization process "identity is latent destiny" because it sets one group apart from others who do not conform to the approved "chosen traits."[5]

To return to Wister's cowpuncher or Virginian is to see this essential American writ large, mirroring the writings of Theodore Roosevelt, who felt that "one common racial ancestor or master-race is the root of all those peoples whose languages belong to the Indo-European family and that in some races (that is, the Teutons) the line of inheritance runs truer." However, just as Wister recognized the variety of peoples arriving in America, so did Roosevelt, who argued that only the "best men" emerged through the rigorous life of the frontier, becoming leaders and rising above the masses. These were the true race, born out of war and struggle, where differences dissolve into the common "blood" so that "the tribal variants are harmonized and blended while their common 'Germanic' root-qualities are reinforced and made into the basis of political unity."[6]

To return to the eating palace with this in mind is to see the tensions in Wister's work between the pull to his essentialized ideal and his fascination with a diasporic West, traveling and nomadic in its bold pioneering of a new nation. Paul Gilroy employs just such tensions in order productively to rethink how essential, racial "roots" can be dialogized by the exploration of "routes" and the hybrid quality of encounter. Gilroy employs the concept of diaspora as a "valuable idea [that] . . . points towards a more refined and more worldly sense of culture than the characteristic notions of soil, landscape and rootedness" that are often used to fix national identity. The likes of Roosevelt, Frederick Jackson Turner, and Wister were Americans rooting the nation in the landscapes of the West and arguing that the "race" was forged (in various ways) in contact with the conditions, rigors, and adventures of that space. In this way, the West became the "natural" American "homeland" where "roots, soil, landscape and natural beauty were used so that nation and citizenship appeared to be natural rather than social phenomena – spontaneous expressions of a distinctiveness that was palpable in a deep inner harmony between people and their dwelling-places." Diaspora reassesses this thinking about identity as essential and absolute and "problematizes the cultural and historical mechanics of belonging" by disrupting the mythic, "explanatory links between place, location and consciousness."[7]

Diaspora can also challenge primordial concepts of identity rooted in an idealized past where the race was formed, like Wister's Saxon myth-ideal, for under diaspora, identity is constructed as dynamic, interlinked, and hybrid. There is no authentic single "home place" in which one's roots are planted, for identity is formed by the "routes" that it travels and the contacts that it makes in that process as much as by any settlement that might take place. Identity has to be seen as "spatial" and not locked into a version of "tradition" imagined by Wister as, as Hall would put it, "a one-way transmission belt; an umbilical cord, which connects us to our culture of origin." The latter produces only a closed, linear version of culture, whereas diaspora redefines it as circular and spatial, "as moving, not in a line but through different circuits."[8] However, Wister laments a "lost" epic time when the West was unchanged by "Progress," immigration, and movement and when behavior and justice were uncluttered by ambiguity or doubt. This view sees culture as ever more diluted the further it moves away from its "roots" and its origins. Conversely, however, one can see change as dynamic and productive, with identity "traveling" and encountering cultural experiences along its complex "routes" of diasporization and "identities . . . constantly producing and reproducing themselves anew, through transformation and difference."[9] James Clifford has developed these ideas to emphasize the importance of "travel" – of "routes" as well as "roots" – so "that specific dynamics of dwelling/travelling be understood comparatively," questioning culture as simply "a rooted body that grows, lives, dies, and so on," and seeing instead "disputed historicities, sites of displacement, interference, and interaction" where negotiations take place between groups.[10]

As the scene at the eating palace demonstrates, Wister was interested in showing the "negotiations" of the mixed West, but only as a parade passing by on the way to becoming one nation defined and ruled by the Anglo-Saxon "overseers." His discomfort at any "mongrelization" is described metaphorically in an essay about taming ponies demonstrating the importance of control and order over potential "chaos." The horses "intertangle as in cross-tag, pushing between your design and its victim, mingling confusedly like a driven mist. . . . But when the desired one is at last taken, and your successful rope is on his neck, you would not dream he had ever wished for anything else. He stands submitting absent-mindedly to bit and blanket, mild as any unconscious lamb, while placid-ity descends once more upon the herd."[11] The challenge is to bring order and authority to the unruly, just as Wister suggests that the evolution of the cowpuncher is part of a process bringing controlled, racially destined democracy to the mixture of the frontier.

The struggle between "intertangling" and "design" is an accurate rep-resentation of the ethnic and gender battles played out on Wister's fron-tier, yet in reading this description one is struck by the longing implied in the phrase "mingling confusedly like a driven mist," as if the hidden de-sire to mix with the abandon of these ponies is retreated from only be-cause of the perceived necessity for a "new order" of defined roles.[12] Wis-ter resists the possibility of exchange or encounter as a dialogic process because it implies that meaning (and identity) can be negotiated and, therefore, unfixed, preferring instead to resort to the colonial positions of acquisition, incorporation, and violent suppression as the natural way to deal with frontier experiences. If the "intertangled" could be brought to heel and healed of its inherent differences, then, for Wister, it had to be through the charismatic, mythic "tamer of the West" exercising the des-tiny of his evolved Anglo-Saxon character on behalf of national order.

Clifford's work values, in contrast to Wister's fear of difference, dialogi-cally "tangled cultural experiences," seeing the frontier as a contact zone of "intersecting histories – discrepant detours and returns." His defini-tion of *diaspora* extends the point: "Diaspora . . . involves dwelling, main-taining communities . . . [and] articulates, or bends together, both roots and routes to construct . . . alternate public spheres, forms of community consciousness and solidarity that maintain identifications outside the na-tional time/space in order to live inside, with a difference."[13] Clifford, like Homi Bhabha, sees a "need to think beyond narratives of originary and initial subjectivities [like those of Wister] and to focus on those mo-ments or processes that are produced in the articulation of cultural differ-ences" since it is in these "in-between spaces" that "new signs of identity, and innovative sites of collaboration," are initiated.[14] In my reading of *The Virginian*, having given the reader a brief glimpse of some alternative cultural order, "in-between," where identity is formed in a dialogized contact zone between roots and routes, Wister retreats into an originary, nationalist mythos that reinforces a particular gendered and racist vision.

Thus, Wister's tentative "prismatic" identity with its possibility of hybrid, collaborative visions of the West indicates, if only briefly, a more tolerant understanding of differences and an appreciation of the plural contributions to the creation of America that speak of a valuable and potent redefinition of equality. However, the novel's retreat is, in the manner that Bhabha describes, back to origins and to a version of, in Wister's words, "true aristocracy" that equates "the best man" with "winning" and assumes that people have "equal liberty to find [their] own level" (91).

At its extreme points, Wister's work has a racist "contempt for the foreigner" while valorizing an Anglo-Saxon ideal epitomized by the perfect white male standing against the poisoning of the nation by "debased and mongrel . . . hordes of encroaching alien vermin, that turn our cities into Babels and our citizenship to a *hybrid farce*" (emphasis added).[15] However, despite decrying hybridity, his work hints at another kind of history and cultural identity much closer to Hall's antiessentialism, one in which difference "constitute[s] 'what we really are'; or rather – since history has intervened – 'what we have become.' " In this formulation, cultural identity is not fixed and essential, buried in the past and awaiting rediscovery, but diasporic and 'undergo[ing] constant transformation . . . subject to the continuous 'play' of history, culture and power."[16] Despite himself, Wister recognized the hybrid nature of America as "motley," "unmatched," "divers [*sic*]," and "from various points of the compass," yet he cannot acknowledge that any non-Anglo-Saxon cultural differences might be, in themselves, productive in the creation of the nation. Instead, Wister dismisses the effect of "others" as a "hybrid farce" and raises their presence only in order to contain their importance, as with the Mexican *vaquero*, who, he admits, was the "original cow-boy," but who, he claims, "the American improved on."[17]

Although Wister's pattern of dismissal reduces any contribution of the non-Anglo-Saxon (or of women), there remains a dialogic process presenting alternative ideas alongside these overt reductionist sentiments. For example, in his discussion of language development as emblematic of the "evolutionary" process, he argues that the cowpuncher, "not only built, but *borrowed* his own [language] wherever he found it" (emphasis added). Wister's analysis comes close to contemporary notions of the productive hybridization or "creolization" of language or dialogic exchanges between different groups in the creation of new structures and forms that both resist the centralized, official language and demonstrate the active, regenerative nature of identity freed from an essentialized definition. Wister writes of the "translations" and "transfers from the Mexican," "trickles" of French and Spanish that with English "melt into two separate amalgams" and "drift everywhere . . . in the cow-puncher's dialect."[18] This rumination on language identifies a powerful, polyglossic mixing of words on the western frontier, among different cultural identities in a manner that recent postcolonial studies analyzes in relation to theories of diaspora, hybridization, and new ethnicities.[19] However, Wister's description of a fluid process of interactive cultures in the contact zone of the frontier quickly retreats into his racialized and gendered hierarchy by asserting that the cowpunchers' taking of these fragments of language and "making a useful verb" proved their "individuality" and asserted the "need for quick thinking and doing."[20] In a bizarre masturbatory image, as Tatum has called it, Wister goes on to write: "Any young strong race will always lay firm hands on language and squeeze juice from it," asserting the masculine imperialism of these frontier identities and rejecting the "Babel" of many voices in favor of the dominant, all-conquering singular voice of the Anglo-Saxon.[21]

In *The Virginian* these tensions form dialogues between movement and stasis, nature and civilization, migration and settlement, hybridity and essentialism, and at the heart of the dialogues is the figure of the eponymous hero, an outsider circling around within the novel's space, moving from the margins to the center until he is married and belongs at its social center. In this diasporic world, the Virginian is a migrant, "recently back from havin' a look at Arizona" (18); marked by travel, having "plainly come many miles from somewhere across the vast horizon and the dust upon him showed" (3); an outsider whose southern drawl indicates his otherness in a community of others.

Wister often uses images of ships and the sea to suggest these tensions, relating them to the narrator, the Virginian, and the landscape itself. Hence, in a key early description of a tense scene between Trampas and the Virginian, Wister writes, "This level of smooth relaxation hinted no more plainly of what lay beneath than does the surface tell the depth of the sea" (19). Between the "surface" of the text and its "depth" exist other stories of contradiction and unease, where alternative American identities jostle with the "smooth" surface of the myth. Traveling and contact articulate these tensions, as people move across space, interacting and exchanging. For example, the narrator initially feels he has come on "a sort of ship" and been "marooned in a foreign ocean" at the very edge of "the unending gulf of space," but traveling beyond the town, he sees a different West, one bathed in "the air of creation's first morning," "a world of crystal light, a land without end, a space across which Noah and Adam might come straight from Genesis" (5, 8). Beyond the town "nothing was there but the road we had come; it lay like a ship's wake across the huge ground swell of the earth. We were swallowed in a vast solitude" (33).

Travel, or displacement, literally "broadens the mind," providing experiences of vision and feeling that can transform identity, challenge assumptions, and unsettle ideologies, just as it will with the narrator, who is transformed in the course of the novel to "manhood" able to cross "unmapped spaces with no guidance" (236). To Clifford, travel represents "practices of crossing and interaction that troubled the localism of many common assumptions about culture" and, therefore, stood out against notions of "dwelling" and settlement as the primary modes of cultural formation. For embedded in this is the assumption that "roots always precede routes" and that travel is significant only because it leads us to a place in which to settle. Perhaps, therefore, it might be more productive to view culture as "as much a site of travel encounters as of residence . . . like a hotel lobby, urban café, ship or bus," where people are engaged in different forms of interaction and exchange.[22]

This is *The Virginian*'s space of relations, crossed and recrossed by the endlessly described "chronotopes" and routes of movement: railroads, stages, trails, hotels, junctions, ships (or metaphors of ships), and letters.[23] The novel begins with scenes of transit and encounter at the railroad station, with the comings and goings of a transient, shallow-rooted community of outsiders and "foreigners" who are endlessly roving around sharing towels and beds. There are travelers everywhere; men traveling for brides; salesmen and "drummers" of all ethnicities; outlaws; landladies sleeping with cowboys but married to freight conductors; and cowboys themselves wandering the cattle trails and frontier ranches for work. In an early scene at the railhead town of Medicine Bow, the Virginian is at the heart of a carnivalesque moment when all these different travelers engage in a "reel" that literally uproots the "tenderfoot" narrator – "my own feet left the earth" – until he "sped like a bobbing cork into this mill race, whirling . . . in the wake of the others" (25). In an excessive, mobile cohesion of differences, the men dance together without prejudice, drawing everyone into the throng, "swept along . . . *routed* from their own bed" to join the "procession" (26; emphasis added).

What is crucial about this carnival moment is that in its temporary quality it belongs to the wider "motion/stasis" pattern of Wister's novel. For at the very point of potential chaos, order and domesticity are resumed, "Medicine Bow gradually went *home*," and as the Virginian states, "I have got to stay responsible" (26; emphasis added). Excited by this very non-eastern activity, the narrator finds, however, a "bar" to any further "approaches" shutting him off from any contact with the Virginian, whose sudden stillness and reserve is reflected in the stasis of the town: "So still, that through the air the deep whistles of the freight trains came from below the horizon across great miles of silence" (27).

Wister, in fact, describes a diasporic America forming around this pattern of traveling and dwelling, motion and stasis, with the East seen as a "settled place" (9) where the idea of "home" (16) is well established, in contrast to the West, where "a man's home is apt to be his saddle blanket" (32). The Virginian is constantly identified with "moving," for since leaving "home" in the South at fourteen, he had "seen Arkansas, Texas, New Mexico, Arizona, California, Oregon, Idaho, Montana, and Wyoming . . . [for] he was one of the thousands drifting and living thus," with "no hunger for home." In being "homeless," the Virginian has traversed the nation from South to North and West to East, coming into contact with the varieties of the nation and forming an identity out of those contacts: "Everywhere he had taken care of himself, and survived" (33). At ease in all company, he is a man always "equal to the situation," ruthless, yet always just and fair, for as he says, "travellin' learns a man many customs" (120).

However, Wister cannot allow the Virginian to remain a "homeless" "bachelor of the saddle" (61), so his travels must become focused on specific interrelated goals and "responsibilities": the winning of Molly Stark Wood and his self-improvement as an entrepreneur. The Virginian is, like many American heroes, full of youthful vigor finding perfect expression on the frontier, yet Wister's pull to stasis and responsibility equates with his hero's "rites of passage."[24] The Virginian is associated with youth and travel throughout the novel and identifies with the young heroes of the books he reads – Hal in *Henry IV* and David in *David Copperfield* – but as with the heroes of all bildungsromans, he must leave his wild wanderings behind for marriage, responsibility, and social authority.[25] In discussing *Henry IV*, which he terms a "bed-rock" play, the Virginian comments that it is about a shift from "travelling with trash," via regrettably killing "another jim-dandy," to being a "man" (217). This mirrors the Virginian's own evolutionary path as he moves to stability and responsibility by kill-

ing Steve and Trampas, both reminders of his youthful wanderings and alternative identities.

To some extent, Molly is described in terms of travel and dispersal too,
for she has traveled from the East in search of a new (if temporary) life in
the West, yet Wister associates her with the specific dispersal of seeds, being "the seed of love" that "had floated across wide spaces, and was bid-
ing its time in his heart" (39), waiting to select the Virginian for "rootedness" and for social growth. Her role is to save his "seed" and to ensure
that it finds its proper and rightful "place" in the American soil, for "fe-
cund nature begets and squanders thousands of these rich seeds in the
wilderness of life" (87). The "coupling" of Molly and the Virginian implies a potential new identity joining their two characters and breaking
the boundaries of traditional gender and class divisions, but in actuality
there is a "melting" rather than an "adding" since Molly's often contradictory desires must be conquered by her "master," the Virginian, as he
accepts his new "responsibility."[26] Wister recoils from any true, equal
mixing of Molly and the Virginian, for as with his fear of ethnic mixing
discussed earlier, it would seem to imply a weakening of his epic hero to
her New Womanism.

The "hide-and-seek" (82) relationship of Molly and the Virginian is
marked by contradictions and indecision of all kinds, with expectations
as likely to be turned upside down as confirmed.[27] These are revealed in
their contrasting dreams: Molly dreams, "The Virginian had ridden his
horse into the railroad car, and sat down beside her, the fire in the great
stone chimney of her cabin flicker[ing] quietly," while he dreams, "I ain't
too old for education. Maybe she will lend me books. And I'll watch her
ways and learn . . . [to] stand still" (84). Hers is a sexualized ("the great
stone chimney") romance of motion (horse and railroad), while his is a
static dream of education and self-improvement. She is drawn to the West
but feels that the East is still the measure of all that is good and civilized,
so in denying the Virginian, she imagines that she is denying the wilderness and its values. Ironically, as we have seen, the Virginian is "mobile"
and already engaged in a rejection of the "Trampas West" in favor of an
upward entrepreneurial spirit supported by a "necessary" commitment
to a version of justice derived from the chivalry of the frontier.[28] Thus,
their "journeys" are apparently moving in opposite directions.

In theory their marriage and sexual contact might create for Wister a
hybridized identity, an ideal type fit for the new nation, yet uncomfort-

able with any kind of "mongrelization," he displaces it once again and resorts to associating Molly with traditional notions of containment, domesticity, and the family and the Virginian with the opposite. The values of the New Woman that Molly wishes to assert out West are "fighting a battle" (159) with her "heart" (200), but as Wister wrote, "The frontier is just ourselves expressed in unbridled terms."[29] Her independent feelings cannot be "unbridled," for she must find her destiny through the Virginian only. Thus, Wister reveals, in another way, his fear of hybridization – whether between races or genders – in his desperate need to assert marriage as an unequal meeting rather than a hybrid mixing. To borrow a phrase from the novel itself, Wister is engaged in "rewrapping *Kenilworth*" (126) to demonstrate the construction, or "evolution," of his conventional epic hero and his suitable heroine.

As Molly is "bridled" and contained, the Virginian's wanderlust becomes increasingly channeled by Wister into ambition and the need to gain respect, authority, and status within the West, "the newest part of a new world" (139). He wants to be the "fore-man" in the future West, rather than work as a hired hand for the judge, and Molly seems to motivate this ambition, for it is her conversation on equality that draws out his statement about his own upward mobility. Here, moving, associated throughout the novel with the Virginian, takes on a very specific, new meaning. Mobility now is social mobility. He says, "I am the kind that moves up. I am goin' to be your best scholar." He cannot remain a simple cowboy, as she might want him to be (in her romantic image), for in order to win her, as he sees it, his "seed" must ripen in this new climate: "Yu' might as well ask fruit to stay green" (90), he says. The idea of becoming foreman (or "fore-man") "meant everything to him: recognition, higher station, better fortune, a separate house of his own, and – perhaps – one step nearer to the woman he wanted" (145). The Virginian will literally move out of the bunkhouse into his new physical space, "a house . . . of his own," and simultaneously move into new social, economic, and cultural space that will bring him ever closer to the ideal of Wister's America.

No longer marked by travel, the nomad now stays closer to home in his separate space, building his career, surrounded by images of stasis, "imprisoned" in a "snowbound" landscape of "silence . . . and patience," "his fingers . . . coated with ink," "enveloped" by education at a desk from which he "did not move" (165–66). He no longer reads the texts of youthful passage, for "instead of Shakespeare and fiction school books lay open on his cabin table," and his powers of storytelling have been transformed to "various exercises" (165) of spelling and penmanship. In a sphere associated more with women, the Virginian is apparently learning to live differently, between worlds of motion and stasis, as an uneasy hybrid, able to read and ride, a killer-philosopher, unlike the figures of Trampas or Shorty ("the lost dog" [171]), whose lives are fixed in the old ways – "fooling around the earth, jumping from job to job, and helling all over town between whiles" (170). The Virginian's wandering is tempered by a new set of values born of hard work, self-worth, and thrift: "Take my land away tomorrow, and I'll still have my savings in bank. . . . I had to work right hard gathering them in. . . . I settled down and did it" (171). Wister now directs and tames the Virginian's youthful instincts toward very specific ideological ends – the work ethic and domestic settlement.

These shifts in the Virginian's character – his "phases of going" – are resolved most noticeably in the scenes following the Indian ambush when he is saved and cared for by Molly.[30] The "wandering work" (175) that has dominated the Virginian's youthful, carefree, diasporic days is paralleled in these scenes with the feverish aftermath of his wounding, which is also referred to as a "wandering" (212).[31] During this scene, as the fever "masters" him he must be held down and "tamed" as if his old life is likened to aberrant madness, a delirium from which he must awake. In fact, earlier, when describing his days of wandering, the Virginian says that "his strong heart" had not "yet waked up to any hunger for a home" (33). However, as he does come round from his temporary insanity, with its crazed "language of the round-up," he feels displaced, asking "how he came here," and more significantly, finding that there was not "anything left in his memory" to aid him with a return to what he had been. Of course, this is precisely the point, for the Virginian has been transformed by his "awakening" and now moves unswervingly toward his clear goals, his essential "deep, untainted strength" (213), and "nearer [the] certainty" (212) of a life with Molly. He has been purged, literally and metaphorically, by the "clean water treatment" (212) of his wounds, showing that "illness, so far from veiling, more often quickens, the perceptions" (214), and from it the Virginian sheds the delirium of his youthful wanderings to accept his new, "natural" responsibility to "home," like the inevitability of Prince Hal maturing into King Henry or the "lost" Americans finding their Anglo-Saxon roots in the West.

Appropriately, Molly says, "There's no need to move him" (212), as if to reinforce her new role as "nurse" and "sweetheart" anchoring him to home and reminding us of the Virginian's new, static persona. For Molly too has "awakened" from her own sickness to discard her independent dreams; she "forgot everything to listen to him, as he forgot himself . . . and grew talkative to her" (219). Despite the potentially hybrid image of the Virginian wearing "a silk handkerchief . . . to feel respectable again" with a "Navajo blanket . . . around his shoulders . . . with its splendid zigzags of barbarity," in writing to Molly's great-aunt he explains that these oppositional worlds cannot coexist, for a man can be one thing only: "A man like me who has travelled meets many of them [women] as he goes and passes on *but I stopped when I came to Miss Wood*" (234; emphasis added). The Virginian's stasis demands Molly's acceptance of her prescribed role, for their diverse routes must become the roots of settlement and a stable, socially acceptable family life. In seeking to impress Molly's great-aunt, the Virginian now draws, not on his Western experiences of travel, but on the roots of his family, who "have always stayed at the same place" and can trace their heritage back to "Virginia English and Scotch Irish" (233).

Thus, as this couple approach their wedding day, Wister describes "their journey's end" with the town "beneath them like a map . . . set out in *order clearly*, shining extensive and *motionless* in the sun" (279; emphasis added). Their journey toward settling down brings them into the mixed landscape of "Wyoming space," with its "watered fields," "tawny plain," "blue gulfs of pine" (279–80), and distant mountains, but Molly now admits that "their positions had been exchanged," that "her better birth and schooling that had once been weapons to keep him at his distance . . . had given way before the onset of the natural man himself." She is now "powerless" before her "master," who is "more than ever she could be" (281). The Virginian is Wister's ideal aristocrat, a natural man risen, not because of his name (after all, he has none), but by hard work, single-minded individualism, and innate honorable decency. For all her eastern breeding and education, Molly cannot compete with his singular vision, and to that extent she is conquered by him. Yet she is far from irrelevant to the Virginian's "emergence," for we are reminded, "they exchanged and shared. It was a new bliss to her to know a man's talk and thoughts . . . and to him it was a bliss still greater to melt from that reserve his lonely life had bred in him." The Virginian changes in contact with Molly, bringing out all that "had been stored away in him, unexpressed till now" (312), yet these aspects of their relationship tend to be overlooked in the concentration on her secondary role. These subtle inclusions, however downplayed, remind us again of the novel's fascination with the possibilities of hybridity while ultimately favoring the apparent authority of the dominant white male.

Having killed Trampas in town and symbolically killed off his "tramp-like," wandering self, the Virginian takes his bride away to "the unsurveyed and virgin wilderness" along "road[s] less worn with travel" where the map-like order of their descent into town "lay in another world from this where they rode now" (304–5). This final, nomadic journey takes them back to a primal space beyond cultural order where "no hand but nature's had sown these crops of yellow flowers" (305) and where it is "natural" that "she obeyed him" (307). As Adam and Eve, they find an Eden in the woods away from the burgeoning communities of the plain, and here, watching a beaver playing in the water, the Virginian admits that such a place "has made me want to become the ground, become the water, become the trees, mix with the whole thing. Not know myself from it. Never unmix again" (310). The Virginian desires a mixing fusion with nature, a dissolution of the self and an abandonment of the responsibility and social mobility that has been his recent goal in favor of a return to the freedoms of the trail. As with all "mixing" and its connotations of hybridity and "intertangling" in the novel, it is short-lived, becoming merely a dream that purges the Virginian of all ambiguity until he is an innocent youth again and he and Molly are like "two children" – "his face changed by her to a boy's, and she leavened with him" (311). The Virginian's youthful rites of passage are purged again in this pastoral romance of new beginning in which Wister authors his American Adam and Eve – he innocent and masterful, she "leavened" and obedient, and all dreams of mixing and dialogue gone, displaced by a different future "getting ready for change" (315).

Apparently freed from the "travelling-mind" developed throughout his earlier youthful journeys, the Virginian now transfers his mobile frontier spirit to the new entrepreneurial class. As he proudly states when visiting Molly's home in the East, "I am well fixed for the new conditions," for he has taken land "where there is coal" (315) to feed the needs of the railroads and the industries that they bring West. Of course, in another sense the Virginian is indeed "fixed," for he has given up the migrant's traveling mind, and all the possibilities of hybridity, to take up the place that Wister believed was the inevitable one for a true American: "The nomadic, bachelor West is over, the housed, married West is established."[32] In fact, as we see this "new" man, purged of the past "wild-west show" and beginning his new life, he is increasingly associated with the settled East and with the Old World, wearing "*Scotch home*spun" and acknowledging that he had "a heap to learn" (emphasis added). In a telling comment, he says, "I was very young then, or maybe not so young, as very – as what you saw I was when you first came to Bear Creek" (313). The hesitation shows that he is no longer either a youth or uneducated, for both changes have been the consequences of his new, rooted existence, which enables him to identify the East and the West as both having "something to do with making our country" (316).

Wister's avoidance of dialogue between the multiple possibilities of the West confirms his preferred monologic vision of settlement and fixity locating American identity within a particular class and gender hierarchy. However, en route the process of the Virginian's "becoming," and the tensions that the text articulates, leaves another path for the reader to follow. In this respect, *The Virginian* is part of a tradition in American literature that links youth, the road, and the journey West with a longing for particular ideological visions of freedom, equality, democracy, escape, nonconformity, and rebellion. Of course, this is a diverse tradition, one including the poetry of Walt Whitman, *The Adventures of Huckleberry Finn*, *On the Road, Zen and the Art of Motorcycle Maintenance,* and *Easy Rider,* in which often contradictory desires give rise to many dramatic opportunities. In the case of *The Virginian*, youthful "rebellion" and mischief are sanctioned and accommodated until the hero's travels are contained as mere "phases" in his process of becoming a bourgeois subject fulfilling his "rags-to-riches" destiny.

There is no sense of the Virginian wanting to "move on" or "light out for the Territory" at the end of the novel since his "phases of going" have been a very measured approach to his precise goals of settlement and fixed identity, unlike Trampas, the migrant soul and "out-law," who must be killed off to clear this path to closure and resolution. The Virginian's ultimate social responsibility and normative behavior are marked by maturity, marriage, family, home, and education and overseen by Judge Henry (and, hence, by lawfulness), making him socially acceptable and unthreatening and defining a very specific vision of American identity. Just as the tenderfoot narrator must become a man under the mentoring of the Virginian, so the mentor learns the values of the wider world to which his contained identity belongs. He is rather like Tom Sawyer, whose youthful rebellion is ultimately sanctioned by another judge (Judge Thatcher) as he welcomes the boy as his "surrogate" son and begins to process his institutionalized future in business, the law, or the army. The road traveled has led the Virginian, like many other American rebels, to containment and socialization, and his waywardness been translated into the admired, productive bourgeois values of competition, stability, success, and authority. Wister's overarching sense of identity flirted with motion and hybridity only in order to reassert the social value of an American identity rooted in a vision of the past, without cultural exchange, where the road is never unending and multiple but always unidirectional and clear, forming what he called the "American story" (vii).

Yet as we have seen, in the diasporic journey underpinning the novel there remains an ambiguous and contradictory trail, full of movement and change, leading to a different understanding of this process of identity formation. The Virginian can be "read" as a hybrid, migrant man, "trying to face (at least) two ways at once," one who mixes and "travels" between many different groups and contact zones inscribing an alternative American western identity that counteracts, to a degree, the preferred Anglo-Saxon model of Wister's essays.[33] The complex "third space" that the novel approaches and then, ultimately avoids, has the potential, in Bhabha's words, of "remaking the boundaries, exposing the limits of any claim to a singular or autonomous sign of difference – be it class, gender, or race. Such assignations of social differences – where difference is neither One nor the Other but something else besides, inbetween – find their agency in a form of the 'future' where the past is not originary, where the present is not simply transitory."[34] Of course, as we have seen, this space "in between" is consistently repressed, as is the Virginian's desire to "mix" with nature or to enter into a full "exchange" in his relationship with Molly, in favor of an altogether different vision of normalized identity and hierarchical social order. It is finally Wister's fear of "something else besides" that leads him back to origins, to roots rather than routes, and to the figure of his aristocratic epic hero building a new America with a single vision.

The dissatisfaction and debate about the ending of The Virginian is a response to the dialogues established and then denied in the novel, to the representation of a West constructed by movement and interaction finally reordered as stasis and fixity, and to the feeling that an opportunity was missed to tell a more complex and multifaceted story of the West as a mix of routes and roots where hybrid, diasporic identities provide, not the nation's weakness, as Wister believed, but its very strength. In many ways, this was a story that others would take up, placing the emphasis less on the social importance of closure and more on the mobile, hybrid nature of the West as a complex space of unequal relations and struggles over power, culture, and identity. In so doing, it is fair to see *The Virginian* as the intertextual fulcrum for subsequent western texts in which the very point of closure for its hero – settlement, family, business, and the symbolic giving up of his horse – would become the focus for the existential restlessness of the western genre and of its characters endlessly searching for the very things that the Virginian has given up or lost.[35] Thus, in repressing the tensions between motion and stasis and providing the reader instead with a resolution built on the social incorporation of the cowpuncher and his youthful wanderings, Wister gave generations of future western artists a set of surprisingly powerful patterns, themes, and images to contest and explore dialogically in their various works.

NOTES

1. These terms derive from Mikhail Bakhtin's work (in *The Dialogical Imagination*) on dialogue in language and, by extension, culture, work that informs much of this essay and that is very important to the theories of Hall, Gilroy, Bhabha, and Clifford also referred to in this essay.

2. Wister, *The Virginian* (Signet, 1979), x. Page numbers for subsequent citations will be given in the text.

3. Davis, *Owen Wister's West*, 43, 37, 56.

4. Hall, "Cultural Identity and Diaspora," 223.

5. Gilroy, "Diaspora and Detours of Identity," 308.

6. Slotkin, *Gunfighter Nation*, 43, 44.

7. Gilroy, "Diaspora and Detours of Identity," 328, 331.

8. Hall, "New Cultures for Old," 207.

9. Hall, "Cultural Identity and Diaspora," 235.

10. Clifford, *Routes*, 24, 25.

11. Wister, "The Evolution of the Cow-Puncher," 46–47.

12. In *The Virginian*, the hero sleeps with a woman whose morality is clearly questioned since "impropriety lurked noiselessly all over her . . . [I]t was interblended with her sum total" (29). It is as if the idea of "interblending" always suggests immorality or corruption to Wister.

13. Clifford, *Routes*, 2, 30, 251. Clifford develops these arguments in his *Predicament of Culture* and in Clifford and Marcus, eds., *Writing Culture*.

14. Bhabha, *The Location of Culture*, 1–2.

15. Wister, "The Evolution of the Cow-Puncher," 42, 37.

16. Hall, "Cultural Identity and Diaspora," 225.

17. Wister, "The Evolution of the Cow-Puncher," 43, 50.

18. Wister, "The Evolution of the Cow-Puncher," 47, 48.

19. See Hall, "Cultural Identity and Diaspora"; Gilroy, *The Black Atlantic*; Clifford, *Routes*; and Bhabha, *The Location of Culture*.

20. Wister, "The Evolution of the Cow-Puncher," 49. The idea of the *contact zone* in the way in which I use it here is best explored and defined in Pratt's *Imperial Eyes*, a book clearly influenced by the work of Bakhtin, who employs the related concept of a *zone of contact* in his writings (see Bakhtin, *The Dialogical Imagination*).

21. Tatum, "Topographies of Transition in Western American Literature"; Wister, "The Evolution of the Cow-Puncher," 49.

22. Clifford, *Routes*, 3, 25.

23. The chronotope is "a setting or scene organizing time and space in representable whole form" (Clifford, *Routes*, 25) or "an optic for reading texts as x-rays of the forces at work in the culture system from which they spring" (Bakhtin, *The Dialogical Imagination*, 426).

24. The "rites of passage" tradition is a key component of the American literary tradition and has particular connections with the West since the West was so often the geographic point of desire for the journeying heroes, from Huck Finn, to Sal Paradise in *On the Road*, to Billy and Wyatt in *Easy Rider*.

25. The novel makes many references to youth, suggesting that both the West and the Virginian's experiences are "youthful" and, therefore, engaged in a process of growth toward maturity. This is an important effect in the patterns of the novel and in the way in which Wister resolves his hero's changes. Wister's "To the Reader" claims the West as "the true fountain of youth" (ix), and in the novel it is referred to as "this great playground of young men" (41).

26. Stuart Hall ("What Is This 'Black' in Black Popular Culture," 472) discusses the concept of "coupling," claiming that "the logic of coupling rather than the logic of a binary opposition" allows for being more than one thing, hence "black and British" or, in Molly and the Virginian's case, "male and female," "East and West," etc.

27. Space is too limited to examine the full role of Molly and her relationship with the Virginian in the novel, but in a number of exchanges she is seen as an important voice in his transformation. Molly is drawn to many of the western qualities that she admires in the Virginian ("his roughness was a pleasure to her" [88]), saying that she had "always wanted to be a man" (83), and in part she wants him to remain exactly as he is when she first knows him. She also educates him and provides a tentative dialogue with him on matters of violence and other masculine pursuits.

28. The novel has much to say about justice. The figure of Judge Henry, of

course, has developed a whole theory of frontier Western justice, which he tells to Molly to justify the Virginian's lynching of Steve: "The ordinary citizens . . . are where the law comes from. . . . [T]hey chose the delegates who made the Constitution. . . . [W]hen they lynch they only take back what they once gave" (273).

29. Wister, "Concerning 'Bad Men,'" 91.

30. "The phrase "phases of going" used in the title is taken from Wister's "The Evolution of the Cow-Puncher" (1987/1995), 49, where he is discussing cowboys as nomads and hoboes.

31. The idea of wandering is also associated with the Indians who have wounded the Virginian, for they have wandered off the reservation. Thus, in rejecting wandering the Virginian also rejects the savagery and disorder associated with the tribes.

32. Wister, preface to *Members of the Family*, 142.

33. Gilroy, *The Black Atlantic*, 3.

34. Bhabha, *The Location of Culture*, 219. The concept *third space* is an idea that I have discussed at length elsewhere (see Campbell, *The Cultures of the American New West*) and names the space "in between," a new, hybrid space in which binaries are collapsed and identities coexist simultaneously.

35. I am thinking in particular of the work of Cormac McCarthy's *Blood Meridian*. This novel, in ironic reference to Wister's seminal text, named its demonic central character Judge Holden.

11   WISTER AND THE "NEW WEST"   *Susan Kollin*

In Susan Kollin's essay Neil Campbell's nineteenth-century transients have morphed into those yuppie western settlers "amenity migrants" as Kollin explores the "convergence of the Old West and the New." Her essay is a fitting conclusion to this volume, for she argues most forcefully for the novel's contemporary significance: "what is striking about Wister's Old West portrayal are the ways in which the problems plaguing the novel's regional vision," "problems involving land use, tenure rights, and race relations," are still central to the region's evolving identity. As Kollin makes clear, today's policies are shaped by the fictions of the past: "The most powerful arguments have tended to come from the cultural level, where they are based in ideas shaped by a nostalgia for a mythic western past." As a cultural critic, Kollin focuses less on the novel than on "the debates that it has fostered since it was published," and her essay demonstrates the ongoingness of those debates and how a reading of The Virginian *provides a point of departure for serious discussion of the twenty-first-century West.*

This is how we prefer to see him, standing alone in the long sundown of our collective imagination . . . a heroic silhouette rising from the lengthening shadows of Main Street as if snipped out of the history that falls away and out of the picture. Homeless, ancestorless, his name itself is a kind of genre, his presence is as ancient and unanswerable as the granite peaks that catch the last of the dying light beyond him. . . . Like any myth, the Western myth is an artifact, a tool made by human beings to do a certain work. Yet every artifact . . . raises an appropriate question: whom does it serve, and who pays the price?

ZEESE PAPANIKOLAS, *Trickster in the Land of Dreams*

At high noon it's easier to get espresso in Bozeman, Montana, than it is to find an available spittoon. . . . The West as a home for dust-chewing cowboys, lonely ranchers and strong-willed miners and loggers has all but disappeared. But the West as a theme park built around its legends is stronger than ever. Nearly a hundred years after the American frontier was pronounced dead by historians like Frederick Jackson Turner, a new generation of faux ranchers, urban cowboys and high-country artists are getting rich helping to develop a new economy out of the enduring icons of the old West. . . . They make their living not from tearing apart the scenery or wrestling with the elements, but from selling an image that Americans refuse to let go of.

TIMOTHY EGAN, "The Mild West"

Ex-urbanite telecommuters dwell in one-acre ranchettes featuring *Sunset* magazine front-room vistas. Small-town food co-ops offer organic bison to their health-conscious middle-class consumers. Newly erected horse corrals butt against vinyl-sided buildings, which themselves butt against the town's local two-lane highway. Satellite dishes connecting the rural West to the global community and sports utility vehicles delivering weekend recreationalists to ski resorts grace the yards and driveways of gated communities and subdivisions alike. Ralph Lauren–clad professionals and New Age enthusiasts join forces to prevent the building of yet one more Wal-Mart or strip mall in their communities. Snowmobilers, skiers, mountain bikers, and out-of-state tourists clash with each other over trail use and other outdoor etiquette in national and state parks.

Anyone who has lived in the western United States during the last decade or so can probably tell you about these strange new scenarios, about the demographic and economic transformations that have brought profound changes to the region in recent years. Beginning in the 1990s, writers, critics, historians, and geographers have made much of the growing popularity of the American West and have pointed to the ways in which a recent surge of interest in the region has brought with it more than just a dramatic boom in population as documented by the most recent census. Many residents and scholars, in fact, have begun addressing the emergence of what they call the *New West*, with newspaper articles, academic essays, and even an atlas published by the Center for the American West at the University of Colorado in Boulder all documenting the far-reaching changes that the region underwent in the late twentieth century.[1]

As a terrain that purportedly offers an escape from an all-encompassing modernity, the American West has in recent years been radically altered by the forces of global capitalism, by a new postindustrial service-sector economy, and by a booming migration that shows no signs of abating. The New West, we are told, is a region undergoing the forces of hyperdevelopment, a place transformed by amenity migrants, dot-com million-aires, trophy homes, ranchette estates, ski resorts, espresso bars, and a burgeoning New Age movement.[2]

During the past decade Westerners have experienced a clash of cul-tures as the legacy of ranching, mining, and logging from the previ-ous century has given way to a high-stakes computer industry and an amenities-dependent, recreation-based economy that relies heavily on outside tourist dollars to keep it afloat.

While the term *New West* continues to be used in a variety of settings to describe shifts that have appeared throughout the region in recent years, problems arise in discussing the emergence of this New West, primarily because the concept risks establishing a radical break between "old" and "new," between the identity of the region today and the shape and con-tour of the region as it seemingly once was. A dichotomy between old and new, for instance, threatens to overlook the ways in which the New West might not be so new after all. As various writers and critics have argued, one of the defining features of the New West is its almost parasitic relation with the region's past. If the Old West was thought to be an antidote to modernity, a space of refuge for disaffected urbanites, then what has been called the *New West* simply extends this promise for a postmodern era. Even critics who have enthusiastically adopted the term find themselves questioning the stark divisions that supposedly mark these two worlds. In describing the dynamics of this strange new beast, for instance, the histo-rian Patricia Limerick comments on the peculiar New West enthusiasm for things old, pointing out that in recent years New Western industries have begun turning a profit by fashioning shrines out of Old West land-marks. In the 1990s, the New West as frontier theme park has come to op-erate as one of the region's most prosperous tourist inventions.[3]

The slippage between past and present Wests is not the only problem troubling the dichotomy between old and new. The dualism also tends to assign a false sense of difference to the New West, implying that it holds a critical perspective outside regional myths while consigning the Old West to forever occupying an unreflective place in American history. In this sense, cultural production associated with the Old West is presented as being completely unmarked by self-knowledge, while cultural production associated with the New West somehow remains untouched by illusion. A quick perusal of the short stories of Stephen Crane and Bret Harte, the western writings of Mark Twain, or even the scores of settler narratives in-dicates that nineteenth-century Americans and many "Old Westerners" themselves often regarded the region as a fantasy space, an invention of overly optimistic national hopes and dreams.[4] In the same way, a look at recent television and cinematic productions celebrating the West indicates that the romance of the region continues to hold strong today, even in our media-savvy, postmodern era.

Finally, by declaring a New West departure from the Old, scholars threaten to dehistoricize the immense changes that have shaped the region for the past several hundred years. As one contributor to the *Atlas of the New West* points out, the American Indian West at the end of the pre-contact era certainly underwent massive transformations on the arrival of European settlers. The subsequent fur-trading and mining West also saw vast changes as each economy rose and fell in a series of boom-and-bust cycles. Even the cowboy and ranching West was altered into something new as the advent of technology in the early twentieth century dramatically altered the relations that white settlers had previously forged with the land.[5] In fact, the profound changes shaping the region at the turn of the century serve as a subtheme in *The Virginian*, which, even as it invented an enduring vision of the West for American readers, already lamented the passing of an era. Later, by the mid-twentieth century, the war effort created yet another West as industrial development, urbanization, and migration continued to transform the region. All these regional changes may lead us to wonder whether contemporary discussions of the New West are merely the lamentations of a late-twentieth-century white middle-class populace now finding itself displaced, strangely located in much the same position as the American Indians who, a century earlier, were themselves removed from and dispossessed of their ancestral homes.[6]

The continuing popularity of Wister's Old West novel may be examined for what it reveals about the problems and possibilities offered by discussions of the New West. Over the years, *The Virginian* has remained a popular choice for university courses in western American literature and the modern American novel. Credited with introducing the figure of the modern cowboy into American literary history, *The Virginian* has continually been regarded as an archetypal western narrative even though, as Lee Clark Mitchell and other critics point out, subsequent westerns developed along very different lines, making the novel a strange exemplar in the history of the genre, particularly in the ways in which it foregrounds heterosexual romance and treats the main character's linguistic abilities.[7] The story has also been filmed numerous times, beginning in the silent era with Cecil B. DeMille's 1914 version, and most recently in 2000 by TNT, the television production company founded by the media mogul Ted Turner, himself a New West icon and one of today's most successful frontier promoters.

On the eve of the hundredth anniversary of Wister's novel, it becomes time perhaps to look back on the text for the ways in which its major concerns have managed to cross an Old West/New West divide. Although *The Virginian* was produced in a particular era under specific social and political conditions, what is striking about Wister's Old West portrayal are the ways in which the problems plaguing the novel's regional vision – problems involving land use, tenure rights, and race relations – are concerns that are still being worked out by critics, writers, and residents throughout the region. If New West scholars have difficulty upholding clear distinctions between the old and the new, Wister's novel likewise faces problems delivering on what it argues for – an understanding of the West as a unique and promising terrain, a site offering escape from a corrupting civilized East, and an important locale to regenerate a threatened Anglo masculinity. By novel's end the notion that the West offers a radical break from history, from the traditions of the East, and from the forces of corruption that plague other U.S. regions cannot be sustained as the distinctions upholding the West as an exceptional space, a place set off from larger social forces, begin to break down. Wister's problem is thus the dilemma of many New West critics who likewise have been shaped by the very elements against which they define themselves but who are unable to acknowledge these quite real and powerful connections.

"WHOM DOES IT SERVE? WHO PAYS THE PRICE?"

One of the ways in which *The Virginian* forces a reconsideration of Old West/New West dichotomies appears in its treatment of the struggle over land rights, a concern that resonates in the region today to the extent that one historian points to land use as the "hottest issue" presently shaping the American West.[8] In a reading of *The Virginian*, Zeese Papanikolas follows other critics in arguing that the novel performs important cultural work in debates over land tenure at the turn of the century. More specifically, the novel may be read as a defense of the brutal Johnson County Range War of 1892, which pitted the region's major cattle ranchers against the small homesteaders who were accused of fencing the open range, thus threatening the economic futures of the powerful stock growers. Cattle ranchers in the region went so far as to hire Texas gunmen to tame the homesteaders who were thought to be curtailing the freedom of the range. While arguing that the novel functions as an apology for lynch law "in a frontier situation where vigilantism is the only law that 'works,'" Papanikolas examines the ways in which Wister's cowboy myth operated in another sense to sell a whitewashed view of capitalist ownership to a concerned American public. In Wister's text, the laboring but noble proletariat on the ranch functioned in an important way to make an unstable and inequitable social order appear acceptable. As Papanikolas argues, the myth of the cowboy that was perfected by Wister came to serve as a "sort of forlorn wish for an 'innocent' capitalism far from the tooth-and-claw economics of Wall Street . . . so busy creating fortunes for the few and misery for the many."[9] For Papanikolas and other critics, *The Virginian* deserves attention less for how it functions in the development of the western than for the ways in which it intervened in debates during the period concerning labor, economy, and American national identity.

The myth of the cowboy and the romance of the ranch continue to shape how many Americans regard the region today, a legacy whose power has proved to be difficult to dismantle. Perhaps no one knows this lesson better than Debra L. Donahue, formerly a biologist and currently a professor at the University of Wyoming's Law School. Donahue completed a study a few years ago entitled *The Western Range Revisited* in which she argued for a reconsideration of federal grazing policies and the removal of livestock on federal lands in the arid and semiarid West, a logic that directly reverses the major sentiments that Wister expressed in his novel.[10] Donahue's book was based on years of training in the field, first as a wildlife-science major at Utah State University, then as a graduate student in wildlife biology at Texas A&M University, and later as a scientist working for the Bureau of Land Management in three western states. In chapter after chapter, *The Western Range Revisited* suggests "the unthinkable," as she puts it, by cataloging the economic, ecological, and social problems that cattle ranching causes on the arid and semiarid Western range. In the face of mounting evidence that public land grazing is "economically inefficient and inequitable and causes severe, sometimes irreversible, impacts to the land," Donahue argues that to continue allowing cattle and sheep to graze on public lands is an increasingly insupportable agricultural practice.[11]

Donahue is very clear about her argument: throughout her study, she contends that cattle ranching on arid lands is ecologically unsound and unquestionably detrimental to the health of the western range and that no convincing economic argument for sustaining the practice can be made. As she argues, over the years, the most powerful arguments have tended to come from the cultural level, where they are based in ideas shaped by a nostalgia for a mythic western past. In particular, the most vociferous arguments that she has encountered involve concerns about sustaining a frontier way of life. Proponents of these arguments contend that western ranching functions as a regional tradition that needs to be sustained and preserved, not further restricted or abolished. By way of critique, Donahue spends much of her book reexamining these responses, which, she argues, are based in a culturally enduring romance – that of the cowboy as the quintessential American hero whose preservation is tied up with ideas of the nation itself.[12] In particular, Donahue addresses the argument that getting rid of ranching as we know it will have a negative effect on tourism across the region, currently one of the New West's biggest industries. The claim is that tourists will be less attracted to a West that no longer delivers the sites and scenes nostalgically associated with the region. As she notes, however, present-day agricultural practices have themselves been highly destructive of tourism by contributing to the decline of biodiversity in the region, damaging watersheds, and causing further desertification of public lands.[13]

In romantic views of the Old West, Donahue contends, ranchers are cowboys who have somehow come to embody the very meaning of the region itself. Yet as she goes on to explain, ranchers have never historically "filled the boots of the mythical cowboy – the independent, freedom-loving, self-reliant figure of the open range." Instead, many of them historically have been too quick to replace their own cowboys

with new-fangled balers and four-wheelers and snowmobiles . . . [while] appeal-[ing] to public sentiment and nostalgia to help preserve their traditional way of life. Arguing that the economy of their local community depends on their staying in business, they "moonlight" to make ends meet. The animals they raise on the range deplete the very capital upon which their, and the animals', living depends. They call themselves the "original conservationists," but they have a rifle slung behind the seat of their pickups for picking off coyotes and other "varmints." They poison prairie dogs and willows and sagebrush and replace native meadows with water-guzzling alfalfa.[14]

Although she concedes that some ranchers may operate their businesses differently and thus escape her critique, Donahue clearly holds powerful beliefs about the culture of ranching in the West today, recasting romantic views of cattle owners in much the same way that Papanikolas and other critics have sought to recast popular understandings of the cattle-ranching west in *The Virginian.*

Given the thrust of her argument and her no-holds-barred description of stock growers, one should not be surprised to learn that Donahue's study has not won her many friends in the cattle industry. In fact, if anything, the opposite has been true. As she explains, while there may be current support for a change in public land use, there are difficulties in implementing these more economically and environmentally sound ranching practices, largely because ranchers wield much more political power in the West than perhaps their numbers represent.[15] Some of this power was unleashed in a rather dramatic manner with the publication of her book in 1999. On the floor of the Wyoming legislature, for instance, Donahue's study was bitterly denounced with discussion going so far as to call for the closure of the University of Wyoming's Law School. In subsequent months, a flurry of letters appeared in major newspapers across the state, touching off a heated controversy over the implications of Donahue's argument.[16]

In many ways, *The Western Range Revisited* takes us full circle, back to Owen Wister's novel and the debates that it has fostered since it was published. In Wister's text, the conflicts over land tenure and the role of violence in defending private property remain powerful issues shaping public discussions about the western range today. The bitter land debate generated by Donahue's study and the violent responses that have ensued indicate precisely the extent to which concerns introduced by *The Virginian* remain unresolved in the present era. To a certain degree, however, the critical treatment of Wister's text and the discussions following the publication of Donahue's study tend to overlook another issue shaping land use in the West, one that has yet to be adequately addressed. While critics have focused attention on the novel's uses of frontier violence in protecting a certain class order, another form of violence seems to go unnoticed. The attention in the novel on whether western lynching can be any more justified than southern lynching, I would argue, functions as kind of a structuring silence that overlooks a previous violence occurring in the region. While *The Virginian* concerns itself with unresolved questions of how the western range should be used, another problem appearing in the novel stems from the ongoing displacement of the region's Indian population. Missing from the debate over Donahue, too, is a vision of an alternative land use, a sense of how the region's indigenous inhabitants forged different relations with the land.

Pierre Macherey has argued that the speech of any narrative always comes from a particular silence. No book is ever fully "self-sufficient"; each is "necessarily accompanied by a certain absence, without which it would not exist." As he goes on to explain, a "knowledge of the book must include a consideration of this absence."[17] Macherey's observations encourage us not only to look at the structuring absences of narrative but also to assess what makes these gaps necessary to the successful operations of the text. John G. Cawelti has commented on the absence of Indians in the classic western, arguing that that absence serves a necessary function in the logic of the genre. The more Indians are featured in the western, he argues, the more ambivalent the whole narrative project becomes. As soon as the western devotes space to Indians and their concerns, readers' sympathy threatens to be hijacked, a movement that violates the central logic of the western, which traditionally consigns Native Americans to the role of savagery, as the element that is always on the way out, always vanishing in the face of white progress and civilization.[18] The disregard for what might be thought of as an "originary violence" – the displacement of Indians from western lands – is thus required for the successful operations of the western. In *The Virginian*, the attention to the problems of cattle rustling and the debate over the subsequent lynching of a cowboy redirects readers from the original violence of white settlement – the problems of land theft and genocide – in order to focus attention on the threat posed to the Anglo settlement of the region. As a result, the silences and absences structuring the text ultimately operate to safeguard a larger social order, the hegemony of the Anglo landowning population.

If, as Amy Kaplan has argued, a "disavowal of empire" has traditionally shaped American literature as a whole, then perhaps readers should not be surprised to note that a similar silence shapes the classic western.[19] At its core, the genre has been plagued with questions of expansion and empire. Its resolution has often been either to unmap the land, erasing the signs of the region's previous inhabitants, or to reinvent the victim of theft as the Anglo settler. Both these elements structure Wister's Old West narrative in important ways.

In *The Virginian*, for instance, Native Americans are no longer the subjects of dispossession and displacement; instead, white settlers have taken their place as the region's wronged party. At one point in the novel, the greenhorn narrator explains with some relief that a band of marauding

Indians has finally been taken into custody. "They had come unpermitted from a southern reservation," he tells us, "hunting . . . thieving."[20] Here, Indians function as agents of theft, with the white population serving as the vulnerable and, therefore, innocent party, in a rather odd reversal of actual historical events. Wister uses various tropes to justify this displacement and naturalize the presence of Anglo newcomers while underplaying the absence of tribal peoples in his regional vision. Throughout the novel, for instance, the narrator lavishes praise on the heroic qualities of the Virginian, using an over-the-top language to describe the character as an exceptionally capable and exemplary Westerner. In the novel's opening sequence as the train slows down at the platform station at Medicine Bow, the narrator likens the Virginian to an exotic tiger, his movements "smooth and easy, as if his muscles flowed beneath his skin" (1). Seated in the company of other curious sight-seers, he catches the Virginian at the height of his powers, as the latter skillfully ropes a reluctant cow pony in a scene that makes the hero into a romantic spectacle, an object of consumption for the fascinated eastern tourists. This exoticizing language continues as the narrator refers to the "tiger undulations" of the hero's body, describing him as a man with a "wild calling," whose "tiger limberness" and "beauty were rich with unabated youth" (43), a "Bengal tiger" (144) whose quick "spring" (193) delivers rightful justice to his enemies.

While the animal trope functions to naturalize the Virginian's brand of masculinity, it does so in an odd way, by employing a creature that is not itself native to the American West. It is important to note too that Wister's use of the exotic animal trope does not end with references to the hero as a Bengal tiger but continues as he presents cattle themselves as somehow also native to the West, referring to Wyoming as "Cattle Land" (31, 64) and "cowland" (135) as if the presence of ranch life is an unquestionable given in the region. Wister in effect uses exotic animals – tigers and cattle – to justify the Virginian's actions and the growing presence of the cattle industry in the West; that neither animal is native to the region seems not to matter much as the narrative works to naturalize a way of life that displaces and silences the West's actual native inhabitants.

Wister's treatment of sexuality in the novel operates in ways that are relevant to my discussion of absence and presence, empire and expansion, and land use and race relations in the West. Recently, critics have begun reexamining the relationship between the protagonist and other male characters in the novel in order to draw attention to the queer subtext of

The Virginian. Scholars have, for instance, focused on the cowboy hero's friendship with Steve, the only figure in the novel who calls him by a nickname ("Jeff"), and his relationship with the tenderfoot narrator, who frequently adopts a feminized position in the text.[21] In various places, for instance, the narrator lingers over the Virginian's body, his gaze fascinated by the figure that he describes and by opportunities to "peep through the keyhole at his inner man" (69). Throughout the text, the narrator frequently expresses despair at his inadequate powers of description and, at times, laments his fate in not having been born "a woman myself" (160). At another point, Molly accuses the Virginian of being a dandy. She remarks on the cowboy hero's preoccupation with his physical appearance, telling him that she has made an important "discovery" about him – that he is "fonder of good clothes" (313) than she is.

What is fascinating about the novel is that even as it offers a vision of American masculinity needed to counter the feminizing forces of eastern urban culture, it breaks down gender divisions themselves, with masculinity and femininity becoming fully intertwined entities in various characters. The Virginian himself constantly vacillates between the two; while the preface assures us that the ungoverned hours of his job do not "unman" him in any way, the hero is continually made into a feminized object of a sexual gaze as the narrator eyes the Virginian's body, here described as belonging to a "slim young giant, more beautiful than pictures." Using a comparison usually confined to the female body, the narrator at one point goes so far as to suggest that the hero's physical features remind him of "ripe peaches" (3). In another sequence, Em'ly, the confused hen who so desperately wants to mother any stray object that comes along her path, is likewise described as "sure manly-lookin'" and "near being a rooster" (45). Meanwhile, during the scene with the hen, our tenderfoot narrator, still recovering from his earlier humiliation as the butt of a joke between the ranch hands, describes himself as being "a little ruffled" (44) at his treatment, employing a phrase that feminizes by drawing connections between Em'ly and himself. Later, Scipio enters the bunkhouse and catches the narrator off guard. "Don't look so bashful," he calls out to the Easterner. "There's only us girls here" (148). Along with the later scenes of cross-dressed babies who are swapped at the town dance, these instances help confuse the gender boundaries that Wister's novel purportedly sought to stabilize.

Sexuality also becomes caught up with larger issues debated in the text. Early in the story, Wister takes what seems to be a long digression in order to stage a scene in the sleeping room where much is made of the male ranch hands sharing beds. "Well, they have got ahead of us," the Virginian remarks on entering the room. "They have staked out their claims" (13). The cowboy hero, however, manages to jump these "claims" by manipulating one of the workers out of his bed. Although he initially seems willing to share space with the other man, the Virginian later warns his bed companion not to touch him lest he become startled and turn violently while sleeping. "I'm dreamin' of Indians when I do that," he explains. "And if anything touches me then, I'm liable to grab my knife right in my sleep" (24). The Virginian's ruse eventually proves successful as his would-be bed mate relinquishes his "claim" in the sleeping room, thus allowing the hero to occupy it himself.

This interlude, I would argue, functions as more than an instance in which the heroic cowboy demonstrates his abilities to outwit other workers by managing to trick a man out of his bed. In the classic western, claim jumping is typically presented as an action perpetrated by the greedy outlaw or other less-than-reputable character. Here, however, the cowboy hero manages to smooth talk a drummer out his "claim" in a manner that supposedly speaks more about his intellectual and verbal abilities than about his shifty and underhanded ways. Critics have typically regarded the Virginian's claim jumping in the context of the text's homosociality while saying little about how the scene might play into another reading of the novel. The idea of *claim jumping* and even the term *claim*, however, open up a range of possibilities here. What does it mean to *stake a claim* in this particular context, and who indeed is a rightful *claimant* to these western lands? Claim jumping in this sense might serve as a useful metaphor describing white settlement in the West, the displacement and dispossession of the region's indigenous inhabitants. For the most part, however, these ideas are left unexamined as it becomes clear that Anglo ownership of a certain sort is a given in the novel. Cleverness and heroism are qualities needed to ensure that land is occupied by the rightful figure and that a particular social order prevails. In the text, the Virginian thus gets his "claim" by announcing his abilities as a successful Indian fighter, a frontiersman whose dreams are haunted by dangerous encounters with a ghostly enemy. Staged in this fashion, the sleeping room interlude reveals a great deal about the staging of western conquest in the novel and the ways in which the text helps reposition the victim of land theft as the heroic Anglo settler.

In this way, *The Virginian* functions very much in the tradition of the western in its insistence on recasting victims and restaging history through silences. Such uses of absences and gaps in the classic western have not, however, gone unnoted by Indian writers and critics over the years. Recently, one of the more interesting efforts to redirect debates in western literature has appeared in the work of the Cherokee/German/Canadian writer Thomas King. In his recent novel, *Truth and Bright Water* (1999), the character Monroe, a Blackfoot artist and painter, devises a clever solution to the problems of colonial conquest and white land theft. He devotes himself to various recovery efforts across the world, at one point restoring the bones of Indians dug up by archaeologists and anthropologists in a triumphant moment of forced repatriation of tribal property. He explains: "Took me years to collect them. . . . I stole them from lots of museums. Toronto. New York. Paris. London. Berlin. You name the museum, I've probably been there. . . . Children. . . . I found them in drawers and boxes and stuck away on dusty shelves. Indian children. . . . Happens all the time. . . . Anthropologists and archaeologists dig the kids up, clean them off, and stick them in drawers. Every ten years or so, some bright graduate student opens the drawer, takes a look, writes a paper, and shuts the drawer. . . . So I rescued them." As an artist, Monroe is hired by museums throughout Europe to restore old paintings that have been collected over the years. He remembers with great fondness how one of his jobs involved a landscape piece entitled *Sunrise on Little Turtle Lake.* In the tradition of the nineteenth-century pastoral, the painting features a scene of "nature" with all signs of its native inhabitants erased. "You know what I did?" Monroe asks another character. "I painted the village and Indians back into the painting."[22] Here, Monroe provides a fascinating twist on the concept of landscape "restoration"; in this case, Monroe's actions operate to replace, not what the artist originally painted, but what the artist originally left out. King's novel thus reminds us what has been removed from European visions of the land and what in fact needs to be restored.

From Wister's emphasis on claim jumping and property rights to King's focus on reclamation and tribal sovereignty, it becomes clear that land use continues to be as contested in the New West as it was in the Old West and that divisions marking a New West departure from Old West concerns are distinctions that ultimately cannot be upheld. Like Wister and the larger cohort of Easterners at the turn of the century who sought to make the West into a place where larger national problems could be resolved, a number of figures today are currently repositioning the region as a site where the country can both escape from and find its history. The strength of the New West tourist industry, for instance, shows how powerful the desire remains for locating a frontier American past in the present era. Yet Wister's Old West novel actually reveals how a similar desire operated a hundred years ago. At one point in the text, a train carrying cattle and tourists through Montana is delayed on the tracks until a problem is resolved further down the line. In this scene, the travelers are left to fend for themselves with little to occupy them until Indians from the nearby Crow reservation approach the crowds of stranded tourists, offering them "painted bows and arrows and shiny horns" (115). In this scene, the Crow – now emptied of their threat – become incorporated into the tourist spectacle, no longer symbols of frontier danger, but part of the western landscape to be enjoyed and consumed by curious sight-seers. With the Indians already incorporated into the tourism industry in *The Virginian*, divisions erected between the Old West and the New begin to be dismantled. In both cases, the desire to consume an imagined past, the nostalgic yearning for a seemingly vanished way of life, shapes attitudes toward the region and its native inhabitants.

The convergence of the Old West and the New is perhaps nowhere more visibly enacted today than in the appearance of the West's new gentleman rancher, Ted Turner. And, of course, the importance of this "second coming" of Turner in the late twentieth century has not escaped scholars' attention. Patricia Limerick has recently suggested, for instance, that the West in the present era is now, "more than ever, a Turnerian West, but 'Ted' has replaced 'Frederick Jackson'" in this new context.[23] In some ways a most unlikely heir to Wister's displaced southern hero, Ted Turner has sparked attention across the region and the nation for his distinct land-use policies. Touting bison as the answer to the problems of the western range (and echoing what Indians have long known), Turner represents an interesting blend of the old with the new, becoming the intrepid rancher who announces his plans to replace cattle with bison on his vast landholdings in the West while turning a profit at it too. "I'm going to have the biggest bison operation in the world, and I'm going to show you can do something compatible with nature and still make money doing it," he once told the press.[24] Bringing his own brand of entrepreneurialism to the West, the media mogul/baseball owner/avid United Nations supporter hopes to find new economic success in an industry that promises to extend and even challenge what his imaginary predecessor, the Virginian, offered a hundred years ago.

"BISON — IT'S WHAT'S FOR DINNER"

Emerging as a powerful symbolic force in the region, Ted Turner has often been associated directly and indirectly with recent developments in the West, taking on a kind of mythical status akin to what still surrounds Old West figures like Wister, Remington, and Roosevelt. In the process, Turner has not shown much interest in keeping a low profile across the region. Not long after he purchased the Flying D ranch near Bozeman, Montana, for instance, he sold off the previous rancher's equipment and livestock, surprising his neighbors by ordering the removal of all the ranch's barbed wire fencing in order to return the pastures to native grasses.[25] Gaining a reputation for his ranching efforts on the numerous parcels of land that he owns in Nebraska, Montana, New Mexico, South Dakota, and Kansas, Turner has had to battle the press about his western credentials, particularly as owner of the Atlanta Braves, a team whose fans are renowned for their racially insensitive "chop."[26] (When asked to comment on the name of his baseball club and the fans' choice of bandstand cheer, Turner remarked that the term *brave* should not be considered offensive. "There is nothing wrong with Braves," he contended. "It's a compliment. Braves are warriors." Turner did concede to reporters, however, that he would "like to see something done to get rid of the chop.")[27]

In the meantime, Turner has traveled extensively across the West, making few friends and mostly angering the livestock industry for his unabashed support for the replacement of cattle with bison as an ecologically and economically sound agricultural practice. His newfound environmentalism, however, has often proved inconsistent. It was reported that on his ranch in Montana, Turner arranged to have ten feet removed from the top of a distant hill so that the man-made trout pond that he had installed on his land could better capture the reflection of the nearby Spanish Peaks mountain range.[28] Apparently, such drastic acts of landscaping are not confined to the New West. As it turns out, *The Virginian* also features a moment where the characters debate whether to allow a freight train to move back and forth in its tracks in order to shave down a hilltop that is impeding their efforts at moving cattle to the markets of the East. "Now this was an honest engineering fact," Wister writes. "Better'n settin' dudes squintin' through telescopes an' cipherin' over one per cent re-ductions" (114), his hero explains to the other cowboys.

Ted Turner's support for bison has also emerged in rather strange ways over the years. When Ralphie III, the mascot for the University of Colorado, died unexpectedly in 1998, for instance, Turner came to the rescue by replacing him free of charge with a member of his Montana bison ranch.[29] Although his enthusiasm for bison sets him apart from many of his neighbors in the ranching industry, Turner has not completely abandoned tradition. In fact, he has done much to popularize Old West history over the years, with his successful television station broadcasting more classic western films than perhaps any other while developing new productions as well, including recent remakes of popular western narratives such as *The Virginian* and *High Noon*.

Turner's enthusiasm for bison is not without some merit. Bison has long been known to be better for the range, better for western grasses, and better for those concerned about their health and, particularly, their cholesterol levels. Raised free of growth hormones, bison is also considered more flavorful than beef and requires less maintenance in the process. Yet for many in the livestock community, bison are considered a threat to the cowboy legacy of the Old West. Although bison preceded cattle on the western range, the animals have not been able to capture the imagination and sympathy of Anglo cowboys like cattle do. Perhaps some of this reluctance to embrace the animal has to do with the independent nature of bison themselves. The Bozeman writer Todd Wilkinson explains that some cattle ranchers have expressed unease with bison, in part because the animals cannot be tamed and herded like cattle. As the mythic embodiment of frontier individualism and self-reliance, cowboys oddly have not developed an appreciation for the independent nature of bison. While cattle people have largely not been inspired with romantic feelings about bison, the same is not true for Turner. As Wilkinson reports, the origins of his fascination with bison can be traced back to a childhood collection of buffalo nickels. Turner apparently felt sorry for the animals after hearing stories from his father about their plight in the late nineteenth century and how they were almost driven to extinction by white settlers.[30] A certain Old West nostalgia has also shaped the attitudes of Turner's ex-wife, Jane Fonda, who has long shared his enthusiasm for ranch life. According to another reporter, Fonda likewise had strong memories of the region from her youth; she once confessed that as a child she loved horseback riding and confided that the Lone Ranger was one of her early role models.[31]

Many of Turner's efforts at restoring bison to the range have undoubtedly been self-serving. At the same time, however, his work has also had unintended positive consequences for some Westerners. While he is certainly the most famous bison advocate today, Turner is not the only figure working toward a restoration of the animal on the western range. Presently, the West is witnessing a return of the bison on reservations, a development that has created what some see as a "cultural renaissance" for American Indians. "The symbolism of what's taking place is significant beyond words," Mark Heckert, the executive director of the Intertribal Bison Cooperative in Rapid City, says. "Restoring the everyday contact between Indian people and the buffalo has reinvigorated a synergy that existed for thousands of years but sadly has been absent for the last 100." In the meantime, the return of the bison continues to have a profound effect on Indian communities in ways that differ from how Turner envisions their uses. Arvol Looking Horse, a Lakota spiritual leader in Eagle Butte, South Dakota, says that the return of the bison is helping restore Indian spirituality in the communities. "We look to the buffalo for spiritual guidance," he says. "Like Black Elk told us a long time ago, having these animals back with us means that the well-being of our nation will once again be healthy. I have seen the changes in my own people. It is like a new era has arrived."[32]

Bison advocates, however, still face an uphill battle in some quarters. Much of the recent controversy over the reintroduction of bison, for instance, stems from the fear of brucellosis, a disease that causes cattle to abort if they become infected with it. This concern especially affects range use on public lands. In Yellowstone National Park, for instance, bison have crossed out of park boundaries in order to forage on lower-elevation grasses during the winter. During the 1996–97 winter season, nearly eleven hundred Yellowstone bison ended up being slaughtered by the Department of Livestock (DOL) after they moved out of the park into Montana. That season's unusually harsh winter together with the DOL's wildlife policy resulted in a loss of nearly two-thirds of the park's bison, the nation's last wild, free-roaming herd. The next year, volunteers formed a multiracial, grassroots organization called Buffalo Nations in an effort to prevent another season of bison slaughter. Recently renamed the Buffalo Field Campaign, the organization has sent numerous volunteers from across the world to stand with the bison during daylight hours, monitor the DOL's actions, and make sure that no animals are indiscriminately hazed or killed. The organization currently enjoys support from many members of the communities that border the park. Some residents in the area, for instance, have allowed activists to post signs on their property naming their land "buffalo safe zones." The organization has gained support, too, for offering locals a fence-maintenance and -repair service that fixes damage caused by bison and other wildlife.[33]

The Anishinaabe activist, writer, and two-time Green Party vice presidential candidate Winona LaDuke places the struggle over bison in Yellowstone National Park in historical context. For her, the battle surrounding bison is intimately tied to federal Indian policy and events that took place on the plains throughout the nineteenth century. LaDuke explains:

Buffalo determine landscapes. By their sheer numbers, weight, and behavior, they cultivated the prairie, which is the single largest ecosystem in North America. The destruction of the herd set in motion the ongoing ecological and, now, economic crisis that afflicts the Great Plains. Think of it this way: in 1850, 50 million buffalo ranged the prairie system and left it in excellent shape. One hundred percent of all plant and animal species were present without the "benefit" of fences, federal subsidies, elaborate irrigation systems, or powerful pesticides. Today, a century and a half later, the environment is quite different. Industrialized agriculture has transformed land, life, and water. Forty-five and a half million cattle live in this same ecosystem now, but they lack the adaptability of buffalo. Industrial agriculture determines the entire ecosystem, from feed crop monoculture to feedlots, from underpriced public grazing permits (a holdover from old reservation leases) to drawdown of the aquifers, agricultural runoff, and soil erosion. Much of this is for cows. . . . The Great Plains have been stripped of their biodiversity.

As LaDuke goes on to explain, Old West land-use policies continue to shape present-day American Indian life in profound ways. Although it had been designated *Indian territory* by Congress, the area around present-day Yellowstone was seized from Indians in 1872 to create a national park. By the late 1880s, the Indians who lived in the newly established Yellowstone were forced off their lands and placed on reservations. Today, Native Americans have joined other environmental activists in protesting the land-use policies adopted by the park, particularly in regard to the bison. Ranchers, meanwhile, fear the economic repercussions that might arise should the state lose its "brucellosis-free" status. As LaDuke and other writers have pointed out, however, fears about brucellosis are a misplaced concern; not one documented case of transmission from bison to cattle has occurred, even during the forty years that the animals grazed alongside each other. As LaDuke sees it, the recent slaughter in Yellowstone is nothing less than a struggle between bison and cattle, "that age-old mythological conflict between Indians and cowboys."[34]

OLD WEST, NEW WEST, AND THE NEXT HUNDRED YEARS

All this talk about bison in the New West may seem to have taken us far from a discussion of *The Virginian* and the debates that it stages about land use in the Old West. Or perhaps not. As many writers and residents throughout the West would argue, the land controversies that rage across the region today are directly linked to controversies that emerged over the past hundred years. Cowboy myths die hard as Westerners currently debate and battle over the grazing of bison in Yellowstone or whether cattle should be removed from arid public lands in the West, as figures like Winona LaDuke, Debra Donahue, and others argue. Indeed, with such debates in place, and with so many people still hashing out these issues, it might be premature to speak of a New West. To be sure, there have been changes over the years that have forced a reconsideration of how many residents and nonresidents regard the region. The accomplishments of the New Western historians, the work done by the new cultural geographers, the emergence of western American cultural studies among the literary crowd, as well as the growing movements for environmental justice and Indian sovereignty are all developments that presently seek to change how we conceptualize the West and its place in U.S. culture, history, and politics.

This essay has argued for a reconsideration of the absences and presences in our visions of the region, in furthering our discussion of land debates and race relations in readings of the western in general and Wister's novel in particular. As I have suggested here, the overwhelming presence of ranch life and the cattle industry in the western, the genre's focus on cowboy culture as a heroic enterprise, has often signaled the absence of bison as well as the dispossession of the region's native inhabitants. This presence itself has also signaled, as Debra Donahue's study indicates, a biodiversity absence on the western range that has had serious and far-reaching environmental consequences that we are only beginning to understand today. At the dawn of the twenty-first century, Ted Turner's enthusiasm for bison along with American Indian efforts at restoration may perhaps lead, if not to its absence, then to perhaps a deemphasis on the region's cowboy ethos. Although it is impossible to look into the future

and predict the next hundred years of political and cultural developments across the West, it seems likely that discussions about the western
range and struggles for Indian sovereignty and land rights will be concerns that shape the region for a long time ahead. It also seems a good bet
that these debates and issues will remain themes that structure the next
generation of western American literature for some time to come.

NOTES

1. The literature addressing the New West is vast, and most accounts offer diverse explanations for the recent changes shaping the region. For a representative overview, see Egan, "The Mild West"; Wilkinson, "In New West, Buffalo Roam
on Ranches"; Campbell, *Cultures of the American New West*; Comer, *Landscapes of the
New West*; Kittredge, *Who Owns the West?* Limerick, *Something in the Soil*; *Living in the
Runaway West*; Russell, *Kill the Cowboy*; and Riebsame, ed., *Atlas of the New West*.

2. For a discussion of the recent upscaling of the West, see Riebsame, preface to
Atlas of the New West, 12–13.

3. See Limerick, "The Shadows of Heaven Itself," 155. See also Egan, "The
Mild West."

4. Forrest Robinson ("Clio Bereft of Calliope") also makes this point in regard
to the "newness" of New Western history, pointing out that many Old West texts
were actually involved in questioning larger nationalist projects that shaped the
region and its literature. These literary texts often express values that have been
associated or even thought to have emerged with the work of recent New Western historians.

5. Even the writers of the *Atlas of the New West* find it difficult to uphold the existence of a new, radically different West, noting instead that there have been many
Wests throughout history (see Riebsame, ed., *Atlas of the New West*, 94, 151).

6. The reporter Dan Burkhart ("Home on the Range") makes a similar argument, commenting on the new "invasion of outsiders and the ways this development has upset many long-term white residents who now talk about being 'native'
to the West themselves." "Ironically," he suggests, "it may be the closest they've
come to understanding what the Crow, Sioux, Blackfeet, and Cheyenne felt when
the prairie schooners rattled into the territory." The Montana writer William Kittredge also comments on the irony of many New West responses to changes in the
region, noting that many folks whose forefathers took land from the Indians are
now astonished as they confront the same fate: "They are furious, thinking everything their people fought and suffered for, over generations, will be taken away"
(*Who Owns the West?* 112).

7. Mitchell, *Westerns*, 95.

8. Limerick, *Something in the Soil*, 169.

9. Papanikolas, *Trickster in the Land of Dreams*, 76, 77.

10. Other scholars have also contributed to the debate about western agricultural and ranching practices. See, e.g., Knobloch, *The Culture of Wilderness*; and
Russell, *Kill the Cowboy*.

11. Donahue, *The Western Range Revisited*, x, 3. Thanks to Frieda Knobloch for
bringing this book to my attention.

12. In other instances, Wyoming's public image as a cowboy state has had negative repercussions for residents. Beth Loffreda (*Losing Matt Shepard*) argues, e.g.,
that in the wake of Matthew Shepard's death the image of Wyoming as the "hate
state" and Laramie as a "hateful, redneck town" (12) circulated in the mainstream media as a blanket explanation and condemnation of the region's residents. In a complicated study of Shepard's murder, Loffreda – who, like Donahue,
is a professor at the University of Wyoming at Laramie – critiques what she calls
"the textureless generalizations of much rapid-response cultural criticism." She
argues that the idea that Laramie has "a bar called the Cowboy? Well, that tells you
pretty much all you need to know" (xi) is precisely the kind of response that needs
to be reassessed in cultural criticism.

13. See Donahue, *The Western Range Revisited*, 54, 96.

14. Donahue, *The Western Range Revisited*, 5.

15. See Donahue, *The Western Range Revisited*, 67–68.

16. The back cover of Donahue's *The Western Range Revisited* gives more information on the statewide debates sparked by her study.

17. Macherey, *A Theory of Literary Production*, 85.

18. Cawelti, *The Six-Gun Mystique Sequel*, 22.

19. Kaplan, "'Left Alone with America.'" In "Nation, Region, and Empire,"
Kaplan places Wister's popular novel within the romance of empire. Like Papanikolas, she reads *The Virginian* as a text enabling the erasure of the West as a national site for political conflicts over land rights and land use.

20. Wister, *The Virginian* (Signet, 1979), 212. Page numbers for subsequent citations will be given in the text.

21. See Wister, *The Virginian*, 264. Blake Allmendinger (*Ten Most Wanted*, 158)
makes this observation about the Virginian's private name. For queer readings of
the novel, see Robinson, *Having it Both Ways*, 45; and Allmendinger, *Ten Most
Wanted*, 153–70.

22. King, *Truth and Bright Water*, 250–51, 133.

23. Limerick, "The Shadows of Heaven Itself," 165. Thanks to Melody Graulich, who described this development to me as the "second coming" of Turner.

24. Burkhart, "Home on the Range."

25. Burkhart, "Home on the Range."

26. Camilli, "Ted Turner Buying Up America."

27. Grizzard, "How Can Ted Stop the Chop?"

28. Burkhart, "Home on the Range."

29. Guttierrez, "CU Buffalo Mascot Dies."

30. Wilkinson, "Buffalo Baron."

31. Ryckman, "Cable Cowboy."

32. Both Mark Heckert and Arvol Looking Horse quoted in Wilkinson, "In New West, Buffalo Roam on Ranches."

33. This information comes from the organization's publication, *Buffalo Field Campaign*, which is made available by Cold Mountain, Cold Rivers, Box 7941, Missoula MT 59807. The organization may be contacted at P.O. Box 957, West Yellowstone MT 59758; at its website, *www.wildrockies.org/buffalo*, or through email, at *buffalo@wildrockies.org*.

34. LaDuke, *All Our Relations*, 145–46 (first quotation), 151–53 (on nontransmission of brucellosis to cattle), 152 (second quotation).

AFTERWORD   *Stephen Tatum*

What is become of the horseman, the cow-puncher,
the last romantic figure upon our soil?

OWEN WISTER, *The Virginian*

"HIS UNROMANTIC FUTURE"

As for Wister's friend Henry James, he would have had the Virginian
killed in the full flower of his manhood rather than subject him to the domesticating hands of Molly and all her Vermont relations.[1] As for Wister's
mother, who weighs in with various criticisms of *The Virginian* within a few
weeks of the novel's publication, she would have eliminated the novel's
final chapter ("At Dunbarton").[2] And as for Wister himself: well, he
allows, in various letters to family and friends, that such critiques of his
first novel do have a basic rightness about them. As in the critique of his
characterization of Molly Stark Wood, who comes off as something of a ci-
pher, in his and others' eyes in 1902. But with regard to the "At Dunbarton" chapter, Wister trusts his writerly instincts and staunchly defends
its presence. Arguing in response to his mother's critique of the novel,
Wister claims that "it was desirable his [the Virginian's] unromantic future should be indicated in a book of this kind."[3] No "book of this kind,"
in other words, should resemble the tragedy of *Romeo and Juliet* that the
Virginian and Molly read together once upon a time in the West. No: the
point of what Wister called his "colonial romance" is, rather, to dramatize, for better or worse, the evolution of the "nomadic, bachelor West"
into the "housed, married West."[4]

Not a tragic end, then, but rather an "unromantic future": on the novel's final page, Wister's narrator relates how Judge Henry's wedding present to the Virginian was the offer of a full partnership in his ranching operation. And how in 1892, after still another round of the "cattle war," the "thieves" finally ruined themselves as well as ranchers like the judge and the Virginian, "for in a broken country there is nothing left to steal."[5] But not to worry: in remarks that clearly anticipate the trajectory of the West's political economy through the rest of the twentieth century, Wister's narrator also relates that "the railroad came, and built a branch to that land of the Virginian's where the coal was. By that time he was an important man, with a strong grip on many various enterprises, and able to give his wife all and more than she asked or desired" (392). As for his wife, in the novel's final paragraph we learn about Molly's primary anxiety: that the combined stress of the Virginian's ranching and his "many various business enterprises" would lead to his premature death. Significantly, we are also told that "sometimes she missed the Bear Creek days, when she and he had ridden together." So in the end it is her "unromantic future," as well as his, her fate to dwell in the "married, established West" and, as a result, to recall nostalgically the bygone days of romance, of courtship – of freedom. Still, as Wister's narrator brings this narrative down to the present, enough romance has nevertheless occurred between them to produce the son who now rides the Virginian's faithful horse, Monte, across the Wyoming plains.

And "strictly between ourselves," the narrator confides, as if to make Molly's anxiety about her husband's work ethic groundless, the son's father "is going to live a long while" (392). "Long while" indeed: Wister's daughter Fanny Kemble notes that within eight months of its initial publication, *The Virginian* was reprinted fifteen times by Macmillan and that a cheaper edition published by Grosset and Dunlap further increased the novel's fabulous sales figures. And then of course there was the long-running stage production, the several movies (including one of the first "talking" or sound westerns), the television show, the various trade and mass-market paperback printings, the translations of the book into French, Spanish, Polish, and Czech, as well as its circulation through Macmillan's "Colonial Library" to all the remaining British imperial possessions.

As "an important man" with "many various enterprises," as a father and, presumably, a grandfather aging well into the twentieth century, does

Wister's Virginian, dwelling in the midst of "his unromantic future," miss the Bear Creek days of courtship? As a nouveau riche coal baron in "the Cowboy State," could the Virginian have managed to relinquish, in his "long while" to come, the cowboy's proper belief that, to use Cormac Mc-Carthy's words from *All the Pretty Horses*, "other than cattle there was no wealth proper to a man"?[6] We learn something of Molly's emotional life at novel's end. But the Virginian who in the honeymoon camping trip that begins the novel's final chapter talks freely and feelingly about the consequences of mortality – *this* Virginian basically is absent in the novel's final paragraph, distanced by the narrator's externalized portrait and quasi-historical summary. The overall effect is to monumentalize this cowboy figure, present him as an elemental figure seemingly beyond history's grasp, as stable and constant and enduring as the earth that his eldest son and Monte now ride over and across.

Poised at novel's end after making the transition from his noir moment with Trampas to an "unromantic future" organized by the emergent extractive economy of the modern West, the Virginian's mythic stature anticipates the portraits of any number of genre western male protagonists – say, Alan Ladd in *Shane* or Gary Cooper in *The Westerner* – who also seem free of history, seem to have risen fully armed and capable out of the prairie earth or mountainous outcroppings that encompass them. But of course this stylized portrait remains an illusion, for the Virginian's "unromantic future" actually anticipates that of Bick Benedict, scion of the wealthy west Texas ranching family in Edna Ferber's novel *Giant* (1952). Still: whereas the Virginian's transformation of the open range into the open-pit coal mine takes all of two paragraphs in Wister's novel, for Ferber – writing fifty years after *The Virginian* first appeared and not long before Wister's title character was to head up a television series – it takes the Oedipal presence of Jett Rink, the passing of several years in the novel's plot, and the passage of most of the pages of *Giant* before Bick Benedict finally, and reluctantly, sells his mineral leases and thus allows drilling rigs on his land.

Where have all the cowboys gone? Gone to Texas, some of the time. In 1892, at that moment when the fictional Virginian and his partner, Judge Henry, nearly lose their fortunes and their homes on the range, Wister wintered at the Seven Springs Ranch near Brownwood, Texas. Owned by a Philadelphian named Fitzhugh Savage, the ranch was set up mostly to buy horses and then train them to be polo ponies before shipping them back East. On most afternoons the small bachelor group that convened at Savage's ranch that winter would play polo. Most nights they would drink whiskey and play poker. Wister's biographer allows that young Owen held his own on all fronts. During his stay at Savage's ranch Wister hears two tales that he will eventually rework and include in his stories and his cowboy novel: one tale centers on a cowboy who switches around some sleeping babies' clothes while their parents socialize in another room; the other tale centers on the series of misfortunes faced by a gender-confused hen. On still another occasion Wister hears a young cowboy from Brady, Texas, sing a song set to the melody of what sounds like the Irish tune that Wister knows by the title "The Rose of Tralee." Wister likes what he hears. So he carefully writes down what will turn out to be the first transcription of the cowboy song "Whoopee Ti Yi Yo, Git along Little Dogies." Over the next century a succession of singing, drugstore, cosmic, urban, and punk cowboys and cowgirls will cover the song, both earnestly and playfully. In the final moments of her song "Where Have All the Cowboys Gone," Paula Cole for one keens a breathy hybrid of "Yippee Yi Ki Yay" and "Whoopee Ti Yi Yo."

A hundred years after Wister transcribes "Whoopee Ti Yi Yo," and ninety years after *The Virginian* is published, the Texan Ross Perot – another "important man, with a strong grip on many various business enterprises" – launches his Reform Party campaign for the office of president of the United States. In his column that week for *Newsweek* magazine, George Will observes that Perot's public persona and his campaign's emergent themes were anticipated by Wister's cowboy character and book called *The Virginian*.[7] To be sure, there is some truth in Will's comparison: like Wister, Perot – as well as other politicians during this election year – enumerates the challenges that both legal and illegal immigration pose to the political and cultural integrity of the United States. His "Don't Fence Me In" brand of discourse marks his campaign themes of greater individual freedom from a perceived obstructionist and oppressive federal bureaucracy, and at times his speeches sound like they could have been lifted from the novel's views about the artificial social and political supports that constrain the "quality" from ascending to their rightful place of leadership in American life. Amid all the posturing about the need for strong fences, barbed wire or otherwise, to protect our national borders and our so-called American way of life, however, the fact remains that Perot's immense wealth primarily resulted from his development and eventual sale of the Electronic Data Services (EDS) corporation.

The Virginian's and even Bick Benedict's combination of cattle ranching with income derived from lucrative extractive industries (coal; oil and gas) documents a largely "Old West" political economy. By contrast, Perot's EDS enterprise – for years centered on providing networking services and advanced information processing for governments and defense-related industries – represents, at the end of the twentieth century, the political economy of the "New Wired West." Which is to say, Will's comparison of Perot to the Virginian and Wister does not quite get it right. To be sure, Wister's insular equation of the West as the site of the American nation-state's regeneration does get echoed years later by Perot's dominant campaign themes, all of which were fueled by the residual discourse of the Sagebrush Rebellion and the dramatic rise of Sunbelt economies (such as that in Texas) during the post-Vietnam years of periodic economic recessions. Still, EDS's evolution into a global corporate enterprise bound up with computer technology documents multinational late capitalism's incessant erosion of the regional and national boundaries so necessary to Wister's imagination. So just as the end of *The Virginian* records the schizophrenic positioning of Molly and the Virginian between the realities of an emerging New West (trains; extractive industries; recreational tourism; immigration) and a nostalgic desire for the ranching Old West, so too Perot's political campaign and the EDS corporation, based in Dallas, Texas, "talk" Wister's strident brand of regional and national chauvinism while simultaneously walking the "walk" of multinational corporate capitalism.

In the first year of the new millennium, the U.S. Census Bureau released statistical data and other information that it gathered during the year 2000 census, a massive undertaking itself indebted to computer technologies and EDS-style data management. Demographic changes dominated the discussions of scholars, politicians, marketing analysts, and both print and media journalists. Following on the heels of the much-discussed *Atlas of the New West*, analyses of the 2000 census data in the West's newspapers and magazines typically stressed two themes: the American West's ethnoracial, cultural, and economic transformations since the previous census; the contrast between those western states still mired in an Old West economy and other western states experiencing boom times as a result of their successful transition to a largely New West information/technology economy. During all this accounting, as *The Virginian* neared the centennial year of its initial publication, one fact underlined the change that Wister's concluding reference to coal production and his title character's numerous other business affairs signals: Wyoming economists note that in "the Cowboy State" there are now only about fifteen hundred ranching jobs and roughly thirteen thousand jobs devoted to the coal and oil and gas industries. And when compared to the salaries paid to coal miners, the salaries for ranch-related jobs "barely register."[8]

In the "At Dunbarton" chapter, the Virginian successively moves through three topographies: the topography of secluded high-mountain lake and island where he and Molly spend their honeymoon; the interior, mostly domestic spaces of the Stark and Wood homes in Dunbarton; and the "unromantic" space of modern business affairs, which apparently take the Virginian, as they did Judge Henry, to and from his Wyoming coal-bearing land. But amid these topographies, intervening in one sentence of the novel's final paragraph appears a fourth: the space of the Bear Creek romantic moment on which Molly looks back with some fondness. Here at the end of *The Virginian* in this one sentence devoted to Molly's interior life we glimpse a template that anticipates our postmodern "predicaments," a template affirming Susan Kollin's (chap. 11 in this volume) point about the dangers of our conceiving of any "radical break" between the so-called Old and New Wests.

Although neither as complexly elaborated nor as full of pathos as the interior lives of female characters created by Willa Cather and Mari Sandoz, Molly's landscape of desire at the end interestingly braids together the lived, material space of her "unromantic" present with a perceived or imagined dreamscape that is itself based on a "real" past that she and the Virginian shared. Her affective response to her particularly modern predicament is, structurally speaking, similar to our postmodern predicament of dwelling – in the new global cultural economy evinced by such things as EDS – in concurrent ideo(logical)scapes, mediascapes, and finan(cial)scapes.[9] Owing to the more rapid transmission of media images, capital, peoples, and cultural and political ideologies that has occurred since the era of Bick Benedict and the Virginian's presumed grandchildren, the signifier *Wyoming* similarly connotes or braids together different topographies: the state tourism board's glossy circulation of an extant Old West cowboy (and Indian) culture's iconography as part of its promotion of the dude ranch and ski industries; the aesthetic-recreational landscape of the Teton and Yellowstone National Parks; and the "unromantic" present-day "finanscape" largely dominated by the shift of capital (and people) away from rural towns and embodied in the detritus of businesses and related industries that service the open-pit coal mines and the Wyoming oil patch employing approximately thirteen thousand workers.

As memorialized in several works of "newer" western fiction and films like the elegaic *Monte Walsh* (1970), based on a novel by Jack Schaefer, and as confirmed by demographic facts and trends since the mid-century moment of Bick Benedict, the Virginian's children and grandchildren likely married and moved into town, perhaps altogether abandoning, whether by force or by circumstance, the traditional cowboy's way.[10] Or they may have married and moved into town and now commute to the ranch or the leased public grazing land to tend to their animals' needs. "I think it is essentially that movement, from country to subdivision, homeplace to metropolis, that gives life in present-day Texas its passion," writes Larry McMurtry, both delivering his eulogy about the cowboy's passing and describing a major theme of his own novels published during the height of the Vietnam War. The Virginian and Molly's eldest son is said to ride that faithful horse, Monte, at novel's end. In the introduction to his collection of essays titled *In a Narrow Grave* (1968), McMurtry describes seeing his then five-year-old son riding a machine horse before a laundromat, which makes him think of his Uncle Johnny, at a similar age, "sitting on top of the McMurtry barn watching the last trail herd go by. It is indeed a complex distance from those traildrivers who made my father and my uncles determined to be cowboys to the mechanical horse that helps convince my son that he is a cowboy, as he takes a vertical ride in front of a laundrymat [*sic*]."[11]

Within that "complex distance" between a firsthand sighting that makes one "*determined* to be" a cowboy and the mechanical prosthesis "that *helps convince*" one that one "is a cowboy" – regardless of whether such urban cowboys ride such machines in front of a laundromat or inside Gilley's or Billy Bob's saloons – are the glossy coffee-table books of photography about working cowboys with titles typically bearing witness with such words as *vanishing* or *lost* or *end*. Within that "complex distance" between the days of the old trail drivers and those of the urban cowboy are the cowboys, the real "Marlboro men," dead and dying of lung cancer and emphysema.[12] Within that "complex distance" that negotiates the mythic death of the sunburned horseman is Jack Burns's horse Whiskey, struck dead on a highway near Albuquerque by a truck carrying a load of toilets at the conclusion of Abbey's novel *The Brave Cowboy* (1958).

And within that "complex distance" there exist darker, more troubling cultural extrapolations of cowboy mythology. As slang, the term *cowboy* is, in an industrial American popular culture at the end of the twentieth century, often bandied about to connote any self-aggrandizing behavior occasioned by recklessness, impulsivity, or simply roguish actions. Thus *cowboy cops*, who act independently of the law-enforcement team and who traverse the legal frontier, even crossing the line and engaging in criminal behavior themselves to bring a case to closure. Thus *cowboy politics*, as in the Henry Kissinger–style *mano-a-mano* politics of stubborn confrontation during the later stages of the cold war and in the Vietnam War–era peace negotiations. Thus *to cowboy*, as a verb to denote, for better or worse, impromptu, freelance screwing around with some thing or person, for better perhaps but usually for worse.

Moreover, as *The Virginian* begins its second century in print, a coalition of environmentalists, economists, urban Westerners, and animal rights activists have criticized cattlemen and the cattle industry for the depletion of water resources, for damage to riparian habitats and native predators, and for the destruction of public lands and national forests occasioned by shortsighted grazing practices. In today's West those associated with the cattle trade are often derisively called *welfare ranchers* or *welfare cowboys* because such work is often primarily supported by relatively cheap government grazing fees. In *Kill the Cowboy*, Sharman Apt Russell argues that we should attempt what seems to be the impossible, to "balance ecological concerns" with an ageless "desire to ride a horse across a golden plain." But if the legal, political, and cultural conflicts between contemporary ranchers and environmentalists end up killing off the cowboy and his culture, Russell asks, "Who will replace him?" Like McMurtry's son some twenty years earlier, *her* five-year-old son "identified himself as a cowboy ever since he could ride a rocking horse." So Russell speculates that even "if there were no cowboys, my son would have to invent them."

As it did for McMurtry, for Russell the West's changing economy and ecology forces a consideration not only of new laws, new management plans, and "new ways to live in the West." It also means that we need to reinvent old myths as well as invent new myths. The point is not to let go of myth, as if that were possible, but to understand how our mythic stories now require what the land itself now needs to survive: "*biodiversity*."[13]

"RECLAIMING THEIR EMOTIONAL HOMELAND"

As Raymond Williams has argued, *tradition* should not be regarded simply as a relatively inert instance of "the surviving past." It is always at bottom an intentional, which is to say, an active and highly selective, version of the past. Out of all the meanings and practices and texts produced in the past, Williams observes, the fact is that only certain of them get chosen for attention and thus get branded *significant* or *important*. As a result, a good deal of the other meanings and practices and texts get excluded or ignored in the ongoing process of selection, effectively deemed insignificant, and thus relegated to the culture's margins – or to oblivion. Victoria Lamont's essay (chap. 7 in this volume) on the fate of Frances McElrath's *The Rustler* illustrates how this dynamic operates in fiction about the American West at the beginning of the twentieth century. A given "tradition" of whatever sort essentially reveals that particular culture's dominant social and political organization, its contemporary shaping of a vision of the past so as not only to connect with the present but also to ratify the existing order of things, which is to say, validate the existing hierarchical power relations involving gender, race, and class.[14]

The "tradition" that *The Virginian* has typically represented – and arguably inaugurated – is, of course, that of the formula western, which – as William Kittredge has claimed – is mostly bound up with "the myth of The Western: gunslingers and settlers and savages, invading armies and lawbringing." This presiding myth is largely one of "conquest," so on one level the classic western advanced by *The Virginian* connects with "a much older world mythology, that of lawbringing."[15] Even so – as Gary Scharnhorst (chap. 5 in this volume) specifically demonstrates in his reading of "The Game and the Nation" chapters from *The Virginian* – what Kittredge calls *the myth of the Western* importantly provides the expressive iconography underpinning and rationalizing an American nation-state expanding at home and overseas.

For a time – Kittredge says "up until the 1930s" – the predominant myth of lawbringing made it seem as if "there was only one legitimate story to tell about the West,"[16] the story that Jennifer Tuttle (chap. 4 in this volume) redefines as a "taxidermic gesture of conquest" involving a putatively besieged white manhood's violent appropriation of tribal peoples' "primitive" qualities or traits as part of its revitalization. Yet when the fiftieth anniversary of the publication of *The Virginian* occurred in 1952 during the cold war, critical recognition of the racist, sexist, and class-bound ideologies embedded in popular western writing, film and television, and the visual arts in Wister's wake was barely under way. By the time of the novel's centennial – as the essays in this collection attest – such dominant ideologies shaping both the genre and this particular novel have become prime topics for discussion by revisionist literary critics and cultural historians. Following the lead of Lee Clark Mitchell, Jane Tompkins, Richard Slotkin, and Forrest Robinson, western literary critics and cultural historians have begun to critique, for instance, Wister's modeling of an authentic national identity in an absolutist Anglo-Saxon ethnicity, in the process returning to the critical foreground this particular model's suppression of gender, ethnic, and racial difference and its complicity with America's imperialist ambition, whether this arises in Wister's era or during the era of the cold war and the Vietnam War.

Moreover, such revisionist critics – and several "new" western writers themselves – have frequently complained over the past few decades about the anxiety of influence and the historical falsehoods produced by, in Kittredge's words, the traditional western's stylized "morality play."[17] Thus, "newer" western writers and critics have often self-consciously positioned their work against the mythos of the popular or formula western in fiction, film, and advertising campaigns. Thus, writing of her yearning for Wyoming during her visits to New York, Gretel Erlich claims that "in our hellbent earnestness to romanticize the cowboy we've ironically disesteemed his character."[18] Kittredge notes that, in retrospect, he "first began to suspect the West was going to have itself an *adult literature*" (emphasis added) when he reviewed Norman Maclean's *A River Runs through It* (1976) for a local Montana newspaper.[19]

Now, Kittredge's observation is woefully late in dating the possible emergence of an "adult" western writing that refuses simply featuring a magical hero – say, a man with a silver bullet – who "embraces violence" so as to save "our people from the savage forces of lust and greed." Although Kittredge never refers to Wister or *The Virginian* by name, it is as if it will take for him that moment in *High Noon* (1952), fifty years after *The Virginian*, when Gary Cooper leaves Grace Kelly to confront his enemies waiting in the street – a moment bent on replaying and, finally, revising the ending to Wister's archetypal showdown scene – before the stage can finally be set for artists in the West to begin "claiming and reclaiming their emotional homeland."[20] To begin wresting this homeland away from those who, like Wister, worked "inside" the myth, articulating its conventions and iconography. To begin clearing the western landscape for fiction such as "Brokeback Mountain," in Annie Proulx's collection

Close Range: Wyoming Stories (1999), about a same-sex love affair between two cowboys that endures over twenty summers and eventually outlasts all the emotional bonds attached to their wives and children.

So long on the "inside," *The Virginian* seems, as it begins its second century in print, irrevocably now to be on the "outside," to be *discontinuous* with the present as a result of its reactionary sexual politics and racialized discourse, its anachronistic sentimentality and at times overwrought literary style, much less its insular nationalist ideology, seemingly so retrograde in our postmodern moment's global or transnational political and cultural economy and increasingly multiracial societies. The Virginian himself has, as Wister's narrator predicted in 1902, certainly lived "a long while" as an iconic figure in and of American culture. But his future life and the mythic tradition that it fashioned seem uncertain at best, seem highly problematic given the social, political, economic, and cultural developments to which I have alluded in the first section of this afterword.

I do not find it too difficult, then, to speculate that the future of *The Virginian* will recapitulate that of, say, the Leatherstocking novels written by James Fenimore Cooper in the early nineteenth century – that is, to be regarded finally as a quaint period piece. Perhaps, to be sure, it will be considered of some antiquarian interest because of its originary "begetting" of certain genre conventions: like the gunfight scene reworked by *High Noon* and updated and revised by the director Jim Jarmusch in *Ghost Dog* (2000), his cinematic hip-hop cultural fusion of the samurai western and the gangster film; like the topography of homoerotic and even same-sex desire that, as William Handley (chap. 2 in this volume) argues, saturates Wister's novel and later gets reworked in Proulx's "Brokeback Mountain." Or perhaps it will be regarded as a possible resource for this new millennium's faux nostalgia, for its culture of consumption's seemingly insatiable appetite for retro stylings as exemplified by Woody and Jesse, 1950-era cowboy and cowgirl dolls in the Disney *Toy Story* movies marketed for baby boomers and their kids, who, like the five-year-old children of McMurtry and Russell, want to take vertical rides on rocking horses and mechanized horses or bulls powered nowadays by electricity and computer programming.

While for the most part sharing Kittredge's and Erlich's larger concerns about the need to reexamine the West's cultural productions, the essayists in this volume have little interest in prolonging an earlier critical discussion of western American writing that was obsessed with locating the critical divide between romance and realism or between authenticity and inauthenticity. By identifying how traces of racism, misogyny, homoerotic desire, and class anxieties circulate throughout the novel's rhetorical surface, these essays begin both to identify in the novel's "silences" its suppressed relationship to women's writing and to suggest the range of alternative and oppositional cultural productions that speak to Russell's call for recognizing the American West's mythic "biodiversity."[21] *The Virginian* emerges here as anything but a seamless, monolithic text always and inevitably advancing a dream of empire and of a revitalized white male ethnicity. That the novel exists as a force field of competing, even contradictory ideological perspectives is disclosed, for instance, by Handley's (chap. 2 in this volume) discussion of how Wister's conflicted desire for both the nomadic, bachelor West and the married, established West produces the novel's "affective disjunctions" and "formal narrative problems."

And given how specific, even contradictory, sociocultural and political pressures at work in any historical moment get sedimented in a literary text, western literary studies should, as Krista Comer has remarked in another context, understand how, even while "classic myth-producing texts like Cooper's *The Last of the Mohicans* or Wister's *The Virginian* do indeed perform very conservative cultural works, they are also shot through with all kinds of subversions of and challenges to white and male supremacy, female sexlessness, Indian 'savagery,' environmental ruin, the invisibility of women of color, the heterosexist imperative, and so on."[22]

So if it is a commonplace by now that *The Virginian* forwards that familiar story of conquest through some putatively redemptive violent act installing or enforcing patriarchal law and the private-property right, then we should consider how it also expresses, however provisionally, subversions and challenges to its own political unconscious perhaps, even at moments gestures toward, to use Kittredge's phrasing, some "new story with which to order our lives, in which the strong inherit the earth for better reasons than firepower."[23]

Just might begin to gesture toward, say, the possibility of greater social justice or toward, say, some alternative mode of gender relations than that based on competition or oppression. Or just might begin to limn that fragile yet precious interval before firepower comes into play, that interval when the "strong" somehow recover their senses, somehow realize, say, an expansive pastoral dream of kinship and community by which to negotiate the ongoing traumas of our (post)modern burdens.

For Kittredge: even as "we wait to be discovered by a new story with which to order our lives" – note the passive voice in this claim – there nevertheless remains in this waiting, at the heart of one of the genre's most disturbing representations of the myth of violent conquest, glimpses of that desired new story for our supposedly new times. Kittredge refers here to that image, as the credits scroll by in the director Sam Peckinpah's *The Wild Bunch* (1969), of the Wild Bunch departing the pastoral Mexican oasis of Agua Verde, journeying to their death in another place, but in this moment serenaded by the villagers as they slowly trail through the village's main cart path, bannered light stealing through overarching cottonwood trees and momentarily gracing their mounted figures, this overall choreography of song and motion and color speaking to some ancient ritual of hospitality, some intimate goodwill still alive, against all odds perhaps, among all the gathered men and women and animals, all the old and the young and the infirm, confirmed by the green earth with its ceaseless, seasonal rhythms of creation and destruction.

"BETTER THAN OUR DREAMS"

I don't think well of either a picture by Frederic Remington or a picture by Lungren on the cover. Too many Western books have had covers not very dissimilar from the landscape notion you propose. Take this suggestion into your thought. Could the island and the tent and the camp fire be in some way decoratively indicated on the cover to symbolize the honeymoon as described in the last chapter of *The Virginian*?

OWEN WISTER TO GEORGE BRETT, 26 APRIL 1911

So here is a "new" story from a long time back – an image and a dream that forward discovery through a return, that constitute a kind of *back to the future* movement. A story in the end about continuity. But a different kind than the continuing legacy of conquest that – in the face of all that is discontinuous between our time and that of Wister, his moment, and his cowboy novel – still links 1902 and 2002.

In late December 1909 Frederic Remington unexpectedly dies as a result of peritonitis following on a burst appendix. A few weeks later, in the early winter of 1910, Wister travels to a sanatorium in Loma Linda, California. Operated by Seventh-Day Adventists, the sanatorium prescribes a regimen of vegetarian food and frequent purgative baths for the treatment of his recurring vertigo, headaches, fatigue, and mental depression.

As the stageplay of his cowboy novel proceeds with its seventh straight year of production, Wister returns to Philadelphia in early summer. Almost immediately, he plans a trip to Wyoming, the idea being that more exercise and fresh mountain air will help ease his ongoing insomnia and bodily aches. The traveling cure is a long-standing one, an article of faith, in fact, for Wister. For months he has been regularly using aromatic ammonia and veronal to help him sleep, and for a while his August trip to Wyoming does ease his dependency on these potions. Still, he frets continually about what he perceives to be the nation's decline – and he frets as well about his meager output of writing. In his lengthy correspondence with his editor at Macmillan, George Brett, he floats several different ideas for writing projects. Most will never come to fruition. And invariably, he will also ask Brett for updated sales figures for *The Virginian*, as if a "strong grip" on this fact will keep his world from spinning away from him. The recent deaths of his Aunt Fanny and a close cousin only compound his chronic melancholia as the year draws to a close.

Then, in late December 1910 and early January 1911, while negotiating the details for the publication of Wister's *Members of the Family*, Brett proposes to Wister a "new" edition of *The Virginian*, with new illustrations, a new cover, and a new introduction by Wister. As Brett puts it, it is about time that Wister and the Macmillan Company give this best-selling cowboy novel "a fresh appeal to an audience that has grown up since it was first published."[24]

Then in late April Brett suggests to Wister that the new edition's cover display some wide-open landscape scene – in the manner of, if not actually by, Remington. But Wister rebuffs the idea. To his mind, the linkage of the western with a panoramic landscape view had already, in 1911, become a genre cliché. Still, Wister wonders aloud, Could there be instead a decorative cover with, say, an illustration of the "island and the tent and the campfire . . . symboliz[ing] the honeymoon described in the last chapter of *The Virginian*" – could this be worked up? "Do think about this," Wister urges Brett.[25]

In the end, it all seems to come down to this matter of the novel's final chapter. As friends and family members die off, as his writing proceeds slowly, if at all, as his frequent flights to remote locations from Butler Place supposedly to cure his neurasthenia come to be seen for what they are – evasions of his own "unromantic" present and future – Wister clutches at the memory of the Virginian and Molly's honeymoon idyll. Returns in his memory and imagination to that interlude in the final chapter, prior to the couple's journey back East to meet Molly's relations, that moment when the Virginian leads his new bride into the high mountains. Where they spend their honeymoon night together under the buffalo hide and wool blankets, sheltered by a white canvas tent that is itself encircled by green pines on an island that is itself surrounded by an alpine lake. Returns to that moment the next morning, when the Virginian begins to fish the lake for trout, with Molly close at his side, sharing the sun. When he stops fishing to watch with fascination a beaver swim across the blue water, roll on the lake's sandy shore, and then vanish into the nearby trees. Watching this animal at home both on water and on land, the Virginian confides "dreamily" to Molly that often when camping alone in this secluded spot he has desired "to become the ground, become the water, become the trees, mix with the whole thing. Not know myself from it. Never unmix again" (384–85).

The Virginian, of course, has helped capture and lynch his friend Steve for rustling cattle; he has defended his own and Molly's honor, and in the process he has killed Trampas. These experiences, part of the challenges that he has faced during his overall transformation from drifting cowboy to ranch foreman and husband, surely add up to a "gain" in his maturity and responsibility. At least that is the hope. But here at this moment the Virginian wonders aloud whether this "gain" – this firsthand knowledge of death, this disciplining of his libidinous desire to the marriage contract, this awareness of the elusive nature of justice – whether this gain in fact rather constitutes a major "loss." Particularly in comparison to the instinctual life of animals such as beavers, who, the Virginian projects, are not overly burdened with ethical questions about love, duty, honor, and justice – and who presumably are not burdened by a knowledge of their own pending mortality. Such animals probably are not lonely. Such animals probably are not even nervous.

So the Virginian confesses to Molly his desire to dissolve the boundaries of his self and, as a result, recover an intimacy with the world, as if he must compensate for taking Trampas's life by contemplating his own death, his relinquishing of ego and superego and mixing with the earth, water, and currents of air. Right here, for a brief moment, before heading down from the mountains, right here on this shore where water and land meet, where a tent stands, and where his attentive new wife "learned secrets of his heart new to her" (385), right here Wister's Virginian momentarily revises the paradigm of possessive individualism that equates one's

selfhood with one's property or possessions. As he expropriates his egois-
tic identity in this moment – crossing with or being crossed by the land-
forms and animals in that high country – as he talks with Molly "as he had
never talked to any one, not even to himself" (385), the Virginian dreams
again, gives voice to new desires, and ponders a new intimacy, one that is
heightened, made manifest by Molly's nearby presence. So: "after years
they did come, more than once, to keep their wedding day upon the island, and upon each new visit," in the midst of their "unromantic future," they "were able to say to each other, 'Better than our dreams'"
(386).[26]

Back to the future: the final chapter of *The Virginian* dramatizes and anticipates the psychic dislocations that still haunt us at the beginning of the
twenty-first century. The Virginian does not realize how much he "pines"
for the island and the tent and the campfire until he returns to it with his
new bride, and Wister seemingly does not realize how much he yearns to
recover that imagined moment until considering, in 1911, the right cover
for his novel's new edition. There is the trauma of Trampas's and Steve's
and Shorty's deaths behind him as well as his own wounding, and his "unromantic future" looms before him. These happenings are negotiated, as
is the case with the final images in *The Wild Bunch*, via a remembering and
a repeating – and a repenting – in an encompassing green and blue alpine world. To be sure, as Louis Owens (chap. 3 in this volume) discusses,
such a utopian moment depends on a prior violent removal of the Indian – this is one of the burdens of history hovering around the scene's
invocation of Wister's and the Virginian's primitivist longings. And to
be sure, this utopian moment of conversational unburdening eventually
gets constrained by the fact that the Virginian's gaze, much less his future down in the valley and plain, perhaps prevents him from following
through on this burgeoning gesture toward reciprocity.

   But still: consider how the Virginian at this moment becomes entirely
visible and audible so that whatever might be said to define his interior
life becomes, however briefly, publicly available in terms of his body's
movements, his tears, and – most of all – his words. And consider how this
visible exteriority locates itself in an organic collective, a series of ringed
enclosures that essentially represent but an exfoliated image of the dyadic
relationship formed when the Virginian and Molly unburden themselves
to and share each other in this space by a lake. So it finally would be a mistake, I think, for us to chalk up this scene solely to the workings of imperi-

alist nostalgia or simply to a therapeutic escape to nature, a fantasized desire that some believe has no real purchase on everyday life back in the expanding metropolis. It would be a mistake because, like Molly's yearning for the Bear Creek days, the compelling threshold space formed here by the island and the tent and the campfire exists simultaneously alongside their "unromantic" business and domestic future foreshadowed in the final chapter's final paragraphs. It would be a mistake, in other words, because the world as it is and comes to be is positioned against the world as it might be, if not soon, then maybe some time in the future, this world of yearning where a mythos of mastery and control cedes space to a mythos of reciprocity and exchange, of communion. A potential world where experience, as the Virginian and Molly observe to each other in later camping trips to commemorate their wedding anniversary, just might be better than dreams. *Where experiences of whatever kind would be much reduced without such hopes and dreams.*

In the midst of the gender oppression and misfortunes of her "unromantic" domestic present, the voice that we hear in Paula Cole's song successively asks where her John Wayne, her prairie son, her Marlboro Man, her "lonely ranger" – asks where they all have gone. Asks, finally, where all the cowboys have gone. McMurtry refers as well to "the music of departure" that he imagines hearing as the cowboy-god of Texas passes away, that "horseman, and a god of the country," whose "mythos celebrated those masculine ideals appropriate to a frontier."[27] *The Virginian* has for a century now also "celebrated those masculine ideals appropriate to a frontier," and the Virginian's personal turn to coal anticipates the cowboy era's passing as surely as all the traditional cowboy songs foresaw that fate, even as it was still very much then a working proposition. And yet – and yet – there is that moment in Agua Verde, there is that dream of Russell's to ride a horse across a golden plain after it has been restored with grass and birds – and there is that honeymoon scene in the liminal space of the tent on the island in the high-mountain lake. *Whoopie Ti Yi Yo.*

NOTES

1. Payne, *Owen Wister,* 201.

2. Owen Wister to Sarah Butler Wister, 5 July 1902. See also Payne, *Owen Wister,* 201–2.

3. Wister, ed., *Owen Wister Out West,* 18.

4. Wister, preface to *Members of the Family*, 10.

5. Wister, *The Virginian* (1988), 392. Page numbers for subsequent quotations will be given in the text.

6. McCarthy, *All the Pretty Horses*, 127.

7. Will, "The Barefoot Billionaire," 78.

8. Loomis, "Wyoming Mired in 'Old West' Economy," A-8. For an informative and entertaining guide to the Old West–New West conversation, see Johnson, *New Westers*.

9. See Appadurai, "Disjuncture and Difference in the Global Cultural Economy."

10. For a helpful discussion of the transition in cowboy culture from a general identification with an "orphan" mythos to that of the "married, established West," see Allmendinger, *The Cowboy*, chap. 4.

11. McMurtry, *In a Narrow Grave*, xiii, xv.

12. As memorialized by the half-hour television documentary *Death in the West*. For a discussion of this documentary about the fate of real Marlboro Men in the context of recent revisions of the classic genre western film, see Kollin, "Dead Man, Dead West."

13. Russell, *Kill the Cowboy*, 12–13.

14. Williams, *Marxism and Literature*, 115–16.

15. Kittredge, *Owning It All*, 156.

16. Kittredge, *Owning It All*, 171.

17. Kittredge, *Owning It All*, 158.

18. Erlich, *The Solace of Open Spaces*, 49.

19. Kittredge, *Owning It All*, 177.

20. Kittredge, *Owning It All*, 157, 170.

21. Russell, *Kill the Cowboy*, 197.

22. Comer, "Literature, Gender Studies, and the New Western History," 100.

23. Kittredge, *Owning It All*, 164.

24. George Brett to Owen Wister, 7 April 1911.

25. Owen Wister to George Brett, 26 April 1911.

26. For an alternative reading of this scene, see Rosowski, "The Western Hero as Logos."

27. McMurtry, *In a Narrow Grave*, xv.

BIBLIOGRAPHY

Abel, Richard. *The Red Rooster Scare: Making Cinema American, 1900–1910.* Berkeley and Los Angeles: University of California Press, 1999.

Abrams, Ann Uhry. "National Paintings and American Character: Historical Murals in the Capitol Rotunda." In *Picturing History: American Painting, 1770–1930,* ed. William Ayres, 65–80. New York: Rizzoli International, 1993.

Adams, Henry. *The Education of Henry Adams.* 1918. In *Henry Adams: Novels, Mont Saint Michel, the Education,* 715–1181. New York: Library of America, Literary Classics of the United States, 1983.

Allmendinger, Blake. *The Cowboy: Representations of Labor in an American Work Culture.* New York: Oxford University Press, 1992.

———. *Ten Most Wanted: The New Western Literature.* New York: Routledge, 1998.

Appadurai, Arjun. "Disjuncture and Difference in the Global Cultural Economy." *Public Culture* 2 (1990): 1–24.

Aquila, Richard. "The Pop Culture West." In *Wanted Dead or Alive: The American West in Popular Culture,* ed. Richard Aquila. Urbana: University of Illinois Press, 1996.

———, ed. *Wanted Dead or Alive: The American West in Popular Culture.* Urbana: University of Illinois Press, 1996.

Aristotle. *Poetics.* Translated and with an introduction by Gerald F. Else. Ann Arbor: University of Michigan Press, 1967.

Austin, Mary. *The American Rhythm.* New York: Harcourt, Brace, 1923.

Baber, D. F. *The Longest Rope: The Truth about the Johnson County Cattle War, by D. F. Baber, as Told by Bill Walker.* 1940. Caxton ID: Caxton, 1953.

Baker, Paula. "The Domestication of Politics: Women and American Political Society, 1780–1920." In *Unequal Sisters: A Multi-Cultural Reader in U.S. Women's History* (2d ed.), ed. Vicki Ruiz and Ellen Carol DuBois, 85–110. New York: Routledge, 1994.

Bakhtin, Mikhail M. *The Dialogical Imagination: Four Essays.* Translated by Caryl Emerson and Michael Holquist. Edited by Michael Holquist. Austin: University of Texas Press, 1990.

———. *Speech Genres and Other Late Essays.* Translated by Vern McGee. Edited by Caryl Emerson and Michael Holquist. Austin: University of Texas Press, 1990.

Bancroft, Hubert Howe. *The Book of the Fair: An Historical and Descriptive Presentation of the World's Science, Art, and Industry, as Viewed through the Columbian Exposition at Chicago in 1893.* Chicago: Bancroft, 1893.

Barthes, Roland. "The Death of the Author." In *Image, Music, Text,* trans. Stephen Heath. New York: Hill & Wang, 1977.

Bederman, Gail. *Manliness and Civilization: A Cultural History of Gender and Race in the United States, 1870–1917.* Chicago: University of Chicago Press, 1995.

Bell, Malcolm, Jr. *Major Butler's Legacy: Five Generations of a Slaveholding Family.* Athens: University of Georgia Press, 1987.

Best, James J. *American Popular Illustration: A Reference Guide.* Westport CT: Greenwood, 1984.

Bhabha, Homi. *The Location of Culture.* London: Routledge, 1994.

Bly, Robert. *Iron John: A Book about Men.* Reading MA: Addison-Wesley, 1990.

Bold, Christine. "How the Western Ends: Fenimore Cooper to Frederic Remington." *Western American Literature* 17, no. 2 (summer 1982): 117–35.

———. "The Rough Riders at Home and Abroad: Cody, Roosevelt, Remington, and the Imperialist Hero." *Canadian Review of American Studies* 18 (fall 1987): 321–50.

———. *Selling the Wild West: Popular Western Fiction, 1860–1960.* Bloomington: Indiana University Press, 1987. Reprint, Bloomington: Indiana University Press, 1991.

Borges, Jorge Luis. "A Biography of Tadeo Isidoro Cruz (1829–1874)." In *Collected Fictions,* trans. Andrew Hurley. New York: Viking Penguin, 1998.

———. *Collected Fictions.* Translated by Andrew Hurley. New York: Viking Penguin, 1998.

———. "Martín Fierro." In *Collected Fictions,* trans. Andrew Hurley. New York: Viking Penguin, 1998.

Bowser, Eileen. *The Transformation of Cinema, 1907–1915.* Berkeley and Los Angeles: University of California Press, 1990.

Brett, George. Letter to Owen Wister. 7 April 1911. New York Public Library, Manuscripts and Archives Division, Macmillan Company Records.

Brown, Richard Maxwell. "Western Violence: Structure, Values, Myth." *Western Historical Quarterly* 24 (February 1993): 5–20.

Buechler, Steven M. *Women's Movements in the United States: Woman Suffrage, Equal Rights, and Beyond.* New Brunswick NJ: Rutgers University Press, 1990.

Burch, Noel. *Life to Those Shadows.* Translated and edited by Ben Brewster. Berkeley and Los Angeles: University of California Press, 1990.

Burkhart, Dan. "Home on the Range: Ted Turner's Not Exactly One of the Boys in Bozeman, but He's Working on It." *Atlanta Constitution,* 12 November 1991, 1. Available on-line through Lexis-Nexis, Academic Universe, *http://www.lexis-nexis.com* (accessed 28 April 2000 through Renne Library, Montana State University).

Butler, Judith. *Gender Trouble: Feminism and the Subversion of Identity.* New York: Routledge, 1991.

Camilli, Doug. "Ted Turner Buying Up America." *Montreal Gazette,* 11 April 2000, B7. Available on-line through Lexis-Nexis, Academic Universe, *http://www.lexis-nexis.com* (accessed 28 April 2000 through Renne Library, Montana State University).

Campbell, Neil. *The Cultures of the American New West.* Edinburgh: Edinburgh University Press, 2000.

Cather, Willa. *A Lost Lady.* New York: Knopf, 1923. Reprint, London: Virago, 1980.

Cawelti, John G. *Adventure, Mystery, and Romance: Formula Stories as Art and Popular Culture.* Chicago: University of Chicago Press, 1976.

———. *The Six-Gun Mystique.* Bowling Green OH: Bowling Green University Popular Press, 1971.

———. *The Six-Gun Mystique Sequel.* Bowling Green OH: Bowling Green State University Press, 1999.

Chopin, Kate. *The Awakening.* 1899. Reprint, New York: Norton, 1976.

Clausewitz, Carl Von. *On War.* Edited and translated by Michael Howard and Peter Paret. 1976. Reprint, Princeton NJ: Princeton University Press, 1989.

Clifford, James. *The Predicament of Culture: Twentieth Century Ethnography, Literature, and Art.* Cambridge: Harvard University Press, 1988.

———. *Routes: Travel and Translation in the Late Twentieth Century.* Cambridge: Harvard University Press, 1997.

Clifford, James, and George Marcus, eds. *Writing Culture: The Poetics and Politics of Ethnography.* Berkeley and Los Angeles: University of California Press, 1986.

Cobbs, John L. *Owen Wister.* Boston: Twayne, 1984.

Cole, Paula. "Where Have All the Cowboys Gone?" From *This Fire.* Warner Brothers compact disk B000002NB0, 1996.

Comer, Krista. *Landscapes of the New West: Gender and Geography in Contemporary Women's Writing.* Chapel Hill: University of North Carolina Press, 1999.

———. "Literature, Gender Studies, and the New Western History." In *The New Western History: The Territory Ahead,* ed. Forrest G. Robinson. Tucson: University of Arizona Press, 1997.

Cooper, John Milton, Jr. *Pivotal Decades: The United States, 1900–1920.* New York: Norton, 1990.

Cott, Nancy F. "Giving Character to Our Whole Civil Polity: Marriage and the Public Order in the Late Nineteenth Century." In *U.S. History as Women's History: New Feminist Essays,* ed. Linda K. Kerber, Alice Kessler-Harris, and Kathryn Kish Sklar, 107–21. Chapel Hill: University of North Carolina Press, 1995.

Cowley, Malcolm. Introduction to *Hemingway,* vii–xxiv. New York: Viking, 1944.

Darwin, Charles. *Voyage of the Beagle: Charles Darwin's Journal of Researches.* Edited by Janet Browne and Michael Neve. London: Penguin, 1989.

Davis, Robert Murray, ed. *Owen Wister's West: Selected Articles.* Albuquerque: University of New Mexico Press, 1987.

Dead Man. Directed by Jim Jarmusch. Starring Johnny Depp. Miramax Studios, 1996.

Death in the West. 30 minutes. Pyramid Productions, 1976.

Deloria, Philip. *Playing Indian.* New Haven CT: Yale University Press, 1998.

DeVoto, Bernard. "Birth of an Art." *Harper's* 211 (December 1955): 8–9, 12, 14, 16.

Dilworth, Leah. *Imagining Indians in the Southwest: Persistent Visions of a Primitive Past.* Washington DC: Smithsonian Institution Press, 1996.

Donahue, Debra L. *The Western Range Revisited: Removing Livestock from Public Lands to Conserve Native Biodiversity.* Norman: University of Oklahoma Press, 1999.

Dorst, John D. *Looking West.* Philadelphia: University of Pennsylvania Press, 1999.

———. "Owen Wister and Emergent Discourse of the American West." In *"Writing" Nation and "Writing" Region in America,* ed. Theo D'haen and Hans Bertens, 226–34. Amsterdam: VU University Press, 1996.

DuBois, Ellen Carol. *Feminism and Suffrage: The Emergence of an Independent Women's Movement in America, 1848–1869.* Ithaca NY: Cornell University Press, 1978.

Dykes, Jeff C. *Fifty Great Western Illustrators: A Bibliographic Checklist.* Flagstaff AZ: Northland, 1975.

Egan, Timothy. "The Mild West: Tourists Ride into Town, Cowboys Ride into the Sunset." *New York Times,* 5 July 1992, sec. 4, p. 1. Available on-line through Lexis-Nexis, Academic Universe, *http://www.lexis-nexis.com* (accessed 28 April 2000 through Renne Library, Montana State University).

Ellison, Ralph. "Change the Joke and Slip the Yoke." *Partisan Review* 25 (spring 1958): 212–22.

Emert, Scott D. *Loaded Fictions: Social Critique in the Twentieth Century Western.* Moscow: University of Idaho Press, 1997.

Erlich, Gretel. *The Solace of Open Spaces.* New York: Penguin, 1985.

Fass, Paula. *The Damned and the Beautiful.* New York: Oxford University Press, 1977.

Fenin, George N., and William K. Everson. *The Western: From Silents to the Seventies.* Rev. ed. New York: Penguin, 1977.

Fetterly, Judith. *Resisting Reader: A Feminist Approach to American Fiction.* Bloomington: Indiana University Press, 1978.

Fitzgerald, F. Scott. *This Side of Paradise.* 1920. With a preface and notes by James L. W. West III and Lynn Setzer. New York: Simon & Schuster, 1998.

Flagg, Oscar H. *A Review of the Cattle Business in Johnson County, Wyoming, since 1882, and the Causes That Led to the Invasion.* 1892. Cheyenne WY: Vic, 1967. Originally published in installments in the *Buffalo (Wyo.) Bulletin.*

Foucault, Michel. "What Is an Author?" In *Language, Counter-Memory, Practice,* ed. Donald F. Bouchard, trans. Donald F. Bouchard and Sherry Simon. Ithaca NY: Cornell University Press, 1977.

Frantz, Joe B., and Julian E. Choate Jr. *The American Cowboy: The Myth and the Reality.* Norman: University of Oklahoma Press, 1955.

French, Philip. *Westerns: Aspects of a Movie Genre.* London: Secker & Warburg, for the British Film Institute, 1973.

———. *Westerns: Aspects of a Movie Genre.* New York: Viking, 1974.

Funk & Wagnalls. "The Boer Fight for Freedom" (advertisement). *Publishers' Weekly,* 24 May 1902, 1189.

———. "Daniel Everton" (advertisement). *Publishers' Weekly,* 3 May 1901, 1067.

———. "Novels for the Vacation Outfit" (advertisement). *Publishers' Weekly,* 31 May 1902, 1285.

———. "Spring Publications" (advertisement). *Publishers' Weekly,* 15 March 1902, 760.

Gage, Jack R. *The Johnson County War Ain't a Pack of Lies: The Rustlers' Side; and The*

　　　Johnson County War Is a Pack of Lies: The Barons' Side. Cheyenne WY: Flint-
　　　lock, 1967.

Gardner, Mark L. "The Western Photography of Owen Wister." Master's thesis,
　　　University of Wyoming, 1985.

Garvey, Ellen Gruber. *The Adman in the Parlor.* New York: Oxford University Press,
　　　1966.

Gilbert, Sandra, and Susan Gubar. *The Madwoman in the Attic: The Woman Writer
　　　and the Nineteenth-Century Literary Imagination.* New Haven CT: Yale Uni-
　　　versity Press, 1988.

Gilbert-Rolfe, Jeremy. *Beyond Piety: Critical Essays on the Visual Arts, 1986–1993.*
　　　Cambridge: Cambridge University Press, 1995.

Gilman, Charlotte Perkins. "Why I Wrote 'The Yellow Wallpaper.'" In *The Yellow
　　　Wallpaper,* 37–63. New York: Feminist, 1973.

———. *The Yellow Wallpaper.* 1892. New York: Feminist, 1973.

Gilroy, Paul. *The Black Atlantic: Modernity and Double Consciousness.* 1993. Reprint,
　　　London: Verso, 1996.

———. "Diaspora and the Detours of Identity." In *Identity and Difference,* ed. Kath-
　　　ryn Woodward. London: Sage, 1997.

Girard, René. "Lévi-Strauss, Frye, Derrida, and Shakespearean Criticism." *Dia-
　　　critics* 3, no. 3 (1973): 34–38.

Graulich, Melody. Introduction to *Western Trails: A Collection of Short Stories by Mary
　　　Austin,* 1–28. Reno: University of Nevada Press, 1987.

Grizzard, Lewis. "How Can Ted Stop the Chop?" *Houston Chronicle,* 14 December
　　　1991, 2. Available on-line through Lexis-Nexis, Academic Universe,
　　　http://www.lexis-nexis.com (accessed 28 April 2000 through Renne Li-
　　　brary, Montana State University).

Groussac, Paul. *Popular Customs and Beliefs of the Argentine Provinces: Address Deliv-
　　　ered before the World's Folk-Lore Congress Convened in Chicago during the
　　　World's Columbian Exposition, July 14, 1893.* Chicago: Donohue, Henne-
　　　berry, 1893.

Guttierrez, Hector. "CU [Colorado University] Buffalo Mascot Dies: Ted Turner
　　　Donates Ralphie IV." *Denver Rocky Mountain News,* 1 April 1998, 5A.
　　　Available on-line through Lexis-Nexis, Academic Universe, *http://
　　　www.lexis-nexis.com* (accessed 28 April 2000 through Renne Library,
　　　Montana State University).

Hall, Stuart. "Cultural Identity and Diaspora." In *Identity, Community, Culture, Dif-
　　　ference,* ed. Jonathan Rutherford. London: Lawrence & Wishart, 1990.

———. "New Cultures for Old." In *A Place in the World?* ed. Doreen Massey and Pat
　　　M. Jess. Oxford: Oxford University Press, 1995.

―――. *Representation*. London: Sage, 1997.

―――. "What Is This 'Black' in Black Popular Culture?" In *Stuart Hall: Critical Dialogues in Cultural Studies*, ed. D. Morley and K.-H. Chen, 465–75. London: Routledge, 1996.

Haraway, Donna. "Teddy Bear Patriarchy: Taxidermy in the Garden of Eden, New York City, 1908–36." In *Primate Visions: Gender, Race, and Nature in the World of Modern Science*. New York: Routledge, 1989.

Hays, Peter L. "Hemingway's Use of a Natural Resource: Indians." In *Hemingway and the Natural World*, ed. Robert E. Fleming, 45–54. Moscow: University of Idaho Press, 1999.

Heald, George D., ed. *Wyoming Flames of '92: Official Communications during the Johnson County Cattle War.* Oshoto WY: George D. Heald, 1972.

Hernández, José. *The Gaucho Martin Fierro.* 1872. Translated by Walter Owen. New York: Farrar & Rinehart, 1936.

―――. *The Gaucho Martin Fierro.* Translated by Frank G. Carrino, Alberto J. Carlos, and Norman Mangouni. Albany: State University of New York Press, 1974.

―――. *Martín Fierro.* Edited by Francisco H. Montesanto. Buenos Aires: Ediciones Margus, 1997. This edition contains both *El gaucho Martín Fierro* (1872) and *La vuelta de Martín Fierro* (1879).

Herron, Ima Honaker. "Owen Wister as Playwright." *Southwest Review* 47 (summer 1962): vi–vii, 265–66.

Hickey, Dave. *Air Guitar: Essays on Art and Democracy.* Los Angeles: Artissues.Press, 1997.

Higashi, Sumiko. *Cecil B. DeMille and American Culture: The Silent Era.* Berkeley and Los Angeles: University of California Press, 1994.

Horkheimer, Max, and Theodor W. Adorno. *Dialectic of Enlightenment.* Translated by John Cumming. New York: Continuum, 1986.

Howells, W. D. *Heroines of Fiction.* Vol. 2. New York: Harper & Bros., 1901.

Hoxie, Frederick E. *Parading through History: The Making of the Crow Nation in America, 1805–1935.* Cambridge: Cambridge University Press, 1995.

Johnson, Lee Ann. *Mary Hallock Foote.* Boston: Twayne, 1980.

Johnson, Michael L. *New Westers: The West in Contemporary American Culture.* Lawrence: University of Kansas Press, 1996.

Kaplan, Amy. "'Left Alone with America': The Absence of Empire in the Study of American Culture." In *Cultures of United States Imperialism*, ed. Amy Kaplan and Donald Pease, 3–21. Durham NC: Duke University Press, 1993.

―――. "Nation, Region, and Empire." In *The Columbia History of the American*

Novel, ed. Emory Elliott, 240–66. New York: Columbia University Press, 1991.

———. "Romancing the Empire: The Embodiment of American Masculinity in the Popular Historical Novel of the 1890s." *American Literary History* 2, no. 4 (winter 1990): 659–90.

Keen, Sam. *Fire in the Belly: On Being a Man.* New York: Bantam, 1991.

Kimmel, Michael. *Manhood in America: A Cultural History.* New York: Free Press, 1996.

King, Thomas. *Truth and Bright Water.* New York: Harper & Row, 1999.

Kittredge, William. *Owning It All.* St. Paul MN: Graywolf, 1987.

———. *Who Owns the West?* San Francisco: Mercury, 1996.

Knobloch, Frieda. "Creating the Cowboy State: Culture and Underdevelopment in Wyoming since 1867." *Western Historical Quarterly* 32 (summer 2001): 201–21.

———. *The Culture of Wilderness: Agriculture as Colonization in the American West.* Chapel Hill: University of North Carolina Press, 1996.

Kollin, Susan. "Dead Man, Dead West." *Arizona Quarterly* 56 (autumn 2000): 125–54.

Kolodny, Annette. *The Land before Her: Fantasy and Experience of the American Frontiers.* Chapel Hill: University of North Carolina Press, 1984.

Koszarski, Richard. *An Evening's Entertainment: The Age of the Silent Feature Picture, 1915–1928.* Berkeley and Los Angeles: University of California Press, 1994.

LaDuke, Winona. *All Our Relations: Native Struggles for Land and Life.* Boston: South End, 1999.

Lambert, Neal. "Owen Wister's Virginian: The Genesis of a Cultural Hero." *Western American Literature* 6, no. 2 (summer 1971): 99–107.

Larraya, Antonio Pagés. "José Hernández." In *Latin American Writers*, vol. 1, ed. Carlos A. Solé and Maria Isabel Abreu. New York: Scribner's, 1989.

Lears, T. J. Jackson. *No Place of Grace: Antimodernism and the Transformation of American Culture, 1880–1920.* New York: Pantheon, 1981.

Leutrat, Jean-Louis. *L'Alliance brisée: Le Western des années 1920.* Lyon: Presses Universitaires de Lyon, 1985.

Leverenz, David. "The Last Real Man in America: From Natty Bumppo to Batman." In *Fictions of Masculinity: Crossing Cultures, Crossing Sexualities*, ed. Peter F. Murphy, 21- 53. New York: New York University Press, 1994. Reprinted in *The American Literary History Reader*, ed. Gordon Hutner (New York: Oxford University Press, 1995).

Lewis, Robert W. "'Long Time Ago Good, Now No Good': Hemingway's Indian Stories." In *New Critical Approaches to the Short Stories of Ernest Hemingway*, ed. Jackson J. Benson. Durham NC: Duke University Press, 1990.

Limerick, Patricia Nelson. *Living in the Runaway West: Partisan Views from Writers on the Range*. Compiled by *High Country News*. Golden CO: Fulcrum, 2000.

———. *Something in the Soil: Legacies and Reckonings in the New West*. New York: Norton, 2000.

———. "The Shadows of Heaven Itself." In *Atlas of the New West: Portrait of a Changing Region*, ed. William Riebsame, 151–89. Boulder CO: Center for the American West, 1997.

Loffreda, Beth. *Losing Matt Shepard: Life and Politics in the Aftermath of Anti-Gay Murder*. New York: Columbia University Press, 2000.

Loomis, Brandon. "Wyoming Mired in 'Old West' Economy." *Salt Lake Tribune*, 8 March 2001, A-8.

Lopez, David E. "Cowboy Strikes and Unions." *Labor History* 18 (summer 1977): 325–40.

Lutz, Tom. *American Nervousness, 1903: An Anecdotal History*. Ithaca NY: Cornell University Press, 1991.

Lyon, Thomas J., et al., eds. *Updating the Literary West*. Fort Worth: Texas Christian University Press, 1997.

Macherey, Pierre. *A Theory of Literary Production*. 1978. Reprint, New York: Routledge, 1989.

Maguire, James H. "Fiction in the West." In *The Columbia History of the American Novel*, ed. Emory Elliott et al., 437–64. New York: Columbia University Press, 1991.

Mansilla, Lucio V. *A Visit to the Ranquel Indians*. 1870. Translated by Eva Gillies. Lincoln: University of Nebraska Press, 1997.

Marovitz, Sanford E. "Testament of a Patriot: The Virginian, the Tenderfoot, and Owen Wister." *Texas Studies in Literature and Language* 15, no. 3 (1973): 551–75.

McCarthy, Cormac. *All the Pretty Horses*. New York: Knopf, 1992.

———. *Blood Meridian; or, The Evening Redness in the West*. 1985. London: Picador, 1989.

McCracken, Harold. *Portrait of the Old West*. New York: McGraw-Hill, 1952.

McElrath, Frances. *The Rustler: A Tale of Love and War in Wyoming*. New York: Funk & Wagnalls, 1902.

McMurtry, Larry. *In a Narrow Grave: Essays on Texas*. New York: Simon & Schuster, 1968.

McWhorter, Lucullus Virgil. *Yellow Wolf: His Own Story.* Caldwell ID: Caxton, 1986.

Mercer, A. S. *The Banditti of the Plains.* 1894. Reprint, Norman: University of Oklahoma Press, 1954.

Merk, Frederick. *History of the Westward Movement.* New York: Knopf, 1978.

"Meth Labs: Idaho's Panhandle Provides Seclusion for Drug Producers." *Bozeman Daily Chronicle,* 13 February 2000, 6.

Meyer, Susan E. *America's Great Illustrators.* New York: Abrams, 1978.

Meyers, Jeffrey. "Hemingway's Primitivism and 'Indian Camp.'" *Twentieth Century Literature* 34, no. 2 (1988): 211–22.

Miller, J. Hillis. *Illustration.* Cambridge: Harvard University Press, 1992.

Milton, John. *The Novel of the American West.* Lincoln: University of Nebraska Press, 1980.

Mitchell, Lee Clark. "'When You Call Me That . . .': Tall Talk and Male Hegemony in *The Virginian.*" *PMLA* 102, no. 1 (January 1987): 66–77.

———. *Westerns: Making the Man in Fiction and Film.* Chicago: University of Chicago Press, 1996.

Mitchell, S. Weir, M.D. *Nurse and Patient, and Camp Cure.* Philadelphia: Lippincott, 1877.

———. *Wear and Tear; or, Hints for the Overworked.* 1887. 5th ed. Edited by Gerald N. Grob. New York: Arno, 1973.

Modleski, Tania. "A Woman's Gotta Do . . . What a Man's Gotta Do? Cross-Dressing in the Western." *Signs* 22, no. 3 (1997): 519–44.

Mogen, David. "Owen Wister's Cowboy Heroes." In *The Western: A Collection of Critical Essays,* ed. James K. Folsom. Englewood Cliffs NJ: Prentice-Hall, 1979.

Moreland, Kim. *The Medievalist Impulse in American Literature: Twain, Adams, Fitzgerald, and Hemingway.* Charlottesville: University Press of Virginia, 1996.

Nash, Gerald. *Creating the West: Historical Interpretations, 1890–1990.* Albuquerque: University of New Mexico Press, 1991.

Papanikolas, Zeese. *Trickster in the Land of Dreams.* Lincoln: University of Nebraska Press, 1995.

Paxson, Frederic L. *History of the American Frontier, 1763–1893.* New York: Houghton Mifflin, 1924.

Payne, Darwin. *Owen Wister: Chronicler of the West, Gentleman of the East.* Dallas: Southern Methodist University Press, 1985.

Pecora, Vincent P. *Households of the Soul.* Baltimore: Johns Hopkins University Press, 1997.

Pratt, Mary Louise. *Imperial Eyes: Travel Writing and Transculturation.* London: Routledge, 1992.

Proulx, Annie. "Brokeback Mountain." In *Close Range: Wyoming Stories,* 251–83. New York: Scribner's, 1999.

Radway, Janice. "The Utopian Impulse in Popular Literature: Gothic Romances and 'Feminist' Protest." In *Locating American Studies: The Evolution of a Discipline,* ed. Lucy Maddox. Baltimore: Johns Hopkins University Press, 1999.

Riebsame, William E. Preface to *Atlas of the New West: Portrait of a Changing Region,* ed. William Riebsame and James Robb. Boulder CO: Center for the American West, 1997.

Riebsame, William E., ed. *Atlas of the New West: Portrait of a Changing Region.* Boulder CO: Center for the American West, 1997.

Riley, Glenda. *Inventing the American Woman: A Perspective on Women's History, 1865 to the Present.* Arlington Heights IL: Harlan Davidson, 1986.

Robinson, Forrest G. "Clio Bereft of Calliope: Literature and the New Western History." *Arizona Quarterly* 53, no. 2 (summer 1997): 61–98.

———. *Having It Both Ways: Self-Subversion in Popular Western Classics.* Albuquerque: University of New Mexico Press, 1993.

———, ed. *The New Western History: The Territory Ahead.* Tucson: University of Arizona Press, 1997.

Roosevelt, Theodore. *Ranch Life and the Hunting Trail.* 1888. Reprint, Lincoln: University of Nebraska Press, 1983.

———. "True American Ideals." *Forum* 18 (February 1895): 743–50.

———. *The Works of Theodore Roosevelt.* Vol. 14. New York: Scribner's, 1924.

Rosowski, Susan J. "The Western Hero as Logos; or, Unmaking Meaning." *Western American Literature* 32, no. 3 (fall 1997): 268–92.

Rotundo, E. Anthony. *American Manhood: Transformations in Masculinity from the Revolution to the Modern Era.* New York: Basic, 1993.

Rudnick, Lois. "New Women." In *1915, the Cultural Movement: The New Politics, the New Woman, the New Psychology, the New Art, and the New Theatre in America,* ed. Adele Heller and Lois Rudnick. New Brunswick NJ: Rutgers University Press, 1991.

———. "Re-Naming the Land: Anglo Expatriate Women in the Southwest." In *The Desert Is No Lady: Southwestern Landscapes in Women's Writing and Art,* ed. Vera Norwood and Janice Monk, 10–26. New Haven CT: Yale University Press, 1987.

Rush, N. Orwin. *The Diversions of a Westerner.* Amarillo TX: South Pass, 1979.

———. *Fifty Years of "The Virginian," 1902–1952.* Laramie: University of Wyoming Library Association, 1952.

————. Introduction and notes to *The Virginian: A Play in Four Acts*, by Owen Wister and Kirk La Shelle. Tallahassee: n.p., 1958.

Russell, Sharman Apt. *Kill the Cowboy: A Battle of Mythology in the New West.* Reading MA: Addison-Wesley, 1993. Reprint, Lincoln: University of Nebraska Press, 2001.

Ryckman, Lisa Levitt. "Cable Cowboy: Billionaire TV Mogul Ted Turner, Wife Fonda, Relish Their Many Homes on the Western Range." *Denver Rocky Mountain News*, 22 April 1999, 6A. Available on-line through Lexis-Nexis, Academic Universe, *http://www.lexis-nexis.com* (accessed 28 April 2000 through Renne Library, Montana State University).

Sandburg, Carl. *The American Songbag.* New York: Harcourt, Brace, 1927.

Sandweiss, Martha. "Views and Reviews: Western Art and Western History." In *Under an Open Sky: Rethinking America's Western Past*, ed. William Cronon, George Miles, and Jay Gitlin, 185–202. New York: Norton, 1992.

Sarmiento, Domingo F. *Facundo; or, Civilization and Barbarism.* 1845. Translated by Mary Mann. 1868. Reprint, New York: Penguin, 1998. *Civilzación y barbarie: Vida de Don Facundo Quiroga* was originally published serially in the Chilean newpaper *El progreso.*

Scharnhorst, Gary. "The Virginian as a Founding Father." *Arizona Quarterly* 40 (autumn 1984): 227–41.

Schein, Harry. "The Olympian Cowboy." *American Scholar* 24 (summer 1955): 309–17.

Sedgwick, Eve Kosofsky. *Epistemology of the Closet.* Berkeley and Los Angeles: University of California Press, 1990.

Seelye, John. Introduction to *The Virginian: A Horseman of the Plains*, vii–xxxiii. New York: Penguin, 1988.

Slatta, Richard W. *Comparing Cowboys and Frontiers.* Norman: University of Oklahoma Press, 1997.

————. *Gauchos and the Vanishing Frontier.* Lincoln: University of Nebraska Press, 1983.

Slotkin, Richard. *Gunfighter Nation: The Myth of the Frontier in Twentieth-Century America.* New York: Atheneum, 1992. Reprint, New York: Harper Perennial, 1993.

————. "The Movie Western." In *Updating the Literary West*, ed. Thomas J. Lyon et al., 873–82. Fort Worth: Texas Christian University Press, 1997.

————. "Myth and the Production of History." In *Ideology and Classic American Literature*, ed. Sacvan Bercovitch and Myra Jehlen, 70–90. Cambridge: Cambridge University Press, 1986.

Smith, Helena Huntington. *The War on Powder River.* Lincoln: University of Nebraska Press, 1967.

Smith, Paul. *Clint Eastwood: A Cultural Production.* Minneapolis: University of Minnesota Press, 1993.

Splete, Allen P., and Marilyn Splete, eds. *Fredric Remington– Selected Letters.* New York: Abbeville, 1988.

Stanfield, Peter. "The Western, 1909–14: A Cast of Villains." *Film History* 1, no. 2 (1987): 97–112.

Stedman, Arthur. "A Talk with Owen Wister." *San Francisco Examiner,* 8 December 1895, p. 33, cols. 2–4. Reprinted from an 1895 issue of the *New York Journal.*

Stegner, Wallace. *Angle of Repose.* 1991. Reprint. New York: Penguin, 1992.

Stewart, Susan. *On Longing: Narratives of the Miniature, the Gigantic, the Souvenir, the Collection.* Durham NC: Duke University Press, 1993.

Strong, Amy Lovell. "Screaming through Silence: The Violence of Race in 'Indian Camp' and 'The Doctor and the Doctor's Wife.'" In *Ernest Hemingway: Seven Decades of Criticism,* ed. Linda Wagner-Martin, 29–44. East Lansing: Michigan State University Press, 1998.

Studlar, Gaylyn. "Wider Horizons: Douglas Fairbanks and Nostalgic Primitivism." In *Back in the Saddle Again: New Essays on the Western,* ed. Edward Buscombe and Roberta E. Pearson, 63–76. London: British Film Institute, 1998.

Tanner, Louis. "Owen Wister: Public Intellectual." Ph.D. diss., University of New Mexico, Department of History, 1999.

Tatum, Stephen. "The Classic Westerner: Gary Cooper." In *Shooting Stars: Heroes and Heroines of Western Film,* ed. Archie P. McDonald, 60–86. Bloomington: Indiana University Press, 1987.

———. "Topographies of Transition in Western American Literature." *Western American Literature* 33, no. 4 (winter 1998): 310–52.

Taylor, William R. *Cavalier and Yankee: The Old South and American National Character.* 1961. Reprint, New York: Oxford University Press, 1993.

Thoreau, Henry David. *Walden and Resistance to Civil Government.* Edited by William Ross. New York: Norton, 1992.

Tompkins, Jane. *West of Everything: The Inner Life of Westerns.* New York: Oxford University Press, 1992.

Trachtenberg, Alan. *The Incorporation of America: Culture and Society in the Gilded Age.* New York: Hill & Wang, 1982.

———. *Reading American Photographs: Images as History, Mathew Brady to Walker Evans.* New York: Hill & Wang, 1989.

Turner, Frederick Jackson. "The Significance of the Frontier in American History." Paper presented to the American Historical Association, Chicago, 12 July 1893. Reprinted in *The Frontier in American History* (New York: Henry Holt, 1920), 1–38; and in *The Social Record*, vol. 1 of *American Issues*, ed. William Thorpe et al. (Chicago: Lippincott, 1941), 661–74.

Tuttle, Jennifer S. "Rewriting the West Cure: Charlotte Perkins Gilman, Owen Wister, and the Sexual Politics of Neurasthenia." In *The Mixed Legacy of Charlotte Perkins Gilman*, ed. Catherine J. Golden and Joanna S. Zangrando, 103–21. Newark: University of Delaware Press, 2000.

Vizenor, Gerald. *Fugitive Poses: Native American Indian Scenes of Absence and Presence.* Lincoln: University of Nebraska Press, 1998.

Vorphal, Ben Merchant. *My Dear Wister: The Fredric Remington–Owen Wister Letters.* Palo Alto CA: American West, 1972.

———. "Roosevelt, Wister, Turner, and Remington." In *A Literary History of the American West*, ed. J. Golden Taylor et al., 276–94. Fort Worth: Texas Christian University Press, 1987.

Wacquant, Loïc J. D. "Towards a Reflexive Sociology: A Workshop with Pierre Bourdieu." *Sociological Theory* 7, no. 1 (1989): 26–63.

Wallman, Jeffrey. *The Western: Parables of the American Dream.* Lubbock: Texas Tech University Press, 2000.

Ward, George B. *Boone and Crockett National Collection of Heads and Horns.* 2d ed., rev. Cody WY: Buffalo Bill Historical Center, 1993.

Webb, Walter Prescott. Afterword to *The Ox-Bow Incident*, by Walter Van Tilburg Clark, 219–24. New York: Signet, 1960.

Welch, James. *Fools Crow.* New York: Viking Penguin, 1986.

Westbrook, Max. "Bazarov, Prince Hal, and the Virginian." *Western American Literature* 24, no. 2 (summer 1989): 103–11.

Wexman, Virginia Wright. "The Family on the Land: Race and Nationhood in Silent Westerns." In *The Birth of Whiteness: Race and the Emergence of U.S. Cinema*, ed. Daniel Bernardi, 129–69. New Brunswick NJ: Rutgers University Press, 1996.

Whipp, Leslie T. "Owen Wister: Wyoming's Influential Realist and Craftsman." *Great Plains Quarterly* 10 (fall 1990): 245–59.

White, Edward G. *The Eastern Establishment and the Western Experience: The West of Frederick Remington, Theodore Roosevelt, and Owen Wister.* New Haven CT: Yale University Press, 1968. Reprint, Austin: University of Texas Press, 1989.

White, Richard. *"It's Your Misfortune and None of My Own": A New History of the American West.* Norman: University of Oklahoma Press, 1991.

————. "When Frederick Jackson Turner and Buffalo Bill Cody Both Played Chicago in 1893." In *Frontier and Region: Essays in Honor of Martin Ridge*, ed. Robert C. Ritchie and Paul Andrew Hutton, 201–12. San Marino CA: Huntington Library Press; Albuquerque: University of New Mexico Press, 1997.

Wilkinson, Todd. "Buffalo Baron." *Denver Post*, 26 May 1996, 12. Available on-line through Lexis-Nexis, Academic Universe, *http://www.lexis-nexis.com* (accessed 28 April 2000 through Renne Library, Montana State University).

————. "In New West, Buffalo Roam on Ranches." *Christian Science Monitor*, 10 July 1996, 1. Available on-line through Lexis-Nexis, Academic Universe, *http://www.lexis-nexis.com* (accessed 28 April 2000 through Renne Library, Montana State University).

Will, Barbara. "The Nervous Origins of the Western." *American Literature* 70, no. 2 (June 1998): 293–316.

Will, George F. "The Barefoot Billionaire." *Newsweek*, 1 June 1992, 78.

Williams, Raymond. *Marxism and Literature*. Oxford: Oxford University Press, 1977.

Wister, Fanny Kemble, ed. *Owen Wister Out West: His Journals and Letters*. Chicago: University of Chicago Press, 1958.

————, ed. "Letters of Owen Wister, Author of *The Virginian*." *Pennsylvania Magazine of History and Biography* 83 (January 1959): 3–28.

Wister, Owen. "Among the Cow-Boys: Random Notes of a Tenderfoot and Sportsman in Wyoming." 1892. Edited by Louis Tanner. *Journal of the West* 37, no. 2 (1998): 65.

————. "Bad Medicine." In *When West Was West*, 1–48. New York: Macmillan, 1928.

————. "Concerning 'Bad Men.'" 1901. In *Owen Wister's West: Selected Articles*, ed. Robert Murray Davis. Albuquerque: University of New Mexico Press, 1987.

————. "The Evolution of the Cow-Puncher." *Harper's Monthly* 91 (September 1895): 602–17.

————. "The Evolution of the Cow-Puncher." 1895. In *My Dear Wister: The Frederic Remington–Owen Wister Letters*, ed. Ben Merchant Vorpahl, 77–96. Palo Alto CA: American West, 1972.

————. "The Evolution of the Cow-Puncher." In *Owen Wister's West*, ed. Robert Murray Davis, 33–53. Albuquerque: University of New Mexico Press, 1987. Reprint, Albuquerque: University of New Mexico Press, 1995.

————. "The Evolution of the Cow-Puncher." In *The Virginian: A Horseman of the*

Plains, ed. Robert Schulman, 329–44. New York: Oxford University Press, 1998.

———. "The Game and the Nation." *Harper's Monthly* 100 (May 1900): 884–905.

———. "Hank's Woman." *Harper's Weekly,* 27 August 1892, 821–23.

———. "Hank's Woman." In *The Jimmy John Boss and Other Stories.* New York: Harper & Bros., 1900. A revised version of the 1892 story.

———. "The Land of the Free." *Saturday Evening Post,* 29 October 1904, 7.

———. Letter to Mr. Booth [George Brett's assistant]. 7 November 1901. New York Public Library, Manuscripts and Archives Division, Macmillan Company Records.

———. Letter to George Brett. 11 November 1901. New York Public Library, Manuscripts and Archives Division, Macmillan Company Records.

———. Letters to George Brett. 2 April, 16 May 1902. New York Public Library, Manuscripts and Archives Division, Macmillan Company Records.

———. Letter to George Brett. 9 September 1905. New York Public Library, Manuscripts and Archives Division, Macmillan Company Records.

———. Letter to George Brett. 26 April 1911. New York Public Library, Manuscripts and Archives Division, Macmillan Company Records.

———. Letter to Sarah Butler Wister. 5 July 1902. *Owen Wister Out West: His Journals and Letter,* ed. Fanny Kemble Wister, 18. Chicago: University of Chicago Press, 1958.

———. *Members of the Family.* New York: Macmillan, 1911.

———. "The National Guard of Pennsylvania." *Harper's Weekly,* 1 September 1894, 824–26.

———. "Old Yellowstone Days." *Harper's* 172 (March 1936): 471–80.

———. Preface to *Red Men and White.* 1895. In *Owen Wister's West: Selected Articles,* ed. Robert Murray Davis. Albuquerque: University of New Mexico Press, 1987.

———. *Roosevelt: The Story of a Friendship, 1880–1919.* New York: Macmillan, 1930.

———. *The Virginian: A Horseman of the Plains.* 1902. New York: Macmillan, 1929. Reprint, Lincoln: University of Nebraska Press, 1992.

———. *The Virginian: A Horseman of the Plains.* Reprint, New York: Macmillan, 1955.

———. *The Virginian: A Horseman of the Plains.* Reprint, New York: New American Library (NAL), 1979.

———. *The Virginian: A Horseman of the Plains.* Reprint, New York: Signet, 1979.

———. *The Virginian: A Horseman of the Plains.* Reprint, New York: Penguin, 1988.

———. *The Virginian: A Horseman of the Plains.* Edited by Robert Shulman. New York: Oxford University Press, 1998.

————. *The West of Owen Wister: Selected Short Stories*. With an introduction by Robert L. Hough. Lincoln: University of Nebraska Press, 1972.

Wister, Owen, and Kirke La Shelle. *The Virginian: A Play in Four Acts*. With an introduction and notes by N. Orwin Rush. Tallahassee: n.p., 1958.

Wrobel, David M. *The End of American Exceptionalism: Frontier Anxiety from the Old West to the New Deal*. Lawrence: University of Kansas Press, 1993.

Yates, Norris. *Gender and Genre: An Introduction to Women Writers of Formula Westerns*. Albuquerque: University of New Mexico Press, 1995.

Žižek, Slavoj. *The Sublime Object of Ideology*. London: Verso, 1989.

CONTRIBUTORS

NEIL CAMPBELL is head of American studies at the University of Derby. His recent publications are *The Cultures of the American New West* (Edinburgh University Press/Fitzroy Dearborn, 2000), *The Radiant Hour: Youth in American Culture* (Exeter University Press, 2000), and *American Cultural Studies* (Routledge, 1997). He is currently writing on American western landscape photography.

MELODY GRAULICH is professor of English and director of graduate American studies at Utah State University. Since 1997, she has edited *Western American Literature*. Her many publications include essays and books on Mary Austin, Wallace Stegner, Leslie Silko, western American literature, feminist criticism, and women writers and artists. Forthcoming is a cowritten volume, *Trading Gazes: Euro-American Women Photographers among the North American Indians* (Rutgers).

WILLIAM R. HANDLEY teaches American literature at the University of Southern California. His essay derives from his book *Marriage, Violence, and the Nation in the American Literary West* (Cambridge University Press, forthcoming). He is also co-editor of a volume on authenticity and the American West, to be published by University of Nebraska Press.

RICHARD HUTSON is in the English department at the University of California, Berkeley. He is also an affiliated faculty of the American studies program. His primary interest is in American culture after the Civil War, especially the culture of the Great Plains. His current project is a study of writings from the cattle trade.

SUSAN KOLLIN is associate professor of English at Montana State University in Bozeman, where she teaches courses in western American literature, feminist theory, and environmental cultural studies. Her articles have appeared in *Contemporary Literature, Modern Fiction Studies, Arizona Quarterly,* and *American Literary History.* Her book, *Nature's State: Imagining Alaska as the Last Frontier,* was published in 2001 by the University of North Carolina Press. She is currently at work on a book-length study of antiwesterns.

VICTORIA LAMONT teaches American literature at the University of Waterloo in Ontario, Canada. She has published articles in *Western American Literature,* the *Canadian Review of American Studies, a/b: Auto/Biography Studies, Updating the Literary West,* and *American Women Prose Writers, 1870–1920.* Her areas of specialization include western American literature, especially women's writing and gender issues; American popular culture; and cultural theory.

LOUIS OWENS (Choctaw/Cherokee/Irish) was a distinguished writer and critic of American Literature. He is the author of numerous essays, novels, and critical studies on American and Native American literature, including *I Hear the Train: Inventions, Reflections, and Refractions* (2001); *Mixedblood Messages: Literature, Film, Family, Place* (1998), and *Other Destinies: Understanding the American Indian Novel* (1992). He was a generous colleague, teacher, and friend. His death in 2002 left his many readers saddened.

ZEESE PAPANIKOLAS is a member of the liberal arts department of the San Francisco Art Institute. He is the author of *Buried Unsung: Louis Tikas and the Ludlow Massacre* and *Trickster in the Land of Dreams,* both available in University of Nebraska Press Bison Books editions.

GARY SCHARNHORST is professor of English at the University of New Mexico, editor of *American Literary Realism,* and editor in alternating years of *American Literary Scholarship.* He received the Don D. Walker Award of the Western Literature Association (WLA) for the best journal article in western literary studies published in 1996 and the Thomas J. Lyon Award of the WLA for the best book in western literary studies published in 2000.

STEPHEN TATUM teaches in the English department at the University of Utah and is a past president of the Western Literature Association. He is the author of *Inventing Billy the Kid: Visions of the Outlaw in America, 1881–1981* and *Cormac Mc-*

Carthy's "All the Pretty Horses": A Reader's Guide as well as numerous articles about western American literature, film, and popular culture. His essay "The Solace of Animal Faces" (*Arizona Quarterly*) received the 1994 Don D. Walker Award from the Western Literature Association for best article in western American literary studies.

JENNIFER S. TUTTLE is assistant professor of English at the University of New England in Maine, where she serves as the Dorothy M. Healy Chair in Literature and Health and helps oversee the Maine Women Writers Collection. She received her Ph.D. from the University of California, San Diego, in 1996. She is the author of "Rewriting the West Cure: Charlotte Perkins Gilman, Owen Wister, and the Sexual Politics of Neurasthenia" (in *The Mixed Legacy of Charlotte Perkins Gilman*, ed. Catherine Golden and Joanna Zangrando) and the editor of a new scholarly edition of Gilman's 1911 novel *The Crux*. She has also published in *Legacy: A Journal of American Women Writers* and *Popular Culture Review*. Her scholarly interests include women's writing, the American West, and nineteenth-century medical discourse.

INDEX

Page references in italics refer to illustrations.